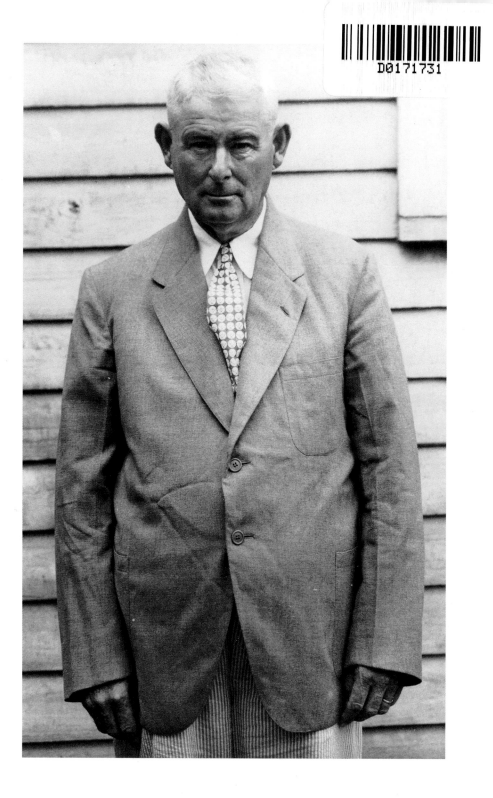

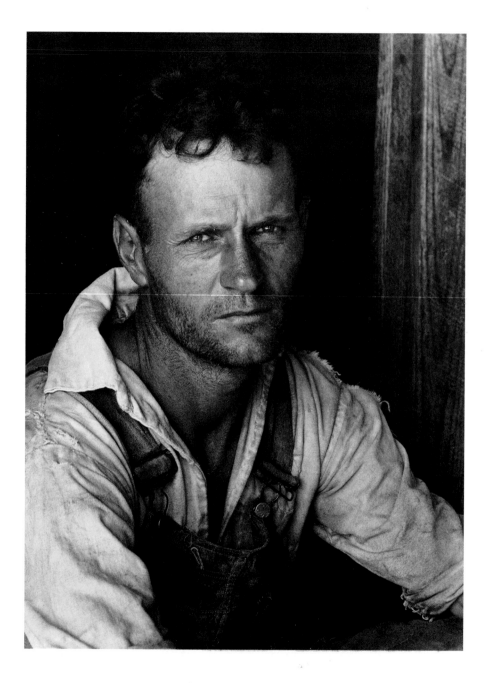

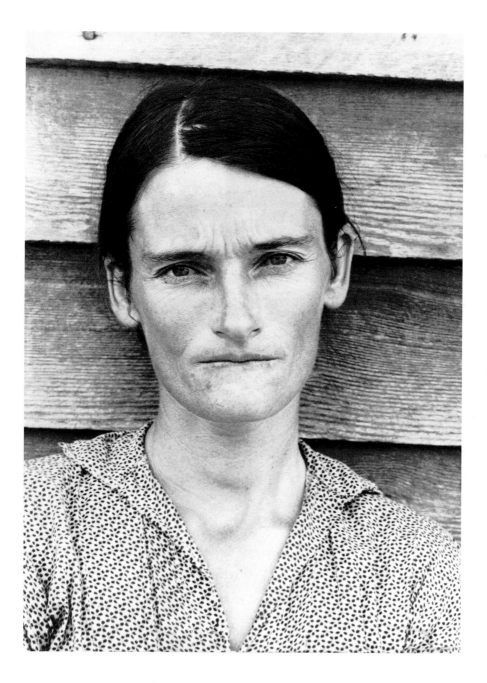

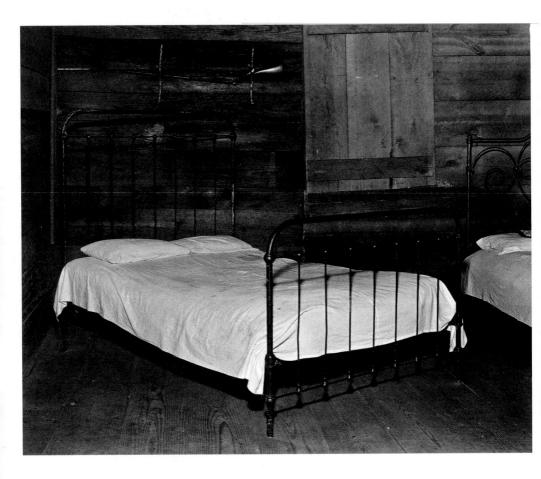

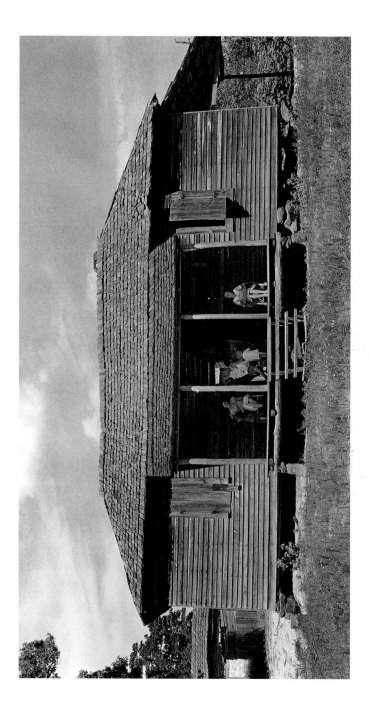

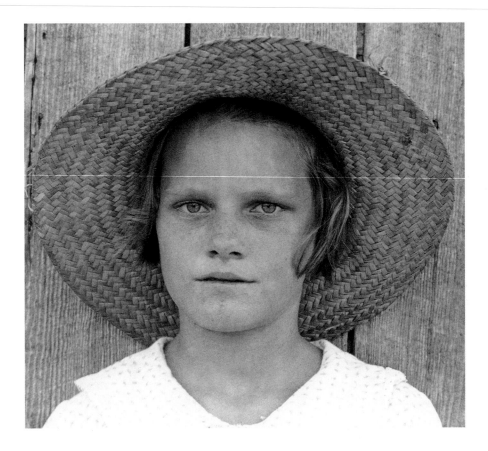

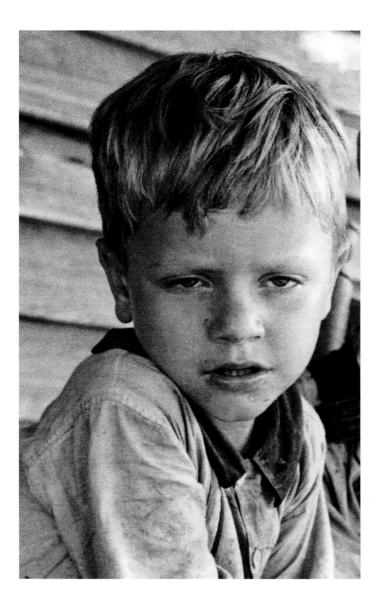

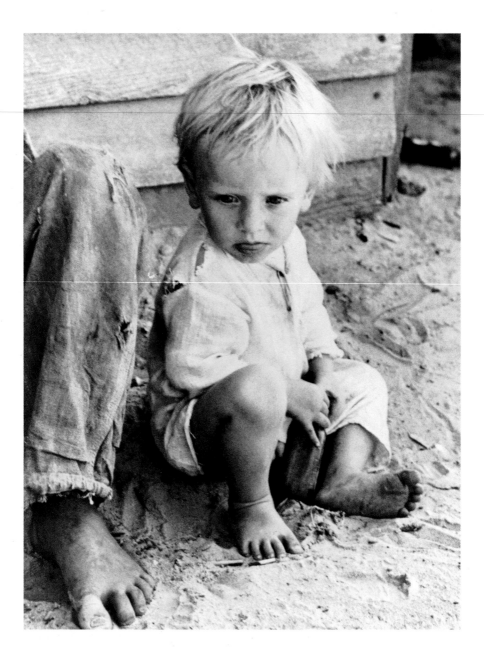

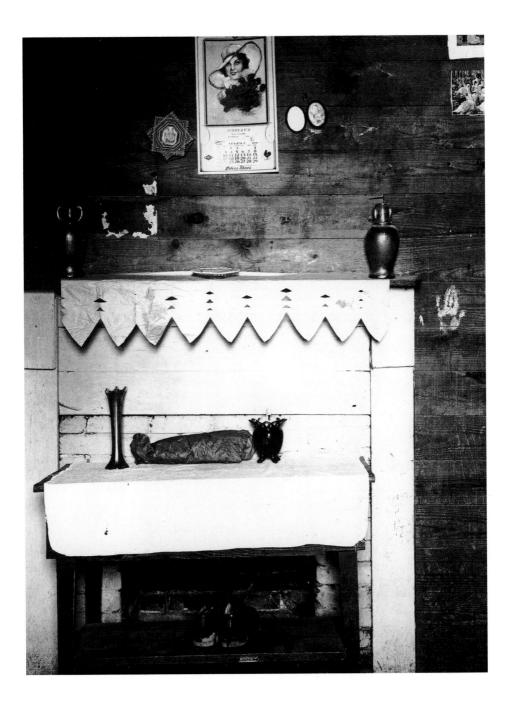

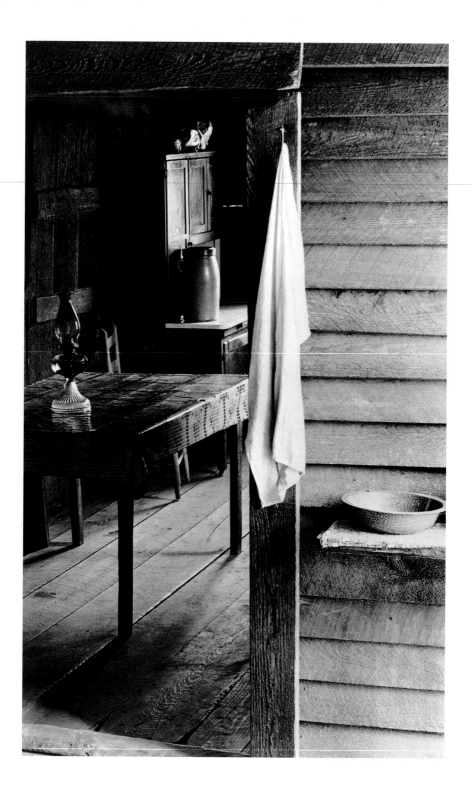

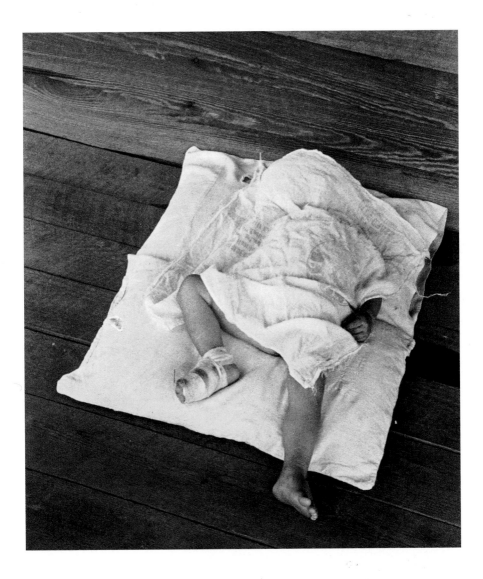

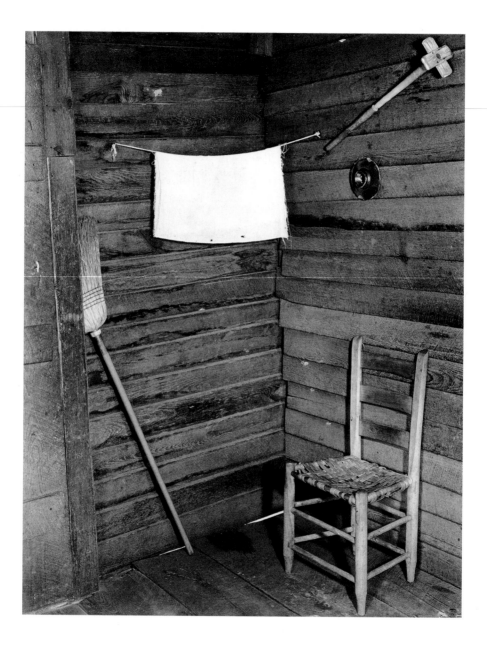

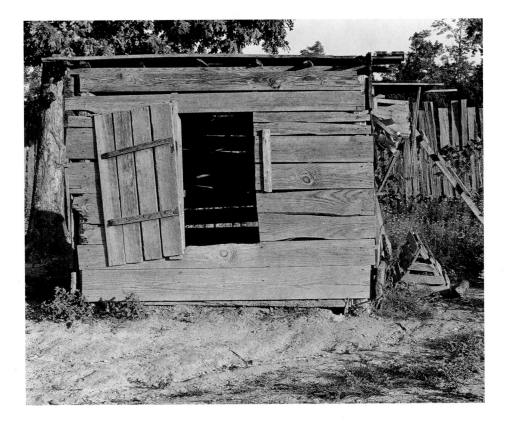

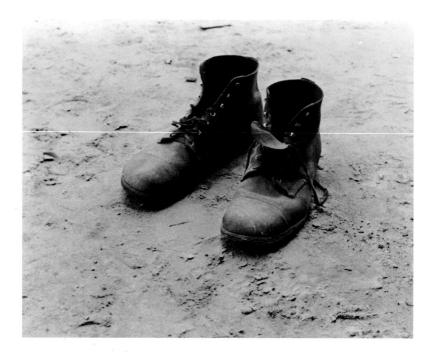

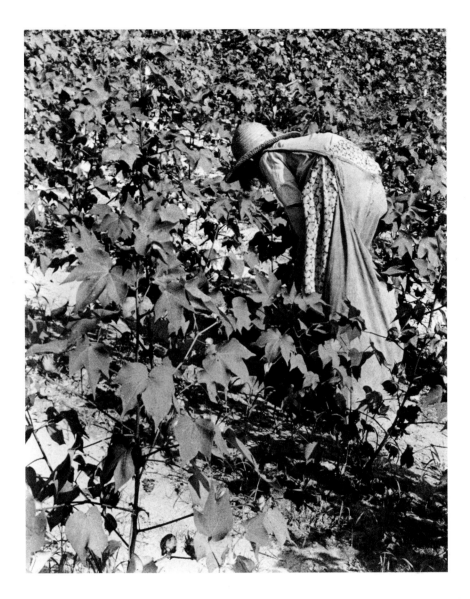

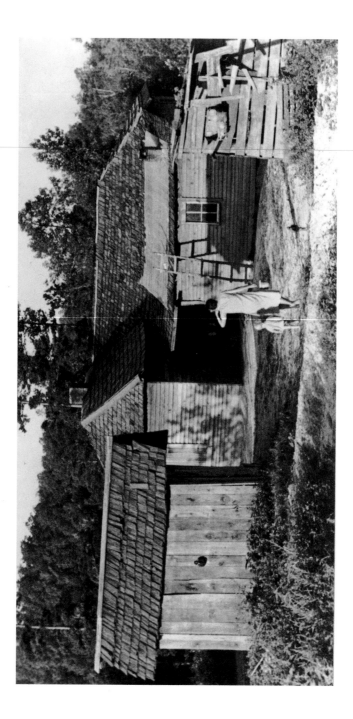

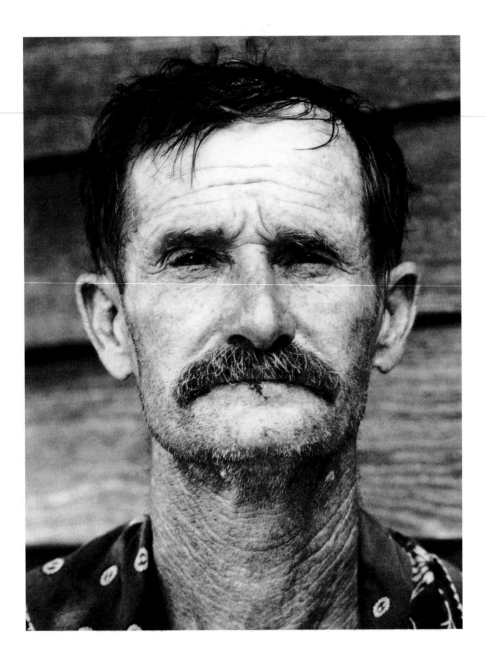

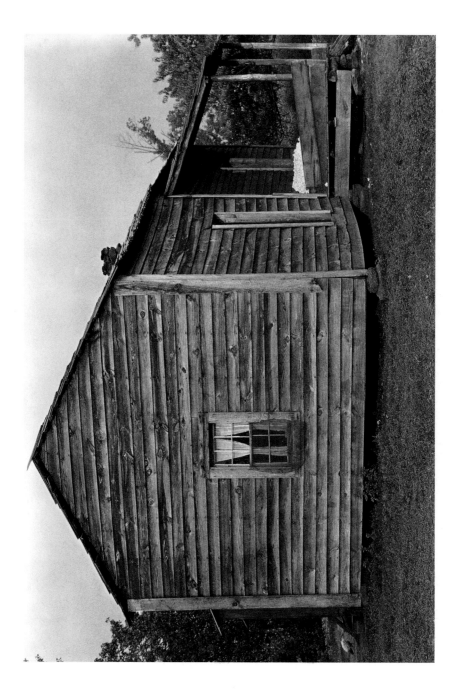

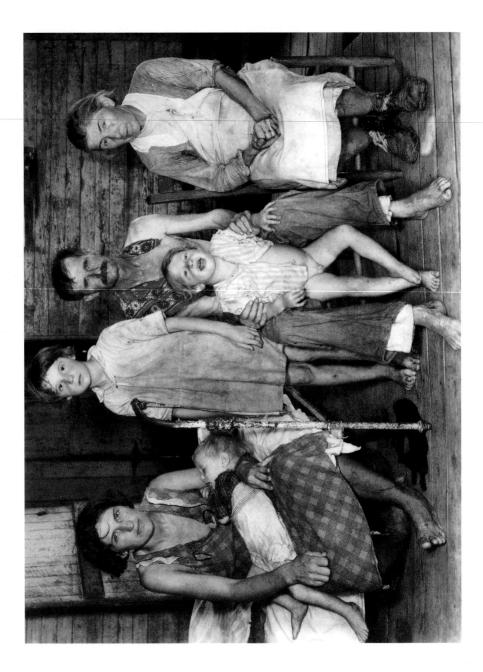

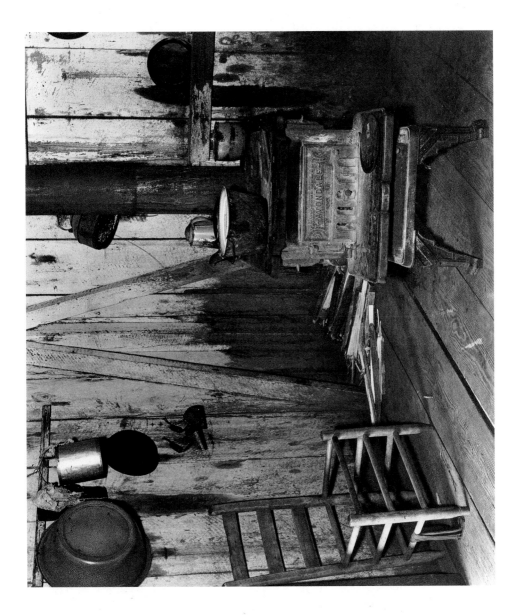

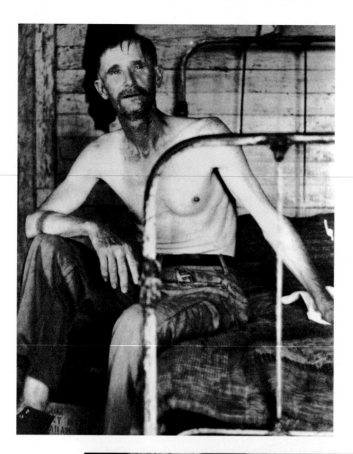

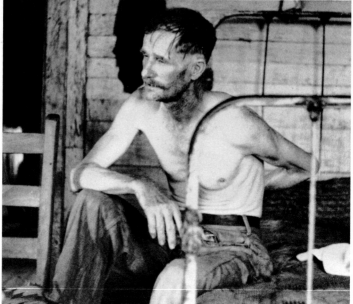

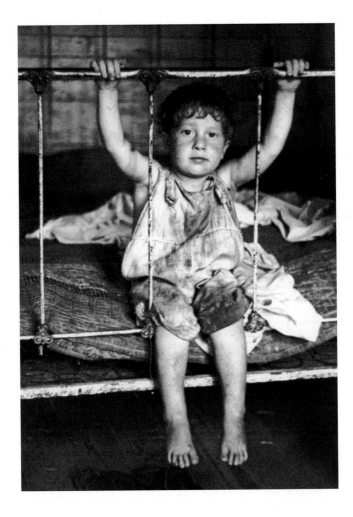

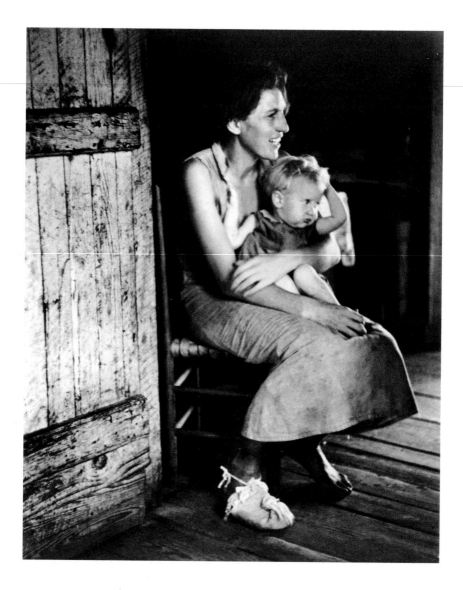

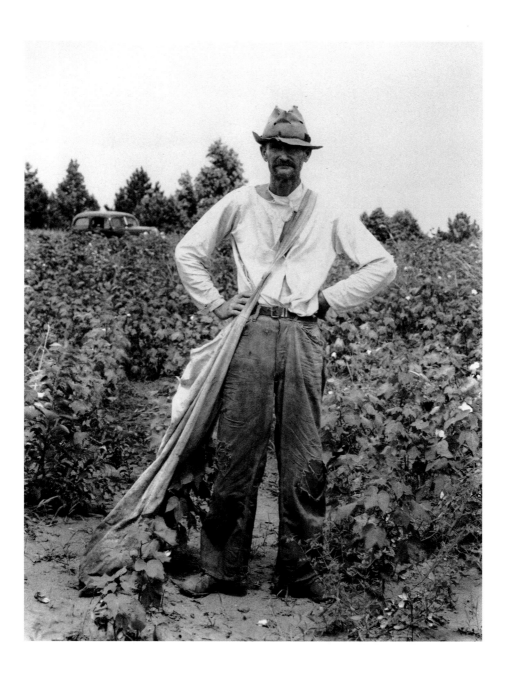

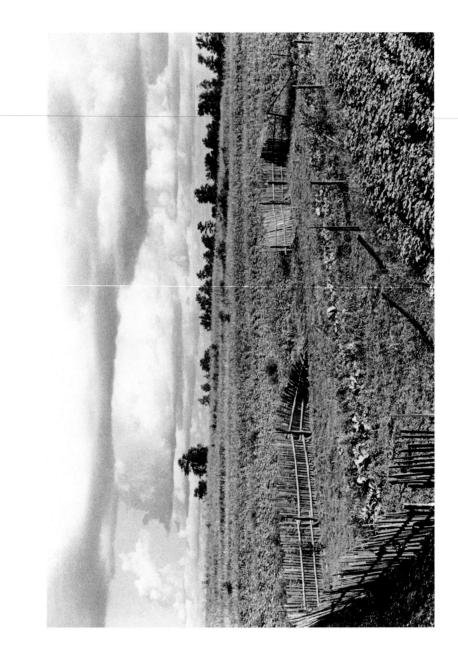

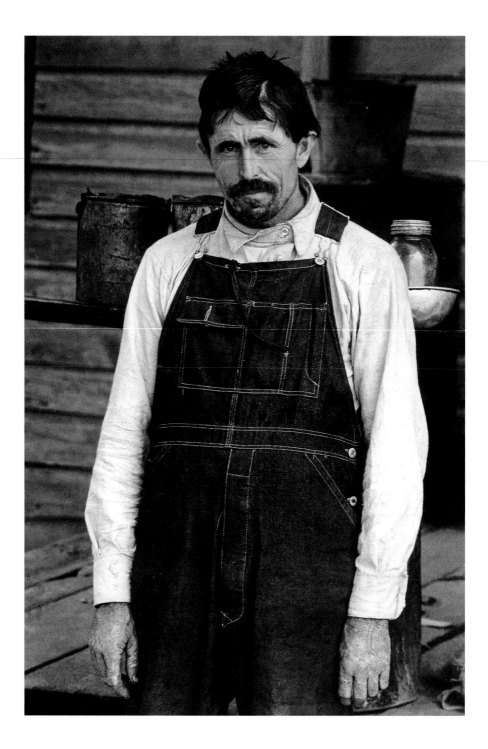

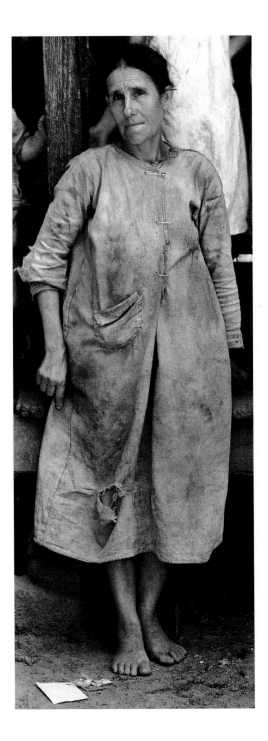

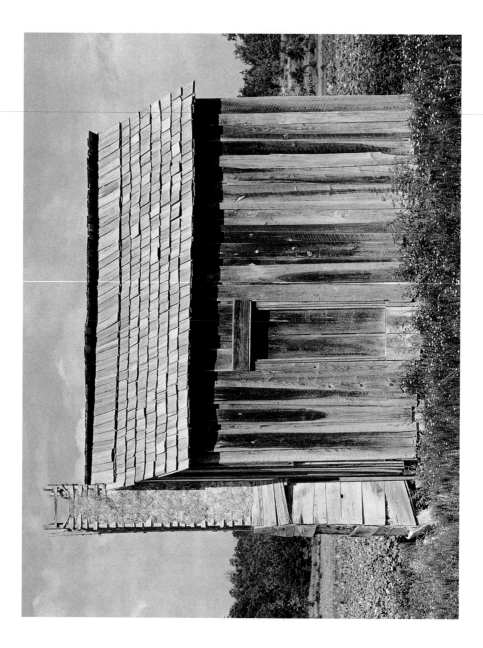

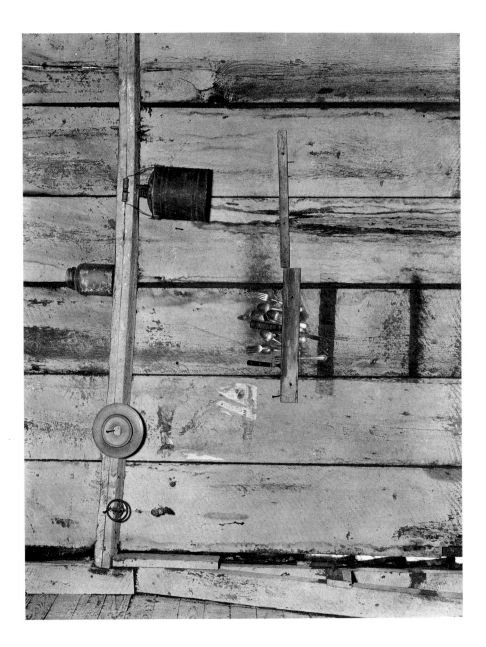

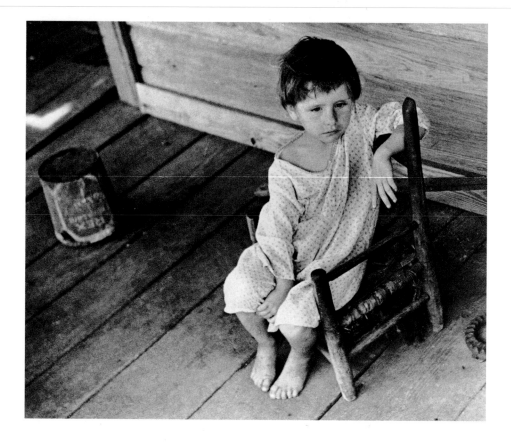

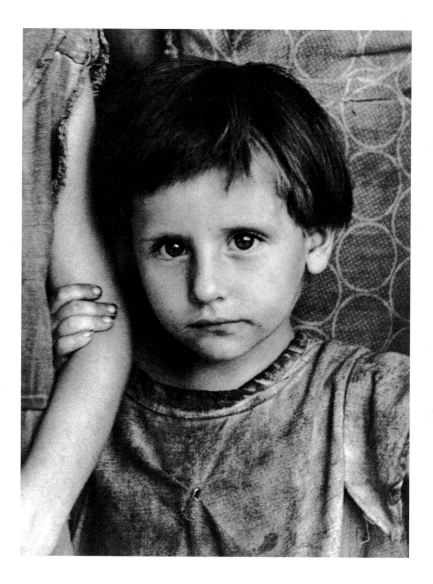

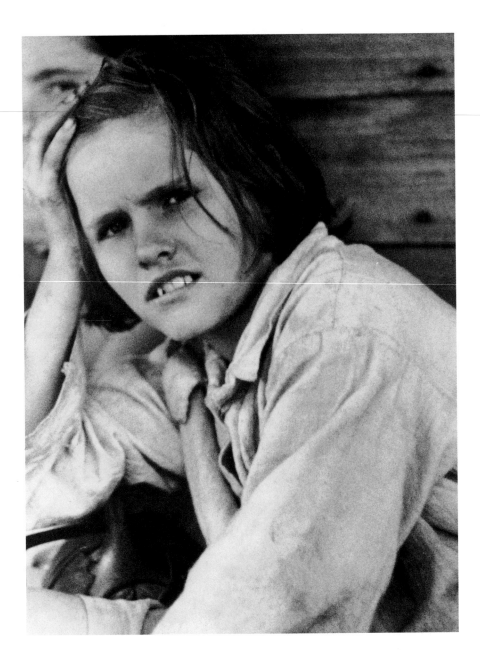

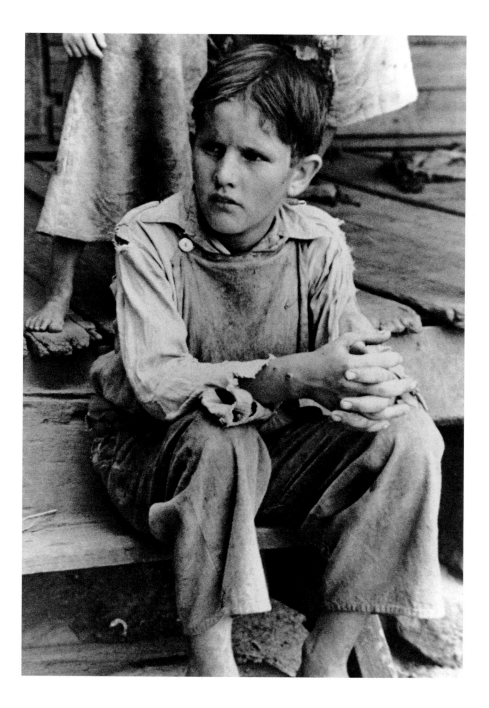

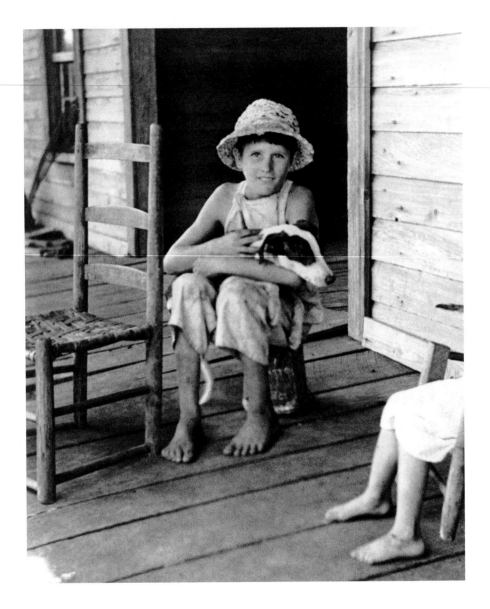

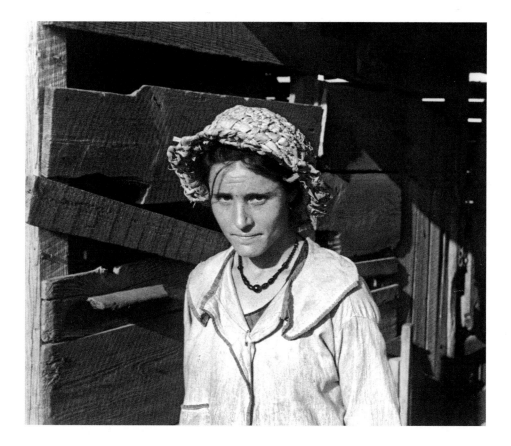

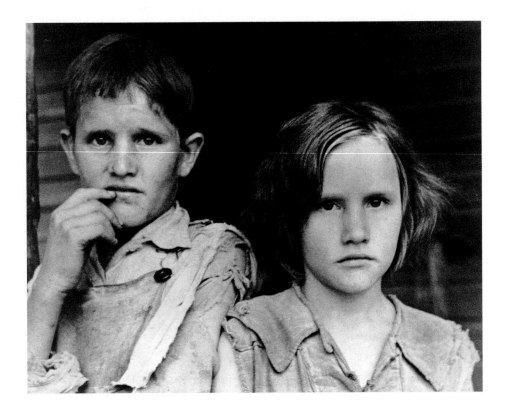

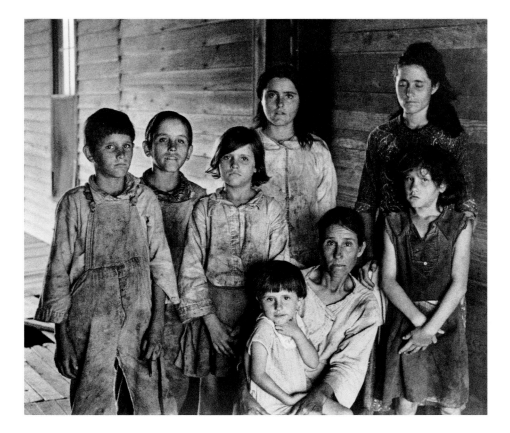

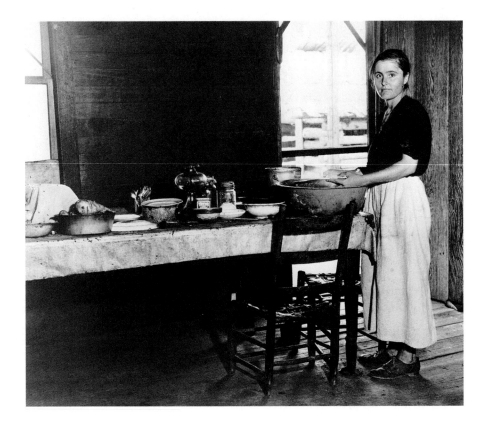

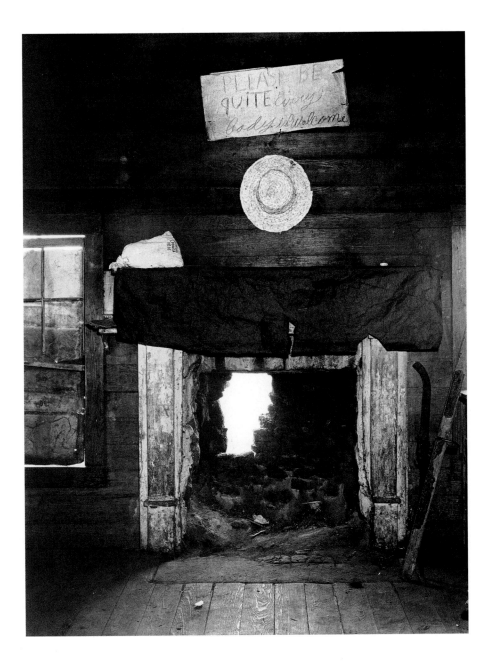

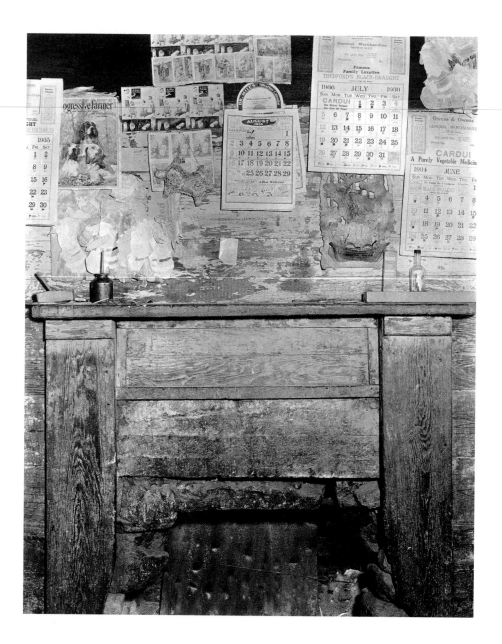

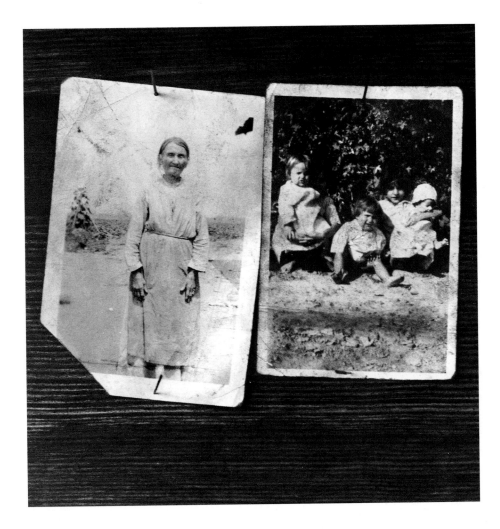

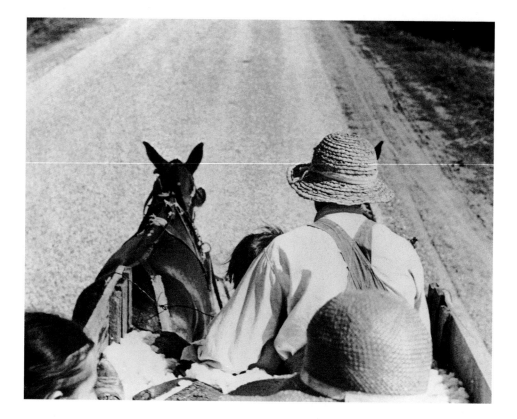

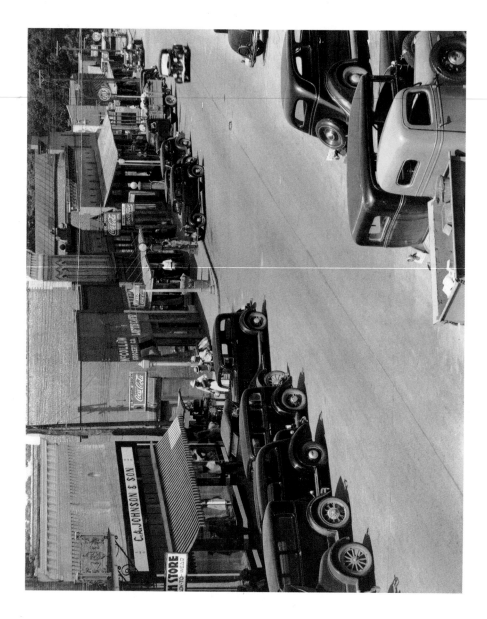

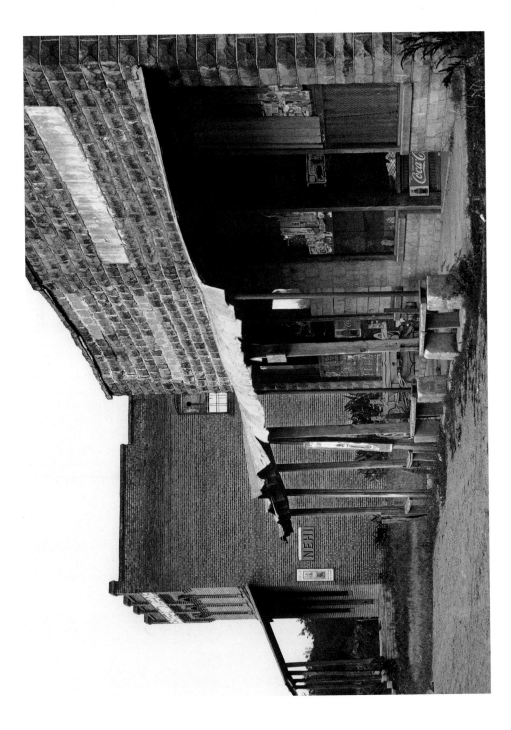

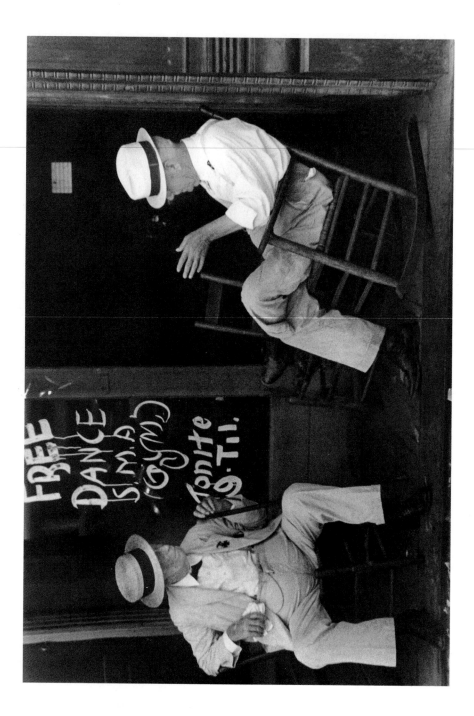

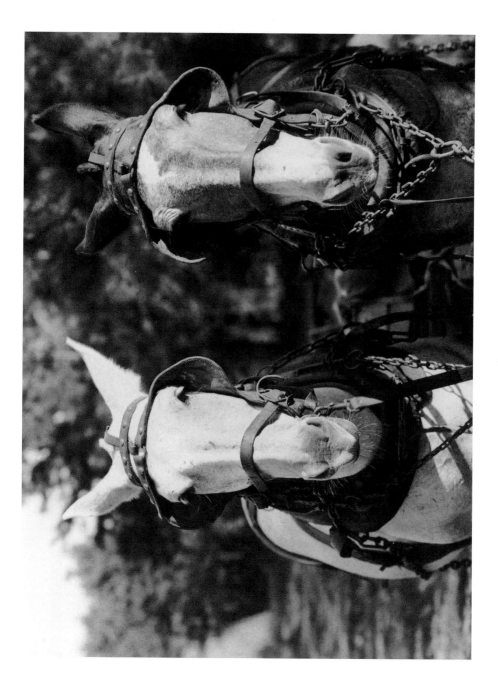

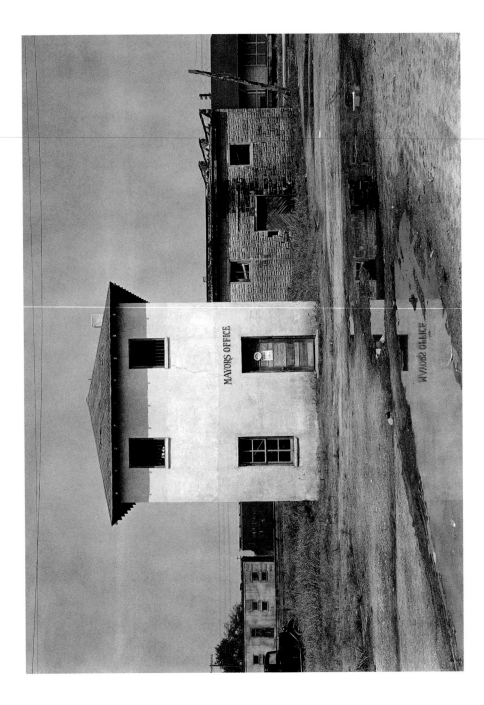

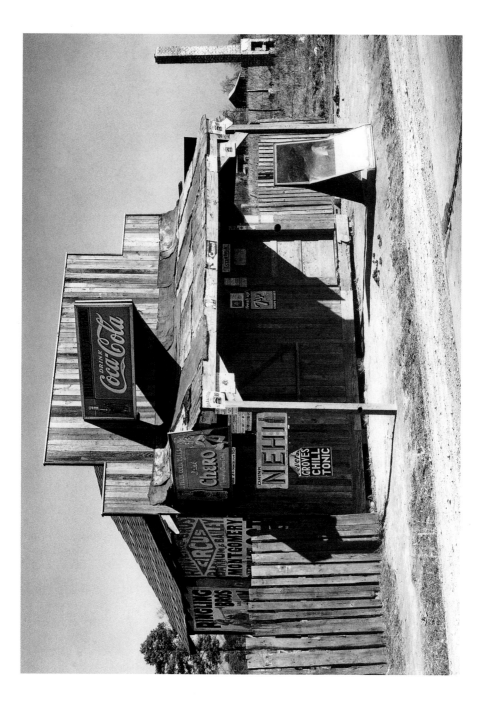

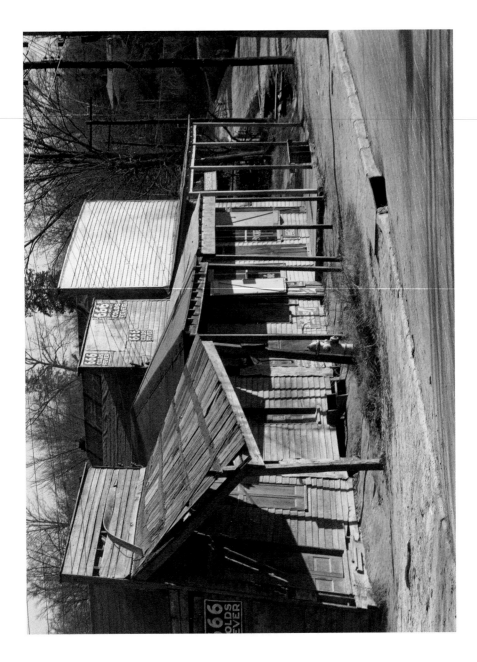

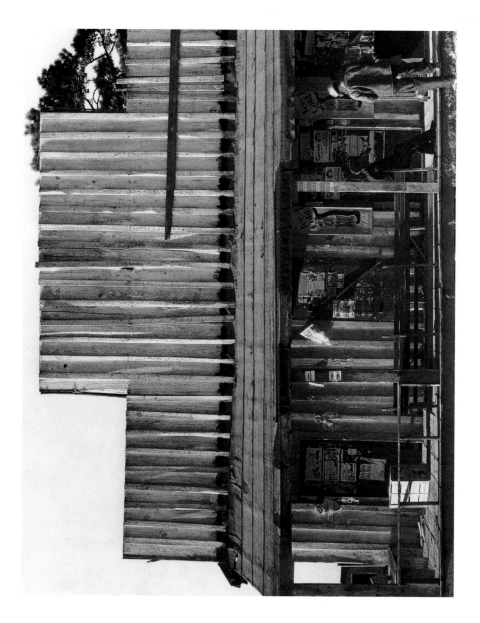

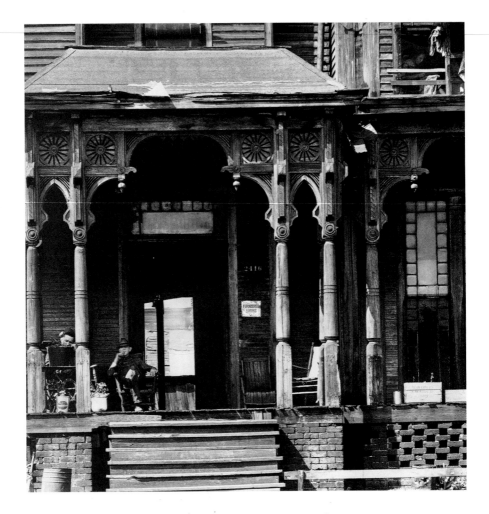

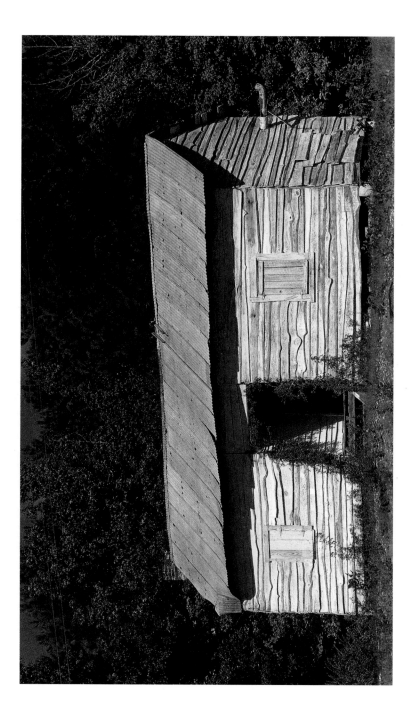

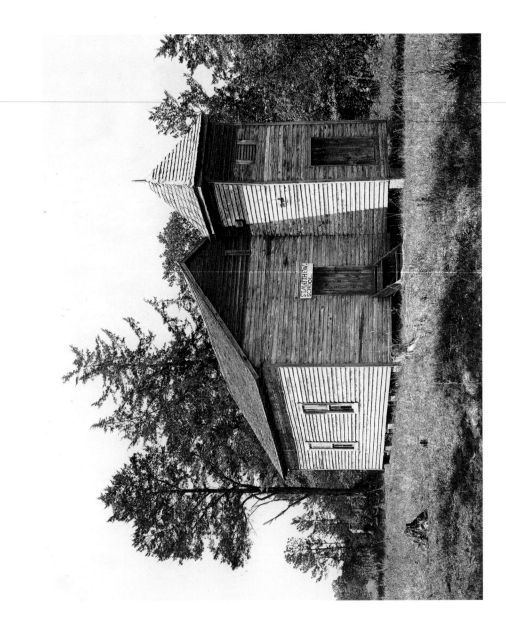

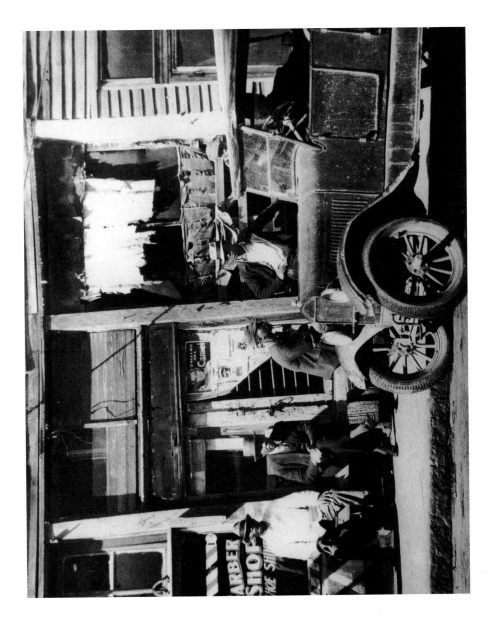

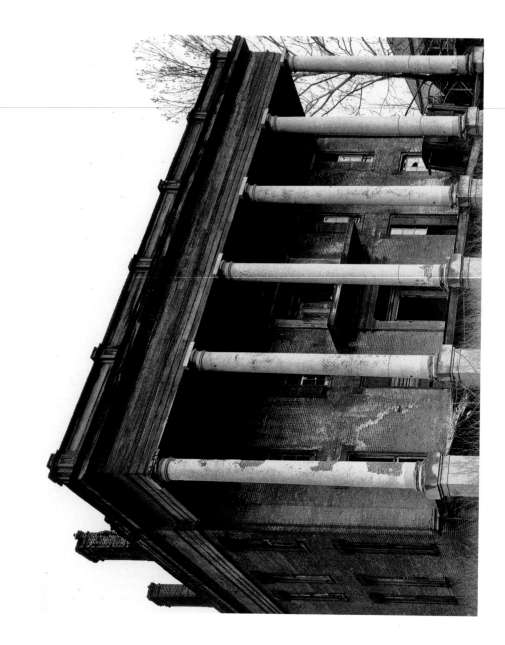

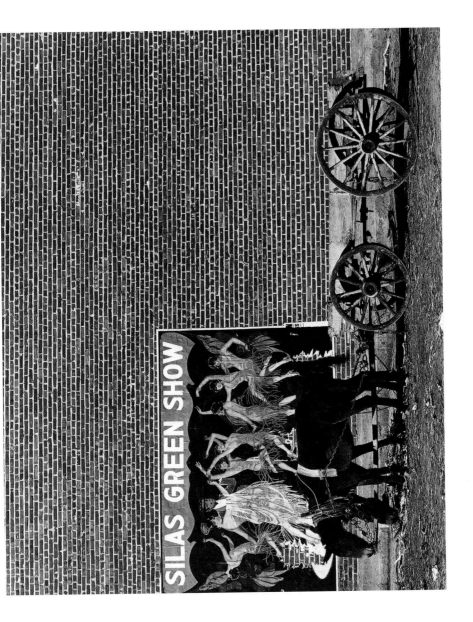

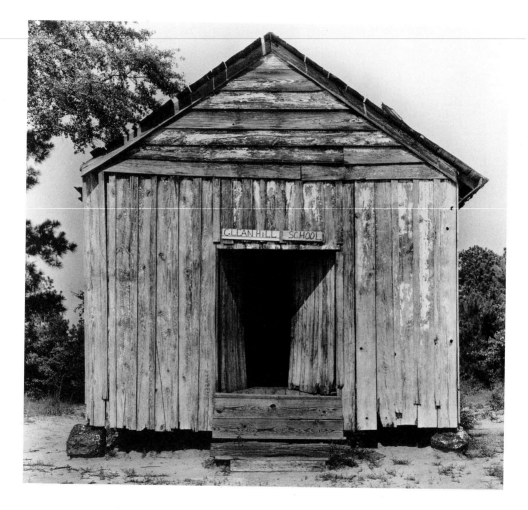

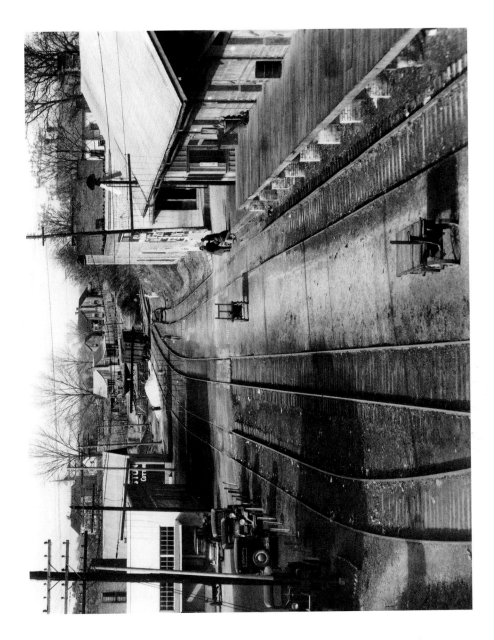

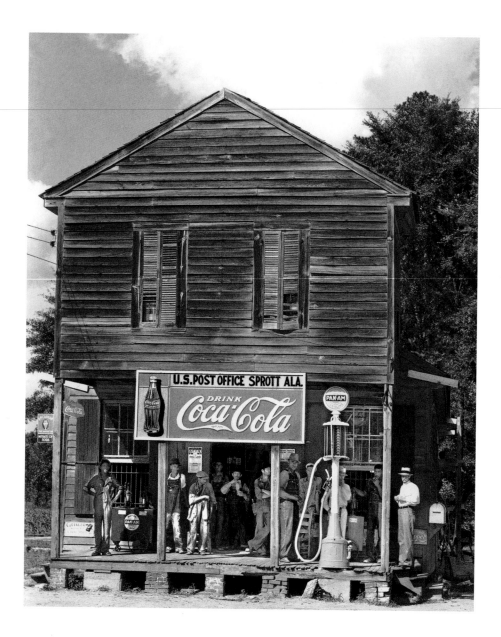

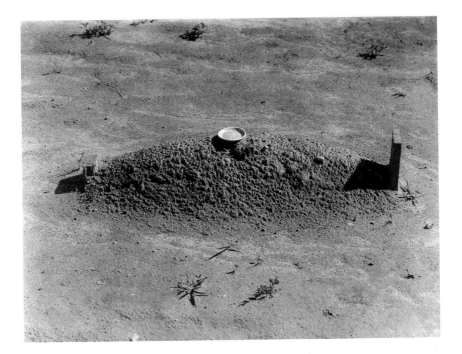

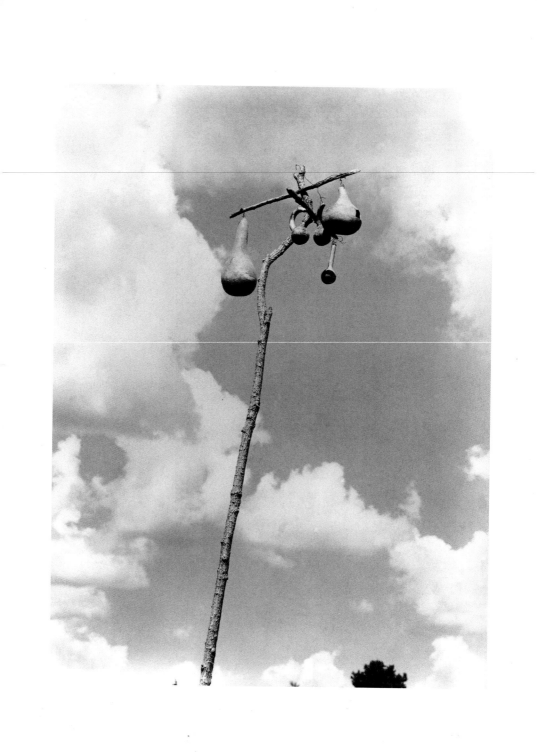

LET US NOW PRAISE FAMOUS MEN

THREE TENANT FAMILIES

LET US NOW PRAISE FAMOUS MEN

James Agee · Walker Evans

A MARINER BOOK
HOUGHTON MIFFLIN COMPANY
BOSTON · NEW YORK

To those of whom the record is made.
In gratefulness and in love.

J. A.
W. E.

———————

First Mariner Books edition 2001

Visit our Web site: www.hmhbooks.com

Library of Congress Cataloging-in-Publication Data
Agee, James, 1909–1955.
Let us now praise famous men : three tenant families / James Agee, Walker Evans
p. cm.
Originally published: Boston : Houghton Mifflin, 1941.
ISBN 0-395-95771-0
ISBN 0-618-12749-6 (pbk.)
1. Alabama – Rural conditions. 2. Agee, James, 1909–1955 – Journeys –
Alabama. 3. Alabama – Description. 4. Farm tenancy – Alabama –
History. I. Evans, Walker, 1903–1975. II. Title.
HN79.A4A535 1988 88–18110
976.1 – dc 19 CIP

Printed in the United States of America

DOC 20 19 18 17 16 15 14

Photographs reproduced through the courtesy of the Library of Congress and the Photography
Collection, Harry Ransom Humanities Research Center, The University of Texas at Austin.
Selected photographs copyright © Walker Evans Archive, The Metropolitan Museum of Art.

Passages from this book appeared in *Common Sense, New Directions,* and *The Atlantic Monthly.*

James Agee in 1936

by Walker Evans

At the time, Agee was a youthful-looking twenty-seven. I think he felt he was elaborately masked, but what you saw right away — alas for conspiracy — was a faint rubbing of Harvard and Exeter, a hint of family gentility, and a trace of romantic idealism. He could be taken for a likable American young man, an above-average product of the Great Democracy from any part of the country. He didn't look much like a poet, an intellectual, an artist, or a Christian, each of which he was. Nor was there outward sign of his paralyzing, self-lacerating anger. His voice was pronouncedly quiet and low-pitched, though not of "cultivated" tone. It gave the impression of diffidence, but never of weakness. His accent was more or less unplaceable and it was somewhat variable. For instance, in Alabama it veered towards country-southern, and I may say he got away with this to the farm families and to himself.

His clothes were deliberately cheap, not only because he was poor but because he wanted to be able to forget them. He would work a suit into fitting him perfectly by the simple method of not taking it off much. In due time the cloth would mold itself to his frame. Cleaning and pressing would have undone this beautiful process. I exaggerate, but it did seem sometimes that wind, rain, work, and mockery were his tailors. On another score, he felt that wearing good, expensive clothes involved him in some sort of claim to superiority of the social kind.

Here he occasionally confused his purpose, and fell over into a knowingly comical inverted dandyism. He got more delight out of factory-seconds sneakers and a sleazy cap than a straight dandy does from waxed calf Peal shoes and a brushed Lock & Co. bowler.

Physically Agee was quite powerful, in the deceptive way of uninsistent large men. In movement he was rather graceless. His hands were large, long, bony, light, and uncared for. His gestures were one of the memorable things about him. He seemed to model, fight, and stroke his phrases as he talked. The talk, in the end, was his great distinguishing feature. He talked his prose, Agee prose. It was hardly a twentieth-century style; it had Elizabethan colors. Yet it had extraordinarily knowledgeable contemporary content. It rolled just as it reads; but he made it sound natural — something just there in the air like any other part of the world. How he did this no one knows. You would have blinked, gaped, and very likely run from this same talk delivered without his mysterious ability. It wasn't a matter of show, and it wasn't necessarily bottle-inspired. Sheer energy of imagination was what lay behind it. This he matched with physical energy. Many a man or woman has fallen exhausted to sleep at four in the morning bang in the middle of a remarkable Agee performance, and later learned that the man had continued it somewhere else until six. Like many born writers who are floating in the illusory amplitude of their youth, Agee did a great deal of writing in the air. Often you had the impulse to gag him and tie a pen to his hand. That wasn't necessary; he was an exception among talking writers. He wrote — devotedly and incessantly.

Night was his time. In Alabama he worked I don't know how late. Some parts of *Let Us Now Praise Famous Men* read as though they were written on the spot at night. Later, in a small house in Frenchtown, New Jersey, the work, I think, was largely night-written. Literally the result shows this; some of the sections read best at night, far in the night. The first passage of *A Country Letter* (page 34) is particularly night-permeated.

Agee worked in what looked like a rush and a rage. In Alabama he was possessed with the business, jamming it all into the days and the nights. He must not have slept. He was driven to see all he could of the families' day, starting, of course, at dawn. In one way, conditions there were ideal. He could live inside the subject, with no distractions. Backcountry poor life wasn't really far from him, actually. He had some of it in his blood, through relatives in Tennessee. Anyway, he was in flight from New York magazine editorial offices, from Greenwich Village social-intellectual evenings, and especially from the whole world of high-minded, well-bred, money-hued culture, whether authoritarian or libertarian. In Alabama he sweated and scratched with submerged glee. The families understood what he was down there to do. He'd explained it, in such a way that they were interested in *his* work. He wasn't playing. That is why in the end he left out certain completed passages that were entertaining, in an acid way. One of these was a long, gradually hilarious aside on the subject of hens. It was a virtuoso piece heightened with allegory and bemused with the pathetic fallacy.

He won almost everybody in those families — perhaps too much — even though some of the individuals were hardbitten, sore, and shrewd. Probably it was his diffidence that took him into them. That non-assurance was, I think, a hostage to his very Anglican childhood training. His Christianity — if an outsider may try to speak of it — was a punctured and residual remnant, but it was still a naked, root emotion. It was an ex-Church, or non-Church, matter, and it was hardly in evidence. All you saw of it was an ingrained courtesy, an uncourtly courtesy that emanated from him towards everyone, perhaps excepting the smugly rich, the pretentiously genteel, and the police. After a while, in a round-about way, you discovered that, to him, human beings were at least possibly immortal and literally sacred souls.

The days with the families came abruptly to an end. Their real content and meaning has all been shown. The writing they induced is, among other things, the reflection of one resolute, private rebellion. Agee's rebellion was unquenchable, self-damaging, deeply principled, infinitely costly, and ultimately priceless.

New York, 1960

Preface

(Serious readers are advised to proceed to the book-proper after finishing the first section of the Preface. A later return will do no harm.)

During July and August 1936 Walker Evans and I were traveling in the middle south of this nation, and were engaged in what, even from the first, has seemed to me rather a curious piece of work. It was our business to prepare, for a New York magazine, * an article on cotton tenantry in the United States, in the form of a photographic and verbal record of the daily living and environment of an average white family of tenant farmers. We had first to find and to live with such a family; and that was the object of our traveling.

We found no one family through which the whole of tenantry in that country could be justly represented, but decided that through three we had come to know, our job might with qualified adequacy be done. With the most nearly representative of the three we lived a little less than four weeks, seeing them and the others intimately and constantly. At the end of August, long before we were willing to, we returned into the north and got our work ready.

---

* Evans was on loan from the Federal Government.

For reasons which will not be a part of this volume the article was not published. At the end of a year it was, however, released to us; and in the spring of 1938 an agreement was reached with a New York publisher for an expansion of the same material in book form. At the end of another year and a half, for reasons which, again, will receive later attention, the completed manuscript was rejected, or withdrawn. In the spring of 1940 it was accepted by those who now publish it, on condition that certain words be deleted which are illegal in Massachusetts.

The authors found it possible to make this concession and, since it rather enhanced a deception, to permit prominence to the immediate, instead of the generic, title.

This volume is designed in two intentions: as the beginning of a larger piece of work; and to stand of itself, independent of any such further work as may be done.

The title of this volume is *Let Us Now Praise Famous Men.*

The title of the work as a whole, this volume included, is *Three Tenant Families.*

The nominal subject is North American cotton tenantry as examined in the daily living of three representative white tenant families.

Actually, the effort is to recognize the stature of a portion of unimagined existence, and to contrive techniques proper to its recording, communication, analysis, and defense. More essentially, this is an independent inquiry into certain normal predicaments of human divinity.

The immediate instruments are two: the motionless camera, and the printed word. The governing instrument — which is also one of the centers of the subject — is individual, anti-authoritative human consciousness.

Ultimately, it is intended that this record and analysis be exhaustive, with no detail, however trivial it may seem, left untouched, no relevancy avoided, which lies within the power of remembrance to maintain, of the intelligence to perceive, and of the spirit to persist in.

Of this ultimate intention the present volume is merely portent and fragment, experiment, dissonant prologue. Since it is intended, among other things, as a swindle, an insult, and a corrective, the reader will be wise to bear the nominal subject, and his expectation of its proper treatment, steadily in mind. For that is the subject with which the authors are dealing, throughout. If complications arise, that is because they are trying to deal with it not as journalists, sociologists, politicians, entertainers, humanitarians, priests, or artists, but seriously.

The photographs are not illustrative. They, and the text, are co-equal, mutually independent, and fully collaborative. By their fewness, and by the impotence of the reader's eye, this will be misunderstood by most of that minority which does not wholly ignore it. In the interests, however, of the history and future of photography, that risk seems irrelevant, and this flat statement necessary.

The text was written with reading aloud in mind. That cannot be recommended; but it is suggested that the reader attend with his ear to what he takes off the page: for variations of tone, pace, shape, and dynamics are here particularly unavailable to the eye alone, and with their loss, a good deal of meaning escapes.

It was intended also that the text be read continuously, as music is listened to or a film watched, with brief pauses only where they are self-evident.

Of any attempt on the part of the publishers, or others, to disguise or in any other way to ingratiate this volume, the authors must express their regret, their intense disapproval, and, as observers awaiting new contributions to their subject, their complaisance.

This is a *book* only by necessity. More seriously, it is an effort in human actuality, in which the reader is no less centrally involved than the authors and those of whom they tell. Those who wish actively to participate in the subject, in whatever degree of understanding, friendship, or hostility, are invited to address the authors in care of the publishers. In material that is used, privately or publicly, names will be withheld on request.

Poor naked wretches, wheresoe'er you are,
That bide the pelting of this pitiless storm,
How shall your houseless heads and unfed sides,
Your loop'd and window'd raggedness, defend you
From seasons such as these? O! I have ta'en
Too little care of this! Take physick, pomp;
Expose thyself to feel what wretches feel,
That thou may'st shake the superflux to them,
And show the heavens more just.

Workers of the world, unite and fight. You have nothing to lose but your chains, and a world to win. *

I. The Great Ball on Which We Live

The world is our home. It is also the home of many, many other children, some of whom live in far-away lands. They are our world brothers and sisters. . . .

2. Food, Shelter, and Clothing

What must any part of the world have in order to be a good home for man? What does every person need in order to live in comfort? Let us imagine that we are far out in the fields. The air is bitter cold and the wind is blowing. Snow is falling, and by and by it will turn into sleet and rain. We are almost naked. We have had nothing to eat and are suffering from hunger as well as cold. Suddenly the Queen of the Fairies floats down and offers us three wishes.

What shall we choose?

'I shall wish for food, because I am hungry,' says Peter.

'I shall choose clothes to keep out the cold,' says John.

'And I shall ask for a house to shelter me from the wind, the snow, and the rain,' says little Nell with a shiver.

Now everyone needs food, clothing, and shelter. The lives of most men on the earth are spent in getting these things. In our travels we shall wish to learn what our world brothers and sisters eat, and where their food comes from. We shall wish to see the houses they dwell in and how they are built. We shall wish also to know what clothing they use to protect themselves from the heat and the cold. *

---

* These are the opening sentences of *Around the World With the Children,* by F. B. Carpenter (published by The American Book Company), a third-grade geography textbook belonging to Louise Gudger, aged ten, daughter of a cotton tenant.

Persons and Places

FRED GARVRIN RICKETTS: a two-mule tenant farmer, aged fifty-four.
SADIE (WOODS) RICKETTS: his wife, aged forty-nine.
 MARGARET: aged twenty.
 PARALEE: aged nineteen.
 JOHN GARVRIN: aged twelve.
 RICHARD: aged eleven.
 FLORA MERRY LEE: aged ten.
 KATY: aged nine.
 CLAIR BELL: aged four.
THOMAS GALLATIN WOODS (BUD): a one-mule tenant farmer, aged fifty-nine.
 IVY WOODS: his second wife; middle twenties.
 MISS-MOLLY: her mother; early fifties.
 GALLATIN: Woods' son by first marriage; a half-cropper; middle thirties.
 EMMA: a daughter of the first marriage; aged eighteen; married.
 PEARL: Ivy's daughter by common-law marriage to a man prior to Woods;
  aged eight.
 THOMAS: son of Woods and second wife; aged three.
 ELLEN: child of second marriage; aged twenty months.
GEORGE GUDGER: a one-mule half-cropper, aged thirty-one.
ANNIE MAE (WOODS) GUDGER: his wife, aged twenty-seven.
 MAGGIE LOUISE: aged ten.
 GEORGE JUNIOR: aged eight.
 BURT WESTLY: aged four.
 VALLEY FEW (SQUINCHY): aged twenty months.

CHESTER BOLES: Gudger's landlord.

T. HUDSON MARGRAVES:
MICHAEL MARGRAVES: } landlords to Woods and Ricketts.

HARMON: a landowner and New Deal executive.

ESTELLE: a middle-class young woman.

JAMES AGEE: a spy, traveling as a journalist.

WALKER EVANS: a counter-spy, traveling as a photographer.

WILLIAM BLAKE
LOUIS-FERDINAND CÉLINE
RING LARDNER
JESUS CHRIST } unpaid agitators.
SIGMUND FREUD
LONNIE JOHNSON
IRVINE UPHAM
OTHERS

BIRMINGHAM: a large Southern industrial city.

CHEROKEE CITY: a county seat; population *c.* 7000.

CENTERBORO: county seat for these tenants; *c.* 1500.

COOKSTOWN: their landlords' town, and theirs; *c.* 300.

MADRID: a crossroads; two stores, four houses.

HOBE'S HILL: a low plateau of clay, where the tenants live.

It is two miles to the highway; three to Madrid; seven to Cookstown; seventeen to Centerboro; twenty-seven to Cherokee City; eighty to Birmingham. Transportation, for these families, is by mule or by mule wagon or on foot. This is not far from the geographic center of the North American Cotton Belt.

Sadie Ricketts is a half-sister of Woods; Annie Mae Gudger is his daughter.

Since none of the characters or incidents of this volume are fictitious, the names of most persons, and nearly all names of places, are altered.

The ages given, and tenses throughout, save where it is otherwise obvious or deliberately ambiguous, are as of the summer of 1936.

LET US NOW PRAISE
FAMOUS MEN

———

Design of the Book

(To Walker Evans.

Against time and the damages of the brain
Sharpen and calibrate. Not yet in full,
Yet in some arbitrated part
Order the façade of the listless summer.

Spies, moving delicately among the enemy,
The younger sons, the fools,
Set somewhat aside the dialects and the stained skins of feigned
    madness,
Ambiguously signal, baffle, the eluded sentinel.

Edgar, weeping for pity, to the shelf of that sick bluff,
Bring your blind father, and describe a little;
Behold him, part wakened, fallen among field flowers shallow
But undisclosed, withdraw.

Not yet that naked hour when armed,
Disguise flung flat, squarely we challenge the fiend.
Still, comrade, the running of beasts and the ruining heaven
Still captive the old wild king.

'I spoke of this piece of work we were doing as "curious." I had better amplify this.

It seems to me curious, not to say obscene and thoroughly terrifying, that it could occur to an association of human beings drawn together through need and chance and for profit into a company, an organ of journalism, to pry intimately into the lives of an undefended and appallingly damaged group of human beings, an ignorant and helpless rural family, for the purpose of parading the nakedness, disadvantage and humiliation of these lives before another group of human beings, in the name of science, of "honest journalism" (whatever that paradox may mean), of humanity, of social fearlessness, for money, and for a reputation for crusading and for unbias which, when skillfully enough qualified, is exchangeable at any bank for money (and in politics, for votes, job patronage, abelincolnism, etc. *; and that these people could be capable of meditating this prospect without the slightest doubt of their qualification to do an "honest" piece of work, and with a conscience better than clear, and in the virtual certitude of almost unanimous public approval. It seems curious, further, that the assignment of this work should have fallen to persons having so extremely

* Money

different a form of respect for the subject, and responsibility toward it, that from the first and inevitably they counted their employers, and that Government likewise to which one of them was bonded, among their most dangerous enemies, acted as spies, guardians, and cheats, * and trusted no judgment, however authoritative it claimed to be, save their own: which in many aspects of the task before them was untrained and uninformed. It seems further curious that realizing the extreme corruptness and difficulty of the circumstances, and the unlikelihood of achieving in any untainted form what they wished to achieve, they accepted the work in the first place. And it seems curious still further that, with all their suspicion of and contempt for every person and thing to do with the situation, save only for the tenants and for themselves, and their own intentions, and with all their realization of the seriousness and mystery of the subject, and of the human responsibility they undertook, they so little questioned or doubted their own qualifications for this work.

All of this, I repeat, seems to me curious, obscene, terrifying, and unfathomably mysterious.

So does the whole course, in all its detail, of the effort of these persons to find, and to defend, what they sought: and the nature of their relationship with those with whom during the searching stages they came into contact; and the subtlety, importance, and almost intangibility of the insights or revelations or oblique suggestions which under different circumstances could never have materialized; so does the method of research which was partly evolved by them, partly forced upon them; so does the strange quality of their relationship with those whose lives they so tenderly and sternly respected, and so rashly undertook to investigate and to record.

So does the whole subsequent course and fate of the work: the causes for its non-publication, the details of its later acceptance else-

---

* Une chose permise ne peut pas être pure.
  L'illégal me va.
— *Essai de Critique Indirecte*

where, and of its design; the problems which confronted the maker of
the photographs; and those which confront me as I try to write of it:
the question, Who are you who will read these words and study these
photographs, and through what cause, by what chance, and for what
purpose, and by what right do you qualify to, and what will you do
about it; and the question, Why we make this book, and set it at large,
and by what right, and for what purpose, and to what good end, or
none: the whole memory of the South in its six-thousand-mile parade
and flowering outlay of the façades of cities, and of the eyes in the
streets of towns, and of hotels, and of the trembling heat, and of the
wide wild opening of the tragic land, wearing the trapped frail flowers
of its garden of faces; the fleet flush and flower and fainting of the
human crop it raises; the virulent, insolent, deceitful, pitying, infinitesimal and frenzied running and searching, on this colossal peasant map,
of two angry, futile and bottomless, botched and overcomplicated
youthful intelligences in the service of an anger and of a love and of an
undiscernible truth, and in the frightening vanity of their would-be
purity; the sustaining, even now, and forward moving, lifted on the lifting of this day as ships on a wave, above whom, in a few hours, night
once more will stand up in his stars, and they decline through lamplight and be dreaming statues, of those, each, whose lives we knew and
whom we love and intend well toward, and of whose living we know
little in some while now, save that quite steadily, in not much possible
change for better or much worse, mute, innocent, helpless and incorporate among that small-moted and inestimable swarm and pollen
stream and fleet of single, irreparable, unrepeatable existences, they are
led, gently, quite steadily, quite without mercy, each a little farther
toward the washing and the wailing, the sunday suit and the prettiest
dress, the pine box, and the closed clay room whose fraily decorated
roof, until rain has taken it flat into oblivion, wears the shape of a ritual scar and of an inverted boat: curious, obscene, terrifying, beyond all
search of dream unanswerable, those problems which stand thickly
forth like light from all matter, triviality, chance, intention, and record
in the body, of being, of truth, of conscience, of hope, of hatred, of

beauty, of indignation, of guilt, of betrayal, of innocence, of forgiveness, of vengeance, of guardianship, of an indenominable fate, predicament, destination, and God.

Therefore it is in some fear that I approach those matters at all, and in much confusion. And if there are questions in my mind how to undertake this communication, and there are many, I must let the least of them be, whether I am boring you, or whether I am taking too long getting started, and too clumsily. If I bore you, that is that. If I am clumsy, that may indicate partly the difficulty of my subject, and the seriousness with which I am trying to take what hold I can of it; more certainly, it will indicate my youth, my lack of mastery of my so-called art or craft, my lack perhaps of talent. Those matters, too, must reveal themselves as they may. However they turn out, they cannot be otherwise than true to their conditions, and I would not wish to conceal these conditions even if I could, for I am interested to speak as carefully and as near truly as I am able. No doubt I shall worry myself that I am taking too long getting started, and shall seriously distress myself over my inability to create an organic, mutually sustaining and dependent, and as it were musical, form: but I must remind myself that I started with the first word I wrote, and that the centers of my subject are shifty; and, again, that I am no better an "artist" than I am capable of being, under these circumstances, perhaps under any other; and that this again will find its measurement in the facts as they are, and will contribute its own measure, whatever it may be, to the pattern of the effort and truth as a whole.

I might say, in short, but emphatically not in self-excuse, of which I wish entirely to disarm and disencumber myself, but for the sake of clear definition, and indication of limits, that I am only human. Those works which I most deeply respect have about them a firm quality of the superhuman, in part because they refuse to define and limit and crutch, or admit themselves as human. But to a person of my uncertainty, undertaking a task of this sort, that plane and manner are not within reach, and could only falsify what by this manner of effort may at least less hopelessly approach clarity, and truth.'

'For in the immediate world, everything is to be discerned, for him who can discern it, and centrally and simply, without either dissection into science, or digestion into art, but with the whole of consciousness, seeking to perceive it as it stands: so that the aspect of a street in sunlight can roar in the heart of itself as a symphony, perhaps as no symphony can: and all of consciousness is shifted from the imagined, the revisive, to the effort to perceive simply the cruel radiance of what is.

This is why the camera seems to me, next to unassisted and weaponless consciousness, the central instrument of our time; and is why in turn I feel such rage at its misuse: which has spread so nearly universal a corruption of sight that I know of less than a dozen alive whose eyes I can trust even so much as my own.'

'If I had explained myself clearly you would realize by now that through this non-"artistic" view, this effort to suspend or destroy imagination, there opens before consciousness, and within it, a universe luminous, spacious, incalculably rich and wonderful in each detail, as relaxed and natural to the human swimmer, and as full of glory, as his breathing: and that it is possible to capture and communicate this universe not so well by any means of art as through such open terms as I am trying it under.

In a novel, a house or person has his meaning, his existence, entirely through the writer. Here, a house or a person has only the most limited of his meaning through me: his true meaning is much huger. It is that he *exists*, in actual being, as you do and as I do, and as no character of the imagination can possibly exist. His great weight, mystery, and dignity are in this fact. As for me, I can tell you of him only what I saw, only so accurately as in my terms I know how: and this in turn has its chief stature not in any ability of mine but in the fact that I too exist, not as a work of fiction, but as a human being. Because of his immeasurable weight in actual existence, and because of mine, every word I tell of him has inevitably a kind of immediacy, a kind of meaning, not at all necessarily "superior" to that of imagination, but of a kind so different that a work of the imagination (however intensely it may draw on "life") can at best only faintly imitate the least of it.'

"The communication is not by any means so simple. It seems to me now that to contrive techniques appropriate to it in the first place, and capable of planting it cleanly in others, in the second, would be a matter of years, and I shall probably try none of it or little, and that very tortured and diluted, at present. I realize that, with even so much involvement in explanations as this, I am liable seriously, and perhaps irretrievably, to obscure what would at best be hard enough to give its appropriate clarity and intensity; and what seems to me most important of all: namely, that these I will write of are human beings, living in this world, innocent of such twistings as these which are taking place over their heads; and that they were dwelt among, investigated, spied on, revered, and loved, by other quite monstrously alien human beings, in the employment of still others still more alien; and that they are now being looked into by still others, who have picked up their living as casually as if it were a book, and who were actuated toward this reading by various possible reflexes of sympathy, curiosity, idleness, et cetera, and almost certainly in a lack of consciousness, and conscience, remotely appropriate to the enormity of what they are doing.

If I could do it, I'd do no writing at all here. It would be photographs; the rest would be fragments of cloth, bits of cotton, lumps of earth, records of speech, pieces of wood and iron, phials of odors, plates of food and of excrement. Booksellers would consider it quite a novelty; critics would murmur, yes, but is it art; and I could trust a majority of you to use it as you would a parlor game.

A piece of the body torn out by the roots might be more to the point.

As it is, though, I'll do what little I can in writing. Only it will be very little. I'm not capable of it; and if I were, you would not go near it at all. For if you did, you would hardly bear to live.

As a matter of fact, nothing I might write could make any difference whatever. It would only be a "book" at the best. If it were a safely dangerous one it would be "scientific" or "political" or "revolutionary." If it were really dangerous it would be "literature" or "religion" or "mysticism" or "art," and under one such name or another might in time achieve the emasculation of acceptance. If it were dangerous enough to be of any remote use to the human race it would be merely "frivolous" or "pathological," and that would be the end of that. Wiser and more capable men than I shall ever be have put their findings before you, findings so rich and so full of anger, serenity, murder, healing, truth, and love that it seems incredible the world were not destroyed and fulfilled in the instant, but you are too much for them: the weak in courage are strong in cunning; and one by one, you have absorbed and have captured and dishonored, and have distilled of your deliverers the most ruinous of all your poisons; people hear Beethoven in concert halls, or over a bridge game, or to relax; Cézannes are hung on walls, reproduced, in natural wood frames; van Gogh is the man who cut off his ear and whose yellows became recently popular in window decoration; Swift loved individuals but hated the human race; Kafka is a fad; Blake is in the Modern Library; Freud is a Modern Library Giant; Dovschenko's *Frontier* is disliked by those who demand that it fit the Eisenstein esthetic; *nobody* reads Joyce any more; Céline is a madman who has incurred the hearty dislike of Alfred Kazin, reviewer for the *New York Herald Tribune* book section, and is, moreover, a fascist; I hope I need not mention Jesus Christ, of whom you have managed to make a dirty gentile.

However that may be, this is a book about "sharecroppers," and is written for all those who have a soft place in their hearts for the laughter and tears inherent in poverty viewed at a distance, and especially for those who can afford the retail price; in the hope that the reader will be edified, and may feel kindly disposed toward any well-thought-out liberal efforts to rectify the unpleasant situation down South, and will somewhat better and more guiltily appreciate the next good meal he eats; and in the hope, too, that he will recommend this little book to really sympathetic friends, in order that our publishers may at least cover their investment and that just the merest perhaps) some kindly thought may be turned our way, and a little of your money fall to poor little us.'

'Above all else: in God's name don't think of it as Art.

Every fury on earth has been absorbed in time, as art, or as religion, or as authority in one form or another. The deadliest blow the enemy of the human soul can strike is to do fury honor. Swift, Blake, Beethoven, Christ, Joyce, Kafka, name me a one who has not been thus castrated. Official acceptance is the one unmistakable symptom that salvation is beaten again, and is the one surest sign of fatal misunderstanding, and is the kiss of Judas.

Really it should be possible to hope that this be recognized as so, and as a mortal and inevitably recurrent danger. It is scientific fact. It is disease. It is avoidable. Let a start be made. And then exercise your perception of it on work that has more to tell you than mine has. See how respectable Beethoven is; and by what right any wall in museum, gallery or home presumes to wear a Cézanne; and by what idiocy Blake or work even of such intention as mine is ever published and sold. I will tell you a test. It is unfair. It is untrue. It stacks all the cards. It is out of line with what the composer intended. All so much the better.

Get a radio or a phonograph capable of the most extreme loudness possible, and sit down to listen to a performance of Beethoven's Seventh Symphony or of Schubert's C-Major Symphony. But I don't mean just sit down and listen. I mean this: Turn it on as loud as you can get it. Then get down on the floor and jam your ear as close into the loudspeaker as you can get it and stay there, breathing as lightly as possible, and not moving, and neither eating nor smoking nor drinking. Concentrate everything you can into your hearing and into your body. You won't hear it nicely. If it hurts you, be glad of it. As near as you will ever get, you are inside the music; not only inside it, you are it; your body is no longer your shape and substance, it is the shape and substance of the music.

Is what you hear pretty? or beautiful? or legal? or acceptable in polite or any other society? It is beyond any calculation savage and dangerous and murderous to all equilibrium in human life as human life is; and nothing can equal the rape it does on all that death; nothing except anything, anything in existence or dream, perceived anywhere remotely toward its true dimension.'

'Beethoven said a thing as rash and noble as the best of his work. By my memory, he said: "He who understands my music can never know unhappiness again." I believe it. And I would be a liar and a coward and one of your safe world if I should fear to say the same words of my best perception, and of my best intention.

Performance, in which the whole fate and terror rests, is another matter.'

The house had now descended

All over Alabama the lamps are out

(On the Porch: 1

The house and all that was in it had now descended deep beneath the gradual spiral it had sunk through; it lay formal under the order of entire silence. In the square pine room at the back the bodies of the man of thirty and of his wife and of their children lay on shallow mattresses on their iron beds and on the rigid floor, and they were sleeping, and the dog lay asleep in the hallway. Most human beings, most animals and birds who live in the sheltering ring of human influence, and a great portion of all the branched tribes of living in earth and air and water upon a half of the world, were stunned with sleep. That region of the earth on which we were at this time transient was some hours fallen beneath the fascination of the stone, steady shadow of the planet, and lay now listing toward the last depth; and now by a blockade of the sun were clearly disclosed those discharges of light which teach us what little we can learn of the stars and of the true nature of our surroundings. There was no longer any sound of the settling or ticking of any part of the structure of the house; the bone pine hung on its nails like an abandoned Christ. There was no longer any sound of the sinking and settling, like gently foundering, fatal boats, of the bodies and brains of this human family through the late stages of fatigue unharnessed or the early phases of sleep; nor was there any

longer the sense of any of these sounds, nor was there, even, the sound
or the sense of breathing. Bone and bone, blood and blood, life and
life disjointed and abandoned they lay graven in so final depth, that
dreams attend them seemed not plausible. Fish halted on the middle
and serene of blind sea water sleeping lidless lensed; their breathing,
their sleeping subsistence, the effortless nursing of ignorant plants;
entirely silenced, sleepers, delicate planets, insects, cherished in amber,
mured in night, autumn of action, sorrow's short winter, water hole
where gather the weak wild beasts; night; night: sleep; sleep.

In their prodigious realm, their field, bashfully at first, less timor-
ous, later, rashly, all calmly boldly now, like the tingling and standing
up of plants, leaves, planted crops out of the earth into the yearly
approach of the sun, the noises and natures of the dark had with the
ceremonial gestures of music and of erosion lifted forth the thousand
several forms of their entrancement, and had so resonantly taken over
the world that this domestic, this human silence obtained, prevailed,
only locally, shallowly, and with the childlike and frugal dignity of a
coal-oil lamp stood out on a wide night meadow and of a star sustained, unraveling in one rivery sigh its irremediable vitality, on the
alien size of space.

Where beneath the ghosts of millennial rain the clay land lay down
in creek and the trees ran thick there disposed upon the sky the cloud
and black shadow of nature, hostile encampment whose fires were
drenched, drawn close, held sleeping, near, helots; and it was feasible
that within a few hours now, at the signaling of the primary changes of
the air, the wave which summer and darkness had already so heavily
overcrested that it leaned above us, snaring its snake-tongued branches, birnam wood, casually would lounge in and suddenly and forever
subdue us: at most, some obscure act of guerrilla warfare, some
prowler, detached from his regiment, picked off in a back country
orchard, some straggling camp whore taken, had; for the sky:

The sky was withdrawn from us with all her strength. Against some
scarcely conceivable imprisoning wall this woman held herself away

from us and watched us: wide, high, light with her stars as milk above our heavy dark; and like the bristling and glass breakage on the mouth of stone spring water: broached on grand heaven their metal fires.

And now as by the slipping of a button, the snapping and failures on air of a spider's cable, there broke loose from the room, shaken, a long sigh closed in silence. On some ledge overleaning that gulf which is more profound than the remembrance of imagination they had lain in sleep and at length the sand, that by degrees had crumpled and rifted, had broken from beneath them and they sank. There was now no further extreme, and they were sunken not singularly but companionate among the whole enchanted swarm of the living, into a region prior to the youngest quaverings of creation.

(We lay on the front porch:

July 1936

Late Sunday Morning

They came into the Coffee Shoppe while we were finishing breakfast, and Harmon introduced the other, whose name I forget, but which had a French sound. He was middle-sized and dark, beginning to grizzle, with the knotty, walnut kind of body and a deeply cut, not unkindly monkey's face. He wore dark trousers, a starched freshly laundered white collarless shirt, and a soft yellow straw hat with a band of flowered cloth. His shoes were old, freshly blacked, not polished; his suspenders were nearly new, blue, with gold lines at the edge. He was courteous, casual, and even friendly, without much showing the element of strain: Harmon let him do the talking and watched us from behind the reflecting lenses of his glasses. People in the street slowed as they passed and lingered their eyes upon us. Walker said it would be all right to make pictures, wouldn't it, and he said, Sure, of course, take all the snaps you're a mind to; that is, if you can keep the niggers from running off when they see a camera. When they saw the amount of equipment stowed in the back of our car, they showed that they felt they had been taken advantage of, but said nothing of it.

Harmon drove out with Walker, I with the other, up a loose wide clay road to the northwest of town in the high glittering dusty sunday late morning heat of sunlight. The man I drove with made steady conversation, in part out of nervous courtesy, in part as if to forestall any questions I might ask him. I was glad enough of it; nearly all his tenants were negroes and no use to me, and I needed a rest from asking questions and decided merely to establish myself as even more easygoing, casual, and friendly than he was. It turned out that I had not been mistaken in the French sound of his name; ancestors of his had escaped an insurrection of negroes in Haiti. He himself, however, was entirely localized, a middling well-to-do landowner with a little more of the look of the direct farmer about him than the average. He was driving a several-years-old tan sedan, much the sort of car a factory worker in a northern city drives, and was pointing out to me how mean the cotton was on this man's land, who thought he could skimp by on a low grade of fertilizer, and how good it was along this pocket and high lift, that somehow caught whatever rain ran across this part of the country, though that was no advantage to cotton in a wet year or even an average; it was good in a drowt year like this one, though; his own cotton, except for a stretch of it along the bottom, he couldn't say yet it was going to do either very good or very bad; here we are at it, though.

A quarter of a mile back in a flat field of short cotton a grove of oaks spumed up and a house stood in their shade. Beyond, as we approached, the land sank quietly away toward woods which ran tendrils along it, and was speckled near and far with nearly identical two-room shacks, perhaps a dozen, some in the part shade of chinaberry bushes, others bare to the brightness, all with the color in the sunlight and frail look of the tissue of hornets' nests. This nearest four-room house we were approaching was the foreman's. We drew up in the oak shade as the doors of this house filled. They were negroes. Walker and Harmon drew up behind us. A big iron ring hung by a chain from the low branch of an oak. A heavy strip of iron leaned at the base of the tree. Negroes appeared at the doors of the two nearest tenant houses. From the third house away, two of them were approaching. One was in clean overalls; the other wore black pants, a white shirt, and a black vest unbuttoned.

Here at the foreman's home we had caused an interruption that filled me with regret: relatives were here from a distance, middle-aged and sober people in their sunday clothes, and three or four visiting children, and I realized that they had been quietly enjoying themselves, the men out at the far side of the house, the women getting dinner, as now, by our arrival, they no longer could. The foreman was very courteous, the other men were non-committal, the eyes of the women were quietly and openly hostile; the landlord and the foreman were talking. The foreman's male guests hovered quietly and respectfully in silence on the outskirts of the talk until they were sure what they might properly do, then withdrew to the far side of the house, watching carefully to catch the landowner's eyes, should they be glanced after, so that they might nod, smile, and touch their foreheads, as in fact they did, before they disappeared. The two men from the third house came up; soon three more came, a man of forty and a narrow-skulled pair of sapling boys. They all approached softly and strangely until they stood within the shade of the grove, then stayed their ground as if floated, their eyes shifting upon us sidelong and to the ground and to the distance, speaking together very little, in quieted voices: it was as if they had been under some sort of magnetic obligation to approach just this closely and to show themselves. The landlord began to ask of them through the foreman, How's So-and-So doing, all laid by? Did he do that extra sweeping I told you? — and the foreman would answer, Yes sir, yes sir, he do what you say to do, he doin all right; and So-and-So shifted on his feet and smiled uneasily while, uneasily, one of his companions laughed and the others held their faces in the blank safety of deafness. And you, you ben doin much coltn lately, you horny old bastard? — and the crinkled, old, almost gray-mustached negro who came up tucked his head to one side looking cute, and showed what was left of his teeth, and whined, tittering, Now Mist So-and-So, you know I'm settled down, married-man, you wouldn't — and the brutal negro of forty split his face in a villainous grin and said, He too *ole*, Mist So-and-So, he don't got no sap lef in him; and everyone laughed, and the landowner said, These yer two yere, colts yourn ain't they? — and the old man said they were, and the landowner said, Musta found *them* in the woods, strappin young niggers as that; and the old man said, No sir, he got the both of them lawful married, Mist So-and-So; and the landowner said that eldest on em looks to be ready for a piece himself, and the negroes laughed, and the two boys twisted their beautiful bald gourdlike skulls in a unison of shyness and their faces were illumined with maidenly smiles of shame, delight and fear; and meanwhile the landowner had loosened the top two buttons of his trousers, and he now reached his hand in to the middle of the forearm, and, squatting with bent knees apart, clawed, scratched and rearranged his genitals.

But now three others stood in the outskirts who had been sent for by a running child; they were young men, only twenty to thirty, yet very old and sedate; and their skin was of that sootiest black which no light can make shine and with which the teeth are blue and the eyeballs gold. They wore pressed trousers, washed shoes, brilliantly starched white shirts, bright ties, and carried newly whited straw hats in their hands, and at their hearts were pinned the purple and gilded ribbons of a religious and burial society. They had been summoned to sing for Walker and for me, to show us what nigger music is like (though we had done all we felt we were able to spare them and ourselves this summons), and they stood patiently in a stiff frieze in the oak shade, their hats and their shirts shedding light, and were waiting to be noticed and released, for they had been on their way to church when the child caught them; and now that they were looked at and the order given they stepped forward a few paces, not smiling, and stopped in rigid line, and, after a constricted exchange of glances among them-selves, the eldest tapping the clean dirt with his shoe, they sang. It was as I had expected, not in the mellow and euphonious Fisk Quartette style, but in the style I have heard on records by Mitchell's Christian Singers, jagged, tortured, stony, accented as if by hammers and cold-chisels, full of a nearly paralyzing vitality and iteration of rhythm, the harmonies constantly splitting the nerves; so that of western music the nearest approach to its austerity is in the first two centuries of polyphony. But here it was entirely instinctual; it tore itself like a dance of sped plants out of three young men who stood sunk to their throats in land, and whose eyes were neither shut nor looking at anything; the screeching young tenor, the baritone, stridulant in the height of his register, his throat tight as a fist, and the bass, rolling the iron wheels of his machinery, his hand clenching and loosening as he tightened and relaxed against the spraining of his ellipses: and they were abruptly silent; totally wooden; while the landowner smiled coldly. There was nothing to say. I looked them in the eyes with full and open respect and said, that was fine. Have you got time to sing us another? Their heads and their glances collected toward a common center, and restored, and they sang us another, a slow one this time; I had a feeling, through their silence before entering it, that it was their favorite and their particular pride; the tenor lifted out his voice alone in a long, plorative line that hung like fire on heaven, or whistle's echo, sinking, sunken, along descents of a modality I had not heard before, and sank along the arms and breast of the bass as might a body sunken from a cross; and the baritone lifted a long black line of comment; and they ran in a long and slow motion and convolution of rolling as at the bottom of a stormy sea, voice meeting voice as ships in dream, retreated, met once more, much woven, digressions and returns of time, quite tuneless, the bass, over and over, approaching, drooping, the same declivity, the baritone taking over, a sort of metacenter, murmuring along monotones between major and minor, nor in any determinable key, the tenor winding upward like a horn, a wire, the flight of a bird, almost into full declamation, then failing it, silencing; at length enlarging, the others lifting, now, alone, lone, and largely, questioning, alone and not sustained, in the middle of space, stopped; and now resumed, sunken upon the bosom of the bass, the head declined; both muted, droned; the baritone makes his comment, unresolved, that is a question, all on one note: and they are quiet, and do not look at us, nor at anything.

The landlord objected that that was too much howling and too much religion on end and how about something with some life to it, they knew what he meant, and then they could go.

They knew what he meant, but it was very hard for them to give it just now. They stiffened in their bodies and hesitated, several seconds, and looked at each other with eyes ruffled with worry; then the bass nodded, as abruptly as a blow, and with blank faces they struck into a fast, sassy, pelvic tune whose words were loaded almost beyond translation with comic sexual metaphor; a refrain song that ran like a rapid wheel, with couplets to be invented, progressing the story; they sang it through four of the probably three dozen turns they knew, then bit it off sharp and sharply, and for the first time, relaxed out of line, as if they knew they had earned the right, with it, to leave.

Meanwhile, and during all this singing, I had been sick in the knowledge that they felt they were here at our demand, mine and Walker's, and that I could communicate nothing otherwise; and now, in a perversion of self-torture, I played my part through. I gave their leader fifty cents, trying at the same time, through my eyes, to communicate much more, and said I was sorry we had held them up and that I hoped they would not be late; and he thanked me for them in a dead voice, not looking me in the eye, and they went away, putting their white hats on their heads as they walked into the sunlight.

At the Forks

On a road between the flying shadows of loose woods toward the middle of an afternoon, far enough thrust forward between towns that we had lost intuition of our balance between them, we came to a fork where the sunlight opened a little more widely, but not on cultivated land, and stopped a minute to decide.

Marion would lie some miles over beyond the road on our left; some other county seat, Centerville most likely, out beyond the road on our right; but on which road the woods might give way to any extension of farm country there was no deducing: for we were somewhere toward the middle of one of the wider of the gaps on the road map, and had seen nothing but woods, and infrequent woods farms, for a good while now.

Just a little behind us on our left and close on the road was a house, the first we had passed in several miles, and we decided to ask directions of the people on the porch, whom, in the car mirror, I could see still watching us. We backed slowly, stopping the car a little short of the house, and I got slowly out and walked back toward them, watching them quietly and carefully, and preparing my demeanors and my words for the two hundredth time.

*

There were three on the porch, watching me, and they must not have spoken twice in an hour while they watched beyond the rarely traveled road the changes of daylight along the recessions of the woods, and while, in the short field that sank behind their house, their two crops died silently in the sun: a young man, a young woman, and an older man; and the two younger, their chins drawn inward and their heads tall against the grained wall of the house, watched me steadily and sternly as if from beneath the brows of helmets, in the candor of young warriors or of children.

They were of a kind not safely to be described in an account claiming to be unimaginative or trustworthy, for they had too much and too outlandish beauty not to be legendary. Since, however, they existed quite irrelevant to myth, it will be necessary to tell a little of them.

The young man's eyes had the opal lightings of dark oil and, though he was watching me in a way that relaxed me to cold weakness of ignobility, they fed too strongly inward to draw to a focus: whereas those of the young woman had each the splendor of a monstrance, and were brass. Her body also was brass or bitter gold, strong to stridency beneath the unbleached clayed cotton dress, and her arms and bare legs were sharp with metal down. The blenched hair drew her face tight to her skull as a tied mask; her features were baltic. The young man's face was deeply shaded with soft short beard, and luminous with death. He had the scornfully ornate nostrils and lips of an aegean exquisite. The fine wood body was ill strung, and sick even as he sat there to look at, and the bone hands roped with vein; they rose, then sank, and lay palms upward in his groins. There was in their eyes so quiet and ultimate a quality of hatred, and contempt, and anger, toward every creature in existence beyond themselves, and toward the damages they sustained, as shone scarcely short of a state of beatitude; nor did this at any time modify itself.

These two sat as if formally, or as if sculptured, one in wood and one in metal, or as if enthroned, about three feet apart in straight chairs tilted to the wall, and constantly watched me, all the while communicating thoroughly with each other by no outward sign of word or glance or turning, but by emanation.

The other man might have been fifty by appearance, yet, through a particular kind of delicateness upon his hands, and hair, and skin — they were almost infantine — I was sure he was still young, hardly out of his twenties, though again the face was seamed and short as a fetus. This man, small-built and heavy jointed, and wandering in his motions like a little child, had the thorny beard of a cartoon bolshevik, but suggested rather a hopelessly deranged and weeping prophet, a D. H. Lawrence whom male nurses have just managed to subdue into a straitjacket. A broken felt hat struck through with grass hair was banged on flat above his furious and leaky eyes, and from beneath its rascally brim as if from ambush he pored at me walleyed while, clenching himself back against the wall, he sank along it trembling and slowly to a squat, and watched up at me.

None of them relieved me for an instant of their eyes; at the intersection of those three tones of force I was transfixed as between spearheads as I talked. As I asked my questions, and told my purposes, and what I was looking for, it seemed to me they relaxed a little toward me, and at length a good deal more, almost as if into trust and liking; yet even at its best this remained so suspended, so conditional, that in any save the most hopeful and rationalized sense it was non-existent. The qualities of their eyes did not in the least alter, nor anything visible or audible about them, and their speaking was as if I was almost certainly a spy sent to betray them through trust, whom they would show they had neither trust nor fear of.

They were clients of Rehabilitation. They had been given a young sick steer to do their plowing with; the land was woods-clearing, but had been used as long as the house (whose wood was ragged and light as pith); no seed or fertilizer had been given them until the end of May. Nothing they had planted was up better than a few inches, and that was now withering faster than it grew. They now owed the Government on the seed and fertilizer, the land, the tools, the house, and probably before long on the steer as well, who was now so weak he could hardly stand. They had from the start given notice of the weakness and youth of the steer, of the nearly total sterility of the soil, and of the later and later withholding of the seed and fertilizer; and this had had a great deal to do with why the seed was given them so late, and they had been let know it in so many words.

The older man came up suddenly behind me, jamming my elbow with his concave chest and saying fiercely *Awnk, awnk*, while he glared at me with enraged and terrified eyes. Caught so abruptly off balance, my reflexes went silly and I turned toward him questioning 'politely' with my face, as if he wanted to say something, and could, which I had not quite heard. He did want urgently to say something, but all that came out was this blasting of *Awnk, awnk*, and a thick roil of saliva that hung like semen in his beard. I nodded, smiling at him, and he grinned gratefully with an expression of extreme wickedness and tugged hard at my sleeve, nodding violently in time to his voice and rooting out over and over this loud vociferation of a frog. The woman spoke to him sharply though not unkindly (the young man's eyes remained serene), as if he were a dog masturbating on a caller, and he withdrew against a post of the porch and sank along it to the floor with his knees up sharp and wide apart and the fingers of his left hand jammed as deep as they would go down his gnashing mouth, while he stayed his bright eyes on me. She got up abruptly without speaking and went indoors and came back out with a piece of stony cornbread and gave it to him, and took her place again in her chair. He took the bread in both hands and struck his face into it like the blow of a hatchet, grappling with his jaws and slowly cradling his head like a piece of heavy machinery, while grinding, passionate noises ran in his throat, and we continued to talk, the young woman doing most of the talking, corroborative and protective of the young man, yet always respectful toward him.

The young man had the asthma so badly the fits of it nearly killed him. He could never tell when he was going to be any good for work, and he was no good for it even at the best, it was his wife did the work; and him – the third – they did not even nod nor shift their eyes toward him; he was just a mouth. These things were said in the voice not of complaint but of statement, quietly stiff with hatred for the world and for living: nor was there any touch of pride, shame, resentment, or any discord among them.

Some niggers a couple of miles down a back road let them have some corn and some peas. Without those niggers there was no saying what they'd be doing by now. Only the niggers hadn't had a bit too much for themselves in the first place and were running very short now; it had been what was left over from the year before, and not much new corn, nor much peas, was coming through the drought. It was –

The older man came honking up at my elbow, holding out a rolled farm magazine. In my effort to give him whatever form of attention could most gratify him I was stupid again; the idea there was something he wanted me to read; and looked at him half-questioning this, and not yet taking what he offered me. The woman, in a voice that somehow, though contemptuous (it implied, You are more stupid than he is), yielded me for the first time her friendship and that of her husband, so that happiness burst open inside me like a flooding of sweet water, said, he wants to give it to you. I took it and thanked him very much, looking and smiling into his earnest eyes, and he stayed at my side like a child, watching me affectionately while I talked to them.

They had told me there was farm country down the road on the right a piece: the whole hoarded silence and quiet of a lonesome and archaic American valley it was to become, full of heavy sunflowers and mediocre cotton, where the women wore sunbonnets without shyness before us and all whom we spoke to were gracious and melancholy, and where we did not find what we sought. Now after a little while I thanked them here on the porch and told them good-bye. I had not the heart at all to say, Better luck to you, but then if I remember rightly I did say it, and, saying it or not, and unable to communicate to them at all what my feelings were, I walked back the little distance to the car with my shoulders and the back of my neck more scalded-feeling than if the sun were on them. As we started, I looked back and held up my hand. The older man was on the dirt on his hands and knees coughing like a gorilla and looking at the dirt between his hands. Neither of the other two raised a hand. The young man lowered his head slowly and seriously, and raised it. The young woman smiled, sternly beneath her virulent eyes, for the first time. As we swung into the right fork of the road, I looked back again. The young man, looking across once more into the woods, had reached his hand beneath the bib of his overalls and was clawing at his lower belly. The woman, her eyes watching us past her shoulder, was walking to the door. Just as I glanced back, and whether through seeing that I saw her I cannot be sure, she turned her head to the front, and disappeared into the house.

Near a Church

It was a good enough church from the moment the curve opened and we saw it that I slowed a little and we kept our eyes on it. But as we came even with it the light so held it that it shocked us with its goodness straight through the body, so that at the same instant we said *Jesus*. I put on the brakes and backed the car slowly, watching the light on the building, until we were at the same apex, and we sat still for a couple of minutes at least before getting out, studying in arrest what had hit us so hard as we slowed past its perpendicular.

It lost nothing at all in stasis, but even more powerfully strove in through the eyes its paralyzing classicism: stood from scoured clay, a light lift above us, no trees near, and few weeds; every grain, each nail-head, distinct; the subtle almost strangling strong asymmetries of that which has been hand wrought toward symmetry (as if it were an earnest description, better than the intended object): so intensely sprung against so scarcely eccentric a balance that my hands of themselves spread out their bones, trying to regiment on air between their strengths its tensions and their mutual structures as they stood subject to the only scarcely eccentric, almost annihilating stress, of the serene, wild, rigorous light: empty, shut, bolted, of all that was now withdrawn from it upon the fields the utter statement, God's mask and wooden skull and home stood empty in the meditation of the sun: and this light upon it was strengthening still further its imposal and embrace, and in about a quarter of an hour would have trained itself ready, and there would be a triple convergence in the keen historic spasm of the shutter.

I helped get the camera ready and we stood away and I watched what would be trapped, possessed, fertilized, in the leisures and shyness which are a phase of all love for any object: searching out and registering in myself all its lines, planes, stresses of relationship, along diagonals withdrawn and approached, and vertical to the slightly off-centered door, and broadside, and at several distances, and near, examining merely the ways of the wood, and the nails, the three new boards of differing lengths that were let in above the left of the door, the staring small white porcelain knob, the solesmoothed stairlifts, the wrung stance of thick steeple, the hewn wood stoblike spike at sky, the old hasp and new padlock, the randomshuttered windowglass whose panes were like the surfaces of springs, the fat gold fly who sang and botched against a bright pane within, and within, the rigid benches, box organ, bright stops, hung charts, wrecked hymnals, the platform, pine lectern doilied, pressed-glass pitcher, suspended lamp, four funeral chairs, the little stove with long swan throat aluminum in the hard sober shade, a button in sun, a flur of lint, a torn card of Jesus among children:

While we were wondering whether to force a window, a young negro couple came past up the road. Without appearing to look either longer or less long, or with more or less interest, than a white man might care for, and without altering their pace, they made thorough observation of us, of the car, and of the tripod and camera. We spoke and nodded, smiling as if casually; they spoke and nodded, gravely, as they passed, and glanced back once, not secretly, nor long, nor in amusement. They made us, in spite of our knowledge of our own meanings, ashamed and insecure in our wish to break into and possess their church, and after a minute or two I decided to go after them and speak to them, and ask them if they knew where we might find a minister or

some other person who might let us in, if it would be all right. They
were fifty yards or so up the road, walking leisurely, and following
them, I watched aspects of them which are less easily seen (as surrounding objects are masked by looking into a light) when one's own
eyes and face and the eyes and face of another are mutually visible and
appraising. They were young, soberly buoyant of body, and strong, the
man not quite thin, the girl not quite plump, and I remembered their
mild and sober faces, hers softly wide and sensitive to love and to
pleasure, and his resourceful and intelligent without intellect and without guile, and their extreme dignity, which was as effortless, unvalued,
and undefended in them as the assumption of superiority which suf-
fuses a rich and social adolescent boy; and I was taking pleasure also
in the competence and rhythm of their walking in the sun, which was
incapable of being less than a muted dancing, and in the beauty in the
sunlight of their clothes, which were strange upon them in the middle
of the week. He was in dark trousers, black dress shoes, a new-laun-
dered white shirt with lights of bluing in it, and a light yellow, soft
straw hat with a broad band of dark flowered cloth and a daisy in the
band; she glossy-legged without stockings, in freshly whited pumps, a
flowered pink cotton dress, and a great sun of straw set far back on her
head. Their swung hands touched gently with their walking, stride by
stride, but did not engage. I was walking more rapidly than they but
quietly; before I had gone ten steps they turned their heads (toward
each other) and looked at me briefly and impersonally, like horses in a
field, and faced front again; and this, I am almost certain, not through
having heard sound of me, but through a subtler sense. By the time I
raised my hand, they had looked away, and did not see me, though
nothing in their looking had been quick with abruptness or surrepti-
tion. I walked somewhat faster now, but I was overtaking them a little
slowly for my patience; the light would be right by now or very soon;
I had no doubt Walker would do what he wanted whether we had 'permission' or not, but I wanted to be on hand, and broke into a trot. At
the sound of the twist of my shoe in the gravel, the young woman's

whole body was jerked down tight as a fist into a crouch from which immediately, the rear foot skidding in the loose stone so that she nearly fell, like a kicked cow scrambling out of a creek, eyes crazy, chin stretched tight, she sprang forward into the first motions of a running not human but that of a suddenly terrified wild animal. In this same instant the young man froze, the emblems of sense in his wild face wide open toward me, his right hand stiff toward the girl who, after a few strides, her consciousness overtaking her reflex, shambled to a stop and stood, not straight but sick, as if hung from a hook in the spine of the will not to fall for weakness, while he hurried to her and put his hand on her flowered shoulder and, inclining his head forward and sidewise as if listening, spoke with her, and they lifted, and watched me while, shaking my head, and raising my hand palm outward, I came up to them (not trotting) and stopped a yard short of where they, closely, not touching now, stood, and said, still shaking my head (*No; no; oh, Jesus, no, no, no!*) and looking into their eyes; at the man, who was not knowing what to do, and at the girl, whose eyes were lined with tears, and who was trying so hard to subdue the shaking in her breath, and whose heart I could feel, though not hear, blasting as if it were my whole body, and I trying in some fool way to keep it somehow relatively light, because I could not bear that they should receive from me any added reflection of the shattering of their grace and dignity, and of the nakedness and depth and meaning of their fear, and of my horror and pity and self-hatred; and so, smiling, and so distressed that I wanted only that they should be restored, and should know I was their friend, and that I might melt from existence: 'I'm *very sorry!* I'm *very* sorry if I scared you! I didn't mean to scare you at all. I wouldn't have done any such thing for anything.'

They just kept looking at me. There was no more for them to say than for me. The least I could have done was to throw myself flat on my face and embrace and kiss their feet. That impulse took hold of me so powerfully, from my whole body, not by thought, that I caught myself from doing it exactly and as scarcely as you snatch yourself from jumping from a sheer height: here, with the realization that it would have frightened them still worse (to say nothing of me) and would have been still less explicable; so that I stood and looked into their eyes and loved them, and wished to God I was dead. After a little the man got back his voice, his eyes grew a little easier, and he said without conviction that that was all right and that I hadn't scared her. She shook her head slowly, her eyes on me; she did not yet trust her voice. Their faces were secret, soft, utterly without trust of me, and utterly without understanding; and they had to stand here now and hear what I was saying, because in that country no negro safely walks away from a white man, or even appears not to listen while he is talking, and because I could not walk away abruptly, and relieve them of me, without still worse a crime against nature than the one I had committed, and the second I was committing by staying, and holding them. And so, and in this horrid grinning of faked casualness, I gave them a better reason why I had followed them than to frighten them, asked what I had followed them to ask; they said the thing it is usually safest for negroes to say, that they did not know; I thanked them very much, and was seized once more and beyond resistance with the wish to clarify and set right, so that again, with my eyes and smile wretched and out of key with all I was able to say, I said I was awfully sorry if I had bothered them; but they only retreated still more profoundly behind their faces, their eyes watching mine as if awaiting any sudden move they must ward, and the young man said again that that was all right, and I nodded, and turned away from them, and walked down the road without looking back.

All over Alabama, the lamps are out. Every leaf drenches the touch; the spider's net is heavy. The roads lie there, with nothing to use them. The fields lie there, with nothing at work in them, neither man nor beast. The plow handles are wet, and the rails and the frogplates and the weeds between the ties: and not even the hurryings and hoarse sorrows of a distant train, on other roads, is heard. The little towns, the county seats, house by house white-painted and elaborately sawn among their heavy and dark-lighted leaves, in the spaced protections of their mineral light they stand so prim, so voided, so undefended upon starlight, that it is inconceivable to despise or to scorn a white man, an owner of land; even in Birmingham, mile on mile, save for the sudden frightful streaming, almost instantly diminished and silent, of a closed black car, and save stone lonesome sinister heelbeats, that show never a face and enter, soon, a frame door flush with the pavement, and ascend the immediate lightless staircase, mile on mile, stone, stone, smooth charted streams of stone, the streets under their lifted lamps lie void before eternity. New Orleans is stirring, rattling, and sliding faintly in its fragrance and in the enormous richness of its lust; taxis are still parked along Dauphine Street and the breastlike, floral air is itchy with the stilettos and embroiderings above black blood drumthroes of an eloquent cracked indiscoverable cornet, which exists only in the imagination and somewhere in the past, in the broken heart of Louis Armstrong; yet even in that small portion which is the infested genitals of that city, never free, neither of desire nor of waking pain, there are the qualities of the tender desolations of profoundest night. Beneath, the gulf lies dreaming, and beneath, dreaming, that woman, that id, the lower American continent, lies spread before heaven in her wealth. The parks of her cities are iron, loam, silent, the sweet fountains shut, and the pure façades, embroiled, limelike in street light are sharp, are still:

Part One

A Country Letter

A Country Letter

It is late in a summer night, in a room of a house set deep and solitary in the country; all in this house save myself are sleeping; I sit at a table, facing a partition wall; and I am looking at a lighted coal-oil lamp which stands on the table close to the wall, and just beyond the sleeping of my relaxed left hand; with my right hand I am from time to time writing, with a soft pencil, into a school-child's composition book; but just now, I am entirely focused on the lamp, and light.

It is of glass, light metal colored gold, and cloth of heavy thread.

The glass was poured into a mold, I guess, that made the base and bowl, which are in one piece; the glass is thick and clean, with icy lights in it. The base is a simply fluted, hollow skirt; stands on the table; is solidified in a narrowing, a round inch of pure thick glass, then hollows again, a globe about half flattened, the globe-glass thick, too; and this holds oil, whose silver line I see, a little less than half down the globe, its level a very little — for the base is not quite true — tilted against the axis of the base.

This 'oil' is not at all oleaginous, but thin, brittle, rusty feeling, and sharp; taken and rubbed between forefinger and thumb, it so cleanses their grain that it sharpens their mutual touch to a new coin edge, or the russet nipple of a breast erected in cold; and the odor is clean, cheerful and humble, less alive by far than that of gasoline, even a shade watery: and a subtle sweating of this oil is on the upward surface of the globe, as if it stood through the glass, and as if the glass were a pitcher of cool water in a hot room. I do not understand nor try to deduce this, but I like it; I run my thumb upon it and smell of my thumb, and smooth away its streaked print on the glass; and I wipe my thumb and forefinger dry against my pants, and keep on looking.

In this globe, and in this oil that is clear and light as water, and reminding me of creatures and things once alive which I have seen suspended in jars in a frightening smell of alcohol — serpents, tapeworms, toads, embryos, all drained one tan pallor of absolute death; and also of the serene, scarved flowers in untroubled wombs (and pale-tanned too, flaccid, and in the stench of exhibited death, those children of fury, patience and love which stand in the dishonors of accepted fame, and of the murdering of museum staring); in this globe like a thought, a dream, the future, slumbers the stout-weft strap of wick, and up this wick is drawn the oil, toward heat; through a tight, flat tube of tin, and through a little slotted smile of golden tin, and there ends fledged with flame, in the flue; the flame, a clean, fanged fan:

I:

The light in this room is of a lamp. Its flame in the glass is of the dry, silent and famished delicateness of the latest lateness of the night, and of such ultimate, such holiness of silence and peace that all on earth and within extremest remembrance seems suspended upon it in perfection as upon reflective water: and I feel that if I can by utter quietness succeed in not disturbing this silence, in not so much as touching this plain of water, I can tell you anything within realm of God, whatsoever it may be, that I wish to tell you, and that what so ever it may be, you will not be able to help but understand it.

It is the middle and pure height and whole of summer and a summer night, the held breath, of a planet's year; high shored sleeps the crested tide: what day of the month I do not know, which day of the week I am not sure, far less what hour of the night. The dollar watch I bought a few days ago, as also from time to time I buy a ten cent automatic pencil, and use it little before I lose all track of it, ran out at seventeen minutes past ten the day before yesterday morning, and time by machine measure was over for me at that hour, and is a monument. I know of the lateness and full height by the quietly starved brightness of my senses, which some while ago made the transition past any need for sleep without taking much notice of it, as, in the late darkness, the

long accustomed liner loses the last black headland, and quietly com-
mends her forehead upon the long open home of the sea: and by a
quality in the night itself not truly apparent to any one of the senses,
yet, by some indirection, to every sense in one, of a most complete and
universally shared withdrawal to source, like that brief paralysis which
enchants a city while wreaths are laid to a cenotaph, and, muted, a
bugle's inscription shines, in the tightening just before the relaxation of
this swarmed, still, silence, till, hats-on, gears grow and smooth, the lifted foot arrested in the stopshot completes its step, once more the white
mane of the drayhorse flurrs in the sunny air: now vibrates all that vast
stone hive: into resumption, reassumption, of casual living.

And it is in these terms I would tell you, at all leisure, and in all
detail, whatever there is to tell: of where I am; of what I perceive.

Lamplight here, and lone, late: the odor is of pine that has stood
shut on itself through the heat of a hot day: the odor of an attic at white
noon: and all of the walls save that surface within immediate touch of
the lamp, where like water slept in lantern light the grain is so sharply
discerned in its retirement beyond the sleep of the standing shape of
pines, and the pastings and pinnings of sad ornaments, are a most dim
scarce-color of grayed silver breathed in yellow red which is the hue
and haze in the room; and above me, black: where, beyond bones of
rafters underlighted, a stomach sucked against the spine in fear, the
roof draws up its peak: and this is a frightening dark, which has again
to do with an attic: for it is the darkness that stands just up the stairs,
sucking itself out of sight of the light, from an attic door left ajar,
noticed on your way to bed, and remembered after you are there: so
that I muse what not quite creatures and what not quite forms are suspended like bats above and behind my bent head; and how far down
in their clustered weight they are stealing while my eyes are on this
writing; and how skillfully swiftly they suck themselves back upward
into the dark when I turn my head: and above all, why they should be
so coy, who, with one slather of cold membranes drooping, could slap

out light and have me: and who own me since all time's beginning. Yet this mere fact of thinking holds them at distance, as crucifixes demons, so lightly and well that I am almost persuaded of being merely fanciful; in which exercise I would be theirs most profoundly beyond rescue, not knowing, and not fearing, I am theirs.

Above that shell and carapace, more frail against heaven than fragilest membrane of glass, nothing, straight to the terrific stars: whereof all heaven is chalky; and of whom the nearest is so wild a reach my substance wilts to think on: and we, this Arctic flower snow-rooted, last matchflame guarded on a windy plain, are seated among these stars alone: none to turn to, none to make us known; a little country settlement so deep, so lost in shelve and shade of dew, no one so much as laughs at us. Small wonder how pitiably we love our home, cling in her skirts at night, rejoice in her wide star-seducing smile, when every star strikes us sick with the fright: do we really exist at all?

> This world is not my home, I'm, only passing through,
> My treasures and my hopes, are, all, beyond the sky,
> I've many, friends, and kindreds, that's gone, along before,
> And I can't, feel, at home, in this world, any, more.

And thus, too, these families, not otherwise than with every family in the earth, how each, apart, how inconceivably lonely, sorrowful, and remote! Not one other on earth, nor in any dream, that can care so much what comes to them, so that even as they sit at the lamp and eat their supper, the joke they are laughing at could not be so funny to anyone else; and the littlest child who stands on the bench solemnly, with food glittering all over his cheeks in the lamplight, this littlest child I speak of is not there, he is of another family, and it is a different woman who wipes the food from his cheeks and takes his weight upon her thighs and against her body and who feeds him, and lets his weight slacken against her in his heavying sleep; and the man who puts another soaked cloth to the skin cancer on his shoulder; it is his wife who is looking on, and his child who lies sunken along the floor with his soft mouth broad open and his nakedness up like a rolling dog, asleep: and the people next up the road cannot care in the same way, not for any of it: for they are absorbed upon themselves: and the negroes down beyond the spring have drawn their shutters tight, the lamplight pulses like wounded honey through the seams into the soft night, and there is laughter: but nobody else cares. All over the whole round earth and in the settlements, the towns, and the great iron stones of cities, people are drawn inward within their little shells of rooms, and are to be seen in their wondrous and pitiful actions through the surfaces of their lighted windows by thousands, by millions, little golden aquariums, in chairs, reading, setting tables, sewing, playing cards, not talking, talking, laughing inaudibly, mixing drinks, at radio dials, eating, in shirtsleeves, carefully dressed, courting, teasing, loving, seducing, undressing, leaving the room empty in its empty light, alone and writing a letter urgently, in couples married, in separate chairs, in family parties, in gay parties, preparing for bed, preparing for sleep: and none can care, beyond that room; and none can be cared for, by any beyond that room: and it is small wonder they are drawn together so cowardly close, and small wonder in what dry agony of despair a mother may fasten her talons and her vampire mouth upon the soul of her struggling son and drain him empty, light as a locust shell: and wonder only that an age that has borne its children and must lose and has lost them, and lost life, can bear further living; but so it is:

A man and a woman are drawn together upon a bed and there is a child and there are children:

First they are mouths, then they become auxiliary instruments of labor: later they are drawn away, and become the fathers and mothers of children, who shall become the fathers and mothers of children:

Their father and their mother before them were, in their time, the children each of different parents, who in their time were each children of parents:

This has been happening for a long while: its beginning was before stars:

It will continue for a long while: no one knows where it will end:

While they are still drawn together within one shelter around the center of their parents, these children and their parents together compose a family:

This family must take care of itself; it has no mother or father: there is no other shelter, nor resource, nor any love, interest, sustaining strength or comfort, so near, nor can anything happy or sorrowful that comes to anyone in this family possibly mean to those outside it what it means to those within it: but it is, as I have told, inconceivably lonely, drawn upon itself as tramps are drawn round a fire in the cruelest weather; and thus and in such loneliness it exists among other families, each of which is no less lonely, nor any less without help or comfort, and is likewise drawn in upon itself:

Such a family lasts, for a while: the children are held to a magnetic center:

Then in time the magnetism weakens, both of itself in its tiredness of aging and sorrow, and against the strength of the growth of each child, and against the strength of pulls from outside, and one by one the children are drawn away:

Of those that are drawn away, each is drawn elsewhere toward another: once more a man and a woman, in a loneliness they are not liable at that time to notice, are tightened together upon a bed: and another family has begun:

Moreover, these flexions are taking place every where, like a simultaneous motion of all the waves of the water of the world: and these are the classic patterns, and this is the weaving, of human living: of whose fabric each individual is a part: and of all parts of this fabric let this be borne in mind:

Each is intimately connected with the bottom and the extremest reach of time:

Each is composed of substances identical with the substance of all that surrounds him, both the common objects of his disregard, and the hot centers of stars:

All that each person is, and experiences, and shall never experience, in body and in mind, all these things are differing expressions of himself and of one root, and are identical: and not one of these things nor one of these persons is ever quite to be duplicated, nor replaced, nor has it ever quite had precedent: but each is a new and incommunicably tender life, wounded in every breath, and almost as hardly killed as easily wounded: sustaining, for a while, without defense, the enormous assaults of the universe:

So that how it can be that a stone, a plant, a star, can take on the burden of being; and how it is that a child can take on the burden of breathing; and how through so long a continuation and cumulation of the burden of each moment one on another, does any creature bear to exist, and not break utterly to fragments of nothing: these are matters too dreadful and fortitudes too gigantic to meditate long and not forever to worship:

Just a half-inch beyond the surface of this wall I face is another surface, one of the four walls which square and collaborate against the air another room, and there lie sleeping, on two iron beds and on pallets on the floor, a man and his wife and her sister, and four children, a girl, and three harmed boys. Their lamp is out, their light is done this long while, and not in a long while has any one of them made a sound. Not even straining, can I hear their breathing: rather, I have a not quite sensuous knowledge of a sort of suspiration, less breathing than that indiscernible drawing-in of heaven by which plants live, and thus I know they rest and the profundity of their tiredness, as if I were in each one of these seven bodies whose sleeping I can almost touch through this wall, and which in the darkness I so clearly see, with the whole touch and weight of my body: George's red body, already a little squat with the burden of thirty years, knotted like oakwood, in its clean white cotton summer union suit that it sleeps in; and his wife's beside him, Annie Mae's, slender, and sharpened through with bone, that ten years past must have had such beauty, and now is veined at the breast, and the skin of the breast translucent, delicately shriveled, and blue, and she and her sister Emma are in plain cotton shifts; and the body of Emma, her sister, strong, thick and wide, tall, the breasts set wide and high, shallow and round, not yet those of a full woman, the legs long thick and strong; and Louise's green lovely body, the dim breasts faintly blown between wide shoulders, the thighs long, clean and light in their line from hip to knee, the head back steep and silent to the floor, the chin highest, and the white shift up to her divided thighs; and the tough little body of Junior, hardskinned and gritty, the feet crusted with sores; and the milky and strengthless littler body of Burt whose veins are so bright in his temples; and the shriveled and hopeless, most pitiful body of Squinchy, which will not grow:

But it is not only their bodies but their postures that I know, and their weight on the bed or on the floor, so that I lie down inside each one as if exhausted in a bed, and I become not my own shape and weight and self, but that of each of them, the whole of it, sunken in sleep like stones; so that I know almost the dreams they will not remember, and the soul and body of each of these seven, and of all of them together in this room in sleep, as if they were music I were hearing, each voice in relation to all the others, and all audible, singly, and as one organism, and a music that cannot be communicated: and thus they lie in this silence, and rest.

Burt half-woke, whimpering before he was awake, an inarticulated soprano speaking through not quite weeping in complaint to his mother as before a sure jury of some fright of dream: the bed creaked and I heard her bare feet slow, the shuffling soles, and her voice, not whispering but stifled and gentle, Go to sleep now, git awn back to sleep, they aint nothin agoin to pester ye, git awn back to sleep, in that cadence of strength and sheltering comfort which anneals all fence of language and surpasses music; and George's grouched, sleepy voice, and hers to him, no words audible; and the shuffling; and a twisting in beds, and grumbling of weak springs; and the whimpering sinking, and expired; and the sound of breathing, strong, not sleeping, now, slowed, shifted across into sleep, now, steadier; and now, long, long, drawn off as lightest lithest edge of bow, thinner, thinner, a thread, a filament; nothing: and once more that silence wherein more deep than starlight this home is foundered.

I am fond of Emma, and very sorry for her, and I shall probably never see her again after a few hours from now. I want to tell you what I can about her.

She is a big girl, almost as big as her sister is wiry, though she is not at all fat: her build is rather that of a young queen of a child's magic story who throughout has been coarsened by peasant and earth living and work, and that of her eyes and her demeanor, too, kind, not fully formed, resolute, bewildered, and sad. Her soft abundant slightly curling brown hair is cut in a square bob which on her large fine head is particularly childish, and indeed Emma is rather a big child, sexual beyond propriety to its years, than a young woman; and this can be seen in a kind of dimness of definition in her features, her skin, and the shape of her body, which will be lost in a few more years. She wears a ten cent store necklace and a sunday cotton print dress because she is visiting, and is from town, but she took off her slippers as soon as she came, and worked with Annie Mae. According to her father she is the spitn image of her mother when her mother was young; Annie Mae favors her father and his people, who were all small and lightly built.

Emma is very fond of her father and very sorry for him, as her sister is, and neither of them can stand his second wife. I have an idea that his marrying her had a lot to do with Emma's own marriage, which her father so strongly advised her against. He married the second time when Emma was thirteen, and for a long while they lived almost insanely, as I will tell you of later, far back in a swamp: and when Emma was sixteen she married a man her father's age, a carpenter in Cherokee City. She has been married to him two years; they have no children.

Emma loves good times, and towns, and people her own age, and he is jealous and mean to her and suspicious of her. He has given her no pretty dresses nor the money to buy cloth to make them. Every minute he is in the house he keeps his eye right on her as if she was up to something, and when he goes out, which is as seldom as he can, he locks her in: so that twice already she has left him and come home to stay, and then after a while he has come down begging, and crying, and swearing he'll treat her good, and give her anything she asks for, and that he'll take to drink or kill himself if she leaves him, and she has gone back: for it isn't any fun at home, hating that woman the way she does, and she can't have fun with anyone else because she is married and nobody will have fun with her that way: and now (and I think it may be not only through the depression but through staying in the house because of jealousy and through fear of living in a town with her, and so near a home she can return to), her husband can no longer get a living in Cherokee City; he has heard of a farm on a plantation over in the red hills in Mississippi and has already gone, and taken it, and he has sent word to Emma that she is to come in a truck in which a man he knows, who has business to drive out that way, is moving their furniture; and this truck is leaving tomorrow. She doesn't want to go at all, and during the past two days she has been withdrawing into rooms with her sister and crying a good deal, almost tearlessly and almost without voice, as if she knew no more how to cry than how to take care for her life; and Annie Mae is strong against her going, all that distance, to a man who leaves her behind and then just sends for her, saying, Come on along, now; and George too is as committal over it as he feels will appear any right or business of his to be, he a man, and married, to the wife of another man, who is no kin to him, but only the sister of his wife, and to whom he is himself unconcealably attracted: but she is going all the same, without at all understanding why. Annie Mae is sure she won't stay out there long, not all alone in the country away from her kinfolks with that man; that is what she keeps saying, to Emma, and to George, and even to me; but actually she is surer than not that she may never see her young sister again, and she grieves for her, and for the loss of her to her own loneliness, for she loves her, both for herself and her dependence and for that softness of youth which already is drawn so deep into the trap, and in which Annie Mae can perceive herself as she was ten years past; and she gives no appearance of noticing the clumsy and shamefaced would-be-subtle demeanors of flirtation which George is stupid enough to believe she does not understand for what they are: for George would only be shocked should she give him open permission, and Emma could not be too well trusted either. So this sad comedy has been going on without comment from anyone, which will come to nothing: and another sort has been going on with us, of a kind fully as helpless. Each of us is attractive to Emma, both in sexual immediacy and as symbols or embodiments of a life she wants and knows she will never have; and each of us is fond of her, and attracted toward her. We are not only strangers to her, but we are strange, unexplainable, beyond what I can begin yet fully to realize. We have acted toward her with the greatest possible care and shyness and quiet, yet we have been open or 'clear' as well, so that she knows we understand her and like her and care for her almost intimately. She is puzzled by this and yet not at all troubled, but excited; but there is nothing to do about it on either side. There is tenderness and sweetness and mutual pleasure in such a 'flirtation' which one would not for the world restrain or cancel, yet there is also an essential cruelty, about which nothing can be done, and strong possibility of cruelty through misunderstanding, and inhibition, and impossibility, which can be restrained, and which one would rather die than cause any of: but it is a cruel and ridiculous and restricted situation, and everyone to some extent realizes it. Everyone realizes it, I think, to such a degree even as this: supposing even that nothing can be helped about the marriage, supposing she is going away and on with it, which she shouldn't, then if only Emma could spend her last few days alive having a gigantic good time in bed, with George, a kind of man she is best used to, and with Walker and with me, whom she is curious about and attracted to, and who are at the same moment tangible and friendly and not at all to be feared, and on the other hand have for her the mystery or glamour almost of mythological creatures. This has a good many times in the past couple of days come very clearly through between all of us except the children, and without fear, in sudden and subtle but unmistakable expressions of the eyes, or ways of smiling: yet not one of us would be capable of trusting ourselves to it unless beyond any doubt each knew all the others to be thus capable: and even then how crazily the conditioned and inferior parts of each of our beings would rush in, and take revenge. But this is just a minute specialization of a general brutal pity: almost any person, no matter how damaged and poisoned and blinded, is infinitely more capable of intelligence and of joy than he can let himself be or than he usually knows; and even if he had no reason to fear his own poisons, he has those that are in others to fear, to assume and take care for, if he would not hurt both himself and that other person and the pure act itself beyond cure.

But here I am going to shift ahead of where I am writing, to a thing which is to happen, or which happened, the next morning (you mustn't be puzzled by this, I'm writing in a continuum), and say what came of it.

The next morning was full of the disorganized, half listless, yet very busy motions of ordinary life broken by an event: Emma's going away. I was going to take her and Annie Mae to her brother Gallatin's house near Cookstown, where she was to meet the man with his truck, and I was waiting around on the front porch in the cool-hot increasing morning sunlight, working out my notes, while the morning housework was done up in special speed. (George was gone an hour or more ago, immediately after the breakfast they had all sat through, not talking much. There had been a sort of lingering in eating and in silences, and a little when the food was done, broken by talk to keep the silences from becoming too frightening; I had let the breakfast start late by telling him I would take him in the car; then abruptly he got up saying, 'Well, Jimmy, if you — ' Whether he would kiss Emma goodbye, as a sort of relative, was on everybody's mind. He came clumsily near it: she half got from her chair, and their bodies were suddenly and sharply drawn toward each other a few inches: but he was much too shy, and did not even touch her with the hand he reached out to shake hers. Annie Mae drawled, smiling, What's wrong with ye George; she ain't agoin' to bite ye; and everyone laughed, and Emma stood up and they embraced, laughing, and he kissed her on her suddenly turned cheek, a little the way a father and an adolescent son kiss, and told her goodbye and wished her good luck, and I took him to work in the car, and came back. And now here I was, as I have said, on the porch.) Here I was on the porch, diddling around in a notebook and hearing the sounds of work and the changing patterns of voices inside, and the unaccustomed noise of shoeleather on the floor, because someone was dressed up for travel; and a hen thudded among dried watermelon seeds on the oak floor, looking, as they usually do, like a nearsighted professor; and down hill beyond the open field a little wind laid itself in a wall against the glistening leaves of the high forest and lay through with a long sweet granular noise of rustling water; and the hen dropped from the ledge of the porch to the turded dirt with a sodden bounce, and an involuntary cluck as her heaviness hit the ground on her sprung legs; and the long lithe little wind released the trees and was gone on, wandering the fringed earth in its affairs like a saturday schoolchild in the sun, and the leaves hung troubling in the aftermath; and I heard footsteps in the hall and Emma appeared, all dressed to go, looking somehow as if she had come to report a decision that had been made in a conference, for which I, without knowing it, seemed to have been waiting. She spoke in that same way, too, not wasting any roundabout time or waiting for an appropriate rhythm, yet not in haste, looking me steadily and sweetly in the eyes, and said, I want you and Mr. Walker to know how much we all like you, because you make us feel easy with you; we don't have to act any different from what it comes natural to act, and we don't have to worry what you're thinking about us, it's just like you was our own people and had always lived here with us, you all are so kind, and nice, and quiet, and easygoing, and we wisht you wasn't never going to go away but stay on here with us, and I just want to tell you how much we all keer about you; Annie Mae says the same, and you please tell Mr. Walker, too, if I don't see him afore I go. (I knew she could never say it over again, and I swore I certainly would tell him.)

What's the use trying to say what I felt. It took her a long time to say what she wanted so much to say, and it was hard for her, but there she stood looking straight into my eyes, and I straight into hers, longer than you'd think it would be possible to stand it. I would have done anything in the world for her (that is always characteristic, I guess, of the seizure of the strongest love you can feel: pity, and the wish to die for a person, because there isn't anything you can do for them that is at all measurable to your love), and all I could do, the very most, for this girl who was so soon going on out of my existence into so hopeless a one of hers, the very most I could do was not to show all I cared for her and for what she was saying, and not to even try to do, or to indicate the good I wished I might do her and was so utterly helpless to do. I had such tenderness and such gratitude toward her that while she spoke I very strongly, as something steadier than an 'impulse,' wanted in answer to take her large body in my arms and smooth the damp hair back from her forehead and to kiss and comfort and shelter her like a child, and I can swear that I now as then almost believe that in that moment she would have so well understood this, and so purely and quietly met it, that now as then I only wish to God I had done it; but instead the most I did was to stand facing her, and to keep looking into her eyes (doing her the honor at least of knowing that she did not want relief from this), and, managing to keep the tears from running down my face, to smile to her and say that there was nothing in my whole life that I had cared so much to be told, and had been so grateful for (and I believe this is so); and that I wanted her to know how much I liked them, too, and her herself, and that I certainly felt that they were my own people, and wanted them to be, more than any other kind of people in the world, and that if they felt that of me, and that I belonged with them, and we all felt right and easy with each other and fond of each other, then there wasn't anything in the world I could be happier over, or be more glad to know (and this is so, too); and that I knew I could say all of the same of Walker (and this, too, I know I was true in saying). I had stood up, almost without realizing I was doing it, the moment she appeared and began to speak, as though facing some formal, or royal, or ritual action, and we stayed thus standing, not leaning against or touching anything, about three feet apart, facing each other. I went on to say that whatever might happen to her or that she might do in all her life I wished her the best luck anyone could think of, and not ever to forget it, that nobody has a right to be unhappy, or to live in a way that makes them unhappy, for the sake of being afraid, or what people will think of them, or for the sake of anyone else, if there is any way they can possibly do better, that won't hurt other people too much. She slowly and lightly blushed while I spoke and her eyes became damp and bright, and said that she sure did wish me the same. Then we had nothing to say, unless we should invent something, and nothing to do, and quite suddenly and at the same instant we smiled, and she said well, she reckoned she'd better git on in and help Annie Mae, and I nodded, and she went, and a half-hour later I was driving her, and Annie Mae, and her father, and Louise, and Junior, and Burt, and the baby, to her brother's house near Cookstown. The children were silent and intent with the excitement of riding in the car, stacked on top of each other around their mother on the back seat and looking out of the windows like dogs, except Louise, whose terrible gray eyes met mine whenever I glanced for them in the car mirror. Emma rode between me and her father, her round sleeveless arms cramped a little in front of her. My own sleeves were rolled high, so that in the crowding our flesh touched. Each of us at the first few of these contacts drew quietly away, then later she relaxed her arms, and her body and thighs as well, and so did I, and for perhaps fifteen minutes we lay quietly and closely side to side, and intimately communicated also in our thoughts. Our bodies were very hot, and the car was packed

with hot and sweating bodies, and with a fine salt and rank odor like
that of crushed grass: and thus in a short while, though I knew speed
was not in the mood of anyone and was going as slowly as I felt I could
with propriety, we covered the short seven mileage of clay, then slag, to
Cookstown, and slowed through the town (eyes, eyes on us, of men,
from beneath hatbrims), and down the meandering now sandy road to
where her brother lived. I had seen him once before, a man in his thirties with a bitter, intelligent, skull-formed face; and his sour wife, and
their gold skinned children: and now here also was another man, forty
or so, leathery-strong, blackshaven, black-hatted, booted, his thin
mouth tightened round a stalk of grass showing gold stained teeth, his
cold, mean eyes a nearly white blue; and he was sardonically waiting,
and his truck, loaded with chairs and bed-iron, stood in the sun where
the treeshade had slid beyond it. He was studying Emma coldly and
almost without furtiveness, and she was avoiding his eyes. It was impossible to go quite immediately. We all sat around a short while and had
lemonade from a pressed-glass pitcher, from which he had already
taken at least two propitiatory glasses. It had been made in some hope
of helping the leavetaking pass off as a sort of party, from two lemons
and spring water, without ice, and it was tepid, heavily sweetened (as
if to compensate the lack of lemons), and scarcely tart; there was half a
glass for each of us, out of five tumblers, and we all gave most of it to
the children. The children of the two families stayed very quiet, shy of
each other; the others, save the black-hatted man, tried to talk, without
managing much; they tried especially hard when Emma got up, as suddenly as if she had to vomit, and went into the next room and shut the
door, and Annie Mae followed her. Gallatin said it was mighty hard on
a girl so young as that leaving her kinfolks so far behind. The man in
the hat twisted his mouth on the grass and, without opening his teeth,
said Yeah-ah, as if he had his own opinions about that. We were trying
not to try to hear the voices in the next room, and that same helpless,
frozen, creaky weeping I had heard before; and after a little it quieted;
and after a little more they came out, Emma flourily powdered straight

to the eyes, and the eyes as if she had cried sand instead of tears; and the man said — it was the first kind gesture I had seen in him and one of the few I suspect in his life, and I am sure it was kind by no intention of his: 'Well, we can't hang around here all day. Reckon you'd better come on along, if you're coming.'

With that, Emma and her father kiss, shyly and awkwardly, children doing it before parents; so do she and her brother; she and Annie Mae embrace; she and I shake hands and say good-bye: all this in the sort of broken speed in which a family takes leave beside the black wall of a steaming train when the last crates have been loaded and it seems certain that at any instant the windows, and the leaned unpitying faces, will begin to slide past on iron. Emma's paper suitcase is lifted into the truck beside the bedsprings which will sustain the years on years of her cold, hopeless nights; she is helped in upon the hard seat beside the driver above the hot and floorless engine, her slippered feet propped askew at the ledges of that pit into the road; the engine snaps and coughs and catches and levels on a hot white moistureless and thin metal roar, and with a dreadful rending noise that brings up the mild heads of cattle a quarter of a mile away the truck rips itself loose from the flesh of the planed dirt of the yard and wrings into the road and chucks ahead, we waving, she waving, the black hat straight ahead, she turned away, not bearing it, our hands drooped, and we stand disconsolate and emptied in the sun; and all through these coming many hours while we slow move within the anchored rondures of our living, the hot, screaming, rattling, twenty-mile-an-hour traveling elongates steadily crawling, a lost, earnest, and frowning ant, westward on red roads and on white in the febrile sun above no support, suspended, sustained from falling by force alone of its outward growth, like that long and lithe incongruous slender runner a vine spends swiftly out on the vast blank wall of the earth, like snake's head and slim stream feeling its way, to fix, and anchor, so far, so wide of the strong and stationed stalk: and that is Emma.

*

But as yet this has not happened, and now she sleeps, here in this next room, among six others dear in their lives to me, and if I were but to section and lift away a part of this so thin shell and protection of wall, there they would be as in a surgery, or a medical drawing, the brain beneath the lifted, so light helmet of the skull, the deep-chambered, powerful and so vulnerable, so delicately ruined, emboweled, most vital organs, behind the placid lovedelighting skin; and a few hours past, they were going to bed, and not long before, they were eating supper, and because of their sadness, and because of the excitement of her being here, supper had in its speaking and its whole manner a tone out of the ordinary, a quality of an occasion, almost of a party, almost of gaiety, with a pale chocolate pudding, made out of cocoa and starch, for dessert, and a sort of made-conversation and joking half forced by fear of sadness, and half genuinely stimulated by her presence and by a shyness and liking for us: and in the middle of the table stood the flower of the lighted lamp, more kind, more friendly in the still not departed withering daylight and more lovely, than may be set in words beneath its fact: and when the supper was finished, it disintegrated without suture or transition into work, sleep, rest: Annie Mae, Emma, Louise, the three women, rising to the work they had scarcely ceased during the meal (for they had served us, eating betweentimes), clearing, scraping, crumbing the damp oilcloth with damp cloth in the light, dishwashing, meanwhile talking (Louise not talking, listening to them, the older women, absorbing, absorbing deeply, grain by grain, ton by ton, that which she shall not escape): the women lifting themselves from their chairs into this work; the children meanwhile sinking and laid out five fathom five mile deep along the exhausted floor: and we, following manners, transferred with George, a few feet beyond the kitchen door, in the open porch hall, leaned back in chairs against the wall, or leaned between our knees and our planted feet, he, with his work shoes off, his feet taking, thirstily drinking like the sunken heads of horses at the trough, the cool and beauty quiet of the grained and gritted boards of the floor; and he talking a little, but too tired for talk, and rolling a damp cigarette and smoking its short sweetness through to the scorching of the stony thumb, with a child's body lifted sleeping between his knees:

and when the women are through, they may or may not come out too, with their dresses wet in front with the dishwashing and their hard hands softened and seamed as if withered with water, and sit a little while with the man or the men: and if they do, it is not for long, for everyone is much too tired, and has been awake and at work since day-light whitened a little behind the trees on the hill, and it is now very close to dark, with daylight scarcely more than a sort of tincture on the air, and this diminishing, and the loudening frogs, and the locusts, the crickets, and the birds of night, tentative, tuning, in that great realm of hazy and drowned dew, who shall so royally embroider the giant night's fragrant cloud of earthshade: and so, too, the talking is sporadic, and sinks into long unembarrassed silences; the sentences, the com-ments, the monosyllables, drawn up from deepest within them without thought and with faint creaking of weight as if they were wells, and spilled out in a cool flat drawl, and quietly answered; and a silence; and again, some words: and it is not really talking, or meaning, but anoth-er and profounder kind of communication, a rhythm to be completed by answer and made whole by silence, a lyric song, as horses who nudge one another in pasture, or like drowsy birds who are heavying a dark branch with their tiredness before sleep: and it is their leisure after work; but it does not last; and in fifteen minutes, or a half-hour at most, it is done, and they draw themselves into motion for bed:

one by one, in a granite-enameled, still new basin which is for that single purpose, they wash their feet in cold water – for this is a very cleanly and decent family – and begin to move into the bedroom: first the children, then the women, last George: the pallets are laid; the lamp is in the bedroom; George sits in the porch dark, smoking another cig-arette. Junior, morose and whimpering and half blind with sleep, un-dresses himself, sliding the straps from his shoulders and the overalls from his nakedness and sinking in his shirt asleep already, along the thin cotton pallet. Burt scarcely half awakens as his sister strips him, a child of dough, and is laid like a corpse beside his cruel brother. Squinchy is drugged beyond doomcrack: his heavy tow head falls back across her bent arm loose as that of a dead bird, the mouth wide open, the eyelids oily gleaming, as his mother slips from his dwarf body the hip length, one-button dress; and the women, their plain shifts lifted from the closet nails, undress themselves, turned part away from each other, and careful not to look: the mother, whose body already at twenty-seven is so wrung and drained and old, a scrawny, infinitely tired, delicate animal, the poor emblems of delight no longer practicable to any but most weary and grunting use: her big young sister, childless still, and dim, soft as a bloomed moon, and still in health, who emanates some disordering or witless violation: and the still inviolate, lyric body of a child, very much of the earth, yet drawn into that short and seraphic phase of what seems unearthliness which it will so soon lose: each aware of herself and of the others, and each hiding what shames or grieves her: and the two elder talking (and the child, the photographic plate, receiving: These are women, I am a woman, I am not a child any more, I am undressing with women, and this is how women are, and how they talk), talking ahead, the two women, in flat, secure, drawled, reedy voices, neither shy nor deliberately communicative, but utterly communicative, the talk loosening out of them serenely and quietly steady and in no restraint of uncertainty of one another like the alternate and plaited music of two slow-dribbling taps; and they are in bed and George throws his cigarette, hurtling its spark into the night yard, and comes in, and they turn their faces away while he undresses; and he takes the clean thin union suit from its nail by the scrolled iron head of the bed; and he slides between the coarse sheets and lets down his weight; and for a little while more, because they are stimulated, they keep talking, while the children sleep, and while Louise lies looking and listening, with the light still on, and there is almost volubility in the talk, and almost gaiety again, and inaudible joking, and little runs of laughter like startled sparrows; and gradually this becomes more quiet, and there is a silence full of muted thought; and George, says; Well; and fluffs out the lamp, and its light from the cracks in my wall, and there is silence; and George speaks, low, and is answered by both women; and a silence; and Emma murmurs something; and after a few seconds Annie Mae murmurs a reply; and there is a silence, and a slow and constrained twisting on springs and extension of a body, and silence; and a long silence in the darkness of the peopled room that is chambered in the darkness of the continent before the unwatching stars; and Louise says, Good night Immer, and Emma says, Good night Louise; and Louise says, Good night mamma; and Annie Mae says, Good night Louise; and Louise says, Good night daddy; and George says, Good night Louise; good night George; night, Immer; night, Annie Mae; night, George; night, Immer; night, Annie Mae; night, Louise; night; good night, good night:

Bring: Bring up:
Thou wound thy mien before the jurying stars:

And wild earth lifted streams in peace so noble, the wide
        dreaming forehead
and water mapped of earth, serene, serene;

O infant skull, back-fallen from an arm upon tall starlight,
        that ran in the bright barnyard:
O world, thou richly peopled, thou sober-steering ark, quiet
        stone, thou granule,
    that finds no ararat:

O thou girl's breast:

II:

There are on this hill three such families I would tell you of: the Gudgers, who are sleeping in the next room; and the Woods, whose daughters are Emma and Annie Mae; and besides these, the Ricketts, who live on a little way beyond the Woods; and we reach them thus:

Leave this room and go very quietly down the open hall that divides the house, past the bedroom door, and the dog that sleeps outside it, and move on out into the open, the back yard, going up hill: between the tool shed and the hen house (the garden is on your left), and turn left at the long low shed that passes for a barn. Don't take the path to the left then: that only leads to the spring; but cut straight up the slope; and down the length of the cotton that is planted at the crest of it, and through a space of pine, hickory, dead logs and blackberry brambles (damp spider webs will bind on your face in the dark; but the path is easily enough followed); and out beyond this, across a great entanglement of clay ravines, which finally solidify into a cornfield. Follow this cornfield straight down a row, go through a barn, and turn left. There is a whole cluster of houses here; they are all negroes'; the shutters are drawn tight. You may or may not waken some dogs: if you do, you will hardly help but be frightened, for in a couple of minutes the whole country will be bellowing in the darkness, and it is over your movements at large at so late and still an hour of the night, and the sound, with the knowledge of wakened people, their heads lifted a little on the darkness from the crackling hard straw pillows of their iron beds, overcasts your very existence, in your own mind, with a complexion of guilt, stealth, and danger:

But they will quiet.

They will quiet, the lonely heads are relaxed into sleep; after a little the whippoorwills resume, their tireless whipping of the pastoral night, and the strong frogs; and you are on the road, and again up hill, that was met at those clustered houses; pines on your left, one wall of bristling cloud, and the lifted hill; the slow field raised, in the soft stare of the cotton, several acres, on the right; and on the left the woods yield off, a hundred yards; more cotton; and set back there, at the brim of the hill, the plain small house you see is Woods' house, that looks shrunken against its centers under the starlight, the tin roof scarcely taking sheen, the floated cotton staring:

The house a quarter-mile beyond, just on the right of the road, standing with shade trees, that is the Ricketts'. The bare dirt is more damp in the tempering shade; and damp, tender with rottenness, the ragged wood of the porch, that is so heavily littered with lard buckets, scraps of iron, bent wire, torn rope, old odors, those no longer useful things which on a farm are never thrown away. The trees: draft on their stalks their clouds of heavy season; the barn: shines on the perfect air; in the bare yard a twelve-foot flowering bush: in shroud of blown bloom slumbers, and within: naked, naked side by side those brothers and sisters, those most beautiful children; and the crazy, clownish, foxy father; and the mother; and the two old daughters; crammed on their stinking beds, are resting the night:

Fred, Sadie, Margaret, Paralee, Garvrin, Richard, Flora Merry Lee, Katy, Clair Bell; and the dogs, and the cats, and the hens, and the mules, and the hogs, and the cow, and the bull calf:

Woods, and his young wife, and her mother, and the young wife's daughter, and her son by Woods, and their baby daughter, and that heavy-browed beast which enlarges in her belly; Bud, and Ivy, and

Miss-Molly, and Pearl, and Thomas, and Ellen, and the nameless plant of unknown sex; and the cat, and the dog, and the mule, and the hog, and the cow, and the hens, and the huddled chickens:

And George, and his wife, and her sister, and their children, and their animals; and the hung wasps, lancing mosquitoes, numbed flies, and browsing rats:

All, spreaded in high quietude on the hill:

Sadie the half-sister of Bud, and drowned in their remembrance: that long and spiral shaft they've climbed, from shacks on shale, rigid as corn on a cob, out of the mining country, the long wandering, her pride of beauty, his long strength in marriage, into this: this present time, and this near future:

George his lost birthright, bad land owned, and that boyhood among cedars and clean creeks where no fever laid its touch, and where in the luminous and great hollow night the limestone shone like sheep: and the strong, gay girls:

Fred, what of him: I can not guess. And Annie Mae, that hat; which still, so broken, the death odor of feathers and silk in menthol, is crumpled in a drawer; and those weeks when she was happy, and to her husband and to her heart it was pleasing to be alive:

She is dreaming now, with fear, of a shotgun: George has directed it upon her; and there is no trigger:

Ivy, and her mother: what are the dreams of dogs?

Margaret, of a husband, and strong land, and ladies nodding in the walks.

And all these children:

These children, still in the tenderness of their lives, who will draw their future remembrance, and their future sorrow, from this place: and the strangers, animals: for work, for death, for food: and the scant crops: doing their duty the best they can, like temperless and feeble-minded children: rest now, between the wrenchings of the sun:

*

O, we become old; it has been a long, long climb; there will not be much more of this; then we will rest: sorrow nor sweating nor aching back, sickness, nor pity, hope gone, heaven's deafness; nothing shall take or touch us more: not thunder nor the rustling worms nor scalding kettle nor weeping child shall rouse us where we rest: these things shall be the business of others: these things shall be the business of our children, and their children; we will rest:

In what way were we trapped? where, our mistake? what, where, how, when, what way, might all these things have been different, if only we had done otherwise? if only we might have known. Where lost that bright health of love that knew so surely it would stay; how, how did it sink away, beyond help, beyond hope, beyond desire, beyond remembrance; and where the weight and the wealth of that strong year when there was more to eat than we could hold, new clothes, a grafanola, and money in the bank? How, how did all this sink so swift away, like that grand august cloud who gathers – the day quiets dark and chills, and the leaves lather – and scarcely steams the land? How are these things?

In the years when we lived down by the river we had all the fish we wanted, and yellow milk, enough to sell, and we bought two mules:

When we moved in here I wanted to make the house pretty, I folded a lot of pattern-paper and cut it into a pretty lace pattern and hung it on the mantelpiece: but now I just don't care any longer, I don't care how anything looks:

My mother made me the prettiest kind of a dress, all fresh for school; I wore it the first day, and everyone laughed and poked fun at me; it wasn't like other dresses, neither the cloth, nor the way it was cut, and I never . . .

I made her such a pretty dress and she wore it once, and she never wore it away from home again:

Oh, thank God not one of you knows how everyone snickers at your father.

*

I reckon we're just about the meanest people in this whole country.

George Gudger? Where'd you dig *him* up? I haven't been back out that road in twenty-five year.

Fred Ricketts? Why, that dirty son-of-a-bitch, he *brags* that he hasn't bought his family a bar of soap in five year.

Ricketts? They're a bad lot. They've got Miller blood mixed up in them. The children are a bad problem in school.

Why, Ivy Pritchert was one of the worst whores in this whole part of the country: only one that was worse was her own mother. They're about the lowest trash you can find.

Why, she had her a man back in the woods for years before *he* married her; had two children by him.

Gudger? He's a fair farmer. Fair cotton farmer, but he hain't got a mite a sense.

None of these people has any sense, nor any initiative. If they did, they wouldn't be farming on shares.

Give them money and all they'll do with it is throw it away.

Why, times when I envy them. No risk, we take all the risk; all the clothes they need to cover them; food coming up right out of their land.

So you're staying out at Gudgers', are you? And how do you like the food they give you? Yeah, aheh-heh-heh-heh, how do you like that fine home cookin'; how do you like that good wholesome country food?

Tell you the honest truth, they owe us a big debt. Now you just tell me, if you can, what would all those folks be doing if it wasn't for us?

*

How did we get caught? Why is it things always seem to go against us? Why is it there can't ever be any pleasure in living? I'm so tired it don't seem like I ever could get rest enough. I'm as tired when I get up in the morning as I am when I lay down at night. Sometimes it seems like there wouldn't never be no end to it, nor even a let-up. One year it'll look like things was going to be pretty good; but you get a little bit of money saved, something always happens.

I tell you *I* won't be sorry when I die. I wouldn't be sorry this minute if it wasn't for Louise and Squinchy-here. Rest vmd git along all right:

(But *I* am young; and I am young, and strong, and in good health; and I am young, and pretty to look at; and I am too young to worry; and so am I, for my mother is kind to me; and we run in the bright air like animals, and our bare feet like plants in the wholesome earth: the natural world is around us like a lake and a wide smile and we are growing: one by one we are becoming stronger, and one by one in the terrible emptiness and the leisure we shall burn and tremble and shake with lust, and one by one we shall loosen ourselves from this place, and shall be married, and it will be different from what we see, for we will be happy and love each other, and keep the house clean, and a good garden, and buy a cultivator, and use a high grade of fertilizer, and we will know how to do things right; it will be very different:) (? :)

((?)   )   :)

How were we caught?

What, what is it has happened? What is it has been happening that we are living the way we are?

The children are not the way it seemed they might be:

She is no longer beautiful:

He no longer cares for me, he just takes me when he wants me:

There's so much work it seems like you never see the end of it:

I'm so hot when I get through cooking a meal it's more than I can do to sit down to it and eat it:

How was it we were caught?

And seeing the multitudes, he went up into a mountain; and when he was set, his disciples came unto him:
And he opened his mouth and taught them, saying:
Blessed are the poor in spirit: for theirs is the kingdom of heaven.
Blessed are they that mourn: for they shall be comforted.
Blessed are the meek: for they shall inherit the earth.
Blessed are they which do hunger and thirst after righteousness: for they shall be filled.
Blessed are the merciful: for they shall obtain mercy.
Blessed are the pure in heart: for they shall see God.
Blessed are the peacemakers: for they shall be called the children of God.
Blessed are they which are persecuted for righteousness' sake: for theirs is the kingdom of heaven.
Blessed are ye when men shall revile you, and persecute you, and shall say all manner of evil against you falsely, for my sake.
Rejoice, and be exceeding glad: for great is your reward in heaven: for so persecuted they the prophets which were before you.

III:

Nevertheless:

Oh, nevertheless:

Spired Europe is out, up the middle of her morning, has brought her embossed cities, her front of country snailed with steel;

the Atlantic globe is burnished, ship-crawled, pathed and paved of air, brightens to blind;

shoulder clean shoulder from their hangar, Brazil and Labrador; flash flame;

from stone shore, bluff-browed tree, birds are drawn sparkling and each plant: erects upon his root, lifts up his head, accepts once more the summer:

and so must these: while the glistening land drives east: they shall be drawn up like plants with the burden of being upon them, their legs heavy, their eyes quiet and sick, the weight of the day watching them quietly from the ceiling, in the sharpening room; they will lift; lift — there is no use, no help for it — their legs from the bed and their feet to the floor and the height of their bodies above their feet and the load above them, and let it settle upon the spine, and the width of the somewhat stooped shoulders, the weight that is not put by; and are drawn loose from their homes a million upon the land, beneath the quietly lifted light, to work:

And here:

Watch from the crackling mattress how the stars, through the roof, though strong, are yet so tired.

The night has dried.

Nothing is yet visible in the room, but one begins again to be aware: of the walls, and their odor and lightness, facing each other; and of the postures of the furniture. The bureau, squared on a corner, and its blind mirror receiving, reflecting, the blindness of the bed. The iron of the bed. The sewing machine, the tin trunk, and the wicker chair. The beauties on the walls.

Outside, from near, there is a new sound. It happens every night, and it is most sorrowful. It is the voice of a blond, fat, and craven rooster, a creature half-frightened of his own wives; and in this poor voice of his, lugubrious, almost surreptitious, he is making a statement he so misbelieves that it is rather a question that expects no answer save the utter scorn and denial of silence; and it gets none: but serves only to remind one of the noises of the night, which perhaps have not at any time ceased.

They have perhaps at no time ceased, but that will never be surely known, they are, after a while, so easily lost: and one hears them once again with a quiet sort of surprise, that only slowly becomes the realization, or near certainty, that they have been there all the while:

They are still there, they still convey to one no merely intimate vicinity, but the whole blind earth dispread: they chainlike stream like water violins, a straight and upward rain extracted from the world: yet they are in this hour so profoundly retired upon themselves, they are scarcely the echo of an echo, music's remembrance in a dying dream, lashed through with weltering whippoorwill, the mourner and genius of great summer night: and even that weeping bird now twice has faltered, and on blurred bark-hued flight has taken his song more deeply among the groves. And the land:

The land, pale fields, black cloudy woodlands, and the late lamps in the central streets of the rare and inexpiable cities: New Orleans; Birmingham; whose façades stand naked in the metal light of their fear:

the land, in its largeness: stretches: is stretched:

it is stretched like that hollow and quietness of water that is formed at the root of a making wave, and it waits: not a leaf, not a grass blade, trembles even: but is stretched: stretched: stretched: and waits (the blood stream stridence meanwhile coursing): waits (the whippoorwill has established in a much nearer tree; one almost knows the feathers that work at his larynx; but he is uncertain):

not suddenly, nor with fright, but certainly with no line of crossing, no beginning, there has been a change in the air, a crisis passed in sleep; for now, that in the same instant it seems was so enchanted still, there is a nearly noiseless trembling of every leaf of the vegetation of all this part of the world, so delicate a turning in fright of sleep as that needle which records a minute disturbance on the far side of the thick planet, and so nearly noiseless, yet so unanimous, it is the indistinguishable and whispered sigh of all the generations of the dead, the crumbling of a world-long wave so distant, that one yard more removed, could not be audible:

yet that shuddering: that of a body hopeless standing, though the air is mild: does not break, but rather intensifies the waiting (this is happening not only here but in a stripe, a few miles wide, straight up through

Canada, and down the Andes): the air darkens to black violet, and the stars refresh:

and casually, and with rending triumph, the signal is delivered on the dusk: the sure wild glittering yell of a rooster; light on a lifted sword.

He is some long distance away, it seems infinite miles, the utmost ledge of the universe, to the east. He has a little while ago awakened, full awake immediately, and intensely aware, as one wakes and is aware, in the total darkness, of someone alien in the room, and his round eye has sharpened on the dark a fierce button, the head cocked, and whole being listening; what is it: what is it; tightening with excitement and premonition, a sort of joyful fear, the hackles roughed with it:

And with the brusqueness of an epileptic seizure a power much stronger than himself has taken him whole; it must be the voice of another rooster, who received it from another, and so to the brim of the continent, where the first, their bright backs warm and splendid in the light, are stabbing at corn; he is taken whole; he clenches the whole strength of his body and his fiery soul deep into one fist, and strives it at the sky, all his strength shuddering:

and it is heard: and distant though it is, it cleaves in its full fortissimo: so valiant a noise as rescuing bugle, or tenor broke his throat for: and no answer:

and then the answer: deep, steep back behind beneath my prostrated head:

(the violet grays; the gray walks through the walls)

silence: the whippoorwill; pleading; deploring:

the first again, much fiercer:

and, almost interrupting him, a third, beyond the woods:

*

('*whip-pawill! whipp-awilll!*)

The second again; at last, our blond, his androgynous voice chortling with fake confidence: a fourth: the first (the country is taking shape): another: now the third (it is emerging like a print in a tank; I see distinctly the walls of the room, and on the earth the medallioned cities): three new ones now: another: now another: strain on their horn' toes and shout.

By now it is full glass light, clean, whitening gray, without shadow, and the air is cold, with an odor of pork and damp earth, and the spiring of the roosters has become a commonplace. The whippoorwill has stayed it out long beyond the last ditch, whispering almost visible from among the distinct gray leaves of a near tree; now he is sunk and gone, and the air is brisk with small and skillful birds, who whistle, and beat metals with light hammers; and a dog comes casually though somewhat stiffly round the corner of the house, and smoke sprowls up from chimneys: and the light still whitens:

But much earlier, while it was not yet light, at about the crowing of the second cock, Annie Mae woke, on her back, and watched up at the ceiling; and at this time Margaret Ricketts is already a half-hour up, and the stove crackling, and she is cooking by lamp before the windows are even pale, for her father suffers from stirrup corns, and has four miles through the woods to walk to work. And Fred, and his wife, and Paralee, lie in their beds collecting their strength, and the children still sleep:

Annie Mae watches up at the ceiling, and she is as sick with sleep as if she had lain the night beneath a just-supportable weight: and watching up into the dark, beside her husband, the ceiling becomes visible, and watching into her eyes, the weight of the day. She has not lacked in utter tiredness, like a load in her whole body, a day since she was a young girl, nor will she ever lack it again; and is of that tribe who by glandular arrangement seem to exhaust rather than renew themselves with sleep, and to whom the act of getting up is almost unendurably painful. But when the ceiling has become visible there is no longer any help for it, and she wrenches herself up, and wriggles a dress on over her head, and shuffles barefooted across the porch to the basin, and ladles out two dippers of water from the bucket, and cups it in her hands, and drenches her face in it, with a shuddering shock that straightens her; and dries on the split flour sack that hangs from a nail; and is capable now of being alive, to work:

Her first work being, to build the fire, and to cook biscuits and eggs and meat and coffee:

With the noise at the stove, George wakes. Without having to look for it, he reaches on the floor by the bed and finds the book of cigarette papers and the tobacco, and the sweatproof matchbox he has made of a truncated Prince Albert tin. In a skillful and beautiful collusion of his stiff, thick fingers he rolls a cigarette, and he props his head, and smokes it, staring through the ornate iron at the wall, while the birds whet and sweeten:

(Ivy is meantime up: she was wakened in the serene quietness of a woods animal, neither tired nor rested, but blank and fresh like water; her fine big feet soothe and seethe the floor, and Bud comes to, lifting his sardonic-gentle, innocent, dimly criminal, birdlike, little-boy's head a little from the pillow, the sheet drawn to his chin: the cleaning light is cool: the children sleep; Pearl, pale, adenoidal, already erotic; and Thomas like a dance, frog-legged, his fists in his eyes; and Ellen, like a baby, fish-mouthed between her enormous cheeks:)

The cleaning light is cool; the older Ricketts are hurrying through breakfast. There is a rapid smattering of feet and Clair Bell sprints in affrighted: that her father has left for work before kissing her good-bye.

They take her on their laps assuring her that he would never do no such a thang, and help her drink her coffee:

I used as a child in the innocence of faith to bring myself out of bed through the cold lucid water of the Cumberland morning and to serve at the altar at earliest lonely Mass, whose words were thrilling brooks of music and whose motions, a grave dance: and there between spread hands the body and the blood of Christ was created among words and lifted before God in a threshing of triplicate bells, and from the rear of the empty church stole forward a serene widow and a savage epileptic, softly blind, and knelt, and on the palms of their hands and at their mouths they took their strength and, blind, retired: and the morning was clangorous with the whole of a roused school when we were done, and out, and that was the peace of a day: and it is in no beauty less that the gestures of a day here begin; and in just such silence and solitude: the iron lids are lifted: the kindling is laid in the grate: and the lids replaced: and a squirting match applied beneath: and the flour is sifted through shaken window-screen, and mixed with lard and water, soda, and a little salt: the coffee is set on the stove, its grounds afloat on the cold water: more wood laid in: the biscuits poured, and stuck into the oven: all these things with set motions, progressions, routines and retracings, of bare feet and of sticklike arms, stick hands, contractions of the sharp body: and the meat sliced and sliding, spitting, in the black skillet; and the eggs broken, and their shells consigned; and the chairs lifted from the porch to the table, and the sorghum set on, and the butter, sugar, salt, pepper, a spoon straightened, the lamp set at the center; the eggs turned; the seething coffee set aside; the meat reheated; the biscuits looked at; the straight black hair, saturated with sweat and smoke of pork, tightened more neatly to the head between four black pins; the biscuits tan, the eggs ready, the coffee ready, the meat ready, the breakfast ready:

and they come in, by order of age, masked with the chill of the water that holds them together, and silent with sleep; and the animals raise themselves out of the floor and establish themselves beneath the table, lifting open heads:

and breakfast is too serious a meal for speaking; and it is difficult and revolting to eat heavily before one is awake; but it is necessary, for on this food must be climbed the ardent and steep hill of the morning, steadily hotter, up to noon, and for Fred and George then a cold lunch only, and resumption, and hours more of work: so that your two halves are held together and erect by this food as by a huge tight buckle as big as the belly, giving no ease but chunk, stone, fund, of strength: endurance in it, or leverage on the day, like a stiff stone: this slowly thaws and is absorbed more evenly throughout the body, and the strength becomes easy leather:

it is much the same at the Woods', a little different; Ivy drawls and chaffers like water, her loose hair lays around on her head; and Pearl's face at the edge of the table is a solemn pouch with swampy eyes; and Woods, his body is elderly, not strong, he must draw it together like strings into a knot; and his eyes look out at the morning, from his intelligent unequipped brain, with a sort of sour part-smiling, hopeless speculation, while he talks a little:

and at the Ricketts', more vivacious, for there are many people; the father talks continuously, and though he has now gone, walking as if barefoot on a field of burrs, there are accidents to food and to children, and enough confusion over who is at what task, to keep them going;

and the breakfasts ended, the houses are broken open like pods in the increase of the sun, and they are scattered on the wind of a day's work.

(How was it we were caught?)

IV:

Four miles back into the northeast, on a relaxation to flatness in the middle of the low, roiling, and tree-mantled hills, there is a long rectangle cut clean of timber, and beyond it, standing pine.

The rectangle is stacked along the middle with fresh lumber that stands in a yellow nimbus. The road splits round it between tall drenched weeds and meets itself at the far end where, still close within the cold, dark, early shade, are the soot-black scaffolded structures of sawmill machinery and of power; the tall black candle of stack torched-off with clear curling heat beneath the stained flag of rust-lighted smoke; and a negro waiting, glancing frequently at his watch with a little left in him, after years of habituation, of a child's excitement in responsibility and in power: and the space is meanwhile struggling full of more and more men, not really many, yet in this woodland and keen morning quietness they seem a crowd, drawn in on rattling wagons and by truck and afoot through the chill hickory smell and fronded shade of the morning forest; and the sun is strong.

It is strong already, and steadfastly strengthening like the held note of a horn. It is lifted square in the middle of the far end among the tops of the black pines and burns a whorl of cobwebs through them, and the pines are sheeted and shredded, carded wool, in a keen mist its brightness refracts among and burns and brightens, so that they are lifted slowly and splendidly in long planes and slashed uncoiling streamers, and there is a sheen on the whole of the clear air of such intensity that it all but hurts the eyes.

Over to the left the brass padlock hangs loosened on the new pine shed of tools and slung harness, and in a barked enclosure behind it are the mules, and along the fence the wagons are ranged in a line, their tongues in the air like a salute of elephants. They are long, low skeleton wagons of tough beams, no sides, for hauling logs; some of them auto-wheeled and rubber-tired; and their oak wood is now blanching with warmth, and their details of metal already warm to the touch. The mules loiter in a hooved muck of tattered water in a tract of brownlighted shadow slivered with sun, a sapling grove licked leafless within their reach, the trunks rubbed slick: very naked-looking and somehow shy without harness, as if they had not quite the right to nature, they stand, they drift, they wait, they glide among the vertical wax saplings in the camouflaging light, and lift back their cynical heads like flowers as the men who master their days lift open the gate and advance toward them: some stand docile, and accept the halter with a kind of sneering meekness; others quietly lift their hoofs in the chopped earth and drift, as a matter of decent form rather than rebellion; two or three draw themselves back as deep among the narrow trees as the squared sharp wire will allow them, and abide a close approach, then slither away, and these are kicked in the belly and slashed along the jaws and across the eyes: there is among these negroes a scarred yet pure white mule, whose presence among them in this magic light is that of an enslaved unicorn: and these are led out and stood along the shafts and harnessed in teams in geometries of leather, rope and bird-jingling metal as sweet in their stresses as the rigging of sloops; and the men now wait quietly and in a casually tense listlessness, talking a little, rolling damp cigarettes, and adjusting the iron violence of their breakfasts inside them; and a negro, harnessing his mules, lifts forth wet-throated, joyfully, three times into the embla-

zoned morning the long black sorrow-foundered and incompleted
phrase of anarchaic mode in whose glorying he begins each day; and
the men still wait; and the trapped mules, twitching the metal flies, con-
niving their long heads: and though the air is still cool, there is now the
cutting odor of grass and weeds, and a cool sweat starts out and faintly stings in patterns upon the forehead, the wrists, the beam of the
shoulders, and the spine; and down in the shortening and uncooling
shade at the black altar of machinery, the negro stands with one hand
hung in a triangular wire and with time like a lake in the palm of the
other, into whose surface he gazes, and on the second, he pulls down
on the wire; and in a stiff standing-out of steam, the air is one rich reeking shriek through which the sunlight is vibrated: and the mules tight-
en; and the negro slides the watch, which is tethered to him by a still
new black shoestring, back into the small pocket at the center of his
chest; and the whistle is cut off like a murder, leaving the aquarium
clearing weak with silence from all sides of which are reflexed in dimin-
ishment the noise like a weltering, withering flat of the contour waves
from a center: they are spread on the hills like the explosive sudden
flowering of a steel rose and it is retracted to the root: and there is a
tightening of strength against harness under slashing of sharp leather
and they move, the long clattering wagons, in a drawn line round the
stacked pine lumber and down the far side of the clearing and on, past
the machinery and uphill to the right along a wide broken trough of
stumps rank weeds iron shade and iron and splendid light, and are
deployed along the ragged and stump-spiked woodlands into the
resumption of yesterday's work: chopping, sawing, snaking, hauling, the
shearing surflike shriek of the saw: and it is now thirty-two minutes
past six, and among these men are George Gudger and —

Colon

Curtain Speech

Colon

But there must be an end to this: a sharp end and clean silence: a steep and most serious withdrawal: a new and more succinct beginning:

Herein I must screen off all mysteries of our comminglings — all these, all such, must be deferred — and must here set in such regard as I can the sorry and brutal infuriate yet beautiful structures of the living which is upon each of you daily: and this in the cleanest terms I can learn to specify: must mediate, must attempt to record, your warm weird human lives each in relation to its world:

Nor may this be lightly undertaken: not lightly, not easily by any means: nor by any hope 'successfully':

For one who sets himself to look at all earnestly, at all in purpose toward truth, into the living eyes of a human life: what is it he there beholds that so freezes and abashes his ambitious heart? What is it, profound behind the outward windows of each one of you, beneath touch even of your own suspecting, drawn tightly back at bay against the backward wall and blackness of its prison cave, so that the eyes alone shine of their own angry glory, but the eyes of a trapped wild animal, or of a furious angel nailed to the ground by his wings, or however else one may faintly designate the human 'soul,' that which is angry, that which is wild, that which is untamable, that which is healthful and holy, that which is competent of all advantaging within hope of human dream, that which most marvelous and most precious to our knowledge and most extremely advanced upon futurity of all flowerings within the scope of creation is of all these the least destructible, the least corruptible, the most defenseless, the most easily and multitudinously wounded, frustrate, prisoned, and nailed into a cheating of itself: so situated in the universe that those three hours upon the cross are but a noble and too trivial an emblem how in each individual among most of the two billion now alive and in each successive instant of the existence of each existence not only human being but in him the tallest and most sanguine hope of godhead is in a billionate choiring and drone of pain of generations upon generations unceasingly crucified and is bringing forth crucifixions into their necessities and is each in the most casual of his life so measurelessly discredited, harmed, insulted, poisoned, cheated, as not all the wrath, compassion, intelligence, power of rectification in all the reach of the future shall in the least expiate or make one ounce more light: how, looking thus into your eyes and seeing thus, how each of you is a creature which has never in all time existed before and which shall never in all time exist again and which is not quite like any other and which has the grand stature and natural warmth of every other and whose existence is all measured upon a still mad and incurable time; how am I to speak of you as 'tenant' 'farmers,' as 'representatives' of your 'class,' as social integers in a criminal economy, or as individuals, fathers, wives, sons, daughters, and as my friends and as I 'know' you? Granted — more, insisted upon — that it is in all these particularities that each of you is that which he is; that particularities, and matters ordinary and obvious, are exactly themselves beyond designation of words, are the members of your sum total most obligatory to human searching of perception: nevertheless to name these things and fail to yield their stature, meaning, power of hurt, seems impious, seems criminal, seems impudent, seems traitorous in the deepest: and to do less badly seems impossible: yet in withholdings of specification I could but betray you still worse.

Let me say, then, how I would wish this account might be constructed.

I might suggest, its structure should be globular: or should be eighteen or twenty intersected spheres, the interlockings of bubbles on the face of a stream; one of these globes is each of you.

The heart, nerve, center of each of these, is an individual human life.

We should first meditate and establish its ancient, then more recent, its spreaded and more local, history and situation: how it is a child of the substance and bowels of the stars and of all space: how it is created forth of an aberration special to one speck and germ and pollen fleck this planet, this young planet, on that broadblown field: how on the youth of this planet it is youngest, scarcely yet breathed-upon yet born, into its future growth: how it is blossomed forth upon that branch most sportive, most precarious, most propitious, potential and most frightful in known creation, of human existence, of human consciousness, of human possibility to build itself ruin or wonder: how it is the bearer of whatever the future shall be: how in itself, no matter which individual mote it is, it is in its beginning capable, in its terms, of health, which is perfection, which is holiness, which is simple and salted, blooded functioning of each animal in his own best: and is capable likewise of all harm to itself and to others: how all that is to make all this difference is circumstance, physical and mental: how there is nothing within consciousness and the receiving of our senses which is not incorporate of this bulk and strength to shape of circumstance, and nothing so minute but that it impounds more power, more importance, more meaning of impingement upon this human life, than most exact or violent words might ever tell:

At this center we set this seed, this flower, whose genealogy we have suggested and whose context in eternal history, his royalty, his miraculousness, his great potentiality: we try at least to suggest also his incomparable tenderness to experience, his malleability, the almost inimaginable nakedness and defenselessness of this wondrous fivewindowed nerve and core: the size, the pity, the abomination of the crimes he is to sustain, against the incredible sweetness, strength, and beauty of what he might be and is cheated of:

Never relaxing the simultaneity of his ancestral and brotherly stars, we bring his sources into a more near convergence in local place of time: how he is brought forth of a chain and weaving, a texture of sorrowful and demented flesh, which in all previous centuries has scarcely in few meaningless hundreds wrought up a head from the blind bottom of the human sea and breathed one cup of brightness and plain air, and in these disadvantagings were drawn up and woven upon the crookedness of one continent and were drawn upon seas and upon a newer to no better faring, and here a few generations have dwelt in the woodlands and dead clays in bestial freedom or in servitude, shaken with fevers, grieved and made sick with foods, wrungout in work to lassitude in the strong sun and to lack of hope or caring, in ignorance of all cause, all being, all conduct, hope of help or cure, saturated in harm and habit, unteachable beliefs, the germens they carry at their groins strained, cracked, split, tainted, vitiate to begin with, a wallet of cheated coinage:

Here we have two, each crucified, further crucify one another upon the shallow pleasure of an iron bed and instigate in a woman's belly a crucifixion of cell and whiplashed sperm: whose creature is our center, our nerve we spoke of; in this instant already his globe is rounded upon him and is his prison, which might have been his kingdom: it is begun in a redblack cherishing of a blind and beating of hurt unvanquishable blood and is informed entirely of the ferment of this blood, of whom likewise hard work is done, indecent diet is taken, there is fright and sorrow in dream, and not much or no love at all, a weaponless mind is meditating as it may; this creature, the motive even of his creation, is sprung, is sprained, is slaved and ordered by a crimesoaked world: for he is made for work, for a misuser, not his own even illusive master nor even mere slave of his parents or a healthful state, but of misuse without which he shall not live at all: and it is in obedience to these pressures that the marriage was made and that he was conceived, and that he is nursed and emboweled among the discouragements of this beating of beaten blood; and it is toward this bondage that the germ unfurls and flowers, climbs from that soft and floated sea through darkness and petting blood the steep ladder through all shifts of nature and, low helmet huge and cowering mild, hands covering lightless eyes, knees, feet drawn tight as if he were receiving the blow of a bayonet in his solar plexus, he floats steadily upward in balance upon his deafness and at length, like the bursting beating of the lungs of a deep diver, is broken forth on gladness of the air

to find himself:

how should he know it, how should these poor parents who so earnestly wish him well, ever suspect it better than a little, how in their ignorance and skinned sadness shall they ever learn, how all the help they would do him is but harm

to find himself:

weakened, internally hurt already beyond all use of estimate, yet still amenable of all goodness were it there:

and defenseless and unknowing, without choice, without knowledge for choice if he had it, without power of choice if he had knowledge

to find himself

Ahh, so set about so pressed upon, so searched to the very soul already by poisons, monsters, all shapes of ruin, smiling jaws of traps, that that true-mythic natural man of racial dream, that self-venturous hero, that strong young man were much more fortunate who at the end of so steep and arduous a journey and flight from the floor of creation revisited, his lungs ready to burst his heart breaking, his body naked, his primal weapons lost that he might swim at all, bursts bleeding into freedom of his breathing element to find, surrounding him, not just in circle on a floor in closured den as Daniel, but in such complex of such circle as blows round him one bubble and sutureless globe, his grinning grincing machinearmed scorcheyed lovetaloned raving foes:

For this man is aware; he may have skill; it is by skill; by consciousness by innocence by intelligence by love, by magic we shall win and only thus; this skill he may have and by this skill may speak; may talk or flute such mild commodious language that these beasts dissolve their brows, yearn sweetly in quaverings and sobs of ardor toward and upon him, roll down before, and undefend their gold inhuman bellies at his feet in all heaven's astonishment:

and if he lack; or if he fail; his death is soon, is done, as a shock of lightning:

whereas this other: *his* death, *his* destroying, it is quiet, subtle, continuous, very slow, in quite great part deluded, in some part the doing of most tenderly intended love, his foes being of this silent, insinuous, and masked kind, and he void of all skill against:

This creature, this center, soul, nerve, see he is now born, and I have said, how he is globed round, with what shall make and harm him: what are the constituents of this globe? What are the several strengths of their forces upon him?

It was beyond all use of hoping to say, while yet he was in his mother's blood scarce conscious, when this globe was at its simplest and least: how then should we say more now, when with a few hours' wrenching he is wrung out of this haven through such cataclysmic change to take forever, no retreat, his uprooted, root-cut and human place in so immane and outrageous, wild, irresponsible, dangerous-idiot a world: how still shall we better than blankly suggest, or lay down, a few possible laws?

Our five or twenty known human senses: there is no reason to assume but they are few, are crudely woven, that swarms of immediacy slide through these nets at best, assisted though they be by dream, by reason, and by those strictures of diamond glass and light whereby we punch steep holes in the bowels of the gliding heavens, taste out the salt small of the earth, step measurements upon the grand estate of being: nevertheless: nevertheless and at their weakest, weakest and most weaponless of these instruments, their taking is titanic beyond exhaustion of count or valuation, and is all but infinitely populous beyond the knowledge of each moment or a lifetime: and that which we receive yet do not recognize, nor hold in the moment's focus, is nevertheless and continuously and strengthfully planted upon our brains, upon our blood: it holds: it holds: each cuts its little mark: each blown leaf of a woodland a quarter-mile distant while I am absorbed in some close exactitude: each of these registers, cuts his mark: not one of these is negligible: and they measure, not only by multitudes within each granular instant, but by iteration, which is again beyond our counting not alone but as well the remotest realization of our flesh and even brain: and with each iteration the little cut is cut a little distincter, a little deeper, a little more of a scar and a shaping of a substance which might have taken other shape and which in each re-registration loses a little more and a little more the power to meet this possibility: and more and more inexorably and fixedly is drawn and shaped into that steepest-sunken of all graves wherein human hope is buried alive, the power and blindness, stiffness and helplessness of habituation, of acceptance, of resignation so totally deep it has sailed beyond memory of resignation or thought of other possibility: a benumbing, freezing, a paralysis, a turning to stone, merciful in the middle of all that storm of torture, relatively resistant of much further keenness of harm, but always in measure of that petrifaction obtusèd ten times over against hope, possibility, cure:

Moreover, these globular damagements are of many kinds and degrees and colors and of an infinite talent for deceit: being of as many kinds as that particular set of senses and that particular intelligence at their heart can perceive and can receive and can react to and reflect upon: all that is 'physical,' all that is of the 'mind,' all that is of the 'emotions,' all that is of the 'economic' and the 'mental' and the 'glandular' and the 'medical' predicament, all that is of 'belief,' and is of 'habit,' and is of 'morality,' and is of 'fear,' 'pride,' need of 'love,' 'warmth,' 'approbation,' all that is attached in the 'meanings' of 'ideas,' 'words,' 'actions,' 'things,' 'symbols': all these apart, all these in orchestral complex wherein they interlock, interform one another, and conspire in their companionship still sharper fiercer stricter subtler more bonebiting traps and equations of destruction than is in the power of any one or five of them independent of one another:

Here, again, in the midst of all these, is this human creature, born, awaiting their touch:

We specialize him a little more: yes, he is of the depth of the working class; of southern alabamian tenant farmers; certain individuals are his parents, not like other individuals; they are living in a certain house, it is not quite like other houses; they are farming certain shapes and strengths of land, in a certain exact vicinity, for a certain landholder: all such things as these qualify this midge, this center, a good deal:

Born otherwise, he would break his shell upon other forms of madness: he might, for instance, have sprung up in the sheltering and soft shame and guilt of money, which in this earth at present is had at the expense of other spirits and of human good, and which brings on its own diseases, so ghastly that one cannot in wisdom and honesty either envy or hate the image, say, of the landowner whom I suggest beside this child: Or otherwise again, in the guilty sheltering even of a little ease, the mind, the spirit, the heart, which in him shall all so swiftly be killed or obtunded, this might have grown its fight, and would discover, and have to bear, something of the true proportions of the savageness of the world, and something of the true weight of responsibility which each human being must learn to undertake for all others, and something of the true magnitude of the terror and the doubt in which in each human being this responsibility must be searched out and undertaken; and might easily have deceived himself, and become an instrument of poison, or, less deceived, have sustained those further agonies of perception so great that one may very doubtfully feel any glad or guiltless embrace of the joys and lacerations of this consciousness short of the whole uncompromised and seldom piercing and intention of 'genius' itself: see, in this 'consciousness,' what a swarm and slime of monsters he would encounter, whose skill, pain, disease, deceitfulness is multiplied in proportion to the reach and edge of this same 'consciousness' which is our one hope, this monster world's one sure, most shriveling enemy: of this particular world of hope and of smile-masked horror he is nearly free, for in his world few such beasts exist, and the instruments whereby he might see them if they did, or of his own born doing; the lenses of these are smashed in his infancy, the adjustment screws are blocked; his is more nearly purely a tactile, a fragrant, a visible, physical world, wherein through his deep isolation these plainfeatured physiques drive and impose their stresses all the more keenly upon him; and should he by faint and most irregular chance make his little, terrific, faithful struggle to escape, into a sphere how much less tortured shall this escape be made: for this human sphere is all one such interlocked and marvelously variegated and prehensile a disease and madness, what man in ten million shall dare to presume he is cleansed of it or more so than another, shall dare better than most hesitantly to venture, that one form of this ruin is more than a millionth preferable to another?

Here then he is, or here is she: here is this tender and helpless human life: subjected to its immediacy and to all the enlargĔd dread of its future: out of a line, weight, and burthen of sorrow and poison of fatigue whereof its blood is stained and beneath which it lifts up its little trembling body into standing, wearing upon its shoulders the weight of all the spreaded generations of its dead: surrounded already, with further pressures, impingements: the sorrow, weariness, and nescience of its parents in their closures above and round it: the ghastly influence of their lovelessness, their lack of knowledge hope or chance, how to love, what is joy, why they are locked together here: his repeated witness of the primal act, that battling and brutality upon a bed which from his pallet on the floor of the same room he lifts his head and hears and sees and fears and is torn open by: their hopeless innocence how to 'raise' him, an ignorance no less enormous than in the parents of the rest of the world, yet not less relevant nor less horrifying on that account: the food which is drawn out of his mother distilled of the garbage she must eat; and the garbage to which he graduates: the further structures of psychological violence, strangling, crippling, which take shape and stress between him and his brothers and his sisters and between all of these and their parents; for of all these all are utterly innocent, totally helpless: the slow, silent, sweet, quiet yet so profoundly piercing enlargement of the physical sensual emotional world whereof, as we have said, not the least detail whose imposure and whose power to trench and habituate is not intense beyond calculation: all such that in the years of his very steepest defenselessness, who shall always be defenseless, and in the years of his extremest malleability, by the time he is five or six years old, he stands at the center of his enormous little globe a cripple of whose curability one must at least have most serious doubt: and now new worlds open upon him in the manifold swift unfoldings of a great flower, and in each opening he is the more firmly shut upon, his first wounds the more salted, the little slit graves of angelic possibility the more savagely danced on and defiled beyond memory of their existence: all accepted, all taken in, all new burdens taken on, the early laboring, subservience, acclimation to insult and slendering of forms of freedom, the hideous jokes of education and their sharp finish into early worse, the learning of one's situation relative to the world and the acceptance of it, the swellings and tremblings of adolescence, the bursting free from home into wandering, the fatal shining and sweet wraths of joy in love and the locked marriage and the work, the constant lack of money, need, leanness, backbroken work, knowledge of being cheated, helplessness to protest or order this otherwise, clothes worn, landlords imposed on one, towns traded in —

*

This is all one colon:

Here at a center is a creature: it would be our business to show how through every instant of every day of every year of his existence alive he is from all sides streamed inward upon, bombarded, pierced, destroyed by that enormous sleeting of all objects forms and ghosts how great how small no matter, which surround and whom his senses take: in as great and perfect and exact particularity as we can name them:

This would be our business, to show them each thus transfixed as between the stars' trillions of javelins and of each the transfixions: but it is beyond my human power to do. The most I can do — the most I can hope to do — is to make a number of physical entities as plain and vivid as possible, and to make a few guesses, a few conjectures; and to leave to you much of the burden of realizing in each of them what I have wanted to make clear of them as a whole: how each is itself; and how each is a shapener.

We undertake not much yet some, to say: to say, what is his house: for whom does he work: under what arrangements and in what results: what is this work: who is he and where from, that he is now here; what is it his life has been and has done to him: what of his wife and of their children, each, for of all these each is a life, a full universe: what are their clothes: what food is theirs to eat: what is it which is in their senses and their minds: what is the living and manner of their day, of a season, of a year: what, inward and outward, is their manner of living; of their spending and usage of these few years' openness out of the black vast and senseless death; what is their manner of life:

All this, all such, you can see, it so intensely surrounds and takes meaning from a certain center which we shall be unable to keep steadily before your eyes, that should be written, should be listed, calculated, analyzed, conjectured upon, as if all in one sentence and spread suspension and flight or fugue of music: and that I shall not be able so to sustain it, so to sustain its intensity toward this center human life, so to yield it out that it all strikes inward upon this center at once and in all its intersections and in the meanings of its interrelations and interenhancements: it is this which so paralyzes me: yet one can write only one word at a time, and if these seem lists and inventories mere- ly, things dead unto themselves, devoid of mutual magnetisms, and if they sink, lose impetus, meter, intension, then bear in mind at least my wish, and perceive in them and restore them what strength you can of yourself: for I must say to you, this is not a work of art or of entertain- ment, nor will I assume the obligations of the artist or entertainer, but is a human effort which must require human co-operation.

That steep withdrawal and silence and meditation of whose need I spoke; we are now drawn back at the peak of in quite silence: whence let me hope the whole of that landscape we shall essay to travel in is visible and may be known as there all at once: let this be borne in mind, in order that, when we descend among its windings and block- ades, into examination of slender particulars, this its wholeness and simultaneous living map may not be neglected, however lost the breadth of the country may be in the winding walk of each sentence.

Part Two

Some Findings
and Comments

Money

You are farmers; I am a farmer myself.

— Franklin Delano Roosevelt

Woods and Ricketts work for Michael and T. Hudson Margraves, two brothers, in partnership, who live in Cookstown. Gudger worked for the Margraves for three years; he now (1936) works for Chester Boles, who lives two miles south of Cookstown.

On their business arrangements, and working histories, and on their money, I wrote a chapter too long for inclusion in this volume without sacrifice of too much else. I will put in its place here as extreme a précis as I can manage.

Gudger has no home, no land, no mule; none of the more important farming implements. He must get all these of his landlord. Boles, for his share of the corn and cotton, also advances him rations money during four months of the year, March through June, and his fertilizer.

Gudger pays him back with his labor and with the labor of his family.

At the end of the season he pays him back further: with half his corn; with half his cotton; with half his cottonseed. Out of his own half of these crops he also pays him back the rations money, plus interest, and his share of the fertilizer, plus interest, and such other debts, plus interest, as he may have incurred.

What is left, once doctors' bills and other debts have been deducted, is his year's earnings.

Gudger is a straight half-cropper, or sharecropper.

Woods and Ricketts own no home and no land, but Woods owns one mule and Ricketts owns two, and they own their farming implements. Since they do not have to rent these tools and animals, they work under a slightly different arrangement. They give over to the landlord only a third of their cotton and a fourth of their corn. Out of their own parts of the crop, however, they owe him the price of two thirds of their cotton fertilizer and three fourths of their corn fertilizer, plus interest; and, plus interest, the same debts on rations money.

Woods and Ricketts are tenants: they work on third and fourth.

A very few tenants pay cash rent: but these two types of arrangement, with local variants (company stores; food instead of rations money; slightly different divisions of the crops) are basic to cotton tenantry all over the South.

From March through June, while the cotton is being cultivated, they live on the rations money.

From July through to late August, while the cotton is making, they live however they can.

From late August through October or into November, during the picking and ginning season, they live on the money from their share of the cottonseed.

From then on until March, they live on whatever they have earned in the year; or however they can.

During six to seven months of each year, then – that is, during exactly such time as their labor with the cotton is of absolute necessity to the landlord – they can be sure of whatever living is possible in rations advances and in cottonseed money.

During five to six months of the year, of which three are the hardest months of any year, with the worst of weather, the least adequacy of shelter, the worst and least of food, the worst of health, quite normal and inevitable, they can count on nothing except that they may hope least of all for any help from their landlords.

Gudger – a family of six – lives on ten dollars a month rations money during four months of the year. He has lived on eight, and on six. Woods – a family of six – until this year was unable to get better than eight a month during the same period; this year he managed to get it up to ten. Ricketts – a family of nine – lives on ten dollars a month during this spring and early summer period.

This debt is paid back in the fall at eight per cent interest. Eight per cent is charged also on the fertilizer and on all other debts which tenants incur in this vicinity.

At the normal price, a half-sharing tenant gets about six dollars a bale from his share of the cottonseed. A one-mule, half-sharing tenant makes on the average three bales. This half-cropper, then, Gudger, can count on eighteen dollars, more or less, to live on during the picking and ginning: though he gets nothing until his first bale is ginned.

Working on third and fourth, a tenant gets the money from two thirds of the cottonseed of each bale: nine dollars to the bale. Woods, with one mule, makes three bales, and gets twenty-seven dollars. Ricketts, with two mules, makes and gets twice that, to live on during the late summer and fall.

What is earned at the end of a given year is never to be depended on and, even late in a season, is never predictable. It can be enough to tide through the dead months of the winter, sometimes even better: it can be enough, spread very thin, to take through two months, and a sickness, or six weeks, or a month: it can be little enough to be completely meaningless: it can be nothing: it can be enough less than nothing to insure a tenant only of an equally hopeless lack of money at the end of his next year's work: and whatever one year may bring in the way of good luck, there is never any reason to hope that that luck will be repeated in the next year or the year after that.

The best that Woods has ever cleared was $1300 during a war year. During the teens and twenties he fairly often cleared as much as $300; he fairly often cleared $50 and less; two or three times he ended the year in debt. During the depression years he has more often cleared $50 and less; last year he cleared $150, but serious illness during the winter ate it up rapidly.

The best that Gudger has ever cleared is $125. That was in the plow-under year. He felt exceedingly hopeful and bought a mule: but when his landlord warned him of how he was coming out the next year, he sold it. Most years he has not made more than $25 to $30; and about one year in three he has ended in debt. Year before last he wound up $80 in debt; last year, $12; of Boles, his new landlord, the first thing he had to do was borrow $15 to get through the winter until rations advances should begin.

Years ago the Ricketts were, relatively speaking, almost prosperous. Besides their cotton farming they had ten cows and sold the milk, and they lived near a good stream and had all the fish they wanted. Ricketts went $400 into debt on a fine young pair of mules. One of the mules died before it had made its first crop; the other died the year after; against his fear, amounting to full horror, of sinking to the half-crop level where nothing is owned, Ricketts went into debt for other, inferior mules; his cows went one by one into debts and desperate exchanges and by sickness; he got congestive chills; his wife got pellagra; a number of his children died; he got appendicitis and lay for days on end under the ice cap; his wife's pellagra got into her brain; for ten consecutive years now, though they have lived on so little rations money, and have turned nearly all their cottonseed money toward their debts, they have not cleared or had any hope of clearing a cent at the end of the year.

It is not often, then, at the end of the season, that a tenant clears enough money to tide him through the winter, or even an appreciable part of it. More generally he can count on it that, during most of the four months between settlement time in the fall and the beginning of work and resumption of rations advances in the early spring, he will have no money and can expect none, nor any help, from his landlord: and of having no money during the six midsummer weeks of laying by, he can be still more sure. Four to six months of each year, in other words, he is much more likely than not to have nothing whatever, and during these months he must take care for himself: he is no responsibility of the landlord's. All he can hope to do is find work. This is hard, because there are a good many chronically unemployed in the towns, and they are more convenient to most openings for work and can at all times be counted on if they are needed; also there is no increase, during these two dead farming seasons, of other kinds of work to do. And so, with no more jobs open than at any other time of year, and with plenty of men already convenient to take them, the whole tenant population, hundreds and thousands in any locality, are desperately in need of work.

A landlord saves up certain odd jobs for these times of year: they go, at less than he would have to pay others, to those of his tenants who happen to live nearest or to those he thinks best of; and even at best they don't amount to much.

When there is wooded land on the farm, a landlord ordinarily permits a tenant to cut and sell firewood for what he can get. About the best a tenant gets of this is a dollar a load, but more often (for the market is glutted, so many are trying to sell wood) he can get no better than half that and less, and often enough, at the end of a hard day's peddling, miles from home, he will let it go for a quarter or fifteen cents rather than haul it all the way home again: so it doesn't amount to much. Then, too, by no means everyone has wood to cut and sell: in the whole southern half of the county we were working mainly in, there was so little wood that the negroes, during the hard winter of 1935–36, were burning parts of their fences, outbuildings, furniture and houses, and were dying off in great and not seriously counted numbers, of pneumonia and other afflictions of the lungs.

WPA work is available to very few tenants: they are, technically, employed, and thus have no right to it: and if by chance they manage to get it, landlords are more likely than not to intervene. They feel it spoils a tenant to be paid wages, even for a little while. A tenant who so much as tries to get such work is under disapproval.

There is not enough direct relief even for the widows and the old of the county.

Gudger and Ricketts, during this year, were exceedingly lucky. After they, and Woods, had been turned away from government work, they found work in a sawmill. They were given the work on condition that they stay with it until the mill was moved, and subject strictly to their landlords' permission: and their employer wouldn't so much as hint how long the work might last. Their landlords quite grudgingly gave them permission, on condition that they pay for whatever help was needed in their absence during the picking season. Gudger hired a hand, at eight dollars a month and board. Ricketts did not need to: his family is large enough. They got a dollar and a quarter a day five days a week and seventy-five cents on Saturday, seven dollars a week, ten hours' work a day. Woods did not even try for this work: he was too old and too sick.

Shelter

I will go unto the altar of God

SHELTER: An Outline

A home in its fields
The spring: the garden: the outbuildings

The Gudger House

    The house is left alone

    In front of the house: its general structure

    In front of the house: the façade
    The room beneath the house

    The hallway
    Structure of four rooms

    Odors
    Bareness and space

I. The Front Bedroom

    General
    Placement of furniture

    The furniture

    The altar
    The tabernacle

II. The Rear Bedroom

    General

    The fireplace

Shelter

A home in its fields

Gerge Gudger has of Chester Boles a little over twenty acres of open farm land, a few more acres of woods and of hillside ravines, a house, a barn, a smokehouse, a henroost, a garden, and a spring, all suspended and emplaced in solitude out at the end of a mile of dwindled branch road, and not within sight nor within a half-mile's walk of any other inhabited house. A little of his land is on the flat crest of the hill; the rest is broken into large patches among ravines and woods along the falling shapes of the hill and into little patches along the road that leads him out. The house and outbuildings, the garden and the spring, stand about midway in the main pieces of this land, and about halfway down the hill.

The top three acres are a long flat rectangle of keenly red clay and are planted in cotton. Between the edge of the hill and his barnyard there is nothing planted, only wild weeds and briars on a scrubbed-looking set of rounded and trenched surfaces, and a narrow path slid winding among them, but from this edge, standing at the edge of the cotton, you see the house and barnyard, resembling a large museum model or an establishment for large dolls, set at the middle of the slope,

back-to-you, facing due west, and the two large fields in front of it and
on its left which make up most of the rest of the farm, the whole bound
in by a bluff horizon of trees. Now and then a faint windy noise of
speed or a noise of grinding, sweeping a western crescent beyond the
trees and through one thin sector of trees, for two seconds, the uncertain glimpse of a gliding bulk: and these are the thinly spaced sedans
and trucks which use a minor artery between two county seats profoundly distant to a walking man.

One of these fields begins very deep behind the house on its left,
and along its left flank the cotton plants nearly touch the wall; it is nearly all in cotton. Back beyond it and beneath it, in a clearing in the tall
woods, is a smaller patch of corn. The field that falls away two hundred
yards in front of the house is all in adolescent corn, softly flashing, ending at tall forest whose leaves run like quicksilver wheat in the lesions
of heated air. Out at the right of the house is the rough stretch of mid-
hill, partly bare, fluted with rain, not planted, sprung with tall weeds
and smoky grasses and with berry briars, young pines and little runs
and islands of young trees, seeming open, yet merged before long in a
solid coastline of well-grown woods. Out along the road that, beginning just below the house, leads out to the right and north, there are
further small floors and slivers of farm land, all but one less than an
acre, and lying much within the moistures of trees during several hours
of the day, in cotton, in corn, in sorghum cane, in peanuts, in water-
melons, and in sweet potatoes. Some of this land of Gudger's is sandy
clay, dullorange to a dead sort of yellow; some is dark sand; a little is
loam. He has in all about eleven acres in cotton, nine in corn, a quarter in sorghum cane, about half an acre divided among the melons,
peanuts, and potatoes, and there are field peas planted in the corn rows.

These fields are workrooms, or fragrant but mainly sterile work-
floors without walls and with a roof of uncontrollable chance, fear,
rumination, and propitiative prayer, and are as the spread and broken
petals of a flower whose bisexual center is the house.

Or the farm is also as a water spider whose feet print but do not break the gliding water membrane: it is thus delicately and briefly that, in its fields and structures, it sustains its entity upon the blind breadth and steady heave of nature.

Or it is the wrung breast of one human family's need and of an owner's taking, yielding blood and serum in its thin blue milk, and the house, the concentration of living and taking, is the cracked nipple: and of such breasts, the planet is thickly and desperately paved as the enfabled front of a goddess of east india.

The fields are organic of the whole, and of their own nature, and of the work that is poured into them: the spring, the garden, the outbuildings, are organic to the house itself.

The spring

The garden

The outbuildings

The spring is out to the rear of the house and above it, about a hundred and fifty yards away to the right, not a short distance to walk for every drop of water that is needed. The path lifts from the end of the back hall between the henroost and the smokehouse to just below the barn, swings left here, parts from the hill path, and runs narrowly, but slick as a scalp, among thick weeds under sunlight and toward trees whose greenbrown gloom and coolness is sudden and whose silence, different from that of the open light, seems to be conscious and to await the repetition of a signal. Not five feet deeper, a delicate yet powerful odor of wetness in constant shade, a broad windless standing-forth of a new coolness as from a refrigerator door, and a diminutive wrinkling noise of water: and ten feet deep within the roof of leaves, low, on the upward right, the spring, the dirt all round dark and strong-rooted and fragrant, tamped smooth as soap with bare feet, and a mottled piece of plank to kneel to water on. The water stands forward from between rounded strata of submerged dark stone as from between lips or rollers, in a look not of motion yet of quiet compulsion, into a basin a foot deep floored with dead oakleaves and shored up with slimy wood. On a submerged shelf small crocks of butter, cream, and milk stand sunken to their eyes, tied over with pieces of saturated floursack. A sapling next the spring has been chopped short to make a stob, and on it hangs a coffee can rusted black and split at the edges. The spring is not cowled so deeply under the hill that the water is brilliant and nervy, seeming to break in the mouth like crystals, as spring water can: it is about the temper of faucet water, and tastes slack and faintly sad, and as if just short of stale. It is not quite tepid, however, and it does not seem to taste of sweat and sickness, as the water does which the Woods family have to use.

Ten feet below, in a little alcove cleared at the edge of the woods, the water lets out through a rusted pipe and rambles loose. There is a brute oak bench here for washtubs, * and burnt stones are squared round the bright ashes of wood fires, and, next these stones, is one of those very heavy and handsome black iron kettles in which people one remove more primitive still make their own soap.

So, at the end of a slim liana of dry path running out of the heart of the house, a small wet flower suspended: the spring.

The garden plot is close on the right rear of the house. It is about the shape and about two thirds the size of a tennis court, and is caught within palings against the hunger and damage of animals. These palings are thin slats of split pine about three and a half feet tall and an inch and a half wide, wired together vertically, about their width apart from each other. The erratic grain and cleavage of this pine have given each of them a different welter and rippling streaming of surface and pattern structure; the weather has made this all as it were a muted silver and silk, exquisitely sensitive to light; and these slats closely

---

* There was also a split, mended washboard whose ribblings were homesawn out of a thick section of pine plank.

approximate yet seldom perfect their perpendiculars; so that when the sun is on them, and with the segments of garden between each of them, there is here such a virtuosity as might be watched by speechless days on end merely for the variety and distinction of their beauty, without thought or any relevant room for thinking, and without possibility of absorbing all that is there to be seen. Outside, the frowsy weeds stand halfway up these walls: inside, the planting is concentrated to the utmost possible, in green and pink-veined wax and velvet butter beans, and in rank tomatoes, hung low, burst against the ground, in hairy buds of okra, all these sprung heavy with weeds and smothered in textured shades of their leaves, blown like nearly exploding balloons in the full spread of the summer, each in its shape and nature, so that the whole of this space is one blowsy bristling pool and splendor of worm- and insect-embroidered plants and the savage odors of their special lusts that sting the face in gathering, nuzzling the paling as the bars of a zoo: waist-deep to wade in, so twined and spired and reached among each other that the paths between rows are discernible only like steps confounded in snow: a paling gate, nearest the kitchen, is bound shut against their bursting with a piece of wire.

Behind the house the dirt is blond and bare, except a little fledging of grass-leaves at the roots of structures, and walked-out rags of grass thickening along the sides. It lifts up gently, perhaps five feet in twenty yards: across the top line of this twenty yards is the barn, set a few feet to the right of center of the rear of the house. Half between the barn and house, symmetrical to the axis of the house, the henroost and the smokehouse face each other across a bare space of perhaps twelve feet of dirt.

These, like the house, are all made of unpainted pine. In some of this wood, the grain is broad and distinct: in some of it the grain has almost disappeared, and the wood has a texture and look like that of weathered bone.

The henroost is about seven feet square and five high, roofed with rotted shingles. It is built rather at random of planks varying in width between a foot and four inches, nailed on horizontally with narrow spaces between their edges. On the uphill side a short pole leans against the roof with chips and sticks nailed along it for steps and a box nailed at the top with straw in it; but most of the eggs are found by the children in places which are of the hens' own selection and return. Inside the roost, three or four sections of saplings, so arranged that the hens will not dirty each other; these poles rubbed smooth by their feet; the strong slits of light between the boards; the odor of closured and heated wood; and the nearly unbearably fetid odor of the feathers and excretions of the hens.

The smokehouse is about eight feet square and about seven tall to the peak of the roof. It is built of vertical boards of uniform width. The door is flush to the wall without a frame and is held shut by a wood button. On the uphill side, at center of the wall and flat to it, hangs a nearly new washtub, the concentrics on its bottom circle like a target. Its galvanized material is brilliant and dryly eating in the sun; the wood of the wall itself is not much less brilliant. The natural usage of a smokehouse is to smoke and store meat, but meat is not smoked here: this is a storage house. Mainly, there are a couple of dozen tin cans here, of many differing sizes and former uses, now holding sorghum; four hoes; a set of sweeps; a broken plow-frame; pieces of an ice-cream freezer; a can of rusty nails; a number of mule shoes; the strap of a white slipper; a pair of greenly eaten, crumpled workshoes, the uppers broken away, the soles worn broadly through, still carrying the odor of feet; a blue coil of soft iron wire; a few yards of rusted barbed wire; a rotted mulecollar; pieces of wire at random: * all those same broken

---

* Invention here: I did not make inventory; there was more than I could remember. I remember for certain only the sorghum cans, the sweeps, the hoes, the workshoes, the nails; with a vaguer remembrance of random pieces of harness and of broken machinery: there may also have been, for instance, a ruined headlight and a boy's soggy worn-out cap. Many of the sorghum cans, by the way, were almost the only bright and new-looking things on the farm. Gudger may have bought them. If so, they are notable, for tenants seldom buy anything new.

creatures of the Ricketts' porch, of uselessness and of almost endless saving.

It should hardly be called a 'barn,' it is too thin an excuse for one: a long low shed divided into three chambers, a wired-in yard, a hog wallow and the hog's dirty little house. One room is made of thick and thin logs, partly stopped with clay, and this is the stall for the mule when he is there: the rest is pine boards. The next partition is for the cow. In one corner of the small wired yard which squares off this part of the barn, in somewhat trampled and dunged earth, is the hogpen, made of logs; beyond that, a room used, in turn, as a corncrib and as a storage house for cotton prior to ginning. There is no hayloft. The whole structure is about twenty feet long and not more than seven high and seven or eight deep. The floor, except of the corncrib, is earth.

Here I must say, a little anyhow: what I can hardly hope to bear out in the record: that a house of simple people which stands empty and silent in the vast Southern country morning sunlight, and everything which on this morning in eternal space it by chance contains, all thus left open and defenseless to a reverent and cold-laboring spy, shines quietly forth such grandeur, such sorrowful holiness of its exactitudes in existence, as no human consciousness shall ever rightly perceive, far less impart to another: that there can be more beauty and more deep wonder in the standings and spacings of mute furnishings on a bare floor between the squaring bourns of walls than in any music ever made: that this square home, as it stands in unshadowed earth between the winding years of heaven, is, not to me but of itself, one among the serene and final, uncapturable beauties of existence: that this beauty is made between hurt but invincible nature and the plainest cruelties and needs of human existence in this uncured time, and is inextricable among these, and as impossible without them as a saint born in paradise.

But I say these things only because I am reluctant to entirely lie. I can have nothing more to do with them now. I am hoping here only to tell a little, only so well as I may, about an ordinary * house, in which I lived a little while, and which is the home, for the time being, of the Gudger family, and is the sort of home a tenant family lives in, furnished and decorated as they furnish and decorate. Since it is so entirely static a subject, it may be slow going. That is as it may be.

---

* The whole problem, if I were trying fully to embody the house, would be to tell of it exactly in its ordinary terms.

The Gudger House

The house is left alone

Slowly they diminished along the hill path, she, and her daughter,
and her three sons, in leisured enfilade beneath the light. The mother
first, her daughter next behind, her eldest son, her straggler, whimpering; their bare feet pressed out of the hot earth gentle explosions of
gold. She carried her youngest child, his knees locked simian across
her, his light hands at her neck, and his erected head, hooded with
night, next hers, swiveled mildly upon the world's globe, a periscope.
The dog, a convoy, plaited his wanderings round them through the briars. She wore the flowerlike beauty of the sunbonnet in which she is
ashamed to appear before us. At length, well up the hill, their talking
shrank and became inaudible, and at that point will give safe warning
on the hill of their return. Their slanted bodies slowly straightened, one
by one, along the brim, and turned into the east, a slow frieze, and sank
beneath the brim in order of their height, masts foundered in a horizon; the dog, each of the walking children, at length; at last, the guile-
less cobra gloatings of the baby, the mother's tall, flared head.

They are gone.

No one is at home, in all this house, in all this land. It is a long while before their return. I shall move as they would trust me not to, and as I could not, were they here. I shall touch nothing but as I would touch the most delicate wounds, the most dedicated objects.

The silence of the brightness of this middle morning is increased upon me moment by moment and upon this house, and upon this house the whole of heaven is drawn into one lens; and this house itself, in each of its objects, it, too, is one lens.

I am being made witness to matters no human being may see.

There is a cold beating at my solar plexus. I move in exceeding slowness and silence that I shall not dishonor nor awaken this house: and in every instant of silence, it becomes more entirely perfected upon itself under the sun. I take warmed water from the bucket, without sound, and it brings the sweat out sharply and I wipe it away, remembering in shame his labor, George, at this instant, hard, in the strenuous heat, and upon the tanned surface of this continent, this awful field where cotton is made, infinitesimal, the antlike glistening of the sweated labors of nine million. I remember how in hot early puberty, realizing myself left alone the whole of a cavernous and gloomed afternoon in my grandfather's large unsentineled home, I would be taken at the pit of the stomach with a most bitter, criminal gliding and cold serpent restiveness, and would wander from vacant room to vacant room examining into every secrecy from fungoid underearth to rarehot roof and from the roof would gaze in anguish and contempt upon the fronded suffocations of the midsummer city; trying to read; trying to play the piano; ravening upon volumes of soft-painted nudes; staring hungrily and hatefully into mirrors; rifling drawers, closets, boxes, for the mere touch at the lips and odor of fabrics, pelts, jewels, switches of hair; smoking cigars, sucking at hidden liquors; reading the piteous enthusiasms of ribboned letters stored in attic trunks: at length I took off all my clothes, lay along the cold counterpanes of every bed, planted my obscenities in the cold hearts of every mirror in foreknowledge, what unseen words and acts lurked ambushed in those deep white seas before the innocent fixtures of a lady's hair: I permitted nothing to escape the fingering of my senses nor the insulting of the cold reptilian fury of the terror of lone desire which was upon me:

It is not entirely otherwise now, in this inhuman solitude, the nakedness of this body which sleeps here before me, this tabernacle upon whose desecration I so reverentially proceed: yet it differs somewhat: for there is here no open sexual desire, no restiveness, nor despair: but the quietly triumphant vigilance of the extended senses before an intricate task of surgery, a deep stealthfulness, not for shame of the people, but in fear and in honor of the house itself, a knowledge of being at work. And by this same knowledge, along with the coldness, the adoration, the pity, the keen guilt at the heart, complete casualness. I am merely myself, a certain young man, standing in my sweated clothes in the rear of a dividing porch of a certain house, foundered as stone in sea in deepest Alabamian rurality, beneath the white scorch of a calm white morning; the leaves, sluicing most gently in their millions what open breadth of earth I see, beneath upward coilings of transparent air, and here, their home; and they have gone; and it is now my chance to perceive this, their home, as it is, in whose hollow heart resounds the loud zinc flickering heartbeat of the cheap alarm two hours advanced upon false time; a human shelter, a strangely lined nest, a creature of killed pine, stitched together with nails into about as rude a garment against the hostilities of heaven as a human family may wear.

We stand first facing it, squarely in front of it, in the huge and peaceful light of this August morning:

And it stands before us, facing us, squarely in front of us, silent and undefended in the sun.

In front of the house: its general structure

Two blocks, of two rooms each, one room behind another. Between these blocks a hallway, floored and roofed, wide open both at front and rear: so that these blocks are two rectangular yoked boats, or floated tanks, or coffins, each, by an inner wall, divided into two squared chambers. The roof, pitched rather steeply from front and rear, its cards met and nailed at a sharp angle. The floor faces the earth closely. On the left of the hall, two rooms, each an exact square. On the right a square front room and, built later, behind it, using the outward weatherboards for its own front wall, a leanto kitchen half that size.

At the exact center of each of the outward walls of each room, a window. Those of the kitchen are small, taller than wide, and are glassed. Those of the other rooms are exactly square and are stopped with wooden shutters.

From each room a door gives on the hallway. The doors of the two front rooms are exactly opposite: the doors of the rear rooms are exactly opposite. The two rooms on either side of the hallway are also connected inwardly by doors through their partition walls.

Out at the left of the house, starting from just above the side window of the front room, a little roof is reached out and rested on thin poles above bare ground: shelter for wagon or for car.

At the right of the house, just beneath the side window of the front room, a commodious toolbox, built against the wall. It is nailed shut.

The hallway yields onto a front porch about five feet long by ten wide, reaching just a little short of the windows at either side, set at dead center of the front of the house. A little tongue of shingles, the same size, is stuck out slightly slanted above it, and is sustained on four slender posts from which most of the bark has been stripped.

Three steps lead down at center; they are of oak: the bottom one is cracked and weak, for all its thickness. Stones have been stacked beneath it, but they have slid awry, and it goes to the ground sharply underfoot. Just below and beyond it is a wide flat piece of shale the color of a bruise. It is broken several ways across and is sunken into the dirt.

The forty-foot square of land in front of the house, the 'front yard,' is bare of any trees or bushes; there is nothing at all near the house of its own height, or bestowing of any shade. This piece of land is hunched a little on itself in a rondure. Through the dry haze of weeds and flowering fennels its dead red yellowness glows quietly, a look of fire in sunlight, and it is visible how intricately it is trenched and seamed with sleavings of rain; as if, the skull lifted off, the brain were exposed, of some aged not intellectual being who had lived a long time patiently and with difficulty.

Where we stand, square toward the front, the house is almost perfectly symmetrical. Its two front walls, square, balanced, each of a size, cloven by hallway; the lifted roof; at center of each wall, a square window, the shutters closed; the porch and its roof and the four little posts like candles:

Each window is framed round with a square of boards.

Ten or twelve feet out in this yard, and precisely in line with these front windows, as if they were projections of them, and of about the same size, two hollow squares of wood are laid upon the earth and are sunk level with it: and these are in fact two projections and are related with these windows, and indeed are windows, of a sort: for they are intended to let through their frames from the blank wall and darkness of the earth a particular and gracious, pleasing light; they are flower-beds. The one at the left is sprung through with the same indiscriminate fennels of the yard; the one on the right, the same. But here among this rambling of bastardy stands up, on its weak stem, one fainting pale magenta petunia, which stares at its tired foot; and this in the acreage of these three farms is the one domestic flower.

Now raising the eyes, slowly, in face of this strength of sun, to look the house in its blind face:

In front of the house: The façade

The porch: stands in its short square shade:

The hall: it is in shadow also, save where one wall, fifteen feet back, is slantingly slashed with light:

At the far end of this well of hall, the open earth, lifted a little, bald hard dirt; the faced frontages of the smokehouse and the henhouse, and a segment of the barn: and all of this framed image a little unnaturally brilliant and vital, as all strongly lighted things appear through corridors of darkness:

And this hall between, as the open valve of a sea creature, steadfastly flushing the free width of ocean through its infinitesimal existence: and on its either side, the square boxes, the square front walls, raised vertical to the earth, and facing us as two squared prows of barge or wooden wings, shadow beneath their lower edge and at their eaves; and the roof:

And these walls:

Nailed together of boards on beams, the boards facing the weather, into broad cards of wood inlet with windows stopped with shutters: walls, horizontals, of somewhat narrow weatherboarding; the windows bounded by boards of that same width in a square: the shutters, of wide vertical boards laid edge to edge, not overlapped: each of these boards was once of the living flesh of a pine tree; it was cut next the earth, and was taken between the shrieking of saws into strict ribbons; and now, which was vertical, is horizontal to the earth, and another is clamped against the length of its outward edge and its downward clamps another, and these boards, nailed tightly together upon pine beams, make of their horizontalities a wall: and the sun makes close horizontal parallels along the edges of these weatherboards, of sharp light and shade, the parallels strengthened here in slight straight-line lapse from level, in the subtle knife-edged curve of warping loose in another place: another irregular 'pattern' is made in the endings and piecings-out of boards:

And the roof:

It is of short hand-hewn boards so thick and broad, they are shingles only of a most antique sort: crosswise upon rigid beams, laths have been nailed, not far apart, and upon these laths, in successive rows of dozens and of hundreds, and here again, though regularly, with a certain shuffling of erratism against pure symmetry, these broad thick shingles are laid down overlapping from the peak to the overhung edge like the plumage of a bird who must meet weather: and not unlike some square and formalized plumage, as of a holy effigy, they seem, and made in profligate plates of a valuable metal; for they have never been stained, nor otherwise touched or colored save only by all habits of the sky: nor has any other wood of this house been otherwise ever touched: so that, wherever the weathers of the year have handled it, the wood of the whole of this house shines with the noble gentleness of cherished silver, much as where (yet differently), along the floors, in the pathings of the millions of soft wavelike movements of naked feet, it can be still more melodiously charmed upon its knots, and is as wood long fondled in a tender sea:

Upon these structures, light:

It stands just sufficiently short of vertical that every leaf of shingle, at its edges, and every edge of horizontal plank (blocked, at each center, with squared verticals) is a most black and cutting ink: and every surface struck by light is thus: such an intensity and splendor of silver in the silver light, it seems to burn, and burns and blinds into the eyes almost as snow; yet in none of that burnishment or blazing whereby detail is lost: each texture in the wood, like those of bone, is distinct in the eye as a razor: each nail-head is distinct: each seam and split; and each slight warping; each random knot and knothole: and in each board, as lovely a music as a contour map and unique as a thumbprint, its grain, which was its living strength, and these wild creeks cut stiff across by saws; and moving nearer, the close-laid arcs and shadows even of those tearing wheels: and this, more poor and plain than bone, more naked and noble than sternest Doric, more rich and more variant than watered silk, is the fabric and the stature of a house.

It is put together out of the cheapest available pine lumber, and the least of this is used which shall stretch a skin of one thickness alone against the earth and air; and this is all done according to one of the three or four simplest, stingiest, and thus most classical plans contrivable, which are all traditional to that country: and the work is done by half-skilled, half-paid men under no need to do well, who therefore take such vengeance on the world as they may in a cynical and part willful apathy; and this is what comes of it: Most naïve, most massive symmetry and simpleness. Enough lines, enough off-true, that this symmetry is strongly yet most subtly sprained against its centers, into something more powerful than either full symmetry or deliberate breaking and balancing of 'monotonies' can hope to be. A look of being most earnestly hand-made, as a child's drawing, a thing created out of need, love, patience, and strained skill in the innocence of a race. Nowhere one ounce or inch spent with ornament, not one trace of relief or of disguise: a matchless monotony, and in it a matchless variety, and this again throughout restrained, held rigid: and of all this, nothing which is not intrinsic between the materials of structure, the earth, and the open heaven. The major lines of structure, each horizontal of each board, and edge of shingle, the strictness yet subtle dishevelment of the shingles, the nail-heads, which are driven according to geometric need, yet are not in perfect order, the grain, differing in each foot of each board and in each board from any other, the many knots in this cheap lumber: all these fluencies and irregularities, all these shadows of pattern upon each piece of wood, all these in rectilinear ribbons caught into one squared, angled, and curled music, compounding a chord of four chambers upon a soul and center of clean air: and upon all these masses and edges and chances and flowerings of grain, the changes of colorings of all weathers, and the slow complexions and marchings of pure light.

Or by another saying:

'In all this house:

'In all of this house not any one inch of lumber being wasted on embellishment, or on trim, or on any form of relief, or even on any doubling of walls: it is, rather, as if a hard thin hide of wood has been stretched to its utmost to cover exactly once, or a little less than once, in all six planes the skeletal beams which, with the inside surface of the weatherboarding, are the inside walls; and no touch, as I have said, of any wash or paint, nor, on the floors, any kind of covering, nor, to three of the rooms, any kind of ceiling, but in all places left bare the plain essences of structure; in result all these almost perfect symmetries have their full strength, and every inch of the structure, and every aspect and placement of the building materials, comes inevitably and purely through into full esthetic existence, the one further conditioner, and discriminator between the functions and proprieties of indoors and out, being the lights and operations of the sky.'

Or by a few further notes:

'On symmetry: the house is rudimentary as a child's drawing, and of a bareness, cleanness, and sobriety which only Doric architecture, so far as I know, can hope to approach: this exact symmetry is sprung slightly and subtly, here and there, one corner of the house a little off vertical, a course of weatherboarding failing the horizontal between parallels, a window frame not quite square, by lack of skill and by weight and weakness of timber and time; and these slight failures, their tensions sprung against centers and opposals of such rigid and earnest exactitude, set up intensities of relationship far more powerful than full symmetry, or studied dissymmetry, or use of relief or ornament, can ever be: indeed, the power is of another world and order than theirs, and there is, as I mentioned, a particular quality of a thing hand-made, which by comparison I can best suggest thus: by the grandeur that comes of the effort of one man to hold together upon one instrument, as if he were breaking a wild monster to bridle and riding, one of the larger fugues of Bach, on an organ, as against the slick collaborations and effortless climaxes of the same piece in the manipulations of an orchestra.'

Or again by materials: and by surfaces and substances: the build and shape of walls, roof, window frames, verticals of shutters, opposals and cleavings of mass as I have said, and the surfaces and substances: 'The front porch of oak two-by-twelves so hard they still carry a strong piercing fell of splinters; the four supporting posts which have the del-

icate bias and fluences of young trees and whose surface is close to that
of rubbed ivory; in the musculatures of their stripped knots they have
the flayed and expert strength of anatomical studies: and the rest of the
house entirely of pine, the cheapest of local building material and of
this material one of the cheapest grades: in the surfaces of these boards
are three qualities of beauty and they are simultaneous, mutually transparent: one is the streaming killed strength of the grain, infinite, talented, and unrepeatable from inch to inch, the florid genius of nature
which is incapable of error: one is the close-set transverse arcs, dozens
to the foot, which are the shadows of the savage breathings and eatings
of the circular saws; little of this lumber has been planed: one is the
tone and quality the weather has given it, which is related one way to
bone, another to satin, another to unpolished but smooth silver: all
these are visible at once, though one or another may be strongly
enhanced by degree and direction of light and by degree of humidity:
moreover, since the lumber is so cheap, knots are frequent, and here
and there among the knots the iron-hard bitter red center is lost, and
there is, instead, a knothole; the grain near these knots goes into con-
vulsions or ecstasies such as Beethoven's deafness compelled; and with
these knots the planes of the house are badged at random, and again
moreover, these wild fugues and floods of grain, which are of the free
perfect innocence of nature, are sawn and stripped across into rigid
ribbons and by rigid lines and boundaries, in the captive perfect innocence of science, so that these are closely collaborated and inter-
involved in every surface: and at points strategic to structure: and reg-
imented by need, and attempting their own symmetries, yet not in perfect line (such is the tortured yet again perfect innocence of men,
caught between the pulls of nature and science), the patternings and
constellations of the heads of the driven nails: and all these things, set
in the twisted and cradling planet, take the benefit of every light and
weather which the sky in their part of the world can bestow, this within its terms being subtly unrepeatable and probably infinite, and are
qualified as few different structures can be, to make full use of these

gifts. By most brief suggestion: in full symmetry of the sun, the surfaces are dazzling silver, the shadows strong as knives and India ink, yet the grain and all detail clear: in slanted light, all slantings and sharpenings of shadow: in smothered light, the aspect of bone, a relic: at night, the balanced masses, patient in the base world: from rain, out of these hues of argent bone the colors of agate, the whole wall, one fabric and mad zebra of quartered minerals and watered silks: and in the sheltered yet open hallway, a granite gray and seeming of nearly granitic hardness, the grain dim, the sawmarks very strong; in the strength of these marks and peculiar sobriety of the color, a look as if there has been a slow and exact substitution of calcium throughout all the substance: within the rooms, the wood holds much nearer its original colors of yellows, reds, and peasant golds drawn deep toward gray, yet glowing quietly through it as the clay world glows through summer.'

But enough.

The room beneath the house

The rear edges of the house rest in part on stacked stones, in part on the dirt; in part they overhang this dirt a little. Beneath the house this dirt sinks gently, so that the flanks and forward edges are lifted to level in part on taller stacks of stone, in part on thick rounded sections of logs. The porch floor, and the forward parts of the house, are about two and a half feet off the ground.

This cold plaque of earth beneath, which wears the shape of the house and is made different from other earth, as·that part of a wall against which a picture has been hung for years: which might have been field, pasture, forest, mere indiscriminate land: by chance:

At a bright time in sun, and in a suddenness alien to those rhythms the land had known these hundred millions of years, lumber of other land was brought rattling in yellow wagonloads and caught up between hammers upon air before unregarding heaven a hollow altar, temple, or

poor shrine, a human shelter, which for the space of a number of seasons shall hold this shape of earth denatured: yet in whose history this
house shall have passed soft and casually as a snowflake fallen on black
spring ground, which thaws in touching.

There in the chilly and small dust which is beneath porches, the
subtle funnels of doodlebugs whose teasing, of a broomstraw, is one of
the patient absorptions of kneeling childhood, and there, in that dust
and the damper dust and the dirt, dead twigs of living, swept from the
urgent tree, signs, and relics: bent nails, withered and knobbed with
rust; a bone button, its two eyes torn to one; the pierced back of an
alarm clock, greasy to the touch; a torn fragment of pictured print; an
emptied and flattened twenty-gauge shotgun shell, its metal green, lettering still visible; the white tin eyelet of a summer shoe; and thinly
scattered, the desiccated and the still soft excrement of hens, who stroll
and dab and stand, shimmying, stabbing at their lice, and stroll out
again into the sun as vacantly as they departed it. And other things as
well: a long and slender infinitesimally rustling creek and system of
ants in their traffic: the underside of the house, so sparsely lifted even
at the front, and meeting the quietly swollen earth so close there is
scarcely light at all at the rear: and here the earth is cold, continually
damp, and in the odors of mold and of a well, and there are cold
insects, sutured and plated, rapid on many feet that run in a rill and
nimbus along their narrow bodies; and strong spiders here, and dead
ones, pale as mushrooms, suspended in the ruins of their lives, or
strong, avid, distinct among their clean constructions, still, slowly pal-
pitant in their thick bodies, watching you with a poison sharpness of
eye you cannot be sure you see, sudden to movement and swift, and
some who jump: and the clean pine underside of the house, blond like
the floor of a turtle, that sun has never and weather has scarcely
touched, so that it looks still new, as if as yet it had sustained no sorrow above, but only a hope that was still in process of approach, as
once this whole house was, all fresh and bridal, four hollowed rooms
brimmed with a light of honey:

*(O therefore in the cleanly quiet, calm hope, sweet odor, awaiting, of each
new dwelling squared by men on air, be sorrowful, as of the sprung trap, the
slim wrist gnawn, the little disastrous fox:*

*It stands up in the sun and the bride smiles: quite soon the shelves are
papered: the new forks taste in the food:*

Ruin, ruin is in our hopes: nor hope, help, any healing:)

it is hung and strung with their frail structures, and closes with the
cool damp dirt in almost darkness: and is of this noiseless and variegated underworld the flat scarce-lifted stone, the roof and firmament:
and above:

This underside, and firmament, and shelter and graveyard of sharp
alien and short lives, and drifting lot of orts of usage, and retirement of
hens, and relief of dogs, and meditation space of children, and grada-
tion of constant shade, and yielder upward of harsh winter damp, slid
through likewise from time to time with snakes, and sterilizer of earth
which contiguous, just beyond its region of rule, sick as it is, streams
and inaudibly shrieks with green violence: this likewise on its upward
surface is the floor and basis of still other living, a wide inch-thick plat
of wood, swept with straws and not seldom scrubbed, soaped and
spreaded with warmth of water, that drains in its seams, and kneeling,
hard breathing, with hard straws scoured and pure: the walls stand up
from its edges and face one another; and its surface sustains the distributed points and weights of the furnishings of living, and the
motions and directions of desire, need, work, and listlessness: a floor, a
sustainer of human living; whereto children and dogs droop in their
tiredness and rest, and sleep, and on a pallet a baby lies, spread over
with a floursack against infringement of flies, and sleeps, and here a
moving camera might know, on its bareness, the standing of the four
iron feet of a bed, the wood of a chair, the scrolled treadle of a sewing
machine, the standing up at right angles of plain wood out of plain
wood, the great and handsome grains and scars of this vertical and
prostrate wood, the huge and noble motions of brooms and of knees

and of feet, and how with clay, and animals, and the leaning face of a woman, these are among the earliest and profoundest absorptions of a very young child.

The hallway

Structure of four rooms

The hallway is long courses of weatherboard facing one another in walls six feet apart, featureless excepting two pair of opposite doors, not ceiled, but beneath the empty and high angling of the roof: perhaps because of the blankness of these walls, and their facing closeness relative to their parallel length, there is here an extremely strong sense of the nakedness and narrowness of their presence, and of the broad openness, exposing the free land, at either end. The floor is laid along beams rather wide apart. In all the rear end it yields to the ground under much weight: the last few feet lie solid to the ground, and this is a strong muck in wet weather.

The one static fixture in the hallway is at the rear, just beyond the kitchen door. It is a wooden shelf, waist-high, and on this shelf, a bucket, a dipper, a basin, and usually a bar of soap, and hanging from a nail just above, a towel. The basin is granite-ware, small for a man's hands, with rustmarks in the bottom. The bucket is a regular galvanized two-gallon bucket, a little dented, and smelling and touching a little of a fishy-metallic kind of shine and grease beyond any power of cleaning. It is half full of slowly heating water which was not very cold to begin with: much lower than this, the water tastes a little ticklish and nasty for drinking, though it is still all right for washing. The soap is sometimes strong tan 'kitchen' soap, sometimes a cheap white gelatinous lavender face soap. It stands on the shelf in a china saucer. The dipper again is granite-ware, and again blistered with rust at the bottom. Sometimes it bobs in the bucket; sometimes it lies next the bucket on the shelf. The towel is half a floursack, with the blue and red and black printing still faint on it. Taken clean and dry, it is the pleasantest cloth I know for a towel. Beyond that, it is particularly clammy, clinging, and dirty-feeling.

A few notes of discrimination may be helpful:

The towels in such a farmhouse are always floursacks. 'Kitchen' towels are of another world and class of farmer, and 'face' and 'turkish' towels of still another.

By no means all poor farmers use any sort of 'toilet' soap. Some seldom use soap at all. When they use other than kitchen soap, it is of one of about three kinds, all of them of the sort available in five-and-tens and small-town general stores. One is 'lava' or 'oatmeal' soap, whose rough texture is pleasing and convincing of cleanliness to a person who works with his hands. The white soaps smell sharply of lye: again, the odor is cleansing. Or if the soap is more fancy, it is a pink or lemon or purple color, strongly and cheaply scented and giving a big lather. No cheap yet somewhat pleasantly scented soap such as lux is used.

Rather more often than not, the basin and the dipper are plain unenameled tin. I expect, but am not sure, that this is a few cents cheaper. In any case the odor, taste, and shiny, greasy texture soon become strong. The use of enamel ware is a small yet sharp distinction and symptom in 'good taste,' and in 'class,' and in a sort of semi-esthetic awareness, choice and will. The use of gray as against white is still another discriminative. That they bought small sizes, which are a very few cents cheaper, speaks for itself. So does the fact that they have afforded still another basin, not quite big enough for its use, to wash their feet in.

At times, there is also a mirror here, and a comb; but more often these are on the bedroom mantel.

The hall and front porch are a kind of room, and are a good deal used. Mrs. Gudger and her children sit in the porch in empty times of the morning and afternoon: back in the rear of the hall is the evening place to sit, before supper or for a little while just after it. There are few enough chairs that they have to be moved around the house to where they are needed, but ordinarily there is a rockingchair on the porch and a straight chair in the rear of the hall next the bedroom door. This rockingchair is of an inexpensive 'rustic' make: sections of hickory sapling with the bark still on. On the hard and not quite even porch floor the rocking is stony and cobbled, with a little of the sound of an auto crossing a loose wooden bridge. Three of the straight chairs are strong, plain, not yet decrepit hickory-bottoms, which cost a dollar and a half new; there is also a kitchen-type chair with a pierced design in the dark scalloped wood at the head, and the bottom broken through.

When we first knew the Gudgers they had their eating-table in the middle of the hall, for only in the hall is there likely to be any sort of breeze, and the kitchen, where nearly all farm families eat, was so hot that they could at times hardly stand to eat in it. This was only an experiment though, and it was not successful. The hall is too narrow for any comfort in it for a whole family clenched round a table. If it were even two feet wider, it would be much more use to them, but this would not have occurred to those who built it, nor, if it had, would anything have been done about it.

Four rooms make a larger tenant house than is ordinary: many are three; many are two; more are one than four: and three of these rooms are quite spacious, twelve feet square. For various reasons, though, all of which could easily enough have been avoided in the building of the house, only two of these rooms, the kitchen and the rear bedroom, are really habitable. There is no ceiling to either of the front rooms, and the shingles were laid so unskillfully, and are now so multitudinously leaky, that it would be a matter not of repairing but of complete relaying to make a solid roof. Between the beams at the eaves, along the whole front of the house, and the top of the wall on which the beams rest, there are open gaps. In the front room on the right, several courses of weatherboarding have been omitted between the level of the eaves and the peak of the roof: a hole big enough for a cow to get through. The walls, and shutters, and floors, are not by any means solid: indeed, and beyond and aside from any amount of laborious calking, they let in light in many dozens of places. There are screens for no windows but one, in the rear bedroom. Because in half the year the fever mosquitoes are thick and there are strong rainstorms, and in the other half it is cold and wet for weeks on end with violent slanted winds and sometimes snow, the right front room is not used to live in at all and the left front room is used only dubiously and irregularly, though the sewing machine is there and it is fully furnished both as a bedroom and as a parlor. The children use it sometimes, and it is given to guests (as it was to us), but storm, mosquitoes and habit force them back into the other room where the whole family sleeps together.

But now I want to take these four rooms one by one, and give at least a certain rough idea of what is in each of them and of what each is 'like,' though I think I should begin this with a few more general remarks.

Odors

Bareness and space

The Gudgers' house, being young, only eight years old, smells a little dryer and cleaner, and more distinctly of its wood, than an average white tenant house, and it has also a certain odor I have never found in other such houses: aside from these sharp yet slight subtleties, it has the odor or odors which are classical in every thoroughly poor white southern country house, and by which such a house could be identified blindfold in any part of the world, among no matter what other odors. It is compacted of many odors and made into one, which is very thin and light on the air, and more subtle than it can seem in analysis, yet very sharply and constantly noticeable. These are its ingredients. The odor of pine lumber, wide thin cards of it, heated in the sun, in no way doubled or insulated, in closed and darkened air. The odor of woodsmoke, the fuel being again mainly pine, but in part also, hickory, oak, and cedar. The odors of cooking. Among these, most strongly, the odors of fried salt pork and of fried and boiled pork lard, and second, the odor of cooked corn. The odors of sweat in many stages of age and freshness, this sweat being a distillation of pork, lard, corn, woodsmoke, pine, and ammonia. The odors of sleep, of bedding and of breathing, for the ventilation is poor. The odors of all the dirt that in the course of time can accumulate in a quilt and mattress. Odors of staleness from clothes hung or stored away, not washed. I should further describe the odor of corn: in sweat, or on the teeth, and breath, when it is eaten as much as they eat it, it is of a particular sweet stuffy fetor, to which the nearest parallel is the odor of the yellow excrement of a baby. All these odors as I have said are so combined into one that they are all and always present in balance, not at all heavy, yet so searching that all fabrics of bedding and clothes are saturated with them, and so clinging that they stand softly out of the fibers of newly laundered clothes. Some of their components are extremely 'pleasant,' some are 'unpleasant'; their sum total has great nostalgic power. When they are in an old house, darkened, and moist, and sucked into all the wood, and stacked down on top of years of a moldering and old basis of themselves, as at the Ricketts', they are hard to get used to or even hard to bear. At the Woods', they are blowsy and somewhat moist and dirty. At the Gudgers', as I have mentioned, they are younger, lighter, and cleaner-smelling. There too, there is another and special odor, very dry and edged: it is somewhere between the odor of very old newsprint and of a victorian bedroom in which, after long illness, and many medicines, someone has died and the room has been fumigated, yet the odor of dark brown medicines, dry-bodied sickness, and staring death, still is strong in the stained wallpaper and in the mattress.

Bareness and space (and spacing) are so difficult and seem to me of such greatness that I shall not even try to write seriously or fully of them. But a little, applying mainly to the two bedrooms.

The floors are made of wide planks, between some of which the daylighted earth is visible, and are naked of any kind of paint or cloth or linoleum covering whatever, and paths have been smoothed on them by bare feet, in a subtly uneven surface on which the polished knots are particularly beautiful. A perfectly bare floor of broad boards makes a room seem larger than it can if the floor is covered, and the furniture too, stands on it in a different and much cleaner sort of relationship. The walls as I have said are skeleton; so is the ceiling in one of these rooms; the rooms are twelve feet square and are meagerly furnished, and they are so great and final a whole of bareness and complete simplicity that even the objects on a crowded shelf seem set far apart from each other, and each to have a particularly sharp entity of its own. Moreover, all really simple and naïve people * incline strongly toward exact symmetries, and have some sort of instinctive dislike that any one thing shall touch any other save what it rests on, so that chairs, beds, bureaus, trunks, vases, trinkets, general odds and ends, are set very plainly and squarely discrete from one another and from walls, at exact centers or as near them as possible, and this kind of spacing gives each object a full strength it would not otherwise have, and gives their several relationships, as they stand on shelves or facing, in a room, the purest power such a relationship can have. This is still more sharply true with such people as the Gudgers, who still have a little yet earnest wish that everything shall be as pleasant and proper to live with as possible, than with others such as the Woods and Ricketts, who are disheveled and wearied out of any such hope or care.

---

* And many of the most complex, and not many between.

I. The Front Bedroom

General: placement of furniture

Its west wall is the front of the house; its north wall, the hallway; its east wall, the partition; its south wall, the side of the house. At the center of the partition wall is a fireplace. At the center of the side wall and of the front wall is an exactly square window, about three feet each way. At the center of the north wall a door leads into the rear bedroom. The doors are very wide vertical planks, not paneled, but crosslaid with planks in a Z. They are held shut by block wood buttons and are kept shut most of the time. The square shutters, hung on sagged and rusted, loud hinges, are less broad verticals. Always at night and nearly always during the day they are drawn shut and secured, one by a leather strap over a nail, the other by a piece of rag over a nail. When they are shut, the room is dark and has a special heat and odor of daylight darkness; but also there is a strong starlight of sunshine with slits and blades and rods of light through the roof and two outward walls and, looking through the floor, the quiet sunless daylighted grain of the earth can be seen, strange to see as at the bottom of a lake; and in this oddly lighted darkness, certain flecks of the room are brilliantly picked out, and every part of it is visible. When one of the shutters is opened, the light is new and uneasy in the room, as if the objects were blinking, or had been surprised in secret acts, or, even, as an archaeologist who first lets daylight into an unviolated Egyptian tomb: and the feeling and odor of its particular darkness never leaves it: and here, on the bare floor, between the squarings of the wide bare walls, the furniture stands: the furniture, its clothing, and each little ornament on wall and shelf, and the contents of each box and drawer, and the cleanliness of the central floor, such that it might be licked with the tongue and made scarcely cleaner, and the lint curled back against itself under the bed and behind the sewing machine and thick beneath the bureau, and the pine walls, which outside are weathered so pure, still holding their reds and yellows among their grays, clear in their grain, and lined in strong parallels on the far sides of the strongly nailed pine two-by-fours, through the sides of which, here and there, nails have split their points among splinters of fresh-looking wood.

The bed, between the hall door and the front wall, in the angle of the two walls, the head toward the wall, about six inches out from each wall, the foot at the window.

On the other side of the hall door, at center between this door and the angle of the partition wall, a 'settee.'

Directly before the fireplace, but not touching it, a small table. Above the fireplace, a mantel.

Again out from the walls, symmetrically across the right angle made by the partition wall and the side wall, its tall mirror erect above it, a bureau.

Exactly beneath the window of the side wall, again a little out from the wall, a trunk:

Exactly across the angle of the side and front walls, and still again, not touching these walls, a sewing machine.

Exactly at center behind and beneath the sewing machine, on the floor, a square-based and square-bowled lamp of clear heavy glass, dusty, and without its chimney, the base broken and the broken piece fitted but not mended into place:

Exactly beneath the center of the table, on a shelf just above the floor, their toes pointed parallel into the center of the fireplace, a large and still nearly new pair of men's black sunday oxfords, the heels clayed and the shining black upward heels narrowly streaked with clay of the color of angry gold.

On the bureau shelf, the mantel, the table and one wall, objects; small, simple and varied: which, the only adorned or decorated creatures of this room, bestow upon its nakedness the quality of an altar.

The furniture

The dark castiron treadle of the sewing machine spells out squarely, in the middle of its curlings, the word CONQUEST. This is repeated in gold on the split wooden hood, but most of the gold has been rubbed off.

The 'settee': rather fancily bent out of thin canes; loud and broken; too uncomfortable to make much use of. The seat is badly broken through. A thin homemade cushion, stuffed with raw cotton; the slip is the frailest and cheapest kind of cotton cloth, dirty white, splotched with wide pink roses.

It is a small, elderly, once gay, now sober, and very pretty trunk, the lid shallowly domed, somewhat tall and narrow, and thus bearing itself in a kind of severe innocence as certain frame houses and archaic automobiles do. It is surfaced with tin which was once colored bright red and bright blue, and this tin, now almost entirely gone brown, is stamped in a thick complex of daisies and studded with small round-headed once golden nails; and the body of the trunk is bound with wood and with two recently nailed ribbons of bluish iron. The leather handles are gray-green and half-rotted, the hinges are loose, the lock is wrenched. Opening this light trunk, a fragrance springs from it as if of stale cinnamon and fever powders and its inward casket is unexpectedly bright as if it were a box of tamed sunlight, in its lining of torn white paper streaked with brown, fresh yellow wood grained through the torn places, the bright white lining printed with large and bright mauve centerless daisies. In this trunk: an old slightly soiled cotton slip; a little boy's stiff cheap gray cap; a baby's dress; a gray-white knit shoe for a baby; a pair of ten-cent hard thin mercerized bold-patterned electric-blue socks, worn through at the heels, with a strip of green checked gingham tied through the top of one, for a garter, and a strip of pink gingham through the other. In one corner of the floor of the trunk, staring blue with black centers, waxed to the ends of a wire wishbone whose juncture is a light lead weight, the eyes of a small doll.

The bed-frame is not tall or at all ornate, as many iron frames are. Its former surface of hard white paint is worn almost entirely away to the bare, blue-brown iron. It is a three-quarter bed, which means a double bed so far as tenant usage is concerned. Because it is the guest and parlor bed, and little used, it is covered with a thin, brittle, magenta spread of chemical silk.

The bureau was at some time a definitely middle-class * piece of furniture. It is quite wide and very heavy, veneered in gloomy red rich-grained woods, with intricately pierced metal plaques at the handles of the three drawers, and the mirror is at least three feet tall and is framed in machine-carved wood. The veneer has now split and leafed loose in many places from the yellow soft-wood base; the handles of the three drawers are nearly all deranged and two are gone; the drawers do not pull in and out at all easily. The mirror is so far corrupted that it is rashed with gray, iridescent in parts, and in all its reflections a deeply sad thin zinc-to-platinum, giving to its framings an almost incalculably ancient, sweet, frail, and piteous beauty, such as may be seen in tintypes of family groups among studio furnishings or heard in nearly exhausted jazz records made by very young, insane, devout men who were soon to destroy themselves, in New Orleans, in the early nineteen twenties. The surface of this bureau is covered with an aged, pebble-grained

---

* More accurately, it would have been a lower-middle-class imitation of a middle-class piece, mimicking weight, bulk, gloom, ornament, and expense.

face towel, too good a fabric to be used in this house for the purposes it was made for. Upon this towel rest these objects: An old black comb, smelling of fungus and dead rubber, nearly all the teeth gone. A white clamshell with brown dust in the bottom and a small white button on it. A small pincushion made of pink imitation silk with the bodiced torso of a henna-wigged china doll sprouting from it, her face and one hand broken off. A cream-colored brown-shaded china rabbit three or four inches tall, with bluish lights in the china, one ear laid awry: he is broken through the back and the pieces have been fitted together to hang, not glued, in delicate balance. A small seated china bull bitch and her litter of three smaller china pups, seated round her in an equilateral triangle, their eyes intersected on her: they were given to Louise last Christmas and are with one exception her most cherished piece of property. A heavy moist brown Bible, its leaves almost weak as snow, whose cold, obscene, and inexplicable fragrance I found in my first night in this house.

I shall not fully list the contents of the bureau drawers. They contain, among other things, schoolbooks; and in one drawer there are a number of pieces of wrapping paper, each folded separately and very carefully to make no more new creases than is necessary. Some of this paper is dark blue with large gold bells and stars and small gold houses on it. Some is red and green holly on a white ground. Some is plain red or white or green or blue tissue. One is plain brown wrapping paper but has glued to it several seals of santaclaus and of scotch terriers and of bells in holly garlands. These papers are now torn in a number of places, rather somber and faded, and are intricately seamed and ridged over all their surfaces with years of wrapping and unfolding. They smell stale and old. There are also red, frayed gold and silver strings here, wound some on spools, some on matches or nails.

And, centered one upon another and at center of their square-spread partition wall, all squarely opposite the square window, the table and the fireplace and the mantel which, with the wall, create a shrine and altar:

The altar

The three other walls are straight and angled beams and the inward surfaces of unplaned pine weatherboards. This partition wall is made of horizontals of narrow and cleanly planed wood, laid tightly edge to edge; the wood is pine of another quality, slenderly grained in narrow yellow and rich iron-red golds, very smooth and as if polished, softly glowing and shining, almost mirroring bulks: and is the one wall of the room at all conducive to ornament, and is the one ornamented wall. At its center the mantel and square fireplace frame, painted, one coat, an old and thin blue-white: in front of the fireplace, not much more than covering the full width of its frame, the small table: and through, beneath it, the gray, swept yet ashy bricks of the fireplace and short hearth, and the silent shoes: and on the table, and on the mantel, and spread above and wide of it on the walls, the things of which I will now tell.

On the table: it is blue auto paint: a white cloth, hanging a little over the edges. On the cloth, at center, a small fluted green glass bowl in which sits a white china swan, profiled upon the north.

On the mantel against the glowing wall, each about six inches from the ends of the shelf, two small twin vases, very simply blown, of pebble-grained iridescent glass. Exactly at center between them, a fluted saucer, with a coarse lace edge, of pressed milky glass, which Louise's mother gave her to call her own and for which she cares more dearly than for anything else she possesses. Pinned all along the edge of this mantel, a broad fringe of white tissue pattern-paper which Mrs. Gudger folded many times on itself and scissored into pierced geometrics of lace, and of which she speaks as her last effort to make this house pretty.

On the wall, pasted or pinned or tacked or printed, set well discrete from one another, in not quite perfected symmetric relations:

A small octagonal frame surfaced in ivory and black ribbons of thin wicker or of straw, the glass broken out: set in this frame, not filling it, a fading box-camera snapshot: low, gray, dead-looking land stretched back in a deep horizon; twenty yards back, one corner of a tenant house, central at the foreground, two women: Annie Mae's sister Emma as a girl of twelve, in slippers and stockings and a Sunday dress, standing a little shyly with puzzling eyes, self-conscious of her appearance and of her softly clouded sex; and their mother, wide and high, in a Sunday dress still wet from housework, her large hands hung loose and biased in against her thighs, her bearing strong, weary, and noble, her face fainted away almost beyond distinguishing, as if in her death and by some secret touching the image itself of the fine head her husband had cared for so well had softly withered, which even while they stood there had begun its blossoming inheritance in the young daughter at her side.

A calendar, advertising —'s shoes, depicting a pretty brunette with ornate red lips, in a wide-brimmed red hat, cuddling red flowers. The title is Cherie, and written twice, in pencil, in a schoolchild's hand: Louise, Louise.

A calendar, advertising easy-payment furniture: a tinted photograph of an immaculate, new-overalled boy of twelve, wearing a wide new straw hat, the brim torn by the artist, fishing. The title is Fishin'.

Slung awry by its chain from a thin nail, an open oval locket, glassed. In one face of this locket, a colored picture of Jesus, his right hand blessing, his red heart exposed in a burst spiky gold halo. In the other face, a picture by the same artist of the Blessed Virgin, in blue, her heart similarly exposed and haloed, and pierced with seven small swords. *

Torn from a child's cheap storybook, costume pictures in bright furry colors illustrating, exactly as they would and should be illustrated, these titles:

---

* If the Gudgers realized that this is Roman Catholic, they would be surprised and shocked and would almost certainly remove it. It is interesting and mysterious to me that they should have found it anywhere in their country, which is as solidly anti-catholic as the Province of Quebec is roman.

The Harper was Happier than a King as He Sat by his Own Fireside. She Took the Little Prince in Her Arms and Kissed Him. ('She' is a goosegirl.)

Torn from a tin can, a strip of bright scarlet paper with a large white fish on it and the words:

SALOMAR

EXTRA QUALITY MACKEREL

At the right of the mantel, in whitewash, all its whorlings sharp, the print of a child's hand.

The Tabernacle

In the table drawer, in this order:

A delicate insect odor of pine, closed sweated cloth, and mildew.

One swooning-long festal baby's dress of the most frail muslin, embroidered with three bands of small white cotton-thread flowers. Two narrow courses of cheap yet small-threaded lace are let in near the edge of the skirt. This garment is hand-sewn in painfully small and labored stitchings. It is folded, but not pressed, and is not quite clean.

One plain baby's dress of white cotton; a torn rag: home-sewn, less studiously; folded.

Another, as plain, save for pink featherstitching at the cuffs. Torn, not folded.

Another, thinlined gray-blue faded checks on a white ground. The silhouettes of two faded yellow rabbits, cut out at home, are stitched on the front, the features are x'd in in pink thread.

A nearly flat blue cloth cat doll, home-made, a blue tail, nearly torn off, the features in black thread.

A broad and stiff-brimmed soft-crowned hat, the brim broken in several places, the fabrics stained and moldered. The crown is gold, of

thin plush or the cheapest velvet. The ribbon is wide plaid woodsilk
weltering lights of orange and of pearl. It is striped white at the edges
and the stripes are edged in gold thread. The brim is bordered an inch
wide with gold brocade. The underbrim is creamcolored mercerized
cotton, marked in one place by an indelible pencil. Through a tear the
pasteboard brim is visible: it was cut out of a shoe-box. The stitching
throughout is patient, devoted, and diminutive. The hat is one broken,
half-moist, moldered chunk.

A blue foursided tall box of Dr. Peters Rose Talcum Powder, empty
save for some small hard object which rattles. The odor of the powder,
a little like that of perfume-machines in theater toilets.

One smallchecked pink and white baby's dress.

One baby's dress, a rag. Blue featherstitching in mercerized thread.

One child's brown cotton glove, for the right hand. The index finger ends in a hole.

A scissored hexagon of newsprint:

GHAM NEWS
hursday afternoon, March 5, 1936
Price: 3 cents
   in G
   (else

Thousa
are on d
througho
cording its

for the Birm

(over two photographs:)
   Glass and night sticks fly in strike

(caption:)

     between police and strike sympathizers now
     York. A cameraman was right o
     venty-second St.

(the photographs, both flashlighted night scenes:)

 1. A man in civilian clothes including gloves, back to, is doing something unidentifiable to what may be an elevator door.

 2. A street. Two policemen. One is balanced in recoil from an action just accomplished. The face signifies uh-huh. The other, glasses, a masterful head, his nightstick just rebounding from the palm-clenched skull of a hatless topcoated civilian whose head is level with his hips. Flashlighted pavement, spotted with grease or blood. On the black background hands, a shirtfront, watch, poised ready to run, beneath a faint oval of hatface bisected by dark hatband.

(To the left:)

     NEW STRIKE MOVE
     EARED AS PEACE
     NFAB SPLITS UP

     fer to Arbitrate is
     Down by Real
     e Group

     s Owners
     f Parley
     Labor
     reat

     ANY EXPANDS ARMAMEN

     HASES
     MPLETION

Program planned
Keep Pace with
Greater Army

(caption above small photograph:)
    Veteran Chinese War
    Lord Prepares For
    Communist Conflict

(below:)
    Marshal Yen Hsi-Suan
    An impending threat of 10,000 Chinese Communists against Tai-
    Yuan, Shensi Province, China, led Marshal Yen Hsi-Suan, veteran
    war lord, to declare an emergency and mobilize an army to halt
    their approach. Twenty-six American missionaries may be in dan-
    ger. (Associated Press Photo.)

    SHAW CONFESSES
    HE'S A 'WASHOUT'
    British satirist admits he's
    a failure, since world
    won't mind him

(Above photograph:)
    TINY TOT FACES

(below:)
    Altho 4 months old Kenneth House, Jr.
    physicians with X-rays are watching progres
    which he swallowed six days ago, to date
    operation will be necessary to remove it.
    its mother, Mrs. Betty House, at Denver, C

National Whirligig
continued from page 1

T O U

Held against the light, the contents of both sides of the paper are visible at once.

The two parts of a broken button.
A small black hook, lying in its eye.
Another small black hook.
In the corners of the pale inward wood, fine gray dust and a sharp-grained unidentifiable brown dust.
In a split in the bottom of the drawer, a small bright needle, pointed north, as the swan above it is.

II. The Rear Bedroom

General

It is half as bright and opened-seeming (and seems more so) as the room we left was and remains dark: all but the window of the side wall, whose shutter is laid back flat, and which is nailed over with a square of fresh gray screening: yet after a minute it seems somewhat somber too; or thus: the floor from the window in a wide fan and all the opposite wall is clearly lighted, none of it in direct sun: but the rear wall and the corner to the right are much less lighted.

There are two beds here, both three-quarter size, set parallel, their heads near the rear wall, their sides near the two side walls. One is directly opposite this partition door, its foot frame comes just short of the kitchen door: the other is directly opposite the door of a very shallow closet built out from the partition. The fireplace, in the partition wall, faces the closed rear shutter down the bare aisle of transverse planks between them: and the two of them together almost fill their side of the room. These beds are both sheeted in tightly drawn white sheets, and at the central head of each, a hard thin white-cased pillow is slightly tilted from the mattress case. On each of these surfaces is a thin constellation of perhaps a dozen black flies. Once in a while several at once will move a sharp inch or two in straight lines, or one will suddenly spiral off and butt the windowscreen: but for minutes on end they all stand still together. Both these beds are iron. This one we face, which is George's bed, and his wife's, the iron is dark and smooth and the pattern is plain, a few round verticals, and taller verticals at the head: the other is of more slender, white rods, bent into balanced curves.

Above the head of this nearer bed, suspended on two forked sticks nailed to the wall, is a light-gauged shotgun.

On a nail just beside the window hangs the white summer union suit George sleeps in.

There is a trunk beneath the side window, very similar to the trunk in the front room.

The fireplace

All the frame and mantel of the fireplace and the rather dark, blank wall, to a squared-off height of perhaps five and a half feet, and some of the wall beyond the frame, are whitewashed, long enough ago that the wash is scarred with matches and the grain is strong through it, yet a very cold and fine white, the edges of the work carefully labored and inexpert. Up by the right of the fireplace, and not balanced on the other side, is a wide vertical board, creating between its structural dominance and the centrality of the fireplace a not wide yet sharp dilemma of symmetries. The whitewash, with bold and fine instinct, is applied to follow the symmetry of the wood, so that the fireplace is sprung a few inches off center within its large white framing; yet, since it still has so strong a central focus in its wall, a powerful vibration is set up between the two centers.

The mantel

On the mantel above this fireplace:
A small round cardboard box:
(on its front:)

> Cashmere Bouquet Face Powder
> Light Rachel

(on its back:)

> The Aristocrat of Face Powders.
> Same quality as 50¢ size.

Inside the box, a small puff. The bottom of the box and the bottom face of the puff carry a light dust of fragrant softly tinted powder.

A jar of menthol salve, smallest size, two thirds gone.

A small spool of number 50 white cotton thread, about half gone and half unwound.

A cracked roseflowered china shaving mug, broken along the edge. A much worn, inchwide varnish brush stands in it. Also in the mug are eleven rusty nails, one blue composition button, one pearl headed pin (imitation), three dirty kitchen matches, a lump of toilet soap.

A pink crescent celluloid comb: twenty-seven teeth, of which three are missing; sixteen imitation diamonds.

A nailfile.

A small bright mirror in a wire stand.

Hung from a nail at the side of the fireplace: a poker bent out of an auto part.

Hung from another nail, by one corner: a square pincushion. Stuck into it, several common pins, two large safety-pins, three or four pins with heads of white or colored glass; a small brooch of green glass in gilded tin; a needle trailing eighteen inches of coarse white thread.

Above the mantel, right of center, a calendar: a picture in red-brown shadows, and in red and yellow lights from a comfortable fireplace. A young darkhaired mother in a big chair by the fire: a little girl in a long white nightgown kneels between her knees with her palms together: the mother's look is blended of doting and teaching. The title is Just a Prayer at Twilight.

The closet

On nails on the inside of the door of the shallow closet:

A short homesewn shift of coarse white cotton, square beneath the arms and across the chest and back: a knot in the right shoulderstrap.

A baby's dress, homemade. The top is gray denim; the collar is trimmed in pink; the skirt, in a thinner material, is small yellow-and-white checks.

A long homemade shift of coarse white cotton, same rectilinear design as above. A tincture of perspiration and of sex.

On the closet floor, to the left, a heap of overalls, dresses, shirts, bedding, etc., ready for laundering.

On a shelf above, three or four patchwork quilts of various degrees of elaborateness and inventiveness of pattern, and in various degrees of raggedness, age, discoloration, dirt absorption, and sense-of-vermin, stuffed with cotton and giving off a strong odor.

On nails along the wall, overalls, dresses, children's clothing; the overalls holding the shape of the knee and thigh; an odor of sweated cloth.

On the floor to the right, folded one on the other, two homemade pallets for children: flat rectangular sacks of thin white cloth thinly padded with cotton.

On the floor at center, two by two, toes to the wall, a pair of women's black slippers, run-over at the low heels. A pair of workshoes, very old, molded to the shape of the feet. A pair of girl's slippers, whited over scrubbed clay and streaked again with clay. A pair of little-boy's high black shoes, broken at the toes and worn through the soles, the toes curled up sharply; looped straps at the heels: thick clay scrubbed off. A pair of little-girl's slightly narrower and softer high tan button shoes, similarly worn and curled, similarly scrubbed. A pair of little-boy's high black button shoes, similarly worn, curled, and scrubbed. One infant's brown sandal. These shoes, particularly those of the children, are somewhat gnawn, and there are rat turds on the floor.

The beds

The children's bed in the rear room has a worn-out and rusted mesh spring; the springs of the other two beds are wire net, likewise rusty and exhausted. Aside from this and from details formerly mentioned, the beds may be described as one. There are two mattresses on each, both very thin, padded, I would judge, one with raw cotton and one with cornshucks. They smell old, stale, and moist, and are morbid with bedbugs, with fleas, and, I believe, with lice. They are homemade. The sheaths are not ticking, but rather weak unbleached cotton. Though the padding is sewn through, to secure it, it has become uncomfortably lumpy in some places, nothing but cloth in others. The sheeting is of a coarse and beautiful unbleached but nearly white cotton, home-sewn down the length of each center with a seam either ridged or drawn apart. It is cloth of a sort that takes and holds body heat rapidly, and which is humid with whatever moisture may be in the air, and the fabric is sharp against the skin. The pillows are store-bought, the cheapest obtainable: thin, hard, crackling under any motion of the head; and seem, like the mattresses, to carry vermin. The pillowcases are homemade, of the sheeting; one is a washed, soft, fifty-pound floursack. The striped ticking shows strongly through the cloth. The beds are insecure enough in their joints that motions of the body must be gentle, balanced, and to some extent thought out beforehand. The mattresses and springs are loud, each in a different way, to any motion. The springs sag so deeply that two or more, sleeping here, fall together at the middle almost as in a hammock. The sheets are drawn tight in making the bed, in part out of housework ritual, in part, I believe, in the wish to make the chronically sagged beds look level. Sometimes this succeeds. At other times the bed, neatly made though it is, looks like an unlucky cake.

Very often, Burt cannot get to sleep except in his mother's arms. During nearly all the year, the whole family sleeps in this one room. The youngest of them never sleeps elsewhere. Even when they are in the next room, the partition is very thin. Even if there were no children, such parents are limited enough that they are deeply embarrassed and disturbed by noises coming of any sexual context and betraying it. Even if there were no noises, the bed frames are insecure, the springs sag weakly, the mattresses are thin and lumpy, the sheets are not very pleasant.

On these beds, however, and among their children, they get whatever sexual good they ever have of each other, as noiselessly and with as little movement as possible; and on these beds, after spending two thirds of their life in hard wearying work and in conscious living in every way hurtful and distortive of the 'mind,' 'emotions,' and 'nerves,' they spend a third of their lives getting the refreshment and rest of sleep.

III. The Kitchen

General

There is a tin roof on the kitchen. It leaks only when the rain is very heavy and then only along the juncture with the roof of the main house. The difficulty is more with heat. The room is small: very little more than big enough to crowd in the stove and table and chairs: and this slanted leanto roof is quite low above it, with no ceiling, and half the tin itself visible. The outdoor sunlight alone is in the high nineties during many hours of one day after another for weeks on end; the thin metal roof collects and sends on this heat almost as powerfully as a burning-glass; wood fires are particularly hot and violent and there is scarcely a yard between the stove and one end of the table: between the natural heat, the cumulated and transacted heat striven downward from the roof, and the heat of the stove, the kitchen is such a place at the noon meal time that, merely entering it, sweat is started in a sheet from the whole surface of the body, and the solar plexus and the throat are clutched into tight kicking knots which relax sufficiently to admit food only after two or three minutes.

This is a leanto room. The forward wall is the former outside of the house. The hall door is at center of its wall; there is another door just beyond the head of the table, about four feet from the far end of the room, leading into the front room; at center of the rear wall is a window; there is another at center of the side wall. These windows are glassed, thin rippled and dimpled panes, and are in two parts, but lacking weights, are held open with stovewood. The stove stands in the corner between them, the 'cupboard' stands against the front wall beyond the door to the storeroom, the table along the front wall between that door and the hall, the meal bin and foot basin in the corner made between the rear and hall walls; the woodbox stands along the near side of the stove; under the stove is the dishpan; the coffee-pot and a kettle stand on it, set back; pots are hung on nails along the walls of the stove-corner; lids are stuck between the walls and a two-by-four; one of the skillets stands out nearly level; its handle is stuck through a rift between two boards of the wall and through this rift a small piece of the outdoors is visible. The broom stands in the corner at the foot of the table and above, on nails, hang the round crockery head of the churn, and the dasher. It is pleasantly bright here, with no sunshine, but an almost cool-looking, strong, calm light, of the sort that takes up residence in any piece of glass without glittering in it.

The room is a little small for comfort, and here, as is unnecessary in the other rooms, everything that can be is blocked back hard against the wall. There are no chairs on the wall side of the table, but a long and quite narrow bench, close against the wall, and the table is brought up close against it so that the children have to climb to their places with a fair amount of difficulty: and in spite of this economizing, the table juts out beyond the hall door, the chairs along that side a little more, and when everyone is seated the room is pretty nearly blocked. The chair at the foot is crowded in close, too, for there is just enough room between the hall door and the storeroom door. The stove has to be set well out from the walls of its corner, a couple of feet from each at least, and this leaves just room and no better between the stove and the corner of the table. In spite of all the open air, the kitchen smells powerfully of the cooking, for the walls are saturated with it.

The 'cupboard,' a carry-all for kitchen implements, china, eating-tools, and the less perishable of the chronic cooking supplies, is never known in the rural south as a cupboard, but always as a safe. * The ordinary safe is a tall, dark, flimsy wood cabinet with several shelves, with double doors faced in rusted tin pierced in ventilative patterns of geometry and of radiant flowers, and smelling stuffily yet rather sweetly of hens, butter, and fried pork and of the cheap metals of its forks. I speak of this because the Gudgers' safe veers so wide of the ordinary as to seem comic or even surrealist in this setting, as a frigidaire might. It is of bright yellow shellacked pine and the doors are white enameled metal in narrow frames, and the door-latches are not buttons shaped like jazz-bows, as in the ordinary nineteenth-century-type safe, but are bright nickel, of the sort used on refrigerators; and it is more capacious than the oldfashioned safe. There is a metal-lined bin for flour, and there are enameled and labeled cans for SUGAR, COFFEE, SALT, TEA, which look to have come with the house. It is a really good piece of furniture; and has a sort of middle-class lovenest look to it which connects it to advertisements in women's magazines and to the recipe voices of radio women, so that it is here peculiarly insulting and pathetic; and already it has picked up tenant-kitchen redolences for which it was never intended.

The stove is of baroque rusting iron, with an oven. It is small, and low enough that it must be leaned above at a rather deep angle. A large black iron kettle stands at the back of it; on nails behind it, in its corner, a few dark pots and flat baking-pans are hung, and a heavy black skillet; the skillet is stuck by its handle through a rift in the wall and extends its round hand flat toward the center of the room.

The mealbin is a fifty-pound lard can half full. It is topped off by a sifter, homemade of windowscreen which is broken, and three

---

* I don't know how this got started, but it seems to me of some interest that farm families, whose most urgent treasures are the food they eat, use for its storage-box the name used among middle-class people for the guardian of money, ledgers, and 'valuable papers.'

trapped flies, covered with meal, brain themselves against the lower side.

The broom is of the cheap thirty-to-forty-cent kind and is nearly new, but do not be misled: the old one, still held in limbo because nothing is thrown away, was well used before it was discarded: it has about the sweeping power of a club foot.

The dasher is made deliciously mild and fragrant by milk and butter, and glows as ivory might against the raw wall.

The chairs sit in exact regiment of uneven heights with the charming sobriety of children pretending to be officers or judges.

The table: the lamp

The table is set for dinner.

The yellow and green checked oilcloth is worn thin and through at the corners and along the edges of the table and along the ridged edges of boards in the table surface, and in one or two places, where elbows have rested a great deal, it is rubbed through in a wide hole. In its intact surfaces it shines prettily and bluntly reflects the window and parts of the objects that are on it, for it has been carefully polished with a wet rag, and it shows also the tracings of this rag. Where it has rubbed through, the wood is sour and greasy, and there are bread crumbs in the seams and under the edges of the cloth, which smell of mold, and these odors are so mingled with that of the oilcloth that they are in total the classic odor of a tenant eating-table.

There are two stainless steel knives and forks with neat black handles which would have cost a dime apiece, and against what little we could do about it these are set at our places: but by actual usage they belong to the two parents.

Aside from these the forks and knives and spoons are of that very cheap, light, and dull metal which seems to be almost universal among working-class families, and in the more charitable and idealistic kinds of institutions, and which impart to every ounce of food they touch their peculiar taste and stench, which is a little like that of a can which has contained strong fish. The tines of nearly all the forks are bent, then rippled back into approximate order; the knives are saw-edged.

Almost no two of the plates, or cups, or glasses, or saucers, are of the same size or pattern. All of the glasses except one are different sizes and shapes of jelly glass. One of the cups is thin, blue, Woolworth's imitation of willow plate: the handle is gone; two others are thick and white, of the sort used in lunchwagons, but of lower quality, flinty, and a little like sandstone at their brims; one of these is chipped; the fourth is a taller cup of the same sort, with a thready split running its full height. Two of the plates are full dinner size, of the same thick lunchwagon china, another is translucent white of a size between saucer and dinnerplate; another, deep cream-colored, netted with brown cracklings, is pressed with a garland of yellow corn and green leaves. The children eat mainly out of saucers and bowls. The food will be served in part out of pans, and in part out of two wide shallow soup plates and a small thick white platter. At the middle of the table is a mason jar of sorghum, a box of black pepper, and a tall shaker of salt whose top is green, all surrounding the unlighted lamp which stands in the bare daylight in the beauty of a young nude girl.

IV. THE STOREROOM

Two essentials

Two essentials, I cannot hope to embody even mildly but must say only, what they are, and what they should be if they could be written: one is of the house as a whole; one may be realized in terms of any single room. The first is true of any house of more than one room. The second is the privilege only of houses such as this one I am talking of.

The first is this: In any house, standing in any one room of it, or standing disembodied in remembrance of it, it is possible, by sufficient quiet and passive concentration, to realize for a little while at a time the simultaneity in existence of all of its rooms in their exact structures and mutual relationships in space and in all they contain; and to realize this not merely with the counting mind, nor with the imagination of the eye, which is no realization at all, but with the whole of the body and being, and in translations of the senses so that in part at least they become extrahuman, become a part of the nature and being of these rooms and their contents and of this house: or in a kind of building-dream, a disembodied consciousness stands in an open platform of floor, no walls nor roof: and in a fluttering of hammers and with wide quiet motions from all sides of this consciousness, at the edges of the platform there

are swept up the wide cards of the wooden walls like the sped closing
of the petals of flowers, and their edges join in a stitching of nails, and
beginning vertical and matched against one another along the ridge-
pole like the closed wings of a butterfly, the great wings of the roof are
spread open and sweep downward either side in darkening, to come to
rest at length along the upward edges of this squared wooden pit: and
where these walls are risen and clasped, their square surfaces face one
another two and two and make an inward square, a chamber, and all
the four rooms of this house where the Gudgers live are here at once
each in its space and each in balance of each other in a chord: and it is
the full bodily recognition of this chord that I speak of particularly,
which can so arrest the heart: and of how all these furnishings and
objects, within these rooms, are squared and enchanted as in amber.

The second, this too is true of any place, yet it is most powerful
where all the materials of structure are bare before one, as they are
here. It is, having examined scientifically or as if by blueprint how such
a house is made from the ground up, in every strictly sized part of its
wood, and in every tightening nail, and with nearly every inch of this
open to the eye as it is within one of these rooms, to let all these things,
each in its place, and all in their relationships and in their full substances, *be, at once,* driven upon your consciousness, one center: and
there is here such an annihilating counterpoint as might be if you could
within an instant hear and be every part, from end to end, of the most
vastly spun of fugues: and this first essence of one of the things a bare
house is, the plain shell, in which the fates of successive families shall
live as they may, can best be realized in this dark room in front of the
kitchen, for it is scarcely used, and is never opened to the open daylight, and is nearly empty, and there reside there mainly the mere walls,
and floor, and roof, facing one another and one center as pine mirrors.

But of this room I can only make these suggestions, and can tell
very little about it, of another kind.

In the room

The way in is by the kitchen door. The hall door and the shutters are nailed shut. Because it is so constantly closed, the heat and darkness and wood odor are different here from elsewhere in the house; and because it is so little used the silence is so powerfully impacted and compounded upon itself that it is almost a solid block, stretching the walls apart. What light there is comes in by the gap above the hall, and by the eaves, and through the many imperfections of the walls and roof, splintering on the floor. There is an odor of sackcloth and a dry odor of storage and of a vault or tomb. Along the north wall there are long shelves with jars on them. From a nail by the kitchen door hang four or five cobs of red and yellow popcorn, years old. Toward the middle of the floor are several sacks, some full, some empty. Up in the high roof a wasp cruises, stricken now and then by sunlight; at such instants he is an electric spark. There are dim smoky cobwebs on beams in corners. Excepting a path along the shelves and to the sacks, it is a floor of gentlest, rat-trailed dust, so full the grain of wood is hardly visible. Nothing else is in the room. One of the sacks is heavy, its head nodded above its belly, it is two-thirds full of cornmeal. Another is part full of dried peas. Another is light, full of unshelled peas. Several lie empty. They will hold peas and meal for the winter. Out at their left are scraps of shattered leaves and twigs. They are peanut leaves, a good feed for stock. There is also a floursack nearly full of dried peaches. Along the shelves, using very little of their space, stand perhaps three dozen mason jars of which about twenty are empty, and fifteen or twenty jelly glasses, of which six or eight are being used: apple and wild berry jellies and jams, and canned peaches, tomatoes, string beans: One or two have already begun to fester. There is almost none of last winter left here now, but at this time of summer, the shelves are beginning to be banked against next winter. By cold weather, every jar here will be used, and every other that Mrs. Gudger can get.

In the Front Bedroom: The Signal

I lie where I lay this dawn.)

If I were not here; and I am alien; a bodyless eye; this would never have existence in human perception.

It has none. I do not make myself welcome here. My whole flesh; my whole being; is withdrawn upon nothingness. Not even so much am I here as, last night, in the dialogue of those two creatures of darkness. What is taking place here, and it happens daily in this silence, is intimately transacted between this home and eternal space; and consciousness has no residence in nor pertinence to it save only that, privileged by stealth to behold, we fear this legend: withdraw; bow down; nor dare the pride to seek to decipher it:

At this certain time of late morning, then, in the full breadth of summer, here in this dark and shuttered room, through a knothole near the sharp crest of the roof, a signal or designation is made each day in silence and unheeded. A long bright rod of light takes to its end, on the left side of the mantel, one of the small vases of milky and opalescent glass; in such a way, through its throat, and touching nothing else, that from within its self this tholed phial glows its whole shape on the obscurity, a sober grail, or divinity local to this home; and no one watches it, this archaic form, and alabastrine pearl, and captured paring of the phosphor moon, in what inhuman piety and silent fear it shows: and after a half minute it is faded and is changed, and is only a vase with light on it, companion of a never-lighted twin, and they stand in wide balance on the narrow shelf; and now the light has entirely left it, and oblates its roundness on the keen thumbprint of pine wall beside it, and this, slowly, slides, in the torsion of the engined firmament, while the round rind of the planet runs in its modulations like a sea, and along faint Oregon like jackstrewn matches, the roosters startling flame from one another, the darkness is lifted, a steel shade from a storefront.

Here also, his noise a long drawn nerve behind him, the violin wasp returns to his house in the angle of the roof, is silent a half minute, and streams out again beneath eaves upon broad light.

But he: he is not unwelcome here: he is a builder; a tenant. He does not notice; he is no reader of signs.

The return

But now on that hill whose mass is hung as a wave behind us I hear her voice and the voices of her children, and in knowledge of those hidden places I have opened, those griefs, beauties, those garments whom I took out, held to my lips, took odor of, and folded and restored so orderly, so reverently as cerements, or priest the blessÈd cloths, I receive a strong shock at my heart, and I move silently, and quickly.

When at length I hear the innocence of their motions in the rear of the hall, the noise of the rude water and the dipper, I am seated on the front porch with a pencil and an open notebook, and I get up and go toward them.

In some bewilderment, they yet love me, and I, how dearly, them; and trust me, despite hurt and mystery, deep beyond making of such a word as trust.

It is not going to be easy to look into their eyes.

On the Woods' and Ricketts' houses I must be much more brief. Do not, through the relative brevity, presume that they are more sparsely furnished, or that they seem to me of less significance, than the Gudgers' house.

THE WOODS' HOUSE

The Woods' house is set quite far back from the road as I have described. It faces south: first a short yard of tough thick grass and weeds, next its garden plot, whose palings are half down, and beyond this a long deep field of very moderately good cotton. Out at the right of the house there are a log corncrib, a small and rotted barn, and a large convulsed apple tree whose yield is small and sour. It is a three-room house: two rooms built end to end and a kitchen leaned-to the far room from the barn. The single, west room had an opening for a front door and the marks of steps which no longer exist. In front of the door into the far room, there is a porch. It is of soft pine, broken through in one place, and ragged at all the outward ends of the boards. During the afternoon a quilt is hung across nails between two of the posts to guard off the sun. There are two windows in the west room, glassed, and with thin white curtains, and three in the east room, glassed, with no curtains, and one glassed window about eighteen inches square in the kitchen, whose main light and ventilation comes through two opposite doors, one into the yard, the other into the front room. The west room is a bedroom, about ten by twelve feet, empty of floor furniture except for a small tin trunk, a broken hickory-bottom chair, and a three-quarter bed of florid iron spread with a mainly white quilt of uncommonly talented pattern. * On the wall beyond this bed hangs a blunt officer's sword in a rusted scabbard; it was used by an ancestor of Mrs. Woods. Next the door there is a mirror in an early to middle nineteenth century frame of pressed and rusty tin: stars, and an eagle grasping crossed thunder javelins. Along the back wall from nails hang overalls, shirts, and a dirty dress, and a clean dress on a wire hanger.

The east room, about ten feet square, is the combined bedroom and sitting-room. The iron bed is so weak in its joints that Woods has nailed it into the wall. It is unmade and is flung over with a wrecked quilt nearly dead-gray with dirt, the dark, crudded cotton leaking from its wounds. Though none of the outside of the house has ever been touched, the walls of this room and of the kitchen have been white-washed and between the resinous streakings of the grain, the wash still thinly shows. There is an iron ice-cream chair here with a homemade seat of fresh bright pine: and on one table, next the lamp, a pot of paper flowers stemmed with still bright tin; and above this, on the wall, 'Just a Prayer at Twilight,' and on the rear wall, a photograph with caption, cut from some inexplicable magazine, of Barbara Drake, aged three, and of John B. Drake III, aged perhaps six, of Chicago, who has already perfected the poisonous expression which in due time will serve him so well in his social-financial-sexual career. The caption is 'The Little Drakes,' and they sit beside water.

The kitchen, eight feet square, contains chiefly a small and heroic wood stove which has already served the lifetime of one family and is well into another. It falls a little further beyond adequate repairing, however, each time they move, and Woods is sure that the rigors of one more moving will end its usefulness for good. In the opposite side of the kitchen is a small bare table from which they eat; and on the walls, what you may see in one of the photographs.

---

* The work of Mrs. Woods' mother. She also excellently embroidered a pair of pillowcases, in pink-ish-brown thread, following out only the simplest lines and dots a child would draw. One was the head of a man, and a balancing flower; the other, with a flower, the head of a woman.

The Woods' spring

Out behind, ten feet or so of scarred red yard, then the dirt is sharply bent and goes steeply down sixty feet to a near-level: and a little out beyond the lower edge of this bank, a small warm spring, guarded in wooden walls. The bank is steep enough that much of it must be climbed on the hands and knees: but that is necessary only when the device for getting water breaks down. This device, which stands close at the edge of the yard, is called a lazyboy. It consists in a windlass, a rope, a bucket, and a heavy rock. The bucket, which is battered nearly shapeless, is let fall rapidly, for the fun of it; the stone ballast insures that it will strike the water right and fill itself. The rope is sectioned together of pieces of sheeting, small rope, and clothesline, and is frayed in several places to parts of a single strand and is knotted and reknotted where it has broken almost in every foot: the windlass is so insecurely mounted that on the uphill winding it is necessary to guard it against collapse with one hand while you wind with the other: and even so, a third to half the water is sloshed out by the time the bucket comes within reach. Sometimes it will go without much trouble as long as two or three days on end; then, as if it had taken it into its head to be contrary, the rope slips its pulley at the far end, or the crank slips loose under the guarding hand, or the rope breaks in mid-climb, and the whole bucket goes banging to hell and has to be gone down after, as many as one trip in any two.

This water, as I have said, is warm and has an ugly, feathery, sickening taste; they believe it is full of fever. And they strongly attribute this sickness of the water to the fact that the spring is also used by a family of negroes who live beneath them in the hollow. For this reason Pearl will hide in watch at the top of her bank and, when the negro children appear (they always come as a pair; they're afraid to come alone), or even the father and mother, pelts down rocks at them which she has collected, and chunks of wood. And in retaliation, the children have a few times had the courage to slip the rope from its pulley, or once, even, to stand there and empty the bucket three times in a row before, coming to their senses, they stopped laughing and ran as hard as they could go into the woods below. But mainly they know better than to fight back, and try simply to come for their water at times of day when they will be least expected.

The Ricketts' House

The Gudgers' and Woods' houses are solidly of the tenant type and were that when they were new and first built. The Ricketts, living in sight of Woods a few hundred yards further up the road, occupy an entirely different sort of place: that is, a house which was originally the property of the man who lived in it, a small-farmer, not a tenant, and designed and constructed in the order of his class. Whereas, for instance, their houses are of the simplest kind of expanded crate construction imaginable, and are low in proportion to their ground space, and are made of knotty lumber which has never been painted or even whitewashed, this Ricketts home is built as an ordinary lower-middle-class frame house is, and simulates both solidity to the earth and the height and bulk of a second floor which it lacks, and the exterior wood is still rubbed with the last dust and scalings of a dull yellow paint with chocolate trim. Moreover, and again as they are not, it is overhung by two strong large shade trees, and there is a flowering bush in the rubbed, bare, and large though shapeless yard; the barn, though it is now shattered into the look of makeshift and weathered white silver, is barn-size, with actual stalls and a hayloft; and beyond the far side of the house there is a wide pit of rocks and rotted planks surrounding a narrower shaft, . . . at the bottom of this shaft, the scummed and sullen

glitter of a former well, and behind the house another pit and other rotted planks and a sudden violent spume of weeds where there was once
a privy: in fact, a very different and at first glance more prosperous type
of establishment; but this man, whoever he may have been, evidently
lost his house and land, however much he may have cared for and tried
to keep it, and probably by foreclosure, and in all probability to the
Margraves brothers, who now own it, and who drew most of their
twenty-six hundred acres from beneath the feet of just such families
and by just such careful observation of the letter of the law: and this
regardless of the fact that it was from just such a family of small-farm-
ers that they themselves came: so now the house and land are let to tenants; and for four years the tenants have been Fred Ricketts and his
family.

The long side lies along the road. First the side porch and kitchen;
next the bedroom, connected with the kitchen by a windowless hall
bedroom just wide and long enough to hold a three-quarter bed and
still allow passage: this bedroom is the front of the house, which is at
right angles to the road. All across the front of it is a wide porch, the
roof so deep and overhanging that little light can get in by the window
on this side: beyond this porch another large square room built in a
unit to itself; and between this and the main house, the porch is
extended fifteen feet or so back along the side of the house, where in
the last five feet its rotted boards are broken beneath a broken roof,
and above a shallow and evil-smelling pit which was once a basement;
and beyond this, an open stretch of high weeds, and the garden palings, and forward and swept wide on the left, a large field of cotton
which joins the Woods' land; and living here, a man and his wife and
seven of the fifteen children they have brought into existence.

The front porch is the social and resting place and is kept nearly
clear of junk. The floor gives very noticeably, with sounds of warning, under the legs or rockers of any chair an adult weight sits in, and
is caved in in a number of places; yet in general it is still safe, and
the unsteady hickory-bottom and the kitchen rocker, its broken seat

stopped with a cushion, which are not needed at the kitchen table, are always there, along with Clair Bell's infant-size chair.

The side porch along the kitchen is utilitarian: it is littered and in one corner stacked high with lard tins, muleshoes, broken pieces of machinery and tools, all such things as cannot properly be called junk because they are here in the idea that a use will be found for them; and the washstand and cistern are also here. The wash basin is an old and dented hub-cap of the wide disk kind, and there is no soap because it is foolish to waste money that can be eaten with on soap when any fool knows there is nothing cleaner than water. The drinking and cooking water is caught off the roof and routed through crumpled gutterpipes into storage beneath the porch. How sound the walls of this cistern are seems to me of possible importance, 'esthetically' at least, because the wide hole in the hall porch above the former basement, about fifteen feet away, is used for nocturnal convenience. Because this cistern water must be used as sparingly as possible even for drinking and cooking if they are to avoid using the fever-water the Woods have to use, and even so is usually exhausted during the hot part of the summer, the laundry is always done at the Woods' spring, a third of a mile and a steep hill away: and because of this, and because, too, degrees of dirt and the bearable or proper are in a sense so highly relative and social in conception, the laundry is almost never done, and beyond their faces and hands the people, and their clothing and bedding, and their pans and dishes, and their house, are generally by standards other than their own insanely or completely dirty, or almost beyond possibility of being dirtier, short of a deliberated or cult-like acquisition of dirtiness.

Here again as at the Gudgers' there are four rooms; but here again that does not mean what it appears to. The room built independent of the house, though it is quite large, and is the best lighted part of the house, is not used to live in. Several of the windowpanes are broken out and though some of these are stopped with rags and with squares of cardboard, that is not enough: for the whole rear wall of the fireplace is burst through, letting in a large hole of daylight, and the stone chimney has fallen in on itself; and so this room is of no use for living, and there is no furniture in it, but only the odor of apples and the nearly fainting munificent odor of warm muskmelons, in their time, or during picking season the terrible ether odor of hot stored cotton. At the center of the stone chimney, between two windows, and in line above the stove-in tunnel of bright gasping country, hang a hat and a sign. The hat is round, and is homemade of brilliant cornshucks. The sign is made on the smooth side of a rectangle of corrugated cardboard, in blue crayon, part in print and part in a lopside running hand, and reads:

PLEAS!

be

QUITE

and is the relic of a religious effort I will speak of later.

So the living is done in three rooms, the kitchen very spacious, perhaps fifteen feet long by twelve wide, so that in its meager and widely spaced furnishing and empty floor it seems larger than it is; and the front bedroom twelve feet square, filled up thick, mainly with two beds; and the third connecting room so small, dark, and stifled that it seems hardly honest to count it as a 'room.'

But all these three rooms are dark, for that matter. It is partly because of the set of the windows, but it is still more that the once whitewashed walls are so dirty. They have in the course of years absorbed smoke and grease and dirt into a rich dark patine so labored into the wood that sweeping and scrubbing affect it as scarcely as if it were iron; so that even in the kitchen, where two windows are not shaded with porch or trees, but are free to the sky's whole blaze, the brightness though powerful is restricted, fragile and chemical like that of a flash bulb, and is blunted or drowned in the iron blackness of every wall.

These faced surfaces also compel upon the room a steel-hard fragrance of their own and in this air amorphous and hairy as Spanish moss, as slab as old wet garments and corrupted meats, hang the odors of the bedding, and of the cooking, and of the people in the sweating and sleeping between whose hands their living is cradled: but this becomes bearable and generalized, indeed nearly unnoticeable, so that the odor of the eating-table, in the kitchen, is a thing in itself: for here the oilcloth is rotted away into scarcely more than a black net, and the cloth and the wood have stored up smoke and rancid grease and pork and corn and meat to a degree which extends a six-foot globe of almost uncombatable nausea thick and filming as sprayed oil.

In the front room, parallel, heads opposite the fireplace, and filling all their part of the room except the path to the door between them, are two beds not of iron but of wood. One of these beds is of simply designed and not very heavy wood; the other is of dark, heavy and ornate victorian wood, high and florid at the head against the dark plank wall, and scarred and chopped with many years of use, and these are spread with nearly black gashed quilts, considerably further gone than are ordinarily found on dump heaps, and at the heads are pillows, some bare and some in slips, in either case the ticking or slipcloths torn and reduced to a festered gray and the urine yellow that is the stain of hair.

The Ricketts' fireplace

The fireplace opposite these beds is broad and high, and handsome in its Greek panelings.

The Ricketts are much more actively fond of pretty things than the other families are, and have lived here longer than they have, and in obedience of these equations the fireplace wall is crusted deep with attractive pieces of paper into the intricate splendor of a wedding cake or the fan of a white peacock: calendars of snowbound and stag-hunting scenes pressed into bas-relief out of white pulp and glittering with a sand of red and blue and green and gold tinsel, and delicately tinted; other calendars and farm magazine covers or advertisements

of dog-love; the blessèd fireside coziness of the poor; indian virgins
watching their breasts in pools or paddling up moonlit aisles of foliage;
fullblown blondes in luminous frocks leaning back in swings, or taking
coca-cola through straws, or beneath evening palmleaves, accepting
cigarettes from young men in white monkey-coats, happy young housewives at resplendent stoves in sunloved kitchens, husbands in tuxedos
showing guests an oil furnace, old ladies leaning back in rocking chairs,
their hands relaxed in their needlework, their faces bemused in lamplight, happy or mischievous or dog-attended or praying little boys and
girls, great rosy blue-eyed babies sucking their thumbs to the bone in
clouds of pink or blue, closeups of young women bravely and purely
facing the gravest problems of life in the shelter of lysol, portraits of
cakes, roasts of beef, steaming turkeys, and decorated hams, little cards
by duplicate and a series depicting incidents in the life of Jesus with
appropriate verses beneath, rich landscapes with rapid tractors in the
foreground, kittens snarled in yarn, or wearing glasses, or squinting
above pink or blue bows, white bulldogs in tophats wearing monocles,
girls in riding-habits making love to the long heads of horses, color
photographs of summer salads, goateed and ruddy colonels smiling
over cups of coffee or receiving Four Roses whiskey from vicariously
delighted negroes, slenderly drawn little girls, boys, adolescent girls,
adolescent boys, and young matrons in new play frocks, rompers, two-
part playsuits, school frocks, school suits, first-party dresses, first long
suits, sports sweaters, house frocks, afternoon frocks, and beach slacks,
dickensians at Christmas dinner, eighteenth-century gentlemen in a
tavern, medievalists at Christmas dinner, country doctors watching
beside sick children, three-quarter views of locomotives at full speed,
young couples admiring newly acquired brown and brocade daven-
ports: all such as these overlaid in complexes and textured with the
names and numberings of days months years and phases of the moon
and with words and phrases and names such as —'s Shoes; —
Furniture, Hay, Grain and Feed, Yellow Stores, Gen'l Merchandise,
Kelvinator, Compliments of, Wist ye not that I am about my Father's

Business, Mazola, Railroad Age, Maxwell House, They Satisfy, Mexico Mexico, The Pause that Refreshes, Birmingham, The Progressive Farmer, After Six, Congoleum, Farm and Fireside, Love's Gift Divine, You Can't Afford *NOT,* Soft, Lovely Hands, You Owe It to Her, You Owe It to Him, You Owe It to Them, Country Gentleman, Daughters of Jerusalem, weep not for me but for your children, and your children's children, Energize, Save, At Last, Don't Be a Stick-in-the-Mud, et cetera. *

The connecting room is entirely furnished and filled by an iron three-quarter bed and, on the facing wall, by clothes very thickly hung from nail-heads. The two eldest daughters sleep here; four of the younger children sleep in the simpler of the two other beds. Mr. and Mrs. Ricketts and Clair Bell sleep in the large bed. The children sleep either in short shirts or entirely naked.

The kitchen contains the table I have spoken of, surrounded by chairs and a bench; another chair stands out in the middle of the room; near the corner opposite the table is a large, very old, nearly unmanageable, and almost inconceivably foul stove, stacked with unwashed pans; and next this a broken table whose unpainted wood surface is coal black and on which the biscuit dough is made. These are the entire contents of the kitchen.

---

* These are in part by memory, in part composited out of other memory, in part improvised, but do not exceed what was there in abundance, variety, or kind. They are much better recorded in photographs for which there is no room in this volume.

Notes

These notes, which might well be the proper device for any amount of expansion, redefinition and linkage, must be just as brief as I can make them. It will probably be necessary to make unsupported statements, and to raise problems rather than to try to answer them. Of the unsupported statements, please know that I have considered their backgrounds as scrupulously as I am able; and of the problems, that I want to 'answer' or at least to consider them as fully as possible in the course of time.

'Beauty'

It is my belief that such houses as these approximate, or at times by chance achieve, an extraordinary 'beauty.' In part because this is ordinarily neglected or even misrepresented in favor of their shortcomings as shelters; and in part because their esthetic success seems to me even more important than their functional failure; and finally out of the uncontrollable effort to be faithful to my personal predilections, I have neglected function in favor of esthetics. I will try after a little to rectify this (not by denial); but at present, a few more remarks on the 'beauty' itself, and on the moral problems involved in evaluating it.

The houses are built in the 'stinginess,' carelessness, and traditions of an unpersonal agency; they are of the order of 'company' houses. They are furnished, decorated and used in the starved needs, traditions and naiveties of profoundly simple individuals. Thus there are conveyed here two kinds of classicism, essentially different yet related and beautifully euphonious. These classicisms are created of economic need, of local availability, and of local-primitive tradition: and in their purity they are the exclusive property and privilege of the people at the bottom of that world. To those who own and create it this 'beauty' is, however, irrelevant and undiscernible. It is best discernible to those who by economic advantages of training have only a shameful and thief's right to it: and it might be said that they have any 'rights' whatever only in proportion as they recognize the ugliness and disgrace implicit in their privilege of perception. The usual solution, non-perception, or apologetic perception, or contempt for those who perceive and value it, seems to me at least unwise. In fact it seems to me necessary to insist that the beauty of a house, inextricably shaped as it is in an economic and human abomination, is at least as important a part of the fact as the abomination itself: but that one is qualified to insist on this only in proportion as one faces the brunt of his own 'sin' in so doing and the brunt of the meanings, against human beings, of the abomination itself.

But consider this merely as a question raised: for I am in pain and uncertainty as to the answers, and can write no more of it here. *

Another question comes up, of course: are things 'beautiful' which are not intended as such, but which are created in convergences of chance, need, innocence or ignorance, and for entirely irrelevant purposes? I can only answer flatly here: first, that intended beauty is far more a matter of chance and need than the power of intention, and that 'chance' beauty of 'irrelevances' is deeply formed by instincts and needs popularly held to be the property of 'art' alone: second, that matters of

---

* The 'sin,' in my present opinion, is in feeling in the least apologetic for perceiving the beauty of the houses.

'chance' and 'nonintention' can be and are 'beautiful' and are a whole universe to themselves. Or: the Beethoven piano concerto #4 *IS* importantly, among other things, a 'blind' work of 'nature,' of the world and of the human race; and the partition wall of the Gudgers' front bedroom *IS* importantly, among other things, a great tragic poem.

Relations and averages

Briefly again, I want to relate these houses to 'the tenant average' (or averages), so far as I know it, and to other relevant southern houses.

By location or setting in the land, the Gudgers' house is far false to the average: the land is much too uneven, the house is too remote, the cultivated land of one farm is closely walled in by thick woods. By all this appearance it better suggests a frontier house in 1800 in newly cleared country, or a 'mountaineer's' home, than a tenant's.

The Woods' and Ricketts' setting is better. A lonely two miles of low hill road, among a dozen used and three or four abandoned houses, it meets very well one important 'average': that of the inhabitants of the little back roads in the rarely traveled, deeply populated and huge country which lies between the inconceivably narrow horizons of the highways. Yet I must emphatically mention that by still another and perhaps more common 'average,' tenants live in nearly flat and much less timbered country, enough houses in sight of one another to give a sense of a world: so that there is, in a two-mile horizon, or the fledging of a lonely road, the 'feeling' of seeing a large yet little part of an enormously populated yet as enormously attenuated one-trade and monotone city: i.e. a city of nine million, stretched thin against a cottonfield which in turn is drawn over earth three hundred miles one way and sixteen hundred the other.

Again, in certain respects of outward frame and appearance, none of these houses meets an average.

The 'averages' might briefly be described thus:

The one-room shack is of vertical planks, a door at center front and center rear, square shuttered glassless windows, a chimney of clay and sticks; the house is, save for the roof, an almost perfect cube.

The two-room is more often than not a three-room, the third being a leanto. This house is most often made of vertical planks, yet quite often of horizontals, clapboards, or even weatherboards or matched edges. Fairly often a small glass window in the kitchen leanto; the others are square and shuttered. The two doors are at center front and rear, and there is usually a small roofed front porch. The rooms, all end-to-end so that the façade is two rooms wide.

All tenant houses have pretty strongly in common these characteristics: wood unpainted and weathered or once whitewashed and weathered; raised off the ground so that earth and daylight are clear under the whole of them; one of two or three of the simplest conceivable designs; hard bare dirt yard; either no shade or that of a bush; no trees near, the low house is much the tallest thing in sight; no flowers or very few; other very similar or even identical houses visible, several at once, yet in each a look of deep remoteness and solitude; the outbuildings small and low beyond proportion to a 'farm'; the house very clearly an enlarged crate or box, scarcely modified to human use; in the whole establishment the look of the utmost possible extreme of flimsiness and nudity.

Such a house can be mistaken for nothing else in its country except, occasionally, the home of the weakest and poorest sort of small-owner. In turn, what you think of as his 'type' of house can easily turn out to be inhabited by a tenant.

By first appearance Ricketts' place is that of a sloppy but by no means hopeless small-farmer. Seen more clearly, it could still as easily as not be the home of an owner at the bottom of the owning class.

Neither the Woods' nor the Gudgers' house would at all likely belong to a small-owner, no matter how small.

On the other hand, and though they fulfill any number of the 'average' tenant characteristics, they differ seriously in this respect: that they lack the rigid and mass-produced look which comes of the near-identities of the most usual forms. The Gudgers' double-house type, with the open hallway, which incidentally is one of the finest designs I know of, is rare, and must be derived of the double houses of square logs which were the homes of the more substantial frontier and mountain farmers. * The Woods' house by outward shape, shallow, with broad façade and leanto, is nearest the standard or class in tenant type; but having begun as a one-room shack it has two front doors, neither of them at center in the purest boxlike fashion: and I could wish, too, that its walls were of verticals and that it was less closely neighbored by trees.

As against other houses in the vicinity: almost no one in the rural and small-town south lives 'well' or 'handsomely'; the houses aren't even 'kept up' as they are, for instance, in Ohio or New England; and by general it would be said that everyone lives in homes equivalent to the homes of those a full category worse off in the economic-social scale than in the north: with the rare splendor and size of the pre-war plantation mansions vanished, and with the tenant-style home emerged beneath the scale of northern analogy; and, by lack of upkeep or a tradition or fear enforcing upkeep, with each category looking a full grade 'poorer' again than it was by original design.

Further comments on relations and averages

The tenant house as a shell is, then, a thing to itself, created by the tenant system, but having much in common with southern company houses in general. But beyond that, to talk as if tenantry as such were respon-

---

* I remember such square-log double houses in mountain parts of Tennessee. Subsequent to writing this I find them mentioned by Victor Tixier, a Frenchman traveling in Missouri in the 1830's. If I remember rightly, Huckleberry Finn describes one, too.

sible, as is often done or seldom guarded against, is dishonest or ridiculous or ignorant, or in any case deceptive and dangerous. It is dangerous because by wrong assignment of causes it persuades that the 'cure' is possible through means which in fact would have little effect save to delude the saviors into the comfortable idea that nothing more needed doing, or even looking-to. It is deceptive because, in point of fact, by furnishing, by decoration, by crudeness of physical function as shelter, by nearly all that is held to be 'disgraceful' or 'disadvantageous' in the tenant homes, these homes have any amount more than less in common with the homes of the whole poorest class of the *owning* cotton farmers, and with the whole tribe and twinned race of the poorest human beings in the rural and small town and in considerable degree in the urban south; the economic source is nothing so limited as the tenant system but is the whole world-system of which tenantry is one modification; and there are in the people themselves, and in the land and climate, other sources quite as powerful but less easy to define, far less to go about curing: and they are, to suggest them too bluntly, psychological, semantic, traditional, perhaps glandular. I may as well add here that this spread beyond responsibility of the tenant system is true also of every other aspect of disadvantage in their physical and mental living. Pardon so much repetition of what must be obvious to anyone of any semblance of intelligence, but I understand that this particular subject of tenantry is becoming more and more stylish as a focus of 'reform,' * and in view of the people who will suffer and be betrayed at the hands of such 'reformers,' there could never be enough effort to pry their eyes open even a little wider.

---

* Now that we are busy buttering ourselves as the last stronghold of democracy, interest in such embarrassments has tactfully slackened off.

Age

None of the tenants and few landlords have any clear idea of the age of any of the houses, nor can this easily be guessed of the houses themselves, for they have been built in exactly the same patterns and of the same materials for generations: Jesse James' birthplace, for instance (1847), is indistinguishable from tens of thousands of houses all over the south today, Gudger's house is very new (1928), and, excepting the hardness of its wood, is already, in the sense of scale that country imposes, timelessly ancient. The oldest part of Woods' house is I would judge forty to sixty years old; Ricketts', about fifty. But former slave quarters are still used here and there, and from the beginning the tenant types have held a primitive common denominator which has had no reason to change.

General habitability

It is very easy, by mention of, for instance, a fireplace, to make a home or room seem more or less well-appointed than it actually is: also, in my enthusiasm for certain aspects, I have neglected others. I want here briefly to review the houses in terms of their function as shelter.

Even when a wall or roof passes the 'daylight' test, i.e., if, in a darkened room, no light leaks through seams, it is a very poor protection indeed against the weather, particularly the wind wet and coldness of winter: for it is only one thin thickness of wood, surrounding a space which cannot be properly heated. Moreover, a tenant house is open to the weather from all six sides, for the floor is raised, and there are seldom protection boards between floor and earth; and ceilings are not at all common. Holes and broken windows are stopped as well as may be with rags, papers, ropes, raw cotton, and cardboard, but none of this is more than a fraction effective. Only the Ricketts have double walls and,

in their bedroom, a big enough fireplace to heat the room. The others
are large enough only to heat their immediate vicinity; their chimneys
are badly made and do not draw well; the fires cannot be kept going
at night; the bedding is ragged and inadequate; the uncarpeted floors
are very cold. * The warmest and best-protected room at the Gudgers'
is the kitchen. It is too warm in summer. The worst room at the Woods'
is the kitchen. It is too cold in winter. The Ricketts' kitchen is too large
for comfort in winter. The only screen on all three farms is one at
Gudger's. Aside from this, windows and doors are shut tight at night,
in winter against cold, in summer by custom, and against 'the night air,'
and against fever mosquitoes. As I have pointed out, two of Gudger's
four rooms are so badly made as to be uninhabitable. There is no possibility of privacy at any time for any purpose. The water facilities are
such as to hold laundering and personal cleanliness at or beneath its
traditional minimum; to virtual nullity during the cold months of the
year, and, in the case of the Ricketts and Woods, the water is very probably unhealthful. The beds, the bedding, and the vermin are such a
crime against sex and the need of rest as no sadistic genius could much
improve on. The furniture in general and the eating implements are all
at or very near the bottom of their scale: broken, insecure, uncomfortable, ill-smelling, all that a man without money must constantly accept,
when he can get it, and be glad of, or make do. Since I have talked of
'esthetics' the least I can do is to add a note on it in their terms: they
live in a steady shame and insult of discomforts, insecurities, and infe-
riorities, piecing these together into whatever semblance of comfortable living they can, and the whole of it is a stark nakedness of
makeshifts and the lack of means: yet they are also, of course, profoundly anesthetized. The only direct opinion I got on the houses as
such was from Mrs. Gudger, and it was, with the tears coming to her
eyes, 'Oh, I do *hate* this house *so bad*! Seems like they ain't nothing in
the whole world I can do to make it pretty.' As for the anesthesia: it

---

* I speak here in part by deduction, in part by winter experience of analogous houses.

seems to me a little more unfortunate, if possible, to be unconscious of an ill than to be conscious of it; though the deepest and most honest and incontrovertible rationalization of the middle-class southerner is that they are 'used' to it.

'Sanitation' and Lighting

I cannot unqualifiedly excite myself in favor of Rural Electrification, for I am too fond of lamplight. Nor in favor of flush toilets, for I despise and deplore the middle-class American worship of sterility and worship-fear of its own excrement. Yet I will grant or for that matter insist it as important that kerosene light is to electric services what foot and mule travel is to travel by auto and airplane, or what plowed clay is to pavement, and that these daily facts and gulfs have incalculably powerful and in many respects disadvantageous influences upon the mind and body. Because it is part of a similar gulf and lag, the lack of a flush toilet is also of great importance. But here I need not be quite so qualified. These families lack not only 'plumbing' but the 'privies' which are by jest supposed to be the property of any American farmer, and the mail-order catalogues which, again with a loud tee-hee, are supposed to be this farmer's toilet paper. They retire to the bushes; and they clean themselves as well as they can with newspaper if they have any around the house, otherwise with corncobs, twigs, or leaves. To say they are forced in this respect to live 'like animals' is a little silly, for animals have the advantage of them on many counts. I will say, then, that whether or not The Bathroom Beautiful is to be preached to all nations, it is not to their advantage in a 'civilized' world to have to use themselves as the simplest savages do.

RECESSIONAL AND VORTEX

Near Woods' barn on the way to the road there is a small wired enclosure of sloping grass, and during this quiet time of the summer three mules, two of them Ricketts', spend most of their time pasturing there. They are bony, very tough, and badly scarred, and have in their eyes and slanted heads the Mongolian look which is common among cruelly used animals. All three show the galled frames of their harness, and large deep red and green sores are eaten against their more prominent bones: one is afflicted all over his back with some festered eruptive disease peculiarly attractive to the largest of the flies, whose stinging is almost as painful as that of hornets, and every three minutes or so, during hour after hour, after trying first to eat, and to walk under low branches, then, after standing twitching all his hide, slashing with his tail, throwing his head around, and stamping and kicking, still trying to chew the sulphur-colored mash, and finally tightening up, trembling all over, with all his strength he bangs himself against the ground in a shock which you think you feel fifty and which you hear two hundred yards away, and hoofs striking loose and wriggling, belly up, grinds his back so hard that the grass in that space is ripped bare.

There is also a cow named Mooly, who, according to Mrs. Woods, would as soon kill the young ones as not, and who one day last winter knocked Mrs. Woods down and stomped on her, cutting her shins badly, the scars still show, and bruising her from head to foot. She is a young cow and has had one calf, and has been crazy in this way ever since she lost him.

There is also a starved, red young hog, and I remember well how one morning he stood by the front steps fumbling, with his jaws, at the tail of a black kitten, who crouched while this happened, and looked back over his shoulder in apprehension, but who was himself too dazzled with hunger to move or to do more, at length, than spread his red mouth in a scratchy, nearly soundless mew; or even very well to understand that he was being tried out for eating. After a little, though, the hog lost interest and went on, and the kitten sat where he had crouched and licked his thin rat's tail smooth of the jaw slime.

In fact each of the families owns and is drawn-round with animals, for work, for food, or by more vague functions: a mule as one kind of center and leverage, a cow as another, a hog as still another, a dog in different meanings of his own, the tolerated tramp's and robber's life of the cat, the three generations of chickens, the peripheral or parasitic or almost unmagnetized spheres of rats, vermin, insects, and serpents, all in turn sprung round with tended and with random vegetation, and finally, those which lounge in the fields, and the many birds, and those who are hunted; and in any proper account it would be necessary to give such a full record of all these in themselves and in their mutual and human meanings and relationships as is impossible here: for, taking even a single center, the human animals alone, they live in an immediate and most elaborate texture of other forms of existence, of the whole need and fear and spread of nature on their part of the surface of the earth; and this fact is of a significance no less powerful and shaping through the mere impossibility of measuring it. Yet here I can make only the briefest sort of tally.

Gudger: the heavy, deranged yellow rooster of whom I have spoken. A clutter of obese, louse-tormented hens whose bodies end dirtily, like sheaves of barley left in rain. Several neat broilers, and a few quilly, half-grown chicks whose heads are still like lizards'. A pair of guineas whose small painted heads and metal bodies thread these surroundings like the exotic glint of naturalistic dreams. A sober, dark-brown, middle-sized dog named Rowdy, who, though he is most strictly suggestible in his resemblance to André Gide, is nevertheless as intensely of his nation, region, and class as Gudger himself. A puppy named Sipco. Two highlegged, rusty, flat-sided young hogs for whom Gudger paid his landlord nine dollars when they were shoats. A cow, tethered from spot to spot in the green stretches, and her calf. A half-grown reptilian cat named Nigger, * so black he is iridescent in the sun. A nameless adolescent tiger cat who just took up with them. And a rented mule, who was not on hand during our time there.

Gudger got the cow in exchange for a grafanola. She has never been much good for milk. The hogs will be fattened and killed in the fall, for next winter. The hens furnish eggs in season and one of them is eaten every now and then. Once in a while they find guinea eggs but guineas are wild and crafty in hiding their nests. In the fall, Gudger usually affords a box of shells for the possibility of fresh meat and goes out to kill it: rabbits, squirrels, or possum. Rowdy is a fair rabbit dog when he puts his mind to it, but good for nothing else; he is kept because dogs are a habit. Sipco is Louise's pet. She picked him up from some people down across the highway. The cats are good for nothing at all; it isn't often they even kill a rat.

Woods' animals, excepting the chickens, I have mentioned. He has no dog, and this alone would set him apart in that country as an unconventional man. The Ricketts, besides their mules, have a good cow and a bull calf, three dogs, very few chickens in ratio to the size of their family, a cat, and a kitten. The dogs are all mongrel rural hounds with the sycophantic eyes and hula hips of their kind in that country, more hopeful and more pleasantly treated than Rowdy, though hungrier. Indeed, they are almost alarmingly rickety: yet they are fatted to bland-

---

* My apologies to the more strict left-wingers: the name is Negro.

ness as compared to the black kitten, not much bigger than a beetle, whose motions along the vast floors are those of an impaired clockwork toy, and whose hide is drawn open red along the entire skeleton. The names of two of the dogs are Sport and Queenie. The cat, whose name is Hazel, which perfectly identifies her, is big enough to get what food she needs. Two of the roosters are named Tom and George. Two of the hens are named Ivy and Annie Mae. This naming of poultry is not common and indicates, if you like, the relative 'primitivism' of the Ricketts; though it also indicates less sociological and more attractive things about them; though these in turn are more difficult to define, or even to understand, and would be merely tiresome to those whose intelligence is set entirely on Improving the Sharecropper, and who feel there's no time to waste on petty detail. These same rapid marchers * in the human vanguard will be equally uninterested in the fact that Mrs. Woods' mother calls babies coons and baby chickens sings, or worse still will nod patronizing 'howsweet' approval or somehow manage to capitalize it politically or against landowners as the unvanquishable poetry of the oppressed, but I will put it on record all the same, and will venture to say that it is more valuable than they think it is, or, for that matter, than they are.

Children are strictly trained not to use cows too roughly: not, for instance, to kick their udders: it is liable to damage the milk supply. A mule is another matter. Even in harnessing him his head is knocked around some, and in all his motions relevant to his users he is used with the gratuitous sort of toughness an American policeman uses against anyone (except the right people) who happens to fall into his power: and this in part for the same 'reasons': get hard before the victim does; or before, in the case of the mule, he gets stubborn or tricky. And in fact mules are in general balky and tricky; I think they are probably in part extremely intelligent and in part insane, and are far less pli-

---

* Wearing Enna Jettick and W. L. Douglas shoes by day, Liggett sandals (made in U.S.A.) and Russian Gift Shop Peasant Pantoufles by night.

able to the reaction of the white, which is to beat, than to that of the negro, which, though with its full share of cruelty, is to converse. In any case if a mule gets tricky, or still worse if he balks, he is in for a physical contest and for hell with any average white farmer; and this farmer is liable to be an expert within the whole range of bullying, battering, and torturing this particular animal, and to have peculiarly urgent egoistic and sexual need to exert full violence and domination over something living, preferably something at least as large and strong as himself. It should be added, in further suggestion, that the mule stands readier victim than any other animal because he is used in the main and most hopeless work, because he is an immediate symbol of this work, and because by transference he is the farmer himself, and in the long tandem harness wherein members and forces of a whole world beat and use and drive and force each other, if they are to live at all, is the one creature in front of this farmer. But any proper set of suggestions, far less statements about this, and about the causes and kinds of sadism in the South, would require more space, time, and understanding than I have at present. Here I can only say that in the people of this country you care most for, pretty nearly without exception you must reckon in traits, needs, diseases, and above all mere natural habits, differing from our own, of a casualness, apathy, self-interest, unconscious, offhand, and deliberated cruelty, in relation toward extra-human life and toward negroes, terrible enough to freeze your blood or to break your heart or to propel you toward murder; and that you must reckon them as 'innocent' even of the worst of this; and must realize that it is at least unlikely that enough of the causes can ever be altered, or pressures withdrawn, to make much difference.

I could tell you details, most of them casual enough, in extension of what I am speaking of, and I could a good deal further explain and guess at the causes, but I think I had better defer all of that until I have more room and understand it better, and here will add only a few short notes.

Animals are fed and cared for in proportion to their usefulness: the

cow and mule and hogs first, then the dogs, et cetera. Cats are casually but thoroughly disliked and are given nothing; they are never fed,
far less caressed; yet their presence and certain forms of theft are tolerated. Or again: dogs are never kindly touched by adults, unless they
are puppies; the children play with them in the usual mixed affection
and torture; the Gudgers feed Rowdy rather irregularly from their
plates, seldom with a floor plate of his own; the Ricketts put down a
plate for their dogs; the cats grab what they can at the end of a meal or
from the dogs' plate. Children are very casually reproved, after the
screaming has become noisy enough, for mistreatment of kittens; dogs,
if they blunder into the way or are slow in obeying an order, are kicked
hard enough to crack their ribs, and, in that manner which has inspired
man to call them, in competition only with his mother, his best friend,
offer their immediate apologies; the sickness or suffering in sickness or
death of any animal which has no function as food or power goes
almost unnoticed, though not at all unkindly so.

The snakes are blacksnakes, garter snakes, milk snakes, hoop
snakes, bull snakes, grass snakes, water moccasins, copperheads, and
rattlers. Milk snakes hang around barns and suck the cows' tits; hoop
snakes take their tails in their mouths and run off like hoops; bull
snakes swell up and roar like a bull when they are cornered; grass
snakes are green, small, and pretty; rattlers are used as amulets by
whites as well as negroes; copperheads are the worst snakes of all. None
of these are common in the sense of daily appearance, but they are by
no means rare, and during the hot months of the year everyone is reasonably watchful where he walks — But it is unhappy to write of animals when there is no time to write of them properly; so likewise with
the plants: and so, in only a few more words, merely the suggestion of
what is textured within any one of these silent and simple-appearing
horizons and of what in and around even one of these blank wood
houses is sewn into these human lives: on the leather land, and sleeping of swamps, and sliding of streamed water, in light and deep shade,
are poured up hickories, red oaks, cottonwoods, pines, junipers, cedars,

chestnuts, locusts, black walnuts, swamp willow, crabapple, wild plum, holly, laurel, chinaberry, May apple, arbutus, honeysuckle, trumpet vine, goldenrod, all kinds of wild daisies, many ferns, corn, cotton, sorghum cane, watermelon vines, muskmelons, peanuts, yams, sweet potatoes, irish potatoes, three kinds of bean, field peas, okra, tomatoes, turnips, fennel, ragweed, jimpson weed: and these are netted through with the traffic and simmering of bees and of wasps and hornets and snakedoctors, and with the needs and the leisures of rabbits, red squirrels, gray squirrels, opossums, raccoons, wild razorbacks, wildcats, perhaps rare foxes, and spiders spread ghosts of suns between branches and start along water, and tadpoles and frogs are in the water and frogs on the earth and trees, and arrowy minnows, and mud turtles, and land tortoises with their curious odor, and the trees are glanded with the nests of birds and the air is streamed and sparkled with their singing, and ribboned and streamered with their flight, the sparrows, ricebirds, thrushes, catbirds, mockingbirds, jays, red-winged blackbirds, cardinals, and groaning and flauting doves, the robins and the sharp wrens, the diamond hummingbirds and their wincing song, sustained in their vibrating spheres, and by night the screechowl and the whippoorwill, the crickets and the roaring frogs, the luna dozing in the daylit swamp, the monarchs and the fields flown low with yellow paper twinkling in the sun, and at the house, the hens who dab and thud at the mealy dung which the puppy or, weightily, the littlest child has disposed on the porch floor, and who, finished, clean their beaks against the oak, their eyes blue with autoerotism, the clatter of the swift and afric guineas, the wasps lance in the eaves and the dark, hot roof, the corn and the trees move as if a great page were being turned, the cat stalks a horned toad who will be too swift, the flies do what they can between now and dinner time, the bedbugs sleep, and so do the rats who tonight will skitter and thump and gnaw and fight the cats, and the dog dozes in shade, and the white puppy, his bowels bursting with petrified food, waddles along the shaded back yard close against the house, his nose to the bare clay, and out toward the spring the cow stands in the shade, working her jaws, and suspending upon creation the wide amber holy lamp of her consciousness, and at a gap in his pen next winter's meat hopefully dilates his slimy disk: and dinner, and they are all drawn into the one and hottest room, the parents; the children; and beneath the table the dog and the puppy and the sliding cats, and above it, a grizzling literal darkness of flies, and spread on all quarters, the simmering dream held in this horizon yet overflowing it, and of the natural world, and eighty miles back east and north, the hard flat incurable sore of Birmingham.

Meanwhile the floor, the roof, the opposed walls, the furniture, in their hot gloom: all watch upon one hollow center. The intricate tissue is motionless. The swan, the hidden needle, hold their course. On the red-gold wall sleeps a long, faded, ellipsoid smear of light. The vase is dark. Upon the leisures of the earth the whole home is lifted before the approach of darkness as a boat and as a sacrament.

(On the Porch: 2

Weelay on the front porch. The boards were unplaned thick oak, of uneven length, pinned down by twenty-penny nails. A light roof stuck out its tongue above us dark and squarely, sustained at its outward edge by the slippery trunks of four young trees from which the bark had been peeled. There were four steps down, oak two-by-twelves; the fourth, when stepped on, touched the ground. These steps were at the middle of the porch. They led, across the porch, into a roofed doorless hallway, about six feet wide, which ran straight through the house and clove it in half. There was a floor to this hallway, of wide unplaned boards. Laid across beams too wide apart, they sagged beneath a heavy foot. For ten feet toward the rear end they were only an inch from the ground. At the end they lay flush on it.

We lay on the front porch to the left of the hall as you enter. One of us lay on the rear seat of a chevrolet sedan, the other on a piece of thin cotton-filled quilting taken from the seat of a divan made of withes. We exchanged these night by night. The problem with the auto seat was its height on one side and lowness on the other, its shortness, and its texture. By letting the center of your weight fall far enough on the high side it was possible to effect a compromise by which you had the benefit of a fair amount of the width of the seat and yet were not rolled off it. Lying with the head on the seat, the lower end gave out abruptly a

few inches above the knee: so you slept best on the back, or, curled, on
the side. Sleeping on the belly, you made sustaining springs of your
feet, and this was slightly and invariably reminiscent of sexual intercourse. A handkerchief or towel under the cheek was helpful while it
lasted but generally managed to slip loose while you slept so that, waking, your cheek was red and burnt with the friction of warmed plush.
Before long, of course, it occurred to us to level up the seat by stacking books under the low side. That was better; but even so, the springs
were strong and large on one side and small and weak on the other.
Our bodies learned to adjust themselves to holding a tension of balance while they were unconscious.

Beyond a not unreasonable phobia that it contained bedbugs, or
lice, or both, there was no difficulty about the pallet. It was thin; the
hard boards and their ridges printed themselves on the flesh distinctly
through it. It was short, but, being so thin, offered no inconvenience to
the length of legbone. Its texture was soft and leaky. Here again you
spread a handkerchief or shirt or towel for your head; and again it was
liable to get away from you. Waking, feeling on your face the almost
slimy softness of loose cotton lint and of fragile, much washed, torn cotton cloth, and immediately remembering your fear of the vermin it
might be harboring, your first reactions were of light disgust and fear,
for your face, which was swollen and damp with sleep and skimmed
with lint, felt fouled, secretly and dirtily bitten and drawn of blood,
insulted. This always wore off within a few moments, but always on
first waking you had it full strength.

We kept exchanging not because one was preferable to the other
but because there was no way of making up our minds that either was
preferable. I perhaps very slightly preferred the pallet, in part because
I like the finality and immediacy of floors and too because the children
were sleeping on pallets. The auto seat, like virtually everything else
about us, was not so near the norm of what we were living in as we
might have wished. But the feeling and sound of the yielding springs,
the always slightly comic postures of your discommoded legs, and the
texture of plush, like a night on a daycoach, under the lips and cheeks,

made it attractive under the body, and brought with it, into a time of celibacy, a pleasing, nostalgic drift of memory and imagination. Even risking the Sportsmanlike way in which this could be misread, and which I despise, neither of them was at all a bad bed.

The dead oak and pine, the ground, the dew, the air, the whole realm of what our bodies lay in and our minds in silence wandered, walked in, swam in, watched upon, was delicately fragrant as a paradise, and, like all that is best, was loose, light, casual, totally *actual*. There was, by our minds, our memories, our thoughts and feelings, some combination, some generalizing, some art, and science; but none of the close-kneed priggishness of science, and none of the formalism and straining and lily-gilding of art. All the length of the body and all its parts and functions were participating, and were being realized and rewarded, inseparable from the mind, identical with it: and all, everything, that the mind touched, was actuality, and all, everything, that the mind touched turned immediately, yet without in the least losing the quality of its total individuality, into joy and truth, or rather, revealed, of its self, truth, which in its very nature was joy, which must be the end of art, of investigation, and of all anyhow human existence.

This situation is possible at any junction of time, space and consciousness: and just as (at least so far as we can know and can be concerned) it is our consciousness alone, in the end, that we have to thank for joy, so too it is our consciousness alone that is defective when we fall short of it. It is curious, and unfortunate, that we find this luck so rarely; that it is so almost purely a matter of chance: yet that, as matters are, becomes inextricably a part of the whole texture of the pleasure: at such a time we have knowledge that we are witnessing, taking part in, being, a phenomenon analogous to that shrewd complex of the equations of infinite chance which became, on this early earth, out of lifelessness, life. No doubt we overvalue the difference between life and lifelessness, but there is a certain difference, just as, in the situation we are speaking of, a difference is remarkable: the difference between a conjunction of time, place and unconscious consciousness and a con-

junction of time, place and conscious consciousness is, so far as we are
concerned, the difference between joy and truth and the lack of joy and
truth. Unless wonder is nothing in itself, but only a moon which glows
only in the mercy of a sense of wonder, and unless the sense of wonder is peculiar to consciousness and is moreover an emotion which, as
it matures, consciousness will learn the juvenility of, and discard, or
only gratefully refresh itself under the power of as under the power of
sleep and the healing vitality of dreams, and all this seems a little more
likely than not, the materials which people any intersection of time and
place are at all times marvelous, regardless of consciousness: and in
either or any case we may do well to question whether there is anything
more marvelous or more valuable in the state of being we distinguish
as 'life' than in the state of being of a stone, the brainless energy of a
star, the diffuse existence of space. Certainly life is valuable; indispen-
sable to all our personal calculations, the very spine of them: but we
should realize that life and consciousness are only the special crutches
of the living and the conscious, and that in setting as we do so high a
value by them we are in a certain degree making a virtue of necessity;
are being provincial; are pleading a local cause: like that small Nevada
town whose pride, because it is its chiefly discernible exclusive distinction, is a mineral spring whose water, assisted by salt and pepper,
tastes remarkably like chicken soup.

This lucky situation of joy, this at least illusion of personal wholeness or integrity, can overcome one suddenly by any one of any number of unpredictable chances: the fracture of sunlight on the façade and
traffic of a street; the sleaving up of chimneysmoke; the rich lifting of
the voice of a train along the darkness; the memory of a phrase of an
inspired trumpet; the odor of scorched cloth, of a car's exhaust, of a
girl, of pork, of beeswax on hot iron, of young leaves, of peanuts; the
look of a toy fire engine, or of a hundred agates sacked in red cheese-
cloth; the oily sliding sound as a pumpgun is broken; the look of a
child's underwaist with its bone buttons loose on little cotton straps;
the stiffening of snow in a wool glove; the odor of kitchen soap, of baby

soap, of scorched bellybands: the flexion of a hand; the twist of a knee; the modulations in a thigh as someone gets out of a chair: the bending of a speeding car round a graded curve: the swollen, blemished feeling of the mouth and the tenacity and thickness of odor of an unfamiliar powder, walking sleepless in high industrial daybreak and needing coffee, the taste of cheap gin mixed with cheap ginger ale without much ice: the taste of turnip greens; of a rotted seed drawn from between the teeth; of rye whiskey in the green celluloid glass of a hotel bathroom: the breath that comes out of a motion-picture theater: the memory of the piccolo notes which ride and transfix Beethoven's pastoral storm: the odor of a freshly printed newspaper; the stench of ferns trapped in the hot sunlight of a bay window; the taste of a mountain summer night: the swaying and shuffling beneath the body of a benighted train; the mulled and branny earth beneath the feet in fall; a memory of plainsong or of the first half hour after receiving a childhood absolution; the sudden re-realization of a light-year in literal, physical terms, or of the shimmering dance and diffuseness of a mass of granite: aside from such sudden attacks from unforeseen directions, gifts which as a rule are as precarious and transient as the returns and illusions of love for a girl one no longer loves, there are few ways it can give itself to you. Wandering alone; in sickness; on trains or busses; in the course of a bad hangover; in any rare situation which breaks down or lowers our habitual impatience, superficial vitality, overeagerness to clinch conclusions, and laziness. We were at this time, and in all the time surrounding it, in such a situation; nor could we for an instant have escaped it, even if we had wished to. At times, exhausted by it, we did wish to and did try, but even when our minds were most exhausted and most deafened such breath as we got, and subsisted on, no matter what its change of constituence and odor (and it now somewhat falsely seems to me that this change occurred with every breath drawn) was the breath of the same continuous excitement; an excitement whose nature seems to me not only finally but essentially beyond the power of an art to convey.

*

We lay on our backs about two feet apart in silence, our eyes open, listening. The land that was under us lay down all around us and its continuance was enormous as if we were chips or matches floated, holding their own by their very minuteness, at a great distance out upon the surface of a tenderly laboring sea. The sky was even larger.

Officially, so far as human beings were concerned; and literally; much of this great surface and pace of land had fallen subject to the instruments and ritual actions of human need. Much of it was cultivated for immediate subsistence or for somebody's profit. It was scattered with houses, most of them more like than unlike the house on whose front porch we lay; thinly scattered with houses; much more thinly with towns; very remotely with cities.

Human beings, with the assistance of mules, worked this land so that they might live. The sphere of power of a single human family and a mule is small; and within the limits of each of these small spheres the essential human frailty, the ultimately mortal wound which is living and the indignant strength not to perish, had erected against its hostile surroundings this scab, this shelter for a family and its animals: so that the fields, the houses, the towns, the cities, expressed themselves upon the grieved membrane of the earth in the symmetry of a disease: the literal symmetry of the literal disease of which they were literally so essential a part.

The prime generic inescapable stage of this disease is being. A special complication is life. A malignant variant of this complication is consciousness. The most complex and malignant form of it known to us is human consciousness. Even in its simplest form this sore raises its scab: all substance is this scab: the scab and the sore are one. Taking shape and complexity precisely in proportion to the shape and complexity of the disease; identical with it, in fact; this identical wound and scab fills out not merely all substance and all process and contrivance of substance but the most intangible reaches of thought, deduction and imagination; the exactitude of its expression may be seen in the skull that scabs a brain, in the deity the race has erected to shield it from the horror of the heavens, in the pressed tin wall of a small restaurant where some of the Greek disease persists through the persistence of a Renaissance disease: in every thing within and probably in anything outside human conception; and in every combination and mutation of these things: and in a certain important sense let it be remembered that in these terms, in terms, that is to say, of the manifestations of being, taken as such, which are always strict and perfect, nothing can be held untrue. A falsehood is entirely true to those derangements which produced it and which made it impossible that it should emerge in truth; and an examination of it may reveal more of the 'true' 'truth' than any more direct attempt upon the 'true' 'truth' itself.

A few words also on symmetry:

On perfectly regular land, of perfectly regular quality, under perfectly regular weather or rhythms of weather, this symmetry would have the simple absoluteness which in fact it approaches in parts of the middle west of this country, just as by other roads, under other pressures, it approaches simple absoluteness under the imposed rigors of a city, a company town, a series of machines, utter poverty, a flower, a strongly organized religion, a sonata, or a beehive. But it is a symmetry sensitive to shape and quality of land, to irregularities and chances of weather, to the chance strength or weakness and productivity of the individual man or mule, to the chance or lack or efficacy or relative obsolescence of machinery, to meteorological, geological, historic, physical, biologic, mental chance: to other matters which I lack the imagination here to consider. Yet of these irregularities of complex equations, which are probably never repeated, inevitabilities infallibly take their shape. Symmetry as we use it here, then, needs a little further examination. Because it is a symmetry sensitive to so many syncopations of chance (all of which have proceeded inevitably out of chances which were inevitable), it is in fact asymmetrical, like Oriental art. * But also, because it is so pliant, so exquisitely obedient before the infinite irreg-

---

* As I have been told is basic to Chinese art.

ularities of chance, it reachieves the symmetry it had by that docility lost on a 'higher' plane: on a plane in any case that is more complex, more comprehensive, born of a subtler, more numerous, less obvious orchestration of causes. This asymmetry now seems to us to extend itself into a worrying even of the rigid dances of atoms and of galaxies, so that we can no longer with any certitude picture ourselves as an egregiously complicated flurry and convolved cloud of chance sustained between two simplicities.

This hearing and seeing of a complex music in every effect and in causes of every effect and in the effects of which this effect will be part cause, and the more than reasonable suspicion that there is at all times further music involved there, beyond the simple equipment of our senses and their powers of reflection and deduction to apprehend, 'gets' us perhaps nowhere. One reason it gets us nowhere is that in a very small degree, yet an absolute one so far as each of us is capable, we are already there: and we take another step still closer when we realize that the symmetry and the disease are identical. In this small but absolute degree then, we are already there. That is one strong argument in favor of art which proves and asserts nothing but which exists, as has been dangerously guessed at, for its own sake. (It could also be said of 'problem' art that severe and otherwise insolvable human and spiritual problems are solved in every performance of, or for that matter in the silent existence of, say, Beethoven's quartet Opus 131.) It is a still stronger part of an argument, which, I grant, cannot apply on all 'levels' in all contexts, against art of any sort from the most 'pure' to the most diluted or the most involved in matters supposedly irrelevant to art. How many, not only of the salient and obvious but more particularly of the casual passages in our experience, carry a value, joy, strength, validity, beauty, wholeness, radiance, of which we must admit not only that they equal in their worthiness as a part of human experience, and of existence, the greatest works of art but, quite as seriously, that the best art quite as powerfully as the worst manages, in the very process of digesting them into art, to distort, falsify and even to obliterate them.

Without any qualification and if necessary with belligerence I respect and believe in even the most supposedly 'fantastic' works of the imagination. I am indeed ready to say, because with fair consistency I believe, that works of the imagination (chiefly because * in a certain degree they create something which has never existed before, they add to and somewhat clarify the sum total of the state of being, whereas the rest of the mind's activity is merely deductive, descriptive, acquisitive or contemplative) advance and assist the human race, and make an opening in the darkness around it, as nothing else can. But art and the imagination are capable of being harmful, and it is probably neither healthy for them nor, which is more to the point, anywhere near true even to the plainest facts, to rate them so singly high. It seems to me there is quite as considerable value (to say nothing of joy) in the attempt to see or to convey even some single thing as nearly as possible as that thing is. I grant the clarifying power in this effort of the memory and the imagination: but they are quite as capable of muddying as of clearing the water and frequently indeed, so frequently that we may suspect a law in ambush, they do both at the same time, clouding in one way the thing they are clearing in another.

George Gudger is a human being, a man, not like any other human being so much as he is like himself. I could invent incidents, appearances, additions to his character, background, surroundings, future, which might well point up and indicate and clinch things relevant to him which in fact I am sure are true, and important, and which George Gudger unchanged and undecorated would not indicate and perhaps could not even suggest. The result, if I was lucky, could be a work of art. But somehow a much more important, and dignified, and true fact about him than I could conceivably invent, though I were an illimitably better artist than I am, is that fact that he is exactly, down to the last inch and instant, who, what, where, when and why he is. He is in those terms living, right now, in flesh and blood and breathing, in an actual part of a world in which also, quite as irrelevant to imagination,

---

* And for many other still more powerful and less 'useful' reasons.

you and I are living. Granted that beside that fact it is a small thing, and granted also that it is essentially and finally a hopeless one, to try merely to reproduce and communicate his living as nearly exactly as possible, nevertheless I can think of no worthier and many worse subjects of attempt.

The same seems to me true of every item in the experience of which I am speaking, and I could say it with equal sincerity of conviction of all human experience. Moreover, and especially if you bear in mind such structures as those of disease and symmetry I sketched out a little, I cannot see how such a piece of work could be small in intensity, 'truth,' complex richness and stature of form and nature, as compared with a work of art. Calling for the moment everything except art Nature, I would insist that everything in Nature, every most casual thing, has an inevitability and perfection which art as such can only approach, and shares in fact, not as art, but as the part of Nature that it is; so that, for instance, a contour map is at least as considerably an image of absolute 'beauty' as the counterpoints of Bach which it happens to resemble. I would further insist that it would do human beings, including artists, no harm to recognize this fact, and to bear it in mind in their seining of experience, and to come as closely as they may be able, to recording and reproducing it for its own, not for art's sake.

One reason I so deeply care for the camera is just this. So far as it goes (which is, in its own realm, as absolute anyhow as the traveling distance of words or sound), and handled cleanly and literally in its own terms, as an ice-cold, some ways limited, some ways more capable, eye, it is, like the phonograph record and like scientific instruments and unlike any other leverage of art, incapable of recording anything but absolute, dry truth.

Who, what, where, when and why (or how) is the primal cliché and complacency of journalism: but I do not wish to appear to speak favorably of journalism. I have never yet seen a piece of journalism which

conveyed more than the slightest fraction of what any even moderately reflective and sensitive person would mean and intend by those
inachievable words, and that fraction itself I have never seen clean of
one or another degree of patent, to say nothing of essential, falsehood.
Journalism is true in the sense that everything is true to the state of
being and to what conditioned and produced it * (which is also, but
less so perhaps, a limitation of art and science): but that is about as far
as its value goes. This is not to accuse or despise journalism for anything beyond its own complacent delusion, and its enormous power to
poison the public with the same delusion, that it is telling the truth
even of what it tells of. Journalism can within its own limits be 'good'
or 'bad,' 'true' or 'false,' but it is not in the nature of journalism even to
approach any less relative degree of truth. Again, journalism is not to
be blamed † for this; no more than a cow is to be blamed for not being
a horse. The difference is, and the reason one can respect or anyhow
approve of the cow, that few cows can have the delusion or even the
desire to be horses, and that none of them could get away with it even
with a small part of the public. The very blood and semen of journalism, on the contrary, is a broad and successful form of lying. Remove
that form of lying and you no longer have journalism.

Nor am I speaking of 'naturalism,' 'realism': though just here may
be the sharpest and most slippery watershed within this first discussion.

Trying, let us say, to represent, to reproduce, a certain city street,
under the conviction that nothing is as important, as sublime, as truly
poetic about that street in its flotation upon time and space as the street
itself. Your medium, unfortunately, is not a still or moving camera, but
is words. You abjure all metaphor, symbol, selection and above all, of

---

* Looked at in this way a page of newspaper can have all the wealth of a sheet of fossils, or a
painting.
† Why not.

course, all temptation to invent, as obstructive, false, artistic. As nearly as possible in words (which, even by grace of genius, would not be very near) you try to give the street *in its own terms:* that is to say, either in the terms in which you (or an imagined character) see it, or in a reduction and depersonalization into terms which will as nearly as possible be the 'private,' singular terms of that asphalt, those neon letters, those and all other items combined, into that alternation, that simultaneity, of flat blank tremendously constructed chords and of immensely elaborate counterpoint which is the street itself. You hold then strictly to materials, forms, colors, bulks, textures, space relations, shapes of light and shade, peculiarities, specializations, of architecture and of lettering, noises of motors and brakes and shoes, odors of exhausts: all this gathers time and weightiness which the street does not of itself have: it sags with this length and weight: and what have you in the end but a somewhat overblown passage from a naturalistic novel: which in important ways is at the opposite pole from your intentions, from what you have seen, from the fact itself.

The language of 'reality' (in the sense of 'reality' we are trying to speak of here) may be the most beautiful and powerful but certainly it must in any case be about the heaviest of all languages. That it should have and impart the deftness, keenness, immediacy, speed and subtlety of the 'reality' it tries to reproduce, would require incredible strength and trained skill on the part of the handler, and would perhaps also require an audience, or the illusion of an audience, equally well trained in catching what is thrown: an audience to whom the complex joke can simply be told, without the necessity for a preceding explanation fifteen times the length of the joke which founders every value the joke of itself has. I know of no one with this particular training or interest who is using words, though one man, at least, is doing even more difficult and more valuable things.

For the camera, much of this is solved from the start: is solved so simply, for that matter, that this ease becomes the greatest danger against the good use of the camera.

Words could, I believe, be made to do or to tell anything within human conceit. That is more than can be said of the instruments of any other art. But it must be added of words that they are the most inevitably inaccurate of all mediums of record and communication, and that they come at many of the things which they alone can do by such a Rube Goldberg articulation of frauds, compromises, artful dodges and tenth removes as would fatten any other art into apoplexy if the art were not first shamed out of existence: and which, in two centrally important and inescapable ways: falsification (through inaccuracy of meaning as well as inaccuracy of emotion); and inability to communicate simultaneity with any immediacy; greatly impairs the value and the integrity of their achievement. It may, however, be added: words like all else are limited by certain laws. To call their achievement crippled in relation to what they have tried to convey may be all very well: but to call them crippled in their completely healthful obedience to their own nature is again a mistake: the same mistake as the accusation of a cow for her unhorsiness. And if you here say: 'But the cow words are trying to be a horse,' the answer is: 'That attempt is one of the strongest laws of language, just as it is no law at all so far as cows are concerned.' In obeying this law words are not, then, at all necessarily accusable, any more than in disobeying it. The cleansing and rectification of language, the breakdown of the identification of word and object, is very important, and very possibly more important things will come of it than have ever come of the lingual desire of the cow for the horse: but it is nevertheless another matter whenever words start functioning in the command of the ancient cow-horse law. Human beings may be more and more aware of being awake, but they are still incapable of not dreaming; and a fish forswears water for air at his own peril.

I doubt that the straight 'naturalist' very well understands what music and poetry are about. That would be all right if he understood his materials so intensely that music and poetry seemed less than his intention; but I doubt he does that, too. That is why his work even at best is never much more than documentary. Not that documentation has not great dignity and value; it has; and as good 'poetry' can be extracted from it as from living itself: but the documentation is not of itself either poetry or music and it is not, of itself, of any value equivalent to theirs. So that, if you share the naturalist's regard for the 'real,' but have this regard for it on a plane which in your mind brings it level in value at least to music and poetry, which in turn you value as highly as anything on earth, it is important that your representation of 'reality' does not sag into, or become one with, naturalism; and in so far as it does, you have sinned, that is, you have fallen short even of the relative truth you have perceived and intended. And if, anti-artistically, you desire not only to present but to talk about what you present and how you try to present it, then one of your first anxieties, in advance of failure foreseen, is to make clear that a sin is a sin.

I feel sure in advance that any efforts, in what follows, along the lines I have been speaking of, will be failures. *

'Description' is a word to suspect.

Words cannot embody; they can only describe. But a certain kind of artist, whom we will distinguish from others as a poet rather than a prose writer, despises this fact about words or his medium, and continually brings words as near as he can to an illusion of embodiment. In doing so he accepts a falsehood but makes, of a sort in any case, better art. It seems very possibly true that art's superiority over science and over all other forms of human activity, and its inferiority to them, reside in the identical fact that art accepts the most dangerous and impossible of bargains and makes the best of it, becoming, as a result, both nearer the truth and farther from it than those things which, like science and scientific art, merely describe, and those things which, like human beings and their creations and the entire state of nature, merely are, the truth.

---

* Failure, indeed, is almost as strongly an obligation as an inevitability, in such work: and therein sits the deadliest trap of the exhausted conscience.

Most young writers and artists roll around in description like honeymooners on a bed. It comes easier to them than anything else. In the course of years they grow or discipline themselves out of it. At best they are undoubtedly right in doing so. But again I suspect that the lust for describing, and that lust in action, is not necessarily a vice. Plain objects and atmospheres have a sufficient intrinsic beauty and stature that it might be well if the describer became more rather than less shameless: if objects and atmospheres for the secret sake of which it is customary to write a story or poem, and which are chronically relegated to a menial level of decoration or at best illumination, were handled and presented on their own merits without either distortion or apology. Since when has a landscape painter apologized for painting landscapes; * and since when, again, should a cow put on a false beard and play horse or, on the other hand, blush and dither over the excellent fact of being a good plain cow, a creature no horse can ever be?

George Gudger is a man, et cetera. But obviously, in the effort to tell of him (by example) as truthfully as I can, I am limited. I know him only so far as I know him, and only in those terms in which I know him; and all of that depends as fully on who I am as on who he is.

I am confident of being able to get at a certain form of the truth about him, *only if* I am as faithful as possible to Gudger as I know him, to Gudger as, in his actual flesh and life (but there again always in my mind's and memory's eye) he is. But of course it will be only a relative truth.

Name me one truth within human range that is not relative and I will feel a shade more apologetic of that.

For that reason and for others, I would do just as badly to simplify or eliminate myself from this picture as to simplify or invent

---

* Cocteau, writing of Picasso and of painting, remarks that the subject is merely the excuse for the painting, and that Picasso does away with the excuse.

character, places or atmospheres. A chain of truths did actually weave itself and run through: it is their texture that I want to represent, not betray, nor pretty up into art. The one deeply exciting thing to me about Gudger is that he is actual, he is living, at this instant. He is not some artist's or journalist's or propagandist's invention: he is a human being: and to what degree I am able it is my business to reproduce him as the human being he is; not just to amalgamate him into some invented, literary imitation of a human being.

The momentary suspension of disbelief is perhaps (and perhaps not) all very well for literature and art: but it leaves literature and art, and it leaves an attempt such as this, in a bad hole. It means that anything set forth within an art form, 'true' as it may be in art terms, is hermetically sealed away from identification with everyday 'reality.' No matter how strong and vivid it may be, its strength and vividness are not of that order which, in the open air of our actual, personal living, we draw in every time we breathe. Even at its very best it is make believe, requiring the killing insult of 'suspension of disbelief,' because it is art. This is in some degree true even of the most 'real' writing I know. It is simply impossible for anyone, no matter how high he may place it, to do art the simple but total honor of accepting and believing it in the terms in which he accepts and honors breathing, lovemaking, the look of a newspaper, the street he walks through. If you think of that a little while, and have any respect for art and for what it is or should be capable of if it is to be held worthy of its own existence, that is a crucially serious matter.

And yet is there any good reason why socalled art cannot, without any complicated wrench of the mind, be accepted as living, as telling of the living 'truth,' so long as art meets you halfway, and tries to tell of nothing else? *

When, in talk with a friend, you tell him, or hear from him, details of childhood, those details are perhaps even more real to you than in

---

* Or even if it is scornful of every such effort.

your solitary memory; and they are real and exciting to both of you in a way no form of art can be, or anyhow is. He is accepting what you say as truth, not fiction. You in turn, and the truth you are telling, are conditioned in some degree by his personality — you are in part, and he knows you are in part, selecting or inventing toward his color — but your whole effort, at which you both may be willing and interested to spend a great deal of time, is to reduce these half-inventions more and more towards the truth. The centrally exciting and important fact, from which ramify the thousand others which otherwise would have no clear and valid existence, is: that was the way it was. What could be more moving, significant or true: every force and hidden chance in the universe has so combined that a certain thing was the way it was.

And why is it that, written, these facts lose so much of their force and reality. Partly the writer's doing: as part-artist he feels the strength of need to select and invent. * Also, he is not aware that the truth is more important than any pretty lie he may tell. And partly the reader's doing: he is so used to the idea that art is a fiction that he can't shake himself of it. And partly the whole weight of art tradition, the deifying of the imagination. All right, go ahead and deify it: I will grant that it is responsible for every great work in any art. What of it! Must it therefore interfere with still another way of seeing and telling of still another form of the truth which is in its own way at least as sound? Is there such a cleavage between the 'scientific' and the 'artistic'? Isn't every human being both a scientist and an artist; and in writing of human experience, isn't there a good deal to be said for recognizing that fact and for using both methods?

I will be trying here to write of nothing whatever which did not in physical actuality or in the mind happen or appear; and my most serious effort will be, not to use these 'materials' for art, far less for journalism, but *to give them as they were and as in my memory and regard they*

---

* Every deadly habit in the use of the senses and of language; every 'artistic' habit of distortion in the evaluation of experience.

are. If there is anything of value and interest in this work it will have to hang entirely on that fact. Though I may frequently try to make use of art devices and may, at other times, being at least in part an 'artist,' be incapable of avoiding their use, I am in this piece of work illimitably more interested in life than in art.

Needless perhaps to say, then, I shall digress, and shall take my time over what may seem to be nonessentials, exactly as seems best.

Make no mistake in this, though: I am under no illusion that I am wringing this piece of experience dry. Nor do I even want to wring it dry. There are reasons of time, judgement and plain desire or, if you like, whim.

Time: It took a great artist seven years to record nineteen hours and to wring them anywhere near dry. Figure it out for yourself; this lasted several weeks, not nineteen hours. I take what I am trying here seriously but there are other pieces of work I want still more to do.

Judgement: Though I do on the one hand seriously believe that the universe can be seen in a grain of sand and that that is as good a lens as any other and a much more practicable one than the universe, I am again not trying any such job here. On too many other counts I simply do not think the experience was important * enough to justify any such effort; and I will consistently hope to keep the effort and method in strict proportion to my own limited judgement of the importance of the experience as a whole and in its parts.

The plain desire or whim must then be self-evident: all I want to do is tell this as exactly and clearly as I can and get the damned thing done with.† I would again be false to the truth if I were false to that.

Very roughly I know that to get my own sort of truth out of the experience I must handle it from four planes:

---

* I am no longer so sure of this.

† This is more complicated now.

That of recall; of reception, contemplation, *in medias res*: for which I have set up this silence under darkness on this front porch as a sort of fore-stage to which from time to time the action may have occasion to return. *

'As it happened': the straight narrative at the prow as from the first to last day it cut unknown water.

By recall and memory from the present: which is a part of the experience: and this includes imagination, which in the other planes I swear myself against.

As I try to write it: problems of recording; which, too, are an organic part of the experience as a whole.

These are, obviously, in strong conflict. So is any piece of human experience. So, then, inevitably, is any even partially accurate attempt to give any experience as a whole.

It seems likely at this stage that the truest way to treat a piece of the past is as such: as if it were no longer the present. In other words, the 'truest' thing about the experience is now neither that it was from hour to hour thus and so; nor is it my fairly accurate 'memory' of how it was from hour to hour in chronological progression; but is rather as it turns up in recall, in no such order, casting its lights and associations forward and backward upon the then past and the then future, across that expanse of experience.†

If this is so the book as a whole will have a form and set of tones rather less like those of narrative than like those of music. ‡

That suits me, and I hope it turns out to be so.

From the amount I am talking about 'this experience' you may have got the idea I think it was of some egregious importance. In that

---

* It still may, but not in this volume.

† I have still to attempt proper treatment of this sort.

‡ The forms of this text are chiefly those of music, of motion pictures, and of improvisations and recordings of states of emotion, and of belief.

case you will be cheated in proportion to your misapprehension. This 'experience' was just a series of various, fairly complicated, and to me interesting, things which I perceived or which happened to me last * summer, that's all. Greater and less things have happened, even to me. And I keep talking so much about it simply because I am respectful of experience in general and of any experience whatever, and because it turns out that going through, remembering, and trying to tell of anything is of itself (not because the Experience was either hot or cold, but of itself, and as a part of the experience) interesting and important to me: and because, as I have said before, I am interested in the actual and in telling of it, and so would wish to make clear that nothing here is invented. The whole job may well seem messy to you. But a part of my point is that experience offers itself in richness and variety and in many more terms than one and that it may therefore be wise to record it no less variously. Much of the time I shall want to tell of particulars very simply, in their own terms: but from any set of particulars it is possible and perhaps useful to generalize. In any case I am the sort of person who generalizes: and if for your own convenience and mine I left that out, I would be faking and artifacting right from the start.

I think there is at the middle of this sense of the importance and dignity of actuality and the attempt to reproduce and analyze the actual, and at the middle of this antagonism toward art, something of real importance which is by no means my discovery, far less my private discovery, but which is a sense of 'reality' and of 'values' held by more and more people, and the beginnings of somewhat new forms of, call it art if you must, of which the still and moving cameras are the strongest instruments and symbols. It would be an art and a way of seeing existence based, let us say, on an intersection of astronomical physics, geology, biology, and (including psychology) anthropology, known and spoken of not in scientific but in human terms. Nothing that springs

---

* The three sections of *On the Porch* were written in 1937.

from this intersection can conceivably be insignificant: everything is most significant in proportion as it approaches in our perception, simultaneously, its own singular terms and its ramified kinship and probable hidden identification with everything else.

Along the lines of this possible 'art' and attitude toward existence, nothing that follows * can pretend to be anything more advanced than a series of careful but tentative, rudely experimental, and fragmentary renderings of some of the salient aspects of a real experience seen and remembered in its own terms.

But if that is of any interest to you whatever, it is important that you should so far as possible forget that this is a book. That you should know, in other words, that it has no part in that realm where disbelief is habitually suspended. It is much simpler than that. It is simply an effort to use words in such a way that they will tell as much as I want to and can make them tell of a thing which happened and which, of course, you have no other way of knowing. It is in some degree worth your knowing what you can of not because you have any interest in me but simply as the small part it is of human experience in general.

It is one way of telling the truth: the only possible way of telling the kind of truth I am here most interested to tell.

Much of this land that lay out around us had been taken over by human beings, who were under and who will perhaps always remain under the infantile delusion that they own it.

But now, in the short yet extreme winter of that shadow of itself through which a continuous half of the earth twists its surface, this fragile and shallow colonization was reduced to its least, the few chilled embers which cities, thanks to their intense concentration of life, man-

---

* I may as well explain that *On the Porch* was written to stand as the beginning of a much longer book, in which the whole subject would be disposed of in one volume. It is here intended still in part as a preface or opening, but also as a frame and as an undertone and as the set stage and center of action, in relation to which all other parts of this volume are intended as flashbacks, foretastes, illuminations and contradictions.

age steadily fainting to sustain clear into the relief of daybreak, and, on the face of the open earth, only the infinitesimal and starlike infrequent glints of sickness here, death and love there. All normal human life was drained away; all creatures of the day time, under the passage and influence of that shadow, were shriveled as unanimously into sleep as when, in the leaning of the northern tracts of the globe away from the sun, all vegetable nature faints like the fading of a blush, the bees are stunned, and on the cold air in glittering swarms the tribal birds drain southward. This whole area of the planet itself, quite as literally as a weary human head, was loosened on its neck, was nodded and yield-ed over to the profound influences and memories, unknown to its sun-blind daytime, of its early childhood, before man became a part of its experience. The blind land itself and the blind water, the sky and the dove-light bombardment of its stars, the air, the shadow, the swarming, sleeping civilizations of the vegetable earth, certain frail insects, certain reptiles, birds, and fur-bearing personalities whose sleep is by day and whose business is dark, these were in complete self-possession. They did not even so much as tolerate the great hypnotized existence, the suspended animation, of human life; they simply ignored it, quite as an ocean is casual of the less than toylike traffic upon it.

I know of course: they ignored it no less in the daylight. I know of course: that whatever triumph I smelled, felt, heard in their presence, and whatever fear, was a merely human, merely personal matter. We bask in our lavish little sun as children in the protective sphere of their parents: and perhaps can never outgrow, or can never dare afford to outgrow, our delusions of his strength and wisdom and of our intelli-gence, competence and safety; and we carry over from him, like a green glow in the eyeballs, these daytime delusions, so inescapably that we can not only never detach ourselves from the earth, even in the per-ception of our minds, but cannot even face the fact of nature without either stone blindness or sentimentality: and we cannot bear, for any length of time, to carry in our minds in any literalness the fact of our small size and our youth. If this were merely the domestic and per-

sonal matter of a father or mother fixation, we would take it very seriously and those of us who could afford it would spend the next two
years talking about ourselves in a shaded room. * It is much more serious than that: it affects the deepest feelings and actions of a whole race
at the very roots; and beyond a couple of psalms and a few almost ac-
cidental artistic trills and semiquavers, what thought have we taken for
it: for that basis of our existence which is even simpler and even more
literal than the need to eat and sleep.

We have known, or have been told that we know, for some centuries now that the sun does not 'set' or 'rise': the earth twists its surface into and out of the light of the sun.

How many poets have become so aware of this fact that it is natural to them to use it.

In its twisting the earth also cradles back and forth, somewhat like
a bobbin, and leans through a very slightly eccentric course, and it is
this retirement out of and a return into a certain proximity to the sun
which causes the change of seasons. As Canada is retired out of summer, the Argentine is restored into summer, as simultaneously, as literally, as the edge of night is balanced by the edge of day, midnight by
noon. Just how much poetry, or art, or plain human consciousness, has
taken this into account. You have only to look at all the autumn art
about death and at all the spring art about life to get an idea: we are
so blindfold by local fact that we cannot even imagine this simultaneity. It is comfortable, and to quite some extent natural, and no doubt to
some extent wise, to be local: and yet in for instance politics we flatter
ourselves we are outgrowing it.

No doubt we are sensible in giving names to places: Canada; the
Argentine. But we would also be sensible to remember that the land

---

* Night is, for some, this shaded room; and in this room these talk of themselves to themselves in
silence, and may sometimes profit of it, and may somewhat break the paralysis of their parentage.
The analyst is the perception toward enigma. Enigma may be called God.

we have given these names to, and all but the relatively very small human population, wear these names lightly.

No doubt we have the 'right' to own and use the earth as seems to us best if we can: but we might be thought to qualify a little better for the job if it ever occurred to us in the least to qualify or question that right.

Even what seem to us our present soundest and most final ideas of justice are noticeably cavalier and provincial and self-centered. What would we have to think of hogs who, having managed to secure justice among themselves, still and continuously and without the undertone of a thought to the contrary exploited every other creature and material of the planet, and who wore in their eyes, perfectly undisturbed by any second consideration, the high and holy light of science or religion.

Sure, these things are simple: so simple, God forbid, that they sound merely whimsical. They are, though, literal facts. Our carelessness of them is literal fact. Any child should be able to grasp them. To grasp such facts, to try to understand them and their application, would seem as primal and as relevant to and influential upon the rest of what we are and do as breathing. Our own inability to grasp them or our negligence, which amounts to the same thing, does not qualify us very highly to handle more difficult facts which are of central importance at very least (to remain provincial) to the good of the human race.

I am a Communist by sympathy and conviction. * But it does not appear (just for one thing) that Communists have recognized or in any case made anything serious of the sure fact that the persistence of what once was insufficiently described as Pride, a mortal sin, can quite as coldly and inevitably damage and wreck the human race as the most total power of 'Greed' ever could: and that socially anyhow, the most dangerous form of pride is neither arrogance nor humility, but its mild, common denominator form, complacency.

---

* *On the Porch* is used without revision. Discussion of this and other issues is projected but postponed.

I am under no delusion that communism can be achieved overnight, if ever; and one's flexibility or patience toward what seem obvious occasions of mishandling should be * as considerable as one's strictness and fearlessness in facing what seem to be the facts of those failures. The fact remains that artists, for instance, should be capable of figuring the situation out to the degree that they would refuse the social eminence and the high pay they are given in Soviet Russia. The setting up of an aristocracy of superior workers is no good sign, either. Certainly, beyond denial, we, human beings, at our best are scarcely entered into the post-diaper stage of our development, and it is common sense to treat us as what we are, and would be as harmful and criminal as it would be foolish to treat ourselves as what we aren't. But it would be bright if the treatment caused us consistently to reach out and grow: you don't clamber out of infantilism by retreating, or staying, or being ordered to retreat, into what any average fool can see is the bedwetting stage.

Certainly we don't know now, and never will, all of even the human truth. But we may as well admit we know a few things, and take full advantage of them. It is probably never really wise, or even necessary, or anything better than harmful, to educate a human being toward a good end by telling him lies.

A couple of hundred yards away I was aware, not by sound but by thinking of it, of the creek bending in the bushes.

We knew this creek a mile away, where it crossed under the highway, and a few yards of it down here near the house. Aside from that we knew nothing of it; it lay only very lightly across our experience and we knew its beginning and course and ending only in a generalized way, a beginning in the sprouting of cold springs, a wandering of the land in sensitive forms, an ending, or a change, at that unknown place where at length it continuously smiled into some stronger stream. These things we knew in imagination and yet could be sure of, but

---

* Or should it.

much differently and more clearly, as if it stood in the warm light of a searchlight beam, we knew of our own part of the creek: the quiet noises and the noiselessnesses with which the burden of its smooth and brown heavy water lay along the flat stones, the sudden deeps, the submerged stumps and the sand and the clay of its patiently fretted trough. The surface of a continent, condensed here and there by chance into the serious infant frowning of mountain systems, is drawn away by the action of water into an enormous and unnaturally slender vine. This vine takes growth not by the radiant outward energy which compels a branched tree to burst still further into branches but always by a sinking away of its energy toward the center, as leaves are drawn into the wake of an auto, or as if a tree should, through the energetic contraction of its sap in autumn, still further pierce the air. As by benefit of that sped-up use of the moving camera through which it is possible to see the act of growth continuous from seed through the falling of the flower, so we may see in five minutes' time the branchings and searchings and innumerable growth of a river system, like a vine feeling out and finding its footholds on a wall, or like those subtlest of all chances which out of the very composture of an acorn ordain upon the growing action of branches in unresisting air certain shapes and not others: this eternal, lithe, fingering, chiseling, searching out the tender groin of the land that the water in a river system is carrying on in ten million parts of a face of earth at once, so that in the least creasing of the land sucked into scars between two stalks of corn you are seeing an organic part of the great body of the Mississippi River. There is no need to personify a river: it is much too literally alive in its own way, and like air and earth themselves is a creature much more powerful, much more basic, than any living thing the earth has borne. It is one of those few, huge, casual and aloof creatures by the mercy of whose existence our own existence was made possible; and at very least as much as it is good to hear the whining of dynamos, the artifacted hearts of our civilization, it is well to hear, to become aware of, the operations of water among whose spider lacings by chance we live: and above all it is well to know of it as nearly as possible in its own terms, wherein the crop it brings up, the destruction it is capable of, the dams and the helmeted brains of generators thrown across it and taking a half-hitch on its personal energy, are small, irrelevant, not even noticed incidents in its more serious career, which is by a continual sagging in all parts of its immense branched vine and by a continual searching out of weakness, the ironing flat and reduction to dead sea level of the wrinkled fabric of the earth. How beautifully then it has drawn our country into pleated valleys, in what language it has written upon the genius forehead of the earth the name and destiny of water, how handsome are the meanderings of its dotage through yellow flats across which is seen in the hard sunlight the broken and glass glistering of a city, are matters less truly important than the wrinkling open of a gully in a cornfield, the cellophane crackle of cold mountain branches, the twinkling spiral of sand that stands out of the heart of a spring, the sleeping and high-breasted sliding along of a milewide river, the great, final, digressive rectal discharge which beneath New Orleans yellows the Mexican Gulf: and the knowledge that such actions, going on intimately in every yard of thousands of miles of land beneath the hoverings and discharges of the sky, are all of one thing, one more than beast.

It was good to be doing the work we had come to do and to be seeing the things we cared most to see, and to be among the people we cared most to know, and to know these things not as a book looked into, a desk sat down to, a good show caught, but as a fact as large as the air; something absolute and true we were a part of and drew with every breath, and added to with every glance of the eye. It was good even, to be doing the limited job we had been assigned. We lay thinking of the unprecedented and unrecorded beauty, and sorrow and honor in the existence of, a child who lay sleeping in the room not far from us, and of the family up the road, and of the other family that lived near them, and remembering hours that were still hardly different from the knowledge of the present, and all the things seen and known and wondered over in those hours.

Out in front of the house the ground was tough, and knotty with thin weeds, in a bulge. Rains had taken its slopings-away violently to pieces. After the series of tricks had been learned, the road as far in as the house was a little more than barely passable in good weather, and gave one the pleasure of any newfound skill. Beyond the house it was a hundred yards of falling ditch full of hunched and convulsed muscles of clay whose levels varied suddenly three and five feet. This ditch fell along the side of the cornfield and flattened abruptly into sand as it lay into the woods. They stood up all along the creek and on the low hill on the far side and swung out deep in front of the house at the far side of another corn patch. From these woods a good way out along the hill there now came a sound that was new to us.

Clothing

Clothing

S unday, George Gudger:

Freshly laundered cotton gauze underwear.

Mercerized blue green socks, held up over his fist-like calves by scraps of pink and green gingham rag.

Long bulb-toed black shoes: still shining with the glaze of their first newness, streaked with clay.

Trousers of a hard and cheap cotton-wool, dark blue with narrow gray stripes; a twenty-five-cent belt stays in them always.

A freshly laundered and brilliantly starched white shirt with narrow black stripes.

A brown, green, and gold tie in broad stripes, of stiff and hard imitation watered silk.

A very cheap felt hat of a color between that of a pearl and that of the faintest gold, with a black band.

The hat is still only timidly dented into shape. Its lining is still brilliant and pearly, with only a faint shadow of oil. The sweatband, and the bright insole of the shoes, will seem untouched for a long time still, and the scarred soles of the shoes are still yellow.

The crease is still sharp in the trousers.

If he were an older man, and faithful in the rural tradition of dressing well rather than in that of the young men in towns, he would wear, not a belt, but suspenders, striped, or perhaps decorated with rosebuds.

These are the only socks he owns.

He does not wear or own a coat and would not want one. What he would like to wear is a pull-over sweater.

He has two suits of the underwear. He will sleep in this suit tonight and during the rest of the week. The other suit will go into the wash and he will put it on next sunday.

His neck seems violently red against the tight white collar. He is freshly shaven, and his face looks shy and naked.

He wears the hat straight awhile, then draws it down a little, but conservatively, over one eye, then pushes it far back on his head so that it is a halo, then sets it on straight again. He is delicate with his hands in touching it.

He walks a little carefully: the shoes hurt his feet.

Saturday, Mrs. Gudger:

Face, hands, feet and legs are washed.

The hair is done up more tightly even than usual.

Black or white cotton stockings.

Black lowheeled slippers with strapped insteps and single buttons.

A freshly laundered cotton print dress held together high at the throat with a ten-cent brooch.

A short necklace of black glass beads.

A hat.

She has two pairs of stockings. She sometimes goes barelegged to Cookstown, on saturdays, but always wears stockings on sundays.

The dress is one of two she would not be ashamed to wear away from home: they are not yet worn-down or ineradicably spotted. In other respects it is like all her other dresses: made at home, of carefully selected printed cotton cloth, along narrow variants of her own designing, which differs from some we saw and is probably a modified inheritance from her mother: short sleeves, a rather narrow skirt several inches longer than is ordinary. No kind of flaring collar, but in some of them, an effort to trim with tape. They are all cut deep at the breast for nursing, as all her dresses must have been for ten years now. The lines are all long, straight, and simple.

The hat is small and shallow, crowned with a waved brim. She must have taken care in its choice. It is a distant imitation of 'gay' or 'frivolous' 'trifles.' It is made of frail glazed magenta straw in a wide mesh through which her black hair shows. It has lost its shape a little in rain. She wears it exactly level, on the exact top of her small and beautifully graven head.

No southern country woman in good standing uses rouge or lipstick, and her face is colorless. There are traces of powder at the wings of her nose and in the seamed skin just in front of her left ear.

She is keenly conscious of being carefully dressed, and carries herself stiffly. Her eyes are at once searching, shy, excited, and hopelessly sad.

Saturday is the day of leaving the farm and going to Cookstown, and from the earliest morning on I can see that she is thinking of it. It is after she has done the housework in a little hurry and got the children ready that she bathes and prepares herself, and as she comes from the bedroom, with her hat on, ready to go, her eyes, in ambush even to herself, look for what I am thinking in such a way that I want to tell her how beautiful she is; and I would not be lying.

She will carry herself in this stiff, gravely watchful, and hopeful way all during the day in town, taking care to straighten her hat, and retiring as deeply as possible behind the wagons to nurse her baby. On the way home in the slow, rattling wagon, she will be tired and drooped, her hat crooked, her eyes silent, and once she will take the smallest child intensely against her, very suddenly.

Sunday: it is not very different from saturday, for she has no really 'sunday' dress, no other dress shoes, no other hat, and no other jewelry. If she is feeling happy, though, she will set into her hair the pink celluloid comb I have spoken of, with the glass diamonds.

George, on saturday, dresses not in his dress clothes but in the newest and cleanest of his work clothes; if there is time, if he is not working until noon, away from home, he shaves that morning and washes his feet. When there is no work to do, in winter and midsummer, he shaves twice a week.

Ricketts, on sunday:

No socks.

Old, black sunday shoes, washed off with water, and slashed with a razor at the broadest part of the feet.

Very old dark trousers with the compound creases of two ironings in them; nearly new white suspenders with narrow blue stripes down the sides and brown dots down the centers, the strap at the right attached to the trousers by a rusty nail.

A nearly new blue work shirt, worn perhaps twice before since laundering; the sleeves rolled down, the cuffs buttoned, the collar buttoned; no tie.

An open vest, too wide and short for him, of heavy, worn-out, gray-and-black wool; his watch and chain joining it across the waist.

A very old and carefully kept dark felt hat with a narrow band and a delicate bow.

A pair of horn-rimmed spectacles.

The spectacles are worn only on sunday and are perhaps mainly symbolic of the day and of his dignity as a reader in church; yet, too, they have strong small lenses. He bought them at a five-and-ten-cent store in Cherokee City.

Woods, on sunday:

Of the head covering I have no certain memory, yet two images. A hat of coarse-grained, strongly yellow straw, shaped by machine as felt hats are by the owner's hands, with a striped band. And: a nearly new, sober plaid, flat cap, of the sort which juts wide above the ears, and of a kind of crackling cheapness which one rain destroys.

Shoes: the oxfords which at one time were his dress shoes, and in which his wife has worked during the week.

Trousers such as seventeen-year-old boys of small towns select for best who can spend no money and want what flash they can get: a coarse-meshed and scratchy cotton-wool, stiffened with glue, of a bright and youthful yellow-gray crossed in wide squares by horizontals of blue-green and verticals of green-blue, and thinly pebbled with small nodules of red, orange, and purple wool. They are a little large for him. The original crease is entirely gone at the knee and is very sharp from knee to cuff. The suspenders are printed with spaced knots of small blue flowers; are worn out, and have been laundered.

A white shirt, starched; thin brown stripes. The sleeves have been cut off just above the elbows and coarsely hemmed. There are rust marks all over it, and the image of a flatiron is scorched just beneath the heart. An originally white piqué detachable collar, blue-gray from laundering, the fray scissored clean. A white cotton tie with two narrow black lines along each edge; about an inch wide throughout; both 'ends' out; the end next the body much longer than the outside end, and showing three or four inches of knitting-wear.

One day's beard; the mustache trimmed neat and short; the temples and the slender, corded, behind-head, trimmed nearly naked and showing the criss-crossed, quilting work of the scissors, and the meekness of the pallid scalp; scraped toast.

The children, washed and combed, barefooted, with clean feet and legs; clean clothes on: I will tell more of them later; so, too, of Mrs. Woods, and Mrs. Ricketts, and of the Ricketts girls: at present, more of the daily clothing.

On monday Gudger puts on cleanly washed workclothes; the other two men, whose laundering is done less often, change their clothing in a more casual cycle, two to several weeks long: I want now to try to describe these work clothes: shoes, overalls, shirts, head coverings:

variants, general remarks: and to speak here perhaps, not of these three men only, but a little more generally as well.

On all the clothing here to be spoken of there are, within the narrow range of availabilities, so many variants that one cannot properly name anything as 'typical,' but roughly align several 'types.' I could say, for instance:

Of shoes: ordinary work shoes, to be described later, may be called 'typical'; but only if you remember that old sunday shoes, tennis sneakers, high tennis shoes, sandals, moccasins, bare feet, and even boots, are not at all rarely used: it should be known, too, that there are many kinds of further, personal treatment of shoes. Mainly, this: Many men, by no means all, like to cut holes through the uppers for foot-spread and for ventilation: and in this they differ a good deal between utility and art. You seldom see purely utilitarian slashes: even the bluntest of these are liable to be patterned a little more than mere use requires: on the other hand, some shoes have been worked on with a wonderful amount of patience and studiousness toward a kind of beauty, taking the memory of an ordinary sandal for a model, and greatly elaborating and improving it. I have seen shoes so beautifully worked in this way that their durability was greatly reduced. Generally speaking, those who do this really careful work are negroes; but again, by no means all of the negroes are 'artists' in this way.

Of overalls, you could say that they are the standard working garment in the country south, and that blue is the standard color. But you should add that old sunday pants in varying degrees of decay are also perhaps half as much used: that striped and khaki overalls sometimes appear and mechanics' coveralls, and dungarees, and khaki work pants:

And again, speaking now of shirts, that though the blue workshirt is standard, there are also gray and brown workshirts; and besides these, old sunday shirts (white or striped), and now and then a home-made shirt, and undershirts, polo shirts, and jerseys:

And again of these categories of body covering, that, though all the variants appear among whites, they are a good deal more frequent among negroes; and again, too, that among the negroes the original predilections for colors, textures, symbolisms, and contrasts, and the subsequent modifications and embellishments, are much more free and notable.

And of hats, you could say that the standard is the ordinary farmers' straw sold at crossroads stores: but here you would be wrong for several reasons. Perhaps half the tenants wear these straws, but even in that category there are many differences in choice of kind at the same price, ranging from hats as conservative in size and shape as the city felts they imitate, through the whole register of what is supposed to be 'typical' to the american farmer, to hats which are only slight modifications of the ten-gallon and of the sombrero. And besides these straws: again there are all kinds of variants: old sunday hats being one whole class; another, caps emulous of small-town and city and factory men: baseball caps, the little caps which are the gifts of flour and paint companies, factory caps; imitation pith helmets imitative of foremen imitative of landowners imitative of the colonists in pith-helmet melodramas; occasionally, too, a homemade hat or cap: and here again, both in choice and in modification, the negroes are much the richer.

There will be no time, though, to go into these variants beyond their mention, nor any time at all to talk of negro work and sunday clothing, which in every respect seems to me, as few other things in this country do, an expression of a genius distributed among almost the whole of a race, so powerful and of such purity that even in its imitations of and plagiarisms on the white race, it is all but incapable of sterility. *

---

* There is a large class of sober, respectable, pious, mainly middle-aged negroes who in every way react intensely against the others of their race, and as intensely toward imitation of the most respectable whites. Their clothing, for instance, has no color in it anywhere, but is entirely black-and-white; and the patterns are equally severe. But even here, the whites are so blazing and starchedly white, and the blacks so waxed-ironed dead, and the clothes are borne in so profound, delicate, and lovely a sobriety, that I doubt the white race has ever approached it.

In all this on negroes, by the way, I am speaking strictly of small towns and of deep country. City negroes, even in the south, are modified; and those of the north are another thing again.

But now having suggested varieties, I want to lay out and tell of 'types,' speaking of the white race.

In general, then: the shoes are either work shoes of one age or another or worn-out sunday oxfords. The body garments are blue overalls and blue work shirts; again, with a wide range of age. The head coverings are straw hats or old sunday hats, or occasionally some more urban form of cap. These things have been bought ready-made, so consistently that any homemade substitute calls for a note to itself. Now a few further notes, on overalls and work shirts.

So far as I know, overalls are a garment native to this country. Subject to the substitutions I have spoken of, they are, nevertheless, the standard or classical garment at very least (to stay within our frame) of the southern rural American working man: they are his uniform, the badge and proclamation of his peasantry. There seems to be such a deep classicism in 'peasant' clothing in all places and in differing times that, for instance, a Russian and a southern woman of this country, of a deep enough class, would be undistinguishable by their clothing: moreover, it moves backward and forward in time: so that Mrs. Ricketts, for instance, is probably undistinguishable from a woman of her class five hundred years ago. But overalls are a relatively new and local garment.

Perhaps little can be said of them, after all: yet something. The basis: what they are: can best be seen when they are still new; before they have lost (or gained) shape and color and texture; and before the white seams of their structure have lost their brilliance.

Overalls

They are pronounced overhauls.

Try – I cannot write of it here – to imagine and to know, as against other garments, the difference of their feeling against your body; drawn-on, and bibbed on the whole belly and chest, naked from the kidneys up behind, save for broad crossed straps, and slung by these straps from the shoulders; the slanted pockets on each thigh, the deep square pockets on each buttock; the complex and slanted structures, on the chest, of the pockets shaped for pencils, rulers, and watches; the coldness of sweat when they are young, and their stiffness; their sweetness to the skin and pleasure of sweating when they are old; the thin metal buttons of the fly; the lifting aside of the straps and the deep slipping downward in defecation; the belt some men use with them to steady their middles; the swift, simple, and inevitably supine gestures of dressing and of undressing, which, as is less true of any other garment, are those of harnessing and of unharnessing the shoulders of a tired and hard-used animal.

They are round as stovepipes in the legs (though some wives, told to, crease them).

In the strapping across the kidneys they again resemble work harness, and in their crossed straps and tin buttons.

And in the functional pocketing of their bib, a harness modified to the convenience of a used animal of such high intelligence that he has use for tools.

And in their whole stature: full covering of the cloven strength of the legs and thighs and of the loins; then nakedness and harnessing behind, naked along the flanks; and in front, the short, squarely tapered, powerful towers of the belly and chest to above the nipples.

And on this façade, the cloven halls for the legs, the strong-seamed, structured opening for the genitals, the broad horizontal at the waist, the slant thigh pockets, the buttons at the point of each hip and on the breast, the geometric structures of the usages of the simpler trades – the complexed seams of utilitarian pockets which are so brightly picked out against darkness when the seam-threadings, double and triple stitched, are still white, so that a new suit of overalls has among its beauties those of a blueprint: and they are a map of a working man.

*

The shirts too; squarely cut, and strongly seamed; with big square pockets and with metal buttons: the cloth stiff, the sweat cold when it is new, the collar large in newness and standing out in angles under the ears; so that in these new workclothes a man has the shy and silly formal charm of a mail-order-catalogue engraving.

The changes that age, use, weather, work upon these.

They have begun with the massive yet delicate beauty of most things which are turned out most cheaply in great tribes by machines: and on this basis of structure they are changed into images and marvels of nature.

The structures sag, and take on the look, some of use; some, the pencil pockets, the pretty atrophies of what is never used; the edges of the thigh pockets become stretched and lie open, fluted, like the gills of a fish. The bright seams lose their whiteness and are lines and ridges. The whole fabric is shrunken to size, which was bought large. The whole shape, texture, color, finally substance, all are changed. The shape, particularly along the urgent frontage of the thighs, so that the whole structure of the knee and musculature of the thigh is sculptured there; each man's garment wearing the shape and beauty of his induplicable body. The texture and the color change in union, by sweat, sun, laundering, between the steady pressures of its use and age: both, at length, into realms of fine softness and marvel of draping and velvet plays of light which chamois and silk can only suggest, not touch; * and into a region and scale of blues, subtle, delicious, and deft beyond what I have ever seen elsewhere approached except in rare skies, the smoky light some days are filmed with, and some of the blues of Cézanne: one could watch and touch even one such garment, study it, with the eyes, the fingers, and the subtlest lips, almost illimitably long, and never fully learn it; and I saw no two which did not hold some world of exquisiteness of its own. Finally, too; particularly athwart the crest and

---

* The textures of old paper money.

swing of the shoulders, of the shirts: this fabric breaks like snow, and is stitched and patched: these break, and again are stitched and patched and ruptured, and stitches and patches are manifolded upon the stitches and patches, and more on these, so that at length, at the shoulders, the shirt contains virtually nothing of the original fabric and a man, George Gudger, I remember so well, and many hundreds of others like him, wears in his work on the power of his shoulders a fabric as intricate and fragile, and as deeply in honor of the reigning sun, as the feather mantle of a Toltec prince.

Gudger has three; it is perhaps four changes of overalls and workshirts. They are, set by set, in stages of age, and of beauty, distinctly apart from one another; and of the three I remember, each should at best be considered separately and at full length. I have room here to say only that they represent medium-early, middle, and medium-late stages, and to suggest a little more about these. The youngest are still dark; their seams are still visible; the cloth has not yet lost all of its hardness, nor the buttons their brightness. They have taken the shape of the leg, yet they are still the doing as much of machinery as of nature. The middle-aged are fully soft and elegantly textured, and are lost out of all machinery into a full prime of nature. The mold of the body is fully taken, the seams are those of a living plant or animal, the cloth's grain is almost invisible, the buttons are rubbed and mild, the blue is at the full silent, greatly restrained strength of its range; the patches in the overalls are few and strategic, the right * knee, the two bones of the rump, the elbows, the shoulders are quietly fledged: the garments are still wholly competent and at their fullness of comfort. The old: the cloth sleeps against all salients of the body in complete peace, and in its loose hangings, from the knee downward, is fallen and wandered in the first full loss of form into foldings I believe no sculptor has ever touched. The blue is so vastly fainted and withdrawn it is discernible

---

* The left knee is rubbed thin and has absorbed irreducibly the gold shadow of the blended colors of the clays of that neighborhood.

scarcely more as blue than as that most pacific silver which the bone wood of the houses and the visage of genius seem to shed, and is a color and cloth seeming ancient, veteran, composed, and patient to the source of being, as too the sleepings and the drifts of form. The shoulders are that full net of sewn snowflakes of which I spoke. The buttons are blind as cataracts, and slip their soft holes. The whole of the seat and of the knees and elbows * are broken and patched, the patches subdued in age almost with the original cloth, drawn far forward toward the feathering of the shoulders. There is a more youthful stage than the youngest of these; Ricketts, in his photograph here, wears such overalls; there are many median modulations; and there is a stage later than the latest here, as I saw in the legs of Woods' overalls, which had so entirely lost one kind of tendency to form that they had gained another, and were wrinkled minutely and innumerably as may best be paralleled by old thin oilskin crumpled, and by the skin of some aged faces.

Shoes

They are one of the most ordinary types of working shoe: the blucher design, and soft in the prow, lacking the seam across the root of the big toe: covering the ankles: looped straps at the heels: blunt, broad, and rounded at the toe: broad-heeled: made up of most simple roundnesses and squarings and flats, of dark brown raw thick leathers nailed, and sewn coarsely to one another in courses and patterns of doubled and tripled seams, and such throughout that like many other small objects they have great massiveness and repose and are, as the houses and overalls are, and the feet and legs of the women, who go barefooted so much, fine pieces of architecture.

---

* Much of the time the sleeves are rolled high and tight at the height of the biceps; but not always. Enough that these patchings are by other comparisons slight, but not so little but that there are large and manifold patches.

They are softened, in the uppers, with use, and the soles are rubbed thin enough, I estimate, that the ticklish grain of the ground can be felt through at the center of the forward sole. The heels are deeply biased. Clay is worked into the substance of the uppers and a loose dust of clay lies over them. They have visibly though to the eye subtly taken the mold of the foot, and structures of the foot are printed through them in dark sweat at the ankles, and at the roots of the toes. They are worn without socks, and by experience of similar shoes I know that each man's shoe, in long enough course of wear, takes as his clothing does the form of his own flesh and bones, and would feel as uneasy to any other as if A, glancing into the mirror, were met by B's eyes, and to their owner, a natural part though enforcement of the foot, which may be used or shed at will. There is great pleasure in a sockless and sweated foot in the fitted leathers of a shoe.

The shoes are worn for work. At home, resting, men always go barefooted. This is no symptom of discomfort, though: it is, insofar as it is conscious, merely an exchange of mutually enhancing pleasures, and is at least as natural as the habituated use and laying by of hats or of 'reading-glasses.'

So far as I could see, shoes are never mended. They are worn out like animals to a certain ancient stage and chance of money at which a man buys a new pair; then, just as old sunday shoes do, they become the inheritance of a wife.

Ricketts' shoes are boldly slashed open to accommodate as they scarcely can the years of pain in his feet. The worst of this pain is in stirrup corns, a solid stripe of stony and excruciating pearls across the ball of each foot; for two years, years ago, he rode mules all of each day. Recognizing my own tendency half-consciously to alter my walk or even to limp under certain conditions of mental insecurity, and believing Ricketts to be one of the most piteously insecure men I have ever known, I suspect, too, that nervous modifications in his walking have had much to do with destroying his feet.

Hats

It happens that not one of the three men uses any form of the farmer's-straw which is popularly thought of as the routine hat; and this may well be, in part (and in many other men), in reaction against a rural-identifying label too glibly applied to them. It is certain of Gudger, anyhow, that his head-covering, like his sunday belt and the pull-over sweater he wants, are city symbols against a rural tradition: indeed, it is industrial, or is the symbol almost of a skilled trade: a handsome twenty-five-cent machinist's cap made of ticking in bold stripes of blue-white and dark blue, drawing all possible elements of his square-chopped, goodlooking, and ineradicably rural face into city and machine suggestions.

Woods wears an exceedingly old felt hat, in which some holes are worn ragged and others cut in diamond shapes for ventilation and in respect for one of the sporty traditions among certain, usually younger, working men – negroes in particular – who reduce hats of a good color to a kind of improved and dashingly worn skullcap, or cut them into the shapes of crowns.

There is greatly among negroes, * and considerably, too, among working-class whites, an apparent reverence for the natural and symbolic dignities of the head (which is generally lost in the softer classes of white): so that, perhaps even more than the rest of the body, it is dressed according to symbolic and imitative enforcements. All symbolisms in clothing are complex and corrupt in this country; they are so specially so in the matter of hats, and the variety of personal choice is so wide, it can easily seem pure casual chance and carelessness, which I am sure it is not. In any case an absolute minimum social and egoistic requirement of a man's hat in this class and country is that it be

---

* Certain of their sculptures in their native continent seem to me to habitually embody this reverence toward the head as other human work does only sporadically, and more confusedly: and this seems to give background and impulse to the beauty of headdress and head-bearing in american country negroes.

ready-made and store bought. And so the fact that Ricketts is willing to work and to appear in public in a home made hat is significant of his abandonment 'beneath' the requirements of these symbologies, both toward himself and toward his world. A hat could be bought for fifteen cents. But he, and his family, all wear identical hats, which they casually exchange among themselves. They are made of cornshucks. These are plaited into a long ribbon; the ribbon is then sewn against its own edges from center outward in concentric spirals. Margaret or Paralee can make one in a day. They are the shape of very shallow cones, about eight inches in diameter, light enough in the crown that they do not stay easily on the head. They are not only unmistakably homemade, and betraying of the most deeply rural class; they suggest also the orient or what is named the 'savage.' The shucks are of a metal-silk brilliance I have never seen in other straw, and in this, its painstaking but unachieved symmetries, and the cone and outward spiral, each hat is an extraordinary and beautiful object: but this is irrelevant to its social meanings, as are nearly all products of honesty, intelligence, and full innocence.

Gudger, then: conventional, middle-aged unslashed work shoes; three suits of overalls and work shirts, all blue, in more uniformity to begin with and in more distinction apart through what is done with them, than any tailor would or could create; a machinist's cap; a modification of the Leyendecker face, brick red, clean shaven; a medium-height, powerful, football player's body modified into the burlings of oak and into slow square qualities blending those of the lion and the ox:

Ricketts: overalls too, I think not more than two suits, one youthful, and one very old; in shirts, a confusion of blues with torn white shirts of sundays ten years foundered; slashed, crippled shoes, standing on the outward rims of his heels; long matted hair on the low forehead, flashing, foxy, crazy eyes, a great frowning scoop of dark mustache; a dirty platinum halo; in all his clothing dirtier; a somehow willowy and part feminine yet powerful body, seeming a little soft at the hips as if he might be girlish white there:

Woods: an old man with a lightly made, still vital and sexually engaging body, the beautiful and light-boned, pleasingly carried, skeptic's unconquered head of those men whose ancestors are birds, not mammals: clothed in fine saggings of blue and flangings of white or, as I will now further indicate:

At home and at leisure, barefooted and naked to the waist, the feet narrow and almost fastidious, showing their bones, the elbows sharp like pulleys, the bones sharp at the peaks of the shoulders, and the ribs; strong clearly made and nearly hairless breasts of the form that seems common in men of India; the muscles of the upper arm weakening; the forearms shaped in ovals; a bandana hung on his sore shoulder; the body freckled and white and firm, then abruptly, at the neck, seamed as a turkey; the weathered face, and the sweated, candy hair, delicate as a baby's, laid on his forehead, and the eyes, glittering with narcotics and intelligence like splintered glass, to which the fringed lashes, which his daughter Emma inherits, give a sleepy look of charming innocence:

At work, he puts on his shoes and shirt and hat.

An overall strap would continually torment this sore which has developed in his shoulder, and may indeed — for in this garment this shoulder is the area of greatest stress and friction in the body — have helped to create it there: and for this reason Woods has cut off the bib of his overalls and holds them up at the waist with a piece of tied harness-leather. They are very old, and hang in a delicateness of wrinklings I have spoken of, and appear to be the only work clothes he owns.

The shoes are of the Gudger type: but of a lighter leather, perhaps two years older, worn through in the soles, and tied up with snaggled and knotted twine, tight on the ankles, for they are big for him.

The hat I have spoken of.

The shirt is home made out of a fertilizer sack. The cloth, by use and washing, is of a heavy and delicious look: as if pure cream were pressed into a fabric an eighth of an inch thick, and were cut and sewn into a garment. The faded lettering and branding is still visible, upside down, in red and blue and black. It is made in earnest imitation of store shirts but in part by heaviness of cloth and still more by lack of skill is enlarged in details such as the collar, and simplified, and improved, and is sewn with tough hand stitches, and is in fact a much more handsome shirt than might ever be bought: but socially and economically, it is of like but less significance with Ricketts' cornshuck hat.

The men's clothes are all ready-made. Any deviation from this is notable.

The women's and girls' clothes and those of the children are made at home, excepting boys' overalls and school clothes, shoes, and head coverings; and with these exceptions all deviations are notable too for one reason and another.

There are standard cloths, cheap cotton prints mainly, and thin white cottons, woven and on sale specifically to make clothing of.

Because there is so exceedingly little money, some wives make use of still other materials in dressing themselves, their children, and less commonly their men, at least for the weekdays, when they are sunken far back in their own country, to be seen by none who differ from themselves. Mrs. Woods has one sort of solution, and Mrs. Ricketts another. It is hard to say what is 'normal' here and what is not. By a general common denominator of memory throughout the summer, I would say it was most nearly 'normal' for there to be about an even mixture, in the week-day clothes, of non-clothing with clothing materials: so that Mrs. Woods, dressing herself and her family in so little that was ever intended for human beings to wear, is 'below normal,' and Mrs. Ricketts 'below' and far aside from it. On the other hand, by the almost complete absence of such adapted materials in her family's outfitting, I am sure that Mrs. Gudger feels intense social and perhaps 'spiritual' distinctions between the kinds of cloth in their meanings: and that with as little money as Mrs. Woods and hardly more than Mrs. Ricketts has, her success in keeping to one side of this line is the result of an effort and strain as intense as her feeling. In this she differs from and is 'above' the 'normal,' as she is too in the designing of the clothes, and in various symbolic reaches into the materials of a 'higher' class.

Three women's dresses

Mrs. Gudger: I have spoken already of her dresses. I think she has at most five, of which two are ever worn further away from home than the Woods'. Three are one-piece dresses; two are in two pieces. By cut they are almost identical; by pattern of print they differ, but are similar in having been carefully chosen, all small and sober, quiet patterns, to be in good taste and to relieve one another's monotony. I think it may be well to repeat their general appearance, since it is of her individual designing, and is so thoroughly a part of the logic of her body, bearing, face and temper. They have about them some shadow of nineteenth century influence, tall skirt, short waist, and a little, too, of imitation of Butterick patterns for housewives' housework-dresses; this chiefly in the efforts at bright or 'cheery,' post-honeymoon-atmosphere trimming: narrow red or blue tape sewn at the cuffs or throat. But by other reasons again they have her own character and function: the lines are tall and narrow, as she is, and little relieved, and seem to run straight from the shoulders to the hem low on the shins, and there is no collar, but a long and low V at the throat, shut narrowly together, so that the whole dress like her body has the long vertical of a Chartres statue.

Mrs. Woods: Two work dresses. They are both made of fertilizer * sacks, one in one piece, the other in two. Except that the one-piece dress hangs unbelted, they are much alike: no sleeves; wide hemmed holes cut for the arms; no collar; a wide triangle cut for nursing, and hemmed, in coarse stitching like the armholes; a broad skirt reaching about two inches below the knee, and falling in thick folds: the grain of the cloth defined here and there in dark grease, the whole garment clayed and sweated; the faded yet bold trademarks showing through in unexpected parts of the material: a garment very little different in some

---

* Fertilizer sacks are used a great deal in place of calico. Since our visit at least one company is making its sacks in calico patterns.

respects from those of the women of the ancient Greeks, and probably very closely matched in Thessaly or on Euboea.

Mrs. Ricketts: I am not sure that she has more than one work dress: in any case there was no change of it during the time that I knew her, and it seemed even at the first to have been worn for a long time. Excepting for the clothes of babies, it is the most primitive sewn and designed garment I have ever seen. It is made of a coarse tan cotton I will speak of later. It is shaped like a straight-sided bell, with a little hole at the top for the head to stick through, the cloth slit from the neck to below the breasts and held together if I remember rightly with a small snarl of shoelace; the bare arms sticking through the holes at the sides, the skirt ending a little below the knee, the whole dress standing out a little from the body on all sides like a child's youngest cartoons, not belted, and too stiffened perhaps with dirt to fall into any folds other than the broadest and plainest, the skirt so broad away from her at the bottom that, with her little feet and legs standing down from inside it, for all their beauty they seem comic sticks, and she, a grievous resemblance to newspaper drawings of timid men in barrels labeled John Q. Public.

Mrs. Ricketts wears one of the corn-shuck hats when she is working. I have never seen her with shoes on.

Mrs. Woods wears a big broken straw when she is working and, occasionally, her husband's oldest shoes.

Mrs. Gudger may have no work shoes; more likely, she uses something cast off by her husband. She worked barefooted most of the time, sometimes in her slippers. She was enough embarrassed to be barefooted that she may well have wished to conceal or avoid the indignity before us of using very old and broken shoes which were twice too big for her. She was shy also of our seeing her in a sunbonnet. I doubt that many headgears have ever been as good or as handsome.

Louise: the dress she wore most was sewn into one piece of two materials, an upper half of faded yellow-checked gingham, and a skirt made of a half-transparent flour sack, and beneath this, the bulk of a pinned, I presume flour sack, clout; and a gingham bow at the small of the back, and trimming at the neck. She has two other dresses, which are worn to Cookstown or for sundays, and are, I imagine, being saved for school. They too are made painstakingly to be pretty, and as much as possible like pattern and ready-made dresses. During the week she is always barefooted and wears a wide straw hat in the sun. Her mother dresses her carefully in the idiom of a little girl a year or two littler than she is. On sundays she wears slippers and socks, and a narrow blue ribbon in her hair, and a many times laundered white cloth hat.

Junior: ready-made overalls, one pair old, one not far from new, the newer cuffs turned up; a straw hat; bare feet, which are one crust of dew-poisoned sores; a ready-made blue shirt; a homemade gray shirt; a small straw hat. On sunday, cleaned feet, clean overalls, a white shirt, a dark frayed necktie, a small, frayed, clean, gray cap.

Burt: two changes of clothes. One is overalls and one of two shirts, the other is a suit. The overalls are homemade out of pale tan cotton. One of the shirts is pale blue, the other is white; they are made apparently, of pillowslip cotton. The collars are flared open: 'sport' collars, and the sleeves end nearer the shoulder than the elbow. The suit, which is old and, though carefully kept, much faded, is either a ready-made 'extravagance' or a hard-worked imitation of one. It is sewn together, pants and an upper piece, the pants pale blue, the upper piece white, with a small rabbit-like collar. There are six large white non-functional buttons sewn against the blue at the waistline.

Valley Few: In making inventory of the contents of a table drawer I described a number of Valley Few's dresses. I would now wish to remind you in particular of one decorated with homemade rabbits, and that most of the others are either plain white or in small utility checks. He also had one of a dark solid blue with red trim at the collar. Relative to the clothing of the rest of the family, there are a great many babies' dresses, I believe for two good reasons. One is that they are kept on for the use of one child after another. The other is that there is so little money to spend. Because there is so little; none at all really for clothes except by luck in the fall; clothes have to be an afterthought, and because of that, in turn, they can be a steady undertone of desire: so that from month to month, with now a dime and now even a quarter to spare, the first thing to come to Mrs. Gudger's mind would be what is to her the most immediate need secondary to food: decent clothes and enough of them. And because there is so little to be had for that money, she is best likely to satisfy herself in the purchase of the materials for one complete garment. If this is so, it is of the pattern of her particular care for clothes; it turns up in neither of the other families.

Valley Few's dresses are like Ellen Woods' and those of most babies here. There is ordinarily no genital genteelism. The dress hangs just to the crotch; it is fastened by one button at the nape of the neck and is open down the back. Often there is some attempt to make it pretty with a collar or pockets or both, or a belt; about as often, it is completely plain. Crawling along the floor, trailing the whole cape to one side, a baby has the comic and foolish look of a dog who has been dressed up by children.

Pearl has a dress made of flour sacks, another made of a fertilizer sack, and a third made of brown-and-blue checked gingham. This is properly her sunday dress, but she is fond of clothes, and is allowed to wear it a fair amount on week-days, along with her brown glass beads, her ring and her white slippers. There will be no time in this volume to tell much of personalities, but I think I will say a little briefly, here. Pearl is much more conscious of clothes than are Louise, Flora Merry Lee, and Katy, who are all near her age, and her mother's casualness is also significant. Mrs. Woods and her mother are of the sexually loose 'stock' of which most casual country and smalltown whoredom comes; and the child, already showing the signs, is effortlessly let drift her own way. I would not suggest that any 'attitude' towards this, on your part or mine, is sound enough to be worth striking; I am merely remarking a detail of the childhood of Pearl's mother and grandmother, who I may add appeared to be by far the best satisfied and satisfying women, of their class or of any other, whom I happened to see during this time in the south.

At home her younger half-brother Thomas goes naked some of the time. More often he wears a wornout undershirt which about covers his ribs, or a dress made by cutting off one end of a broadstriped pillow-sack and cutting in the other end holes for his head and arms.

Mrs. Gudger has exceedingly little money and an intense determination to hold her family's clothing within a certain level of respectability; Mrs. Woods has exceedingly little money and is relaxed into a level of improvisations, perhaps more fully, with less mixture of calicos, than is average; Mrs. Ricketts, with exceedingly little money as compared even with them, has done still otherwise.

Several years ago, judging by appearance, she bought a quantity of a cloth which, though not intended or ordinarily used for clothes, seemed feasible to her: a great many yards of coarse and unbleached cotton, the cheapest available material of which sheets and pillowcases are made at home: in a color somewhere between ivory, pale gray and white: and of this sheeting nearly all the clothes are made, varied only once or twice in its own designing, and by a few worn-out home-made sunday clothes, and by a few equally worn-out store clothes. It seems worth noticing that the old sunday clothes are much more than ordinarily talented, careful, hopeful and ambitious, and that with one or two exceptions the sheeting clothes are almost as if vindictively plain. All this sheeting is deeply grained in the colors and maculations of clay, dark grease and sweat and is stiff with this dirt, and is a good deal patched, in more sheeting, in floursack cloth, and in blue shirttail.

Clair Bell wears a short dress, halfway down the thighs, made of a plain straight sack of this sheeting, frayed holes for the arms and head, and alternate with it, a dress of the same material more tenderly made, with a flared skirt, a belt, and an effort at tucking at the throat, abandoned midway. On sundays, or when she is being taken to town, or sometimes when there is 'company,' she is taken aside and a closefitting pair of pink rayon drawers are drawn onto her. These are among the only three garments which give any evidence of recent purchase: everything else seems at least three or four years old.

Katy and Flora Merry Lee are of the same size and use each other's clothes. They have between them perhaps three dresses made of the sheeting, with short sleeves and widened skirts, and shirts or blouses made of thin washed flour sacking, and each has a pair of sheeting overalls. They wear what I presume are floursack drawers, pinned as a diaper is. They sometimes wear the shirts with the overalls; at other times, excepting the overalls, they go naked. They have no 'sunday' clothes; for sunday they wear the least unclean of these dresses, and a few cheap pins, necklaces and lockets. During the week as well as on sunday they sometimes tie dirty blue ribbons into their hair, and sometimes shoestrings.

Richard and Garvrin have between them a pair of very old ready-made overalls, and three or four shirts made some of sheeting and some of floursacks. Each has a pair of sheeting overalls, and a pair of corduroy pants from which the nap is almost entirely rubbed and washed. They fairly often wear the shirts; more often, they go naked except for the overalls or corduroys. On sundays the corduroys are brushed off and the week's damages are mended, and they wear these with frayed nearly clean white shirts which are saved from week to week, and with frazzled ties.

Paralee, for daily work, usually wears what was once her sunday dress. It is a transparent * blue cotton covered with white and faded gold circles, with a carefully made collar, torn, narrow lace at the sleeves, and at the breast a destroyed ruffle of curtain lace and dirty blue ribbons. The dress is torn at the shoulders and along the sides of the back.

Margaret at her daily work wears sometimes a long wide dark skirt and floursack or sheeting blouse, sometimes a sheeting dress. This latter was, I am quite sure, designed as a 'best' dress. It is carefully made

---

* It is worn over a slip.

throughout to hand and to fit well, and at the left breast and shoulder and across the back of the shoulders, hanging half down the back, is a broad sort of combined collar-and-cape of faded blue cotton.

Paralee sometimes wears black glass beads on weekdays as well as on sundays. Margaret seldom does.

Their clothing too is I presume interchangeable, though there was no overlapping during the time I knew them.

Margaret has two sunday dresses. One was made at home. It is of thin and very cheap white cotton, unskilfully gathered at the breast to a nakedly plain, round, very carefully hemmed throat. It is belted, but does not fit her or hang successfully, and the coarse and somewhat dirty undergarment shows through. Her other dress must I am sure have been bought ready-made and at terrible expense in their scale of money. It is an imitation of the elaborate sort of dress a 'well-preserved,' dark-haired, elegantly well-to-do, middle-aged woman might at some uncertain time during the past twenty years have worn formally: black transparent crêpe, sewn over thickly with a coruscation of small jet beads. But the elaborations are worn down into an almost indistinguishable chaos; the black undergarment is torn in several places; many of the beads are lost, or hang loose on their threads; and the cloth is sweated open irreparably and alarmingly at the armpits, so that when the arms are raised, there is in this somberness the sudden bright dreadfulness of twin yawning cats.

Paralee is much more fortunate. She has a new dress, and it is fully and exactly of the kind which middle class girls of her age wear in town on saturday afternoons. And yet it isn't exactly of that kind. In the wish for brilliance and emphasis and propriety, everything is overstepped. The orange and blue and white stripes are far more anxiously bold than any worn by town girls, save now and then a negress, and the fit is almost too sharp and sporting, and the strength, deftness and flexibility of her body betray her, and the dress, and her deeply tanned, rural, strongly freckled face, her too-carefully-done hair, the use with this garment of all the jewelery she has, and above all the excitement, the blend of confidence and terror, and the desperately searching hope which blaze in her eyes, all these betray her still more hopelessly, so that she would inspire the fear inspired by all who are over-eager or who would 'climb,' and seems almost as if she had stolen the dress.

These are the clothes which these girls must wear to attract men and to qualify as marriageable. Many girls marry at sixteen, not a few at fifteen or even fourteen; nearly all are married by seventeen; by the time they are eighteen, if they are unmarried, they are drifted towards the spinster class, a trouble to their parents, an embarrassment to court and be seen with, a dry agony to themselves: Paralee is nineteen; and Margaret is twenty. Margaret has already the mannerisms and much of the psychic balance of a middle-aged woman of the middle class in the north.

Mrs. Ricketts, sunday:

A long and full skirt of dead black cotton held at the hip by a safetypin. A blouse of the same material, plain at the throat, sleeves to the elbows. No trimming nor any kind of surplus cloth. Spots and streaks, reasserting themselves through the drying moisture with which she has tried to erase them. The hem fallen in a part of the skirt. No ornaments of any kind. No hat, or a straw hat (ready-made). It is thus also that she dressed to ride to Cookstown when cotton was taken to gin.

Mrs. Woods, in Cookstown:

She stands a little apart from everyone in the dark drugstore waiting until the doctor shall be ready to attend to her abscessed tooth, while the men at the soda fountain are turned and watch her. She wears no hat, nor stockings, nor shoes. Her dress is made at home of thin pillowslip cotton, plain at the throat, cut deep for nursing, without sleeves, reaching a little below her knees, belted in with a belt of narrow glazed cracked scarlet leather, all edges of the material frayed, a deep tear along the back, another through which her right knee shows, the design of the whole very much that of the plainest sort of nightgown, the whole fabric a welter of sweat and dirt. She rests her weight on one foot and studies the other while they look at her. She is noticeably though not yet heavily pregnant. She wears a 'slip' beneath this dress but the materials of both are so thin that her dark sweated nipples are stuck to them and show through, and it is at her nipples, mainly, that the men keep looking. It is thus also that she is dressed on sundays.

Mrs. Woods' mother:

A wide short striped skirt, the stripes blue and white: thick-ribbed black cotton stockings, wrinkled on her legs: Keds, the ankles patched, the soles worn through: a man's work shirt, so exceedingly old it is almost white: a red bandana tied at the throat: a man's large new yellow straw hat.

Past:

Mrs. Gudger has, besides the magenta straw she wears at present, two other hats.

One: an omelet shape of crimson straw slanted through with a thick stripped white quill, the coloring ruined with rain. It is at fifteenth remove an imitation of those 'smart' hats which set off 'smart,' incisive, leisured, vicious faces.

Two: this I have formerly described. It is the great-brimmed, triumphal crown I found ruined yet saved in a table drawer, which had been so patiently home made. I will remark now that in its breadth and elaborateness it is reminiscent of the hats which were stylish around 1900, and that it is of such a particular splendor that I am fairly sure it was her wedding hat, made for her, perhaps as a surprise, by her mother. She was sixteen then; her skin would have been white, and clear of wrinkles, her body and its postures and her eyes even more pure than they are today; and she would have been happy, and confident enough in her beauty, to wear it without fear: and in her long white home made marriage dress and in that glory of a hat, with her sister Emma, seven years old, marveling up at her, and her mother standing away and approving her while her image slowly turned upon itself on blank floor and in a glass, she was such a poem as no human being shall touch.

Education

Education

In every child who is born, under no matter what circumstances, and of no matter what parents, the potentiality of the human race is born again: and in him, too, once more, and of each of us, our terrific responsibility towards human life; towards the utmost idea of goodness, of the horror of error, and of God.

Every breath his senses shall draw, every act and every shadow and thing in all creation, is a mortal poison, or is a drug, or is a signal or symptom, or is a teacher, or is a liberator, or is liberty itself, depending entirely upon his understanding: and understanding,* and action proceeding from understanding and guided by it, is the one weapon against the world's bombardment, the one medicine, the one instrument by which liberty, health, and joy may be shaped or shaped towards, in the individual, and in the race.

This is no place to dare all questions that must be asked, far less to advance our tentatives in this murderous air, nor even to qualify so much as a little the little which thus far has been suggested, nor even

---

* Active 'understanding' is only one form, and there are suggestions of 'perfection' which could be called 'understanding' only by definitions so broad as to include diametric reversals. The peace of God surpasses all understanding; Mrs. Ricketts and her youngest child do, too; 'understanding' can be its own, and hope's, most dangerous enemy.

either to question or to try to support my qualifications to speak of it at all: we are too near one of the deepest intersections of pity, terror, doubt, and guilt; and I feel that I can say only, that 'education,' whose function is at the crisis of this appalling responsibility, does not seem to me to be all, or even anything, that it might be, but seems indeed the very property of the world's misunderstanding, the sharpest of its spearheads in every brain: and that since it could not be otherwise without destroying the world's machine, the world is unlikely to permit it to be otherwise.

In fact, and ignorant though I am, nothing, not even law, nor property, nor sexual ethics, nor fear, nor doubtlessness, nor even authority itself, all of which it is the business of education to cleanse the brain of, can so nearly annihilate me with fury and with horror; as the spectacle of innocence, of defenselessness, of all human hope, brought steadily in each year by the millions into the machineries of the teachings of the world, in which the man who would conceive of and who would dare attempt even the beginnings of what 'teaching' must be could not exist two months clear of a penitentiary: presuming even that his own perceptions, and the courage of his perceptions, were not a poison as deadly at least as those poisons he would presume to drive out: or the very least of whose achievements, supposing he cared truly not only to hear himself speak but to be understood, would be a broken heart. *

For these and other reasons it would seem to me mistaken to decry the Alabama public schools, or even to say that they are 'worse' or 'less good' than schools elsewhere: or to be particularly wholehearted in the regret that these tenants are subjected only to a few years of this education: for they would be at a disadvantage if they had more of it, and at a disadvantage if they had none, and they are at a disadvantage in the little they have; and it would be hard and perhaps impossible to say in which way their disadvantage would be greatest.

*

---

* It may be that the only fit teachers never teach but are artists, and artists of the kind most blankly masked and least didactic.

School was not in session while I was there. My research on this subject was thin, indirect, and deductive. By one way of thinking it will seem for these reasons worthless: by another, which I happen to trust more, it may be sufficient.

I saw, for instance, no teachers: yet I am quite sure it is safe to assume that they are local at very least to the state and quite probably to the county; that most of them are women to whom teaching is either an incident of their youth or a poor solution for their spinsterhood; that if they were of much intelligence or courage they could not have survived their training in the State Normal or would never have undertaken it in the first place; that they are saturated in every belief and ignorance which is basic in their country and community; that any modification of this must be very mild indeed if they are to survive as teachers; that even if, in spite of all these screenings, there are superior persons among them, they are still again limited to texts and to a system of requirements officially imposed on them; and are caught between the pressures of class, of the state, of the churches, and of the parents, and are confronted by minds already so deeply formed that to liberate them would involve uncommon and as yet perhaps undiscovered philosophic and surgical skill. I have only sketched a few among dozens of the facts and forces which limit them; and even so I feel at liberty to suggest that even the best of these, the kindly, or the intuitive, the socalled natural teachers, are exceedingly more likely than not to be impossibly handicapped both from without and within themselves, and are at best the servants of unconscious murder; and of the others, the general run, that if murder of the mind and spirit were statutory crimes, the law, in its customary eagerness to punish the wrong person, * might spend all its ingenuity in the invention of deaths by delayed torture and never sufficiently expiate the enormities which through them, not by their own fault, have been committed.

Or again on the curriculum: it was unnecessary to make even such

---

* This is not to suggest there is a 'right person' or that punishment can ever be better than an enhancement of error.

search into this as I made to know that there is no setting before the
students of 'economic' or 'social' or 'political' 'facts' and of their situation within these 'facts,' no attempt made to clarify or even slightly to
relieve the situation between the white and negro races, far less to
explain the sources, no attempt to clarify psychological situations in the
individual, in his family, or in his world, no attempt to get beneath and
to revise those 'ethical' and 'social' pressures and beliefs in which even
a young child is trapped, no attempt, beyond the most nominal, to
interest a child in using or in discovering his senses and judgment, no
attempt to counteract the paralytic quality inherent in 'authority,' no
attempt beyond the most nominal and stifling to awaken, to protect,
or to 'guide' the sense of investigation, the sense of joy, the sense of
beauty, no attempt to clarify spoken and written words whose power of
deceit even at the simplest is vertiginous, no attempt, or very little, and
ill taught, to teach even the earliest techniques of improvement in occu-
pation ('scientific farming,' diet and cooking, skilled trades), nor to
'teach' a child in terms of his environment, no attempt, beyond the most
suffocated, to awaken a student either to 'religion' or to 'irreligion,' no
attempt to develop in him either 'skepticism' or 'faith,' nor 'wonder,' nor
mental 'honesty' nor mental 'courage,' nor any understanding of or delicateness in 'the emotions' and in any of the uses and pleasures of the
body save the athletic; no attempt either to relieve him of fear and of
poison in sex or to release in him a free beginning of pleasure in it, nor
to open within him the illimitable potentials of grief, of danger, and of
goodness in sex and in sexual love, nor to give him the beginnings at
very least of a knowledge, and of an attitude, whereby he may hope to
guard and increase himself and those whom he touches, no indication
of the damages which society, money, law, fear and quick belief have
set upon these matters and upon all things in human life, nor of their
causes, nor of the alternate ignorances and possibilities of ruin or of joy,
no fear of doubtlessness, no fear of the illusions of knowledge, no fear
of compromise: – and here again I have scarcely begun, and am confronted immediately with a serious problem: that is: by my naming of

the lack of such teaching, I can appear too easily to recommend it, to imply, perhaps, that if these things were 'taught,' all would be 'solved': and this I do not believe: but insist rather that in the teaching of these things, infinitely worse damage could and probably would result than in the teaching of those subjects which in fact do compose the curriculum: and that those who would most insist upon one or another of them can be among the deadliest enemies of education: for if the guiding hand is ill qualified, an instrument is murderous in proportion to its sharpness. Nothing I have mentioned but is at the mercy of misuse; and one may be sure a thousand to one it will be misused; and that its misuse will block any more 'proper' use even more solidly than unuse and discrediting could. It could be said, that we must learn a certitude and correlation in every 'value' before it will be possible to 'teach' and not to murder; but that is far too optimistic. We would do better to examine, far beyond their present examination, the extensions within ourselves of doubt, responsibility, and conditioned faith and the possibilities of their more profitable union, to a degree at least of true and constant terror in even our tentatives, and if (for instance) we should dare to be 'teaching' what Marx began to open, that we should do so only in the light of the terrible researches of Kafka and in the opposed identities of Blake and Céline.

All I have managed here, and it is more than I intended, is to give a confused statement of an intention which presumes itself to be good: the mere attempt to examine my own confusion would consume volumes. But let what I have tried to suggest amount to this alone: that not only within present reach of human intelligence, but even within reach of mine as it stands today, it would be possible that young human beings should rise onto their feet a great deal less dreadfully crippled than they are, a great deal more nearly capable of living well, a great deal more nearly aware, each of them, of their own dignity in existence, a great deal better qualified, each within his limits, to live and to take part toward the creation of a world in which good living will be possible without guilt toward every neighbor: and that teaching at present, such as it is, is almost entirely either irrelevant to these possibilities or destructive of them, and is, indeed, all but entirely unsuccessful even within its own 'scales' of 'value.'

Within the world as it stands, however, the world they must live in, a certain form of education is available to these tenant children; and the extent to which they can avail themselves of it is of considerable importance in all their future living.

A few first points about it:

They are about as poorly equipped for self-education as human beings can be. Their whole environment is such that the use of the intelligence, of the intellect, and of the emotions is atrophied, and is all but entirely irrelevant to the pressures and needs which involve almost every instant of a tenant's conscious living: and indeed if these faculties were not thus reduced or killed at birth they would result in a great deal of pain, not to say danger. They learn the work they will spend their lives doing, chiefly of their parents, and from their parents and from the immediate world they take their conduct, their morality, and their mental and emotional and spiritual key. One could hardly say that any further knowledge or consciousness is at all to their use or advantage, since there is nothing to read, no reason to write, and no recourse against being cheated even if one is able to do sums; yet these forms of literacy are in general held to be desirable: a man or woman feels a certain sort of extra helplessness who lacks them: a truly serious or ambitious parent hopes for even more, for a promising child; though what 'more' may be is, inevitably, only dimly understood.

School opens in middle or late September and closes the first of May. The country children, with their lunches, are picked up by busses at around seven-thirty in the morning and are dropped off again towards the early winter darkness. In spite of the bus the children of these three families have a walk to take. In dry weather it is shortened a good deal; the bus comes up the branch road as far as the group of negro houses at the bottom of the second hill and the Ricketts children walk half a mile to meet it and the Gudger children walk three quarters. In wet weather the bus can't risk leaving the highway and the Ricketts walk two miles and the Gudgers a mile and a half in clay which in stretches is knee-deep on a child.

There was talk during the summer of graveling the road, though most of the fathers are over forty-five, beyond road-age. They can hardly afford the time to do such work for nothing, and they and their negro neighbors are in no position to pay taxes. Nothing had come of it within three weeks of the start of school, and there was no prospect of free time before cold weather.

Southern winters are sickeningly wet, and wet clay is perhaps the hardest of all walking. 'Attendance' suffers by this cause, and by others. Junior Gudger, for instance, was absent sixty-five and Louise fifty-three days out of a possible hundred-and-fifty-odd, and these absences were 'unexcused' eleven and nine times respectively, twenty-three of Junior's and a proportionate number of Louise's absences fell in March and April, which are full of work at home as well as wetness. Late in her second year in school Louise was needed at home and missed several consecutive school days, including the final examinations. Her 'marks' had been among the best in her class and she had not known of the examination date, but no chance was given her to make up the examinations and she had to take the whole year over. The Ricketts children have much worse attendance records and Pearl does not attend at all.

School does not begin until the children shall have helped two weeks to a month in the most urgent part of the picking season, and ends in time for them to be at work on the cotton-chopping.

The bus system which is now a routine of country schools is helpful, but not particularly to those who live at any distance from tax-maintained roads.

The walking, and the waiting in the cold and wetness, one day after another, to school in the morning, and home from schools in the shriveling daylight, is arduous and unpleasant.

Schooling, here as elsewhere, is identified with the dullest and most meager months of the year, and, in this class and country, with the least and worst food and a cold noonday lunch: and could be set only worse at a disadvantage if it absorbed the pleasanter half of the year.

The 'attendance problem' is evidently taken for granted and, judging by the low number of unexcused absences, is 'leniently' dealt with: the fact remains, though, that the children lose between a third to half of each school year, and must with this handicap keep up their lessons and 'compete' with town children in a contest in which competition is stressed and success in it valued and rewarded.

The schoolhouse itself is in Cookstown; a recently built, windowy, 'healthful' red brick and white-trimmed structure which perfectly exemplifies the American genius * for sterility, unimagination, and general gutlessness in meeting any opportunity for 'reform' or 'improvement.' It is the sort of building a town such as Cookstown is proud of, and a brief explanation of its existence in such country will be worth while. Of late years Alabama has 'come awake' to 'education,' illiteracy has been reduced; texts have been modernized; a good many old schools have been replaced by new ones. For this latter purpose the counties have received appropriations in proportion to the size of their school population. The school population of this county is five black to one white, and since not a cent of the money has gone into negro schools, such buildings as this are possible: for white children. The negro children, meanwhile, continue to sardine themselves, a hundred and a hundred and twenty strong, into stove-heated one-room pine shacks which might comfortably accommodate a fifth of their number if the walls, roof, and windows were tight. † But then, as one prominent

---

* So well shown forth in 'low-cost' housing.

† Aside from discomfort, and unhealthfulness, and the difficulty of concentrating, this means of course that several 'grades' are in one room, reciting and studying by rotation, each using only a fraction of each day's time. It means hopeless boredom and waste for the children, and exhaustion for the teacher.

landlord said and as many more would agree: 'I don't object to nigrah education, not up through foath a fift grade maybe, but not furdern dat: I'm too strong a believah in white syewpremcy.'

This bus service and this building the (white) children are schooled in, even including the long and muddy walk, are of course effete as compared to what their parents had. * The schooling itself is a different matter, too: much more 'modern.' The boys and girls alike are subjected to 'art' and to 'music,' and the girls learn the first elements of tap dancing. Textbooks are so cheap almost anyone can afford them: that is, almost anyone who can afford anything at all; which means that they are a stiff problem in any year to almost any tenant. I want now to list and suggest the contents of a few textbooks which were at the Gudger house, remembering, first, that they imply the far reaches of the book-knowledge of any average adult tenant.

> *The Open Door Language Series: First Book: Language Stories and Games.*
>
> *Trips to Take.* Among the contents are poems by Vachel Lindsay, Elizabeth Madox Roberts, Robert Louis Stevenson, etc. Also a story titled: 'Brother Rabbit's Cool Air Swing,' and subheaded: 'Old Southern Tale.'
>
> *Outdoor Visits:* Book Two of *Nature and Science Readers.* (Book One is *Hunting.*) Book Two opens: 'Dear Boys and Girls: in this book you will read how Nan and Don visited animals and plants that live outdoors.'
>
> *Real Life Readers: New Stories and Old: A Third Reader.* Illustrated with color photographs.
>
> *The Trabue-Stevens Speller.* Just another speller.
>
> *Champion Arithmetic.* Five hundred and ten pages: a champion psychological inducement to an interest in numbers. The final problem: 'Janet bought 1¼ lbs. of salted peanuts and ½ lb. of salted almonds. Altogether she bought ? lbs. of nuts? '

---

* Their parents would have walked to one-room wooden schoolhouses. I'm not sure, but think it more likely than not, that many of the white children still do today.

Dear Boys and Girls indeed!

Such a listing is rich as a poem; twisted full of contents, symptoms, and betrayals, and these, as in a poem, are only reduced and diluted by any attempt to explain them or even by hinting. Personally I see enough there to furnish me with bile for a month: yet I know that any effort to make clear in detail what is there, and why it seems to me so fatal, must fail.

Even so, see only a little and only for a moment.

These are books written by 'adults.' They must win the approval and acceptance of still other 'adults,' members of school 'boards'; and they will be 'taught' with by still other 'adults' who have been more or less 'trained' as teachers. The intention is, or should be, to engage, excite, preserve, or develop the 'independence' of, and furnish with 'guidance,' 'illumination,' 'method,' and 'information,' the curiosities of children.

Now merely re-examine a few words, phrases and facts:

The Open Door: open to whom. That metaphor is supposed to engage the interest of children.

Series: First Book. Series. Of course The Bobsey Twins is a series; so is The Rover Boys. Series perhaps has some pleasure associations to those who have children's books, which no tenant children have: but even so it is better than canceled by the fact that this is so obviously not a pleasure book but a schoolbook, not even well disguised. An undisguised textbook is only a little less pleasing than a sneaking and disguised one, though. *First Book:* there entirely for the convenience of adults; it's only grim to a child.

Language: it appears to be a *modern* substitution for the word 'English.' I don't doubt the latter word has been murdered; the question is, whether the new one has any life whatever to a taught child or, for that matter, to a teacher.

Stories and Games: both, modified by a school word, and in a school context. Most children prefer pleasure to boredom, lacking our intelligence to reverse this preference: but you must use your imagination or memory to recognize how any game can be poisoned by being 'conducted': and few adults have either.

Trips to Take. Trips indeed, for children who will never again travel as much as in their daily bus trips to and from school. Children like figures of speech or are, if you like, natural symbolists and poets: being so, they see through frauds such as this so much the more readily. No poem is a 'trip,' whatever else it may be, and suffers by being lied about.

The verse. I can readily imagine that 'educators' are well pleased with themselves in that they have got rid of the Bivouac of the Dead and are using much more nearly contemporary verse. I am quite as sure, knowing their kind of 'knowledge' of poetry, that the pleasure is all theirs.

These children, both of town and country, are saturated southerners, speaking dialects not very different from those of negroes. *Brother* Rabbit! *Old Southern Tale!*

Outdoor Visits. Nature and Science. Book One: *Hunting.* Dear Boys and Girls. In this book you will read (oh, I will, will I?). Nan and Don. Visit. Animals and Plants that Live Outdoors. Outdoors. You will pay formal calls on Plants. They live outdoors. 'Nature.' 'Science.' Hunting. Dear Boys and Girls. Outdoor Visits.

Real Life. 'Real' 'Life' 'Readers.' Illustrated by *color* photographs.

Or back into the old generation, a plainer title: *The Trabue-Stevens Speller.* Or the *Champion Arithmetic,* weight eighteen pounds, an attempt at ingratiation in the word champion, so broad of any mark I am surprised it is not spelled *Champeen.*

Or you may recall the page of geography text I have quoted elsewhere: which, I must grant, tells so much about education that this chapter is probably unnecessary.

I give up. Relative to my memory of my own grade-schooling, I recognize all kinds of 'progressive' modifications: Real Life, color photographs, Trips to Take (rather than Journey to Make), games, post-kindergarten, 'Language,' Nan and Don, 'Nature and Science,' Untermeyer-vintage poetry, 'dear boys and girls'; and I am sure of only one thing: that it is prepared by adults for their own self-flattery and satisfaction, and is to children merely the old set retouched, of afflictions, bafflements, and half-legible insults more or less apathetically submitted to.

Louise Gudger is fond of school, especially of geography and arithmetic, and gets unusually good 'marks': which means in part that she has an intelligence quick and acquisitive above the average, in part that she has learned to parrot well and to respect 'knowledge' as it is presented to her. She has finished the third grade. In the fourth grade she will learn all about the history of her country. Her father and much more particularly her mother is excited over her brightness and hopeful of it: they intend to make every conceivable effort by which she may continue not only through the grades but clear through high school. She wants to become a teacher, and quite possibly she will; or a trained nurse; and again quite possibly she will.

Junior Gudger is in the second grade because by Alabama law a pupil is automatically passed after three years in a grade. He is still almost entirely unable to read and write, and is physically fairly skilful. It may be that he is incapable of 'learning': in any case 'teaching' him would be a 'special problem.' It would be impossible in a public, competitive class of mixed kinds and degrees of 'intelligence'; and I doubt that most public-school teachers are trained in it anyhow.

Burt and Valley Few are too young for school. I foresee great difficulty for Burt, who now at four is in so desperate a psychological situation that he is capable of speaking any language beyond gibberish (in which he has great rhythmic and syllabic talent) only after he has been given the security of long and friendly attention, of a sort which markedly excludes his brothers.

Pearl Woods, who is eight, may have started to school this fall (1936); more likely not, though, for it was to depend on whether the road was graveled so she would not have the long walk to the bus alone or within contamination of the Ricketts children. She is extremely sensitive, observant, critical and crafty, using her mind and her senses much more subtly than is ever indicated or 'taught' in school: whether her peculiar intelligence will find engagement or ruin in the squarehead cogs of public schooling is another matter.

Thomas is three years too young for school. As a comedian and narcist dancer he has natural genius; aside from this I doubt his abilities. Natural artists, such as he is, and natural craftsmen, like Junior, should not necessarily have to struggle with reading and writing; they have other ways of learning, and of enlarging themselves, which however are not available to them.

Clair Bell is three years young for school and it seems probable that she will not live for much if any of it, so estimates are rather irrelevant. I will say, though, that I was so absorbed in her physical and spiritual beauty that I was not on the lookout for signs of 'intelligence' or the lack of it, and that education, so far as I know it, would either do her no good or would hurt her.

Flora Merry Lee and Katy are in the second grade. Katy, though she is so shy that she has to write out her reading lessons, is brighter than average; Flora Merry Lee, her mother says, is brighter than Katy; she reads and writes smoothly and 'specially delights in music.' Garvrin and Richard are in the fourth grade. Garvrin doesn't take to schooling very easily though he tries hard; Richard is bright but can't get interested; his mind wanders. In another year or two they will be big enough for full farm work and will be needed for it, and that will be the end of school.

Margaret quit school when she was in the fifth grade because her eyes hurt her so badly every time she studied books. She has forgotten a good deal how to read. Paralee quit soon after Margaret did because she was lonesome. She still reads fairly easily, and quite possibly will not forget how.

The Ricketts are spoken of disapprovingly, even so far away as the county courthouse, as 'problem' children. Their attendance record is extremely bad; their conduct is not at all good; they are always fighting and sassing back. Besides their long walk in bad weather, here is some more explanation. They are much too innocent to understand the profits of docility. They have to wear clothes and shoes which make them the obvious butts of most of the children. They come of a family which is marked and poor even among the poor whites, and are looked down on even by most levels of the tenant class. They are uncommonly sensitive, open, trusting, easily hurt, and amazed by meanness and by cruelty, and their ostracism is of a sort to inspire savage loyalty among them. They are indeed 'problems'; and the 'problem' will not be simplified as these 'over'sexed and anarchic children shift into adolescence. The two girls in particular seem inevitably marked out for incredibly cruel misunderstanding and mistreatment.

Mrs. Ricketts can neither read nor write. She went to school one day in her life and her mother got sick and she never went back. Another time she told me that the children laughed at her dress and the teacher whipped her for hitting back at them, but Margaret reminded her that that was the dress she had made for Flora Merry Lee and that it was Flora Merry Lee and Katy who had been whipped, and she agreed that that was the way it was.

Fred Ricketts learned quickly. He claims to have learned how to read music in one night (he does, in any case, read it), and he reads language a little less hesitantly than the others do and is rather smug about it — 'I was readn whahl back na Pgressive Fahmuh — ' He got as far as the fifth grade and all ways was bright. When his teacher said the earth turned on a axle, he asked her was the axle set in posts, then. She said yes, she reckoned so. He said well, wasn't hell supposed to be under the earth, and if it was wouldn't they be all the time trying to chop the axle post out from under the earth? But here the earth still was, so what was all this talk about axles. 'Teacher never did bring up nothn bout no axles after that. No sir, she never did bring up nothin about no durn axles after that. No sir-ree, she shore never did brang up nufn baout no dad blame axles attah dayut.'

Woods quit school at twelve when he ran away and went to work in the mines. He can read, write, and figure; so can his wife. Woods understands the structures and tintings of rationalization in money, sex, language, religion, law, and general social conduct in a sour way which is not on the average curriculum.

George Gudger can spell and read and write his own name; beyond that he is helpless. He got as far as the second grade. By that time there was work for him and he was slow minded anyway. He feels it is a terrible handicap not to be educated and still wants to learn to read and write and to figure, and his wife has tried to learn him, and still wants to. He still wants to, too, but he thinks it is unlikely that he will ever manage to get the figures and letters to stick in his head.

Mrs. Gudger can read, write, spell, and handle simple arithmetic, and grasps and is excited by such matters as the plainer facts of astronomy and geology. In fact, whereas many among the three families have crippled but very full and real intelligences, she and to a perhaps less extent her father have also intellects. But these intellects died before they were born; they hang behind their eyes like fetuses in alcohol.

It may be that more are born 'incapable of learning,' in this class, or in any case 'incapable of learning,' or of 'using their intelligences,' beyond 'rudimentary' stages, than in economically luckier classes. If this is so, and I doubt the proportion is more than a little if at all greater, several ideas come to mind: Incapable of learning what? And capable of learning what else, which is not available either to them or, perhaps, in the whole field and idea of education? Or are they incapable through incompetent teaching, or through blind standards, or none, on the part of educators, for measuring what 'intelligence' is? Or incapable by what pressures of past causes in past generations? Or should the incapability be so lightly (or sorrowfully) dismissed as it is by teachers and by the middle class in general?

But suppose a portion are born thus 'incapable': the others, nevertheless, the great majority, are born with 'intelligences' potentially as open and 'healthful,' and as varied in pattern and in charge, as any on earth. And by their living, and by their education, they are made into hopeless and helpless cripples, capable exactly and no more of doing what will keep them alive: by no means so well equipped as domestic and free animals: and that is what their children are being made into, more and more incurably, in every year, and in every day.

'Literacy' is to some people a pleasing word: when 'illiteracy' percentages drop, many are pleased who formerly were shocked, and think no more of it. Disregarding the proved fact that few doctors of philosophy are literate, that is, that few of them have the remotest idea how to read, how to say what they mean, or what they mean in the first place, the word literacy means very little even as it is ordinarily used. An adult tenant writes and spells and reads painfully and hesitantly as a child does and is incapable of any save the manifest meanings of any but the simplest few hundred words, and is all but totally incapable of absorbing, far less correlating, far less critically examining, any 'ideas' whether true or false; or even physical facts beyond the simplest and most visible. That they are, by virtue of these limitations, among the only 'honest' and 'beautiful' users of language, is true, perhaps, but it is not enough. They are at an immeasurable disadvantage in a world which is run, and in which they are hurt, and in which they might be cured, by 'knowledge' and by 'ideas': and to 'consciousness' or 'knowledge' in its usages in personal conduct and in human relationships, and to those unlimited worlds of the senses, the remembrance, the mind and the heart which, beyond that of their own existence, are the only human hope, dignity, solace, increasement, and joy, they are all but totally blinded. The ability to try to understand existence, the ability to try to recognize the wonder and responsibility of one's own existence, the ability to know even fractionally the almost annihilating beauty, ambiguity, darkness, and horror which swarm every instant of every consciousness, the ability to try to accept, or the ability to try to defend one's self, or the ability to dare to try to assist others; all such as these, of which most human beings are cheated of their potentials, are, in most of those who even begin to discern or wish for them, the gifts or thefts of economic privilege, and are available to members of these leanest classes only by the rare and irrelevant miracle of born and surviving 'talent.'

Or to say it in another way: I believe that every human being is potentially capable, within his 'limits,' of fully 'realizing' his potentialities; that this, his being cheated and choked of it, is infinitely the ghastliest, commonest, and most inclusive of all the crimes of which the human world can accuse itself; and that the discovery and use of 'consciousness,' which has always been and is our deadliest enemy and deceiver, is also the source and guide of all hope and cure, and the only one.

I am not at all trying to lay out a thesis, far less to substantiate or to solve. I do not consider myself qualified. I know only that murder is being done, against nearly every individual in the planet, and that there are dimensions and correlations of cure which not only are not being used but appear to be scarcely considered or suspected. I know there is cure, even now available, if only it were available, in science and in the fear and joy of God. This is only a brief personal statement of these convictions: and my self-disgust is less in my ignorance, and far less in my 'failure' to 'defend' or 'support' the statement, than in my inability to state it even so far as I see it, and in my inability to blow out the brains with it of you who take what it is talking of lightly, or not seriously enough.

A few notes

Most of you would never be convinced that much can be implied out of little: that everything to do with tenant education, for instance, is fully and fairly indicated in the mere list of textbooks. I have not learned how to make this clear, so I have only myself to thank. On the other hand there are plenty of people who never get anything into their heads until they are brained by twenty years' documentation: these are the same people who so scrupulously obey, insist on, and interpret 'the facts,' and 'the rules.'

I have said a good deal more here on what ought to be than on what is: but God forbid I should appear to say, 'I know what ought to be, and this is it.' But it did and does seem better to shout a few obvious facts (they can never be 'obvious' enough) than to meech. The meechers will say, Yes, but do you realize all (or any) of the obstacles, presuming you are (in general) a little more right than merely raving? The answer is, I am sure I don't realize them all, but I realize more of them, probably, than you do. Our difference is that you accept and respect them. 'Education' as it stands is tied in with every bondage I can conceive of, and is the chief cause of these bondages, including acceptance and respect, which are the worst bondages of all. 'Education,' if it is anything short of crime, is a recognition of these bondages and a discovery of more and a deadly enemy of all of them; it is the whole realm of human consciousness, action, and possibility; it has above all to try to recognize and continuously to suspect and to extend its understanding of its own nature. It is all science and all conduct; it is also all religion. By which I mean, it is all 'good' or 'wise' science, conduct, and religion. It is also all individuals; no less various. It cannot be less and be better than outrageous. Its chief task is fearfully to try to learn what is 'good' and 'why' (and when), and how to communicate, and its own dimensions, and its responsibility.

Oh, I am very well aware how adolescent this is and how easily laughable. I will nevertheless insist that any persons milder, more obedient to or compromising * with 'the obstacles as they are,' more 'realistic,' contented with the effort for less, are dreamy and insuffi-

---

* One of the researches most urgently needed is into the whole problem of compromise and non-compromise. I am dangerously and mistakenly much against compromise: 'my kind never gets anything done.' The (self-styled) 'Realists' are quite as dangerously ready to compromise. They seem never sufficiently aware of the danger; they much too quickly and easily respect the compromise and come at rest in it. I would suppose that nothing is necessarily wrong with compromise of itself, except that those who are easy enough to make it are easy enough to relax into and accept it, and that it thus inevitably becomes fatal. Or more nearly, the essence of the trouble is that compromise is held to be a virtue of itself.

ciently skeptical. Those are the worst of the enemies, and always have been.

I don't know whether negroes or whites teach in the negro schools; I presume negroes. If they are negroes, I would presume for general reasons that many of them, or most, are far superior to the white teachers. By and large only the least capable of whites become teachers, particularly in primary schools, and more particularly in small towns and in the country: whereas with so little in the world available to them, it must be that many of the most serious and intelligent negroes become teachers. But you would have to add: They are given, insofar as they are given any, a white-traditioned education, and are liable to the solemn, meek piousness of most serious and educated negroes in the south; to a deep respect for knowledge and education as they have worked for it; to a piteous mah-people or Uncle Tom attitude towards all life. Even those who are aware of more dangerous attitudes would in the south have to be careful to the point of impotence. Moreover they would be teaching only very young children, in the earliest years of school, in overcrowded classrooms.

Note on all grade-school teachers: that at best they are exceedingly ill-paid, and have also anxiety over their jobs: with all the nervousness of lack of money and of insecurity even in that little: not a good state of mind for a teacher of the young. Nor is the state of mind resulting of sexlessness, or of carefully spotless moral rectitude, whether it be 'innate,' or self-enforced for the sake of the job. Nearly all teachers and clergymen suffocate their victims through this sterility alone.

It would be hard to make clear enough the deadliness of vacuum and of apathy which is closed over the very nature of teaching, over teachers and pupils alike: or in what different worlds words and processes leave a teacher, and reach a child. Children, taught either years beneath their intelligence or miles wide of relevance to it, or both: their intelligence becomes hopelessly bewildered, drawn off its centers, bored, or atrophied. Carry it forward a few years and recognize how soft-brained an american as against a european 'college graduate' is. On the other side: should there be any such thing as textbooks in any young life: and how many 'should' learn to read at all?

As a whole part of 'psychological education' it needs to be remembered that a neurosis can be valuable; also that 'adjustment' to a sick and insane environment is of itself not 'health' but sickness and insanity.

I could not wish of any one of them that they should have had the 'advantages' I have had: a Harvard education is by no means an unqualified advantage.

Adults writing to or teaching children: in nearly every word within these textbooks, for instance, there is a flagrant mistake of some kind. The commonest is this: that they simplify their own ear, without nearly enough skepticism as to the accuracy of the simplification, and with virtually no intuition for the child or children; then write or teach to satisfy that ear; discredit the child who is not satisfied, and value the child who, by docile or innocent distortions of his intelligence, is.

In school a child is first plunged into the hot oil bath of the world at its cruelest: and children are taught far less by their teachers than by one another. Children are, or quickly become, exquisitely sensitive to social, psychologic, and physical meanings and discriminations. The war is bloody and pitiless as that war alone can be in which every combatant is his own sole army, and is astounded and terrified in proportion to the healthfulness of his consciousness. What clothes are worn, for one simple thing alone, is of tremendous influence upon the child who wears them. A child is quickly and frightfully instructed of his situation and meaning in the world; and that one stays alive only by one form or another of cowardice, or brutality, or deception, or other crime.

It is all, needless to say, as harmful to the 'winners' (the well-to-do, or healthful, or extraverted) as to the losers.

The 'esthetic' is made hateful and is hated beyond all other kinds of 'knowledge.' It is false-beauty to begin with; it is taught by sick women or sicker men; it becomes identified with the worst kinds of femininity and effeminacy; it is made incomprehensible and suffocating to anyone of much natural honesty and vitality.

The complete acquaintance of a child with 'music' is the nauseating little tunes you may remember from your own schooltime. His 'art' has equally little to do with 'art.' The dancing, as I have said, is taught to girls: it is the beginning of tap dancing. The spectacle of a tenant's little daughter stepping out abysmal imitations of Eleanor Powell has a certain charm, but it is somehow decadent, to put it mildly. This is not at all to say that madrigals, finger-painting, or morris-dancing are to be recommended: I wish to indicate only that in either case the 'teaching' of 'the esthetic' or of 'the arts' in Cookstown leaves, or would leave, virtually everything still to be desired.

It is hardly to Louise's good fortune that she 'likes' school, school being what it is. Dressed as she is, and bright as she is, and serious and dutiful and well-thought-of as she is, she already has traces of a special sort of complacency which probably must, in time, destroy all in her nature that is magical, indefinable, and matchless: and this though she is one of the stronger persons I have ever known.

Perhaps half the people alive are born with the possibility of moral intuitions far more subtle and excellent than those laid down by law and custom, and most of the others might learn a great deal. As it is they are more than sufficiently destroyed. If beginning at the age of six they were subjected to a daily teaching of law, the damage would be so much the worse. There is a fair parallel in 'consciousness,' in 'intelligence': and the standards of education, which seem even more monstrous than those of law, are thus imposed as law is not, and are made identical with knowledge.

No equipment to handle an abstract idea or to receive it: nor to receive or handle at all complex facts: nor to put facts and ideas together and strike any fire or meaning from them. They are like revolutionists who must fight fire and iron and poison gas with barrel staves and with bare hands: except that they lack even the idea of revolution.

It would be the narrative task of many pages even scarcely to suggest how slowed, blinded, and helpless-minded they are made. Just as with food, they cannot conceive of or be interested in what they have never tasted or heard of. All except the simplest knowledge of immediate materials and of the senses is completely irrelevant to the life they are living. Perhaps fortunately, the one thing the adults could most surely receive and understand is what a good revolutionist could tell them about their immediate situation and what is to be done about it: certainly one would be a fool, and an insulting one, who tried much else, or who tried much else before that was accomplished. The children could learn this and much more.

For various reasons I am not a good revolutionist, and much as I wanted to, could bear in my 'conscience,' or in my respect for what they were as they stood, to do almost none of this, beyond determining what in general they might learn if they were rightly given it. Moreover, though there are revolutionists whom I totally respect, and before the mere thought of whom I hold myself in contempt, I go blind to think what crimes others would commit upon them, and instill into them; and by every appearance and probability these latter, who for all their devotion and courage seem to me among the most dangerous and hideous persons at large, are greatly in the majority, and it is they who own and will always betray all revolutions.

'Sense of beauty': Is this an 'instinct' or a product of 'training.' In either case there appears to be almost no such thing among the members of these three families, and I have a strong feeling that the 'sense of beauty,' like nearly everything else, is a class privilege. I am sure in any case that its 'terms' differ by class, and that the 'sense' is limited and inarticulate in the white tenant class almost beyond hope of description. (This quite aside from the fact that in other classes, where it is less limited, it is almost a hundred per cent corrupted.) They live on land, and in houses, and under skies and seasons, which all happen to seem to me beautiful beyond almost anything else I know, and they themselves, and the clothes they wear, and their motions, and their speech, are beautiful in the same intense and final commonness and purity: but by what chance have I this 'opinion' or 'perception' or, I might say, 'knowledge'? And on the other hand, why do they appear so completely to lack it? This latter, there seem good reasons for. Habit. No basis of comparison. No 'sophistication' (there can be a good meaning of the word). No reason nor glimmer of reason to regard anything in terms other than those of need and use. Land is what you get food out of: houses are what you live in, not comfortably: the sky is your incalculable friend or enemy: all nature, all that is built upon it, all that is worn, all that is done and looked to, is in plain and powerful terms of need, hope, fear, chance, and function. Moreover, the profoundest and plainest 'beauties,' those of the order of the stars and of solitude in darkened and empty land, come at least partly of awe, and such in a simple being is, simply, unformulable fear. It is true that in what little they can obtain of them, they use and respect the rotted prettinesses of 'luckier' classes; in such naïvety that these are given beauty: but by and large it seems fairly accurate to say that being so profoundly members in nature, among man-built things and functions which are almost as scarcely complicated 'beyond' nature as such things can be, and exist on a 'human' plane, they are little if at all more aware of 'beauty,' nor of themselves as 'beautiful,' than any other member in nature, any animal, anyhow. It is very possible, I would believe probable, that many animals are sensitive to beauty in terms of exhilaration or fear or courting or lust; many are, for that matter, accomplished and obvious narcists: in this sense I would also guess that the animals are better equipped than the human beings. I would say too that there is a purity in this existence *in* and *as* 'beauty,' which can so scarcely be conscious of itself and its world as such, which is inevitably lost in consciousness, and that this is a serious loss.

But so are resourcefulness against deceit and against strangling: and so are pleasure, and joy, and love: and a human being who is deprived of these and of this consciousness is deprived almost of existence itself.

Work

Work

To come devotedly into the depths of a subject, your respect for it increasing in every step and your whole heart weakening apart with shame upon yourself in your dealing with it: To know at length better and better and at length into the bottom of your soul your unworthiness of it: Let me hope in any case that it is something to have begun to learn. Let this all stand however it may: since I cannot make it the image it should be, let it stand as the image it is: I am speaking of my verbal part of this book as a whole. By what kind of foreword I can make clear some essential coherence in it, which I know is there, balanced of its chaos, I do not yet know. But the time is come when it is necessary for me to say at least this much: and now, having said it, to go on, and to try to make an entrance into this chapter, which should be an image of the very essence of their lives: that is, of the work they do.

It is for the clothing, and for the food, and for the shelter, by these to sustain their lives, that they work. Into this work and need, their minds, their spirits, and their strength are so steadily and intensely drawn that during such time as they are not at work, life exists for them scarcely more clearly or in more variance and seizure and appetite than it does for the more simply organized among the animals, and for the plants. This arduous physical work, to which a consciousness beyond that of the simplest child would be only a useless and painful encumbrance, is undertaken without choice or the thought of chance of choice, taught forward from father to son and from mother to daughter; and its essential and few returns you have seen: the houses they live in; the clothes they wear: and have still to see, and for the present to imagine, what it brings them to eat; what it has done to their bodies, and to their consciousness; and what it makes of their leisure, the pleasures which are made available to them. I say here only: work as a means to other ends might have some favor in it, even which was of itself dull and heartless work, in which one's strength was used for another man's benefit: but the ends of this work are absorbed all but entirely into the work itself, and in what little remains, nearly all is obliterated; nearly nothing is obtainable; nearly all is cruelly stained, in the tensions of physical need, and in the desperate tensions of the need of work which is not available.

I have said this now three times. If I were capable, as I wish I were, I could say it once in such a way that it would be there in its complete awefulness. Yet knowing, too, how it is repeated upon each of them, in every day of their lives, so powerfully, so entirely, that it is simply the natural air they breathe, I wonder whether it could ever be said enough times.

The plainness and iterativeness of work must be one of the things which make it so extraordinarily difficult to write of. The plain details of a task once represented, a stern enough effort in itself, how is it possibly to be made clear enough that this same set of leverages has been undertaken by this woman in nearly every day of the eleven or the twenty-five years since her marriage, and will be persisted in in nearly every day to come in all the rest of her life; and that it is only one among the many processes of wearying effort which make the shape of each one of her living days; how is it to be calculated, the number of times she has done these things, the number of times she is still to do them; how conceivably in words is it to be given as it is in actuality, the accumulated weight of these actions upon her; and what this cumulation has made of her body; and what it has made of her mind and of her heart and of her being. And how is this to be made so real to you who read of it, that it will stand and stay in you as the deepest and most iron anguish and guilt of your existence that you are what you are, and that she is what she is, and that you cannot for one moment exchange places with her, nor by any such hope make expiation for what she has suffered at your hands, and for what you have gained at hers: but only by consuming all that is in you into the never relaxed determination that this shall be made different and shall be made right, and that of what is 'right' some, enough to die for, is clear already, and the vast darkness of the rest has still, and far more passionately and more skeptically than ever before, to be questioned into, defended, and learned toward. There is no way of taking the heart and the intelligence by the hair and of wresting it to its feet, and of making it look this terrific thing in the eyes: which are such gentle eyes: you may meet them, with all the summoning of heart you have, in the photograph in this volume of the young woman with black hair: and they are to be multiplied, not losing the knowledge that each is a single, unrepeatable, holy individual, by the two billion human creatures who are alive upon the planet today; of whom a few hundred thousands are drawn into complications of specialized anguish, but of whom the huge swarm and majority are made and acted upon as she is: and of all these individuals, contemplate, try to encompass, the one annihilating chord.

But I must make a new beginning:

(Selection from Part I:

The family exists for work. It exists to keep itself alive. It is a coopera-tive economic unit. The father does one set of tasks; the mother an-other; the children still a third, with the sons and daughters serving apprenticeship to their father and mother respectively. A family is called a force, without irony; and children come into the world chiefly that they may help with the work and that through their help the family may increase itself. Their early years are leisurely; a child's life work begins as play. Among his first imitative gestures are gestures of work; and the whole imitative course of his maturing and biologic envy is a steplad-der of the learning of physical tasks and skills.

This work solidifies, and becomes steadily more and more, in greater and greater quantity and variety, an integral part of his life.

Besides imitation, he works if he is a man under three compul-sions, in three stages. First for his parents. Next for himself, single and wandering in the independence of his early manhood: 'for himself,' in the sense that he wants to stay alive, or better, and has no one depend-ent on him. Third, for himself and his wife and his family, under an employer. A woman works just for her parents; next, without a transi-tion phase, for her husband and family.

Work for your parents is one thing: work 'for yourself' is another. They are both hard enough, yet light, relative to what is to come. On the day you are married, at about sixteen if you are a girl, at about twenty if you are a man, a key is turned, with a sound not easily audi-ble, and you are locked between the stale earth and the sky; the key turns in the lock behind you, and your full life's work begins, and there is nothing conceivable for which it can afford to stop short of your death, which is a long way off. It is perhaps at its best during the first two years or so, when you are young and perhaps are still enjoying one another or have not yet lost all hope, and when there are not yet so many children as to weigh on you. It is perhaps at its worst during the next ten to twelve years, when there are more and more children, but none of them old enough, yet, to be much help. One could hardly describe it as slackening off after that, for in proportion with the size of the family, it has been necessary to take on more land and more work, and, too, a son or daughter gets just old enough to be any full good to you, and marries or strikes out for himself: yet it is true, anyhow, that from then on there are a number of strong and fairly responsible people in the household besides the man and his wife. In really old age, with one of the two dead, and the children all married, and the widowed one making his home among them in the slow rotations of a floated twig, waiting to die, it does ease off some, depending more then on the individual: one may choose to try to work hard and seem still capable, out of duty and the wish to help, or out of 'egoism,' or out of the dread of dropping out of life; or one may relax, and live unnoticed, never spoken to, dead already; or again, life may have acted on you in such a way that you have no choice in it: or still again, with a wife dead, and children gone, and a long hard lifetime behind you, you may choose to marry again and begin the whole cycle over, lifting onto your back the great weight a young man carries, as Woods has done.

That is the general pattern, its motions within itself lithe-unfolded, slow, gradual, grand, tremendously and quietly weighted, as a heroic dance: and the bodies in this dance, and the spirits, undergoing their slow, miraculous, and dreadful changes: such a thing indeed should be constructed of just these persons: the great, somber, blooddroned, beansprout helmed fetus unfurling within Woods' wife; the infants of three families, staggering happily, their hats held full of freshly picked cotton; the Ricketts children like delirious fawns and panthers; and secret Pearl with her wicked skin; Louise, lifting herself to rest her back, the heavy sack trailing, her eyes on you; Junior, jealous and lazy, malingering, his fingers sore; the Ricketts daughters, the younger stepping beautifully as a young mare, the elder at the stove with her mouth twisted; Annie Mae at twenty-seven, in her angular sweeping, every motion a wonder to watch; George, in his sunday clothes with his cuffs short on his blocked wrists, looking at you, his head slightly to one side, his earnest eyes a little squinted as if he were looking into a light; Mrs. Ricketts, in that time of morning when from the corn she reels into the green roaring glooms of her home, falls into a chair with gaspings which are almost groaning sobs, and dries in her lifted skirt her delicate and reeking head; Miss-Molly, chopping wood as if in each blow of the axe she held captured in focus the vengeance of all time; Woods, slowed in his picking, forced to stop and rest much too often, whose death is hastened against a doctor's warnings in that he is picking at all: I see these among others on the clay in the grave mutations of a dance whose business is the genius of a moving camera, and which it is not my hope ever to record: yet here, perhaps, if not of these archaic circulations of the rude clay altar, yet of their shapes of work, I can make a few crude sketches:

A man: George Gudger, Thomas Woods, Fred Ricketts: his work is with the land, in the seasons of the year, in the sustainment and ordering of his family, the training of his sons:

A woman: Annie Mae Gudger, Ivy Woods, Sadie Ricketts: her work is in the keeping of the home, the preparation of food against each day and against the dead season, the bearing and care of her children, the training of her daughters:

Children: all these children: their work is as it is told to them and taught to them until such time as they shall strengthen and escape, and, escaped of one imprisonment, are submitted into another.

There are times of year when all these three are overlapped and collaborated, all in the field in the demand, chiefly, of cotton; but more largely, the woman is the servant of the day, and of immediate life, and the man is the servant of the year, and of the basis and boundaries of life, and is their ruler; and the children are the servants of their parents: and the center of all their existence, the central work, that by which they have their land, their shelter, their living, that which they must work for no reward more than this, because they do not own themselves, and without hope or interest, that which they cannot eat and get no money of but which is at the center of their duty and greatest expense of strength and spirit, the cultivation and harvesting of cotton: and all this effort takes place between a sterile earth and an uncontrollable sky in whose propitiation is centered their chief reverence and fear, and the deepest earnestness of their prayers, who read in these machinations of their heaven all signs of a fate which the hardest work cannot much help, and, not otherwise than as the most ancient peoples of the earth, make their plantations in the unpitying pieties of the moon.

WORK 2: COTTON

Cotton is only one among several crops and among many labors: and all these other crops and labors mean life itself. Cotton means nothing of the sort. It demands more work of a tenant family and yields less reward than all the rest. It is the reason the tenant has the means to do the rest, and to have the rest, and to live, as a tenant, at all. Aside from a few negligibilities of minor sale and barter and of out-of-season work, it is his one possible source of money, and through this fact, though his living depends far less on money than on the manipulations of immediate nature, it has a certain royalty. It is also that by which he has all else besides money. But it is also his chief contracted obligation, for which he must neglect all else as need be; and is the central leverage and symbol of his privation and of his wasted life. It is the one crop and labor which is in no possible way useful as it stands to the tenant's living; it is among all these the one which must and can be turned into money; it is among all these the one in which the landowner is most interested; and it is among all these the one of which the tenant can hope for least, and can be surest that he is being cheated, and is always to be cheated. All other tasks are incidental to it; it is constantly on everyone's mind; yet of all of them it is the work in which the tenant has least hope and least interest, and to which he must devote the most energy. Any less involved and self-contradictory attempt to understand what cotton and cotton work 'means' to a tenant would, it seems to me, be false to it. It has the doubleness that all jobs have by which one stays alive and in which one's life is made a cheated ruin, and the same sprained and twilight effect on those who must work at it: but because it is only one among the many jobs by which a tenant family must stay alive, and deflects all these others, and receives still other light from their more personal need, reward, and value, its meanings are much more complex than those of most jobs: it is a strong stale magnet among many others more weak and more yielding of life and hope. In the mind of one in whom all these magnetisms are daily and habituated from his birth, these meanings are one somber mull: yet all their several forces are pulling at once, and by them the brain is quietly drawn and quartered. It seems to me it is only through such a complex of meanings that a tenant can feel, toward that crop, toward each plant in it, toward all that work, what he and all grown women too appear to feel, a particular automatism, a quiet, apathetic, and inarticulate yet deeply vindictive hatred, and at the same time utter hopelessness, and the deepest of their anxieties and of their hopes: as if the plant stood enormous in the unsteady sky fastened above them in all they do like the eyes of an overseer. To do all of the hardest work of your life in service of these drawings-apart of ambiguities; and to have all other tasks and all one's consciousness stained and drawn apart in it: I can conceive of little else which could be so inevitably destructive of the appetite for living, of the spirit, of the being, or by whatever name the centers of individuals are to be called: and this very literally: for just as there are deep chemical or electric changes in all the body under anger, or love, or fear, so there must certainly be at the center of these meanings and their directed emotions; perhaps most essentially, an incalculably somber and heavy weight and dark knotted iron of subnausea at the peak of the diaphragm, darkening and weakening the whole body and being, the literal feeling by which the words a broken heart are no longer poetic, but are merely the most accurate possible description.

Yet these things as themselves are withdrawn almost beyond visibility, and the true focus and right telling of it would be in the exact textures of each immediate task.

Of cotton farming I know almost nothing with my own eyes; the rest I have of Bud Woods. I asked enough of other people to realize that every tenant differs a little in his methods, so nothing of this can be set down as 'standard' or 'correct'; but the dissonances are of small detail rather than of the frame and series in the year. I respect dialects too deeply, when they are used by those who have a right to them, not to be hesitant in using them, but I have decided to use some of Woods' language here. I have decided, too, to try to use my imagination a little, as carefully as I can. I must warn you that the result is sure to be somewhat inaccurate: but it is accurate anyhow to my ignorance, which I would not wish to disguise.

From the end of the season and on through the winter the cotton and the corn stand stripped and destroyed, the cotton black and brown, the corn gray and brown and rotted gold, much more shattered, the banks of woodland bare, drenched and black, the clay dirt sombered wet or hard with a shine of iron, peaceful and exhausted; the look of trees in a once fullblown country where such a burning of war has gone there is no food left even for birds and insects, all now brought utterly quiet, and the bare homes dark with dampness, under the soft and mourning midwinter suns of autumnal days, when all glows gold yet lifeless, and under constrictions of those bitter freezings when the clay is shafted and sprilled with ice, and the aching thinly drifted snows which give the land its shape, and, above all, the long, cold, silent, inexhaustible, and dark winter rains:

In the late fall or middle February this tenant, which of the three or of the millions I do not care — a man, dressed against the wet coldness, may be seen small and dark in his prostrated fields, taking down these sometimes brittle, sometimes rotted forests of last year's crops with a club or with a cutter, putting death to bed, cleaning the land:

and late in February, in fulfillment of an obligation to his landlord, he borrows a second mule and, with a two-horse plow, runs up the levees,* that is, the terraces, which shall preserve his land; this in a softening mild brightness and odoriferousness of presaging spring, and a rustling shearing apart of the heavy land, his mules moving in slow scarce-wakened method as of work before dawn, knowing the real year's work to be not started yet, only made ready for. It is when this is done, at about the first of March, that the actual work begins, with what is planted where, and with what grade and amount of fertilizer, determined by the landlord, who will also, if he wishes, criticize, advise, and govern at all stages of planting and cultivation. But the physical work, and for that matter the knowledge by which he works, is the tenant's, and this is his tenth or his fortieth year's beginning of it, and it is of the tenant I want to tell.

How you break the land in the first place depends on whether you have one or two mules or can double up with another tenant for two mules. It is much better to broadcast if you can. With two mules you can count on doing it all in that most thorough way. But if you have only one mule you break what you have time for, more shallowly, and, for the rest, you bed, that is, start the land.

To broadcast, to break the land broadcast: take a twister, which is about the same as a turning plow, and, heading the mule in concentrics the shape of the field, lay open as broad and deep a ribbon of the stiff dirt as the strength of the mule and of your own guidance can manage: eight wide by six deep with a single-horse plow, and twice that with a double, is doing well: the operation has the staggering and reeling yet steady quality of a small sailboat clambering a storm.

Where you have broadcast the land, you then lay out the furrows three and a half feet apart with a shovel plow; and put down fertilizer; and by four furrows with a turning plow, twist the dirt back over the

---

* These farms are the width of a state and still more from the river. Is levee originally a land or a river word? It must be a river word, for terracing against erosion is recent in America. So the Mississippi has such power that men who have never seen it use its language in their work.

fertilized furrow. But if, lacking mule power, you have still land which is not broken, and it is near time to plant, you bed the rest. There are two beddings. The first is hard bedding: breaking the hard pan between the rows.

Hard bedding: set the plow parallel to the line of (last year's) stalks and along their right, follow each row to its end and up the far side. The dirt lays open always to the right. Then set the plow close in against the stalks and go around again. The stubble is cleaned out this second time round and between each two rows is a bed of soft dirt: that is to say, the hard pan is all broken. That is the first bedding.

Then drop guano along the line where the stalks were, by machine or by horn. Few tenants use the machine; most of them either buy a horn, or make it, as Woods does. It is a long tin cone, small and low, with a wood handle, and a hole in the low end. It is held in the left hand, pointed low to the furrow, and is fed in fistfuls, in a steady rhythm, from the fertilizer sack, the incipient frock, slung heavy along the right side.

After you have strowed the gyewanner you turn the dirt back over with two plowings just as before: and that is the second bedding. Pitch the bed shallow, or you won't be able to work it right.

If you have done all this right you haven't got a blemish in all your land that is not broke: and you are ready to plant.

But just roughly, only as a matter of suggestion, compute the work that has been done so far, in ten acres of land, remembering that this is not counting in ten more acres of corn and a few minor crops: how many times has this land been retraced in the rolling-gaited guidance and tensions and whippings and orderings of plowing, and with the steadily held horn, the steady arc of the right arm and right hand fisting and opening like a heart, the heavy weight of the sack at the right side?

Broadcasting, the whole unbroken plaque slivered open in rectilinear concenters, eight inches apart and six deep if with one mule, sixteen apart and twelve deep if with two: remember how much length of line is coiled in one reel or within one phonograph record: and then each furrow, each three and a half feet, scooped open with a shovel plow: and in each row the fertilizer laid: and each row folded cleanly back in four transits of its complete length: or bedding, the first bedding in four transits of each length; and then the fertilizer: and four more transits of each length: every one of the many rows of the whole of the field gone eight times over with a plow and a ninth by hand; and only now is it ready for planting.

Planting

There are three harrs you might use but the spring-toothed harr is best. The long-toothed section harrow tears your bed to pieces; the short-toothed is better, but catches on snags and is more likely to pack the bed than loosen it. The springtooth moves lightly but incisively with a sort of knee-action sensitiveness to the modulations of the ground, and it jumps snags. You harrow just one row at a time and right behind the harrow comes the planter. The planter is rather like a tennis-court marker: a seed bin set between light wheels, with a little plow protruded from beneath it like a foot from under a hoopskirt. The little beak of the plow slits open the dirt; just at its lifted heel the seed thrills out in a spindling stream; a flat wheel flats the dirt over: a light-traveling, tender, iron sexual act entirely worthy of setting beside the die-log and the swept broad-handed arm. *

Depending on the moisture and the soil, it will be five days to two weeks before the cotton will show.

Cultivating begins as soon as it shows an inch.

---

* I am unsure of this planting machine; I did not see one there; but what Woods described to me seemed to tally with something I had seen, and not remembered with perfect clearness, from my childhood. The die-log is still used, Woods says, by some of the older-fashioned farmers and by some negroes. I'm not very clear about it either, but I am interested because according to Woods its use goes a *way* on back. My 'impression' is that it's simple enough: a hollow homemade cylinder of wood with a hole in it to regulate and direct the falling stream of seed as would be more difficult by hand.

Cultivation:

Barring off: the sweepings: chopping: laying by:

The first job is barring off.

Set a five- to six-inch twister, the smallest one you have, as close in against the stalks as you can get it and not damage them, as close as the breadth of a finger if you are good at it, and throw the dirt to the middle. Alongside this plow is a wide tin defender, which doesn't allow a blemish to fall on the young plants.

Then comes the first of the four sweepings. The sweeps are blunt stocks shaped a good deal like stingrays. Over their dull foreheads and broad shoulders they neither twist nor roll the dirt, but shake it from the middle to the beds on either side. For the first sweeping you still use the defender. Use a little stock, but the biggest you dare to; probably the eighteen-inch.

Next after that comes the chopping, and with this the whole family helps down through the children of eight or seven, and by helps, I mean that the family works full time at it. Chopping is a simple and hard job, and a hot one, for by now the sun, though still damp, is very strong, hot with a kind of itchy intensity that is seldom known in northern springs. The work is, simply, thinning the cotton to a stand; hills a foot to sixteen inches apart, two to four stalks to the hill. It is done with an eight to ten-inch hoeblade. You cut the cotton flush off at the ground, bent just a little above it, with a short sharp blow of the blade of which each stroke is light enough work; but multiplied into the many hundreds in each continuously added hour, it aches first the forearms, which so harden they seem to become one bone, and in time the whole spine.

The second sweeping is done with the twenty to twenty-two-inch stock you will use from now on; then comes hoeing, another job for the whole family; then you run the middles; that is, you put down soda by hand or horn or machine; soda makes the weed, guano puts on the fruit; then comes the third sweeping; and then another hoeing. The first and second sweepings you have gone pretty deep. The stuff is small and you want to give loose ground to your feed roots. The third sweeping is shallow, for the feed roots have extended themselves within danger of injury.

The fourth sweeping is so light a scraping that it is scarcely more than a ritual, like a barber's last delicate moments with his muse before he holds the mirror up to the dark side of your skull. The cotton has to be treated very carefully. By this last sweeping it is making. Break roots, or lack rain, and it is stopped dead as a hammer.

This fourth sweeping is the operation more properly known as laying by. From now on until picking time, there is nothing more a farmer can do. Everything is up to the sky, the dirt, and the cotton itself; and in six weeks now, and while the farmer is fending off such of its enemies as he can touch, and, lacking rations money to live on, is desperately seeking and conceivably finding work, or with his family is hung as if on a hook on his front porch in the terrible leisure, the cotton is making, and his year's fate is being quietly fought out between agencies over which he has no control. And in this white midsummer, while he is thus waiting however he can, and defending what little he can, these are his enemies, and this is what the cotton is doing with its time:

Each square points up. That is to say: on twig-ends, certain of the fringed leaves point themselves into the sharp form of an infant prepuce; each square points up: and opens a flat white flower which turns pink next day, purple the next, and on the next day shrivels and falls, forced off by the growth, at the base of the bloom, of the boll. The development from square to boll consumes three weeks in the early summer, ten days in the later, longer and more intense heat. The plants are well fringed with pointed squares, and young cold bolls, by the time the crop is laid by; and the blooming keeps on all summer. The development of each boll from the size of a pea to that point where, at the size of a big walnut, it darkens and dries and its white contents silently explode it, takes five to eight weeks and is by no means ended when the picking season has begun.

And meanwhile the enemies: bitterweed, ragweed, Johnson grass;

the weevil, the army worm; the slippery chances of the sky. Bitterweed
is easily killed out and won't come up again. Ragweed will, with another prong every time. That weed can suck your crop to death. Johnson grass, it takes hell and scissors to control. You can't control it in
the drill with your plowing. If you just cut it off with the hoe, it is high
as your thumb by the next morning. The best you can do is dig up
the root with the corner of your hoe, and that doesn't hold it back any
too well.

There is a lot less trouble from the weevils * than there used to be,
but not the army worms. Army worms are devils. The biggest of them
get to be the size of your little finger. They eat leaves and squares and
young bolls. You get only a light crop of them at first. They web up in
the leaves and turn into flies, the flies lay eggs, the eggs turn into army
worms by the millions and if they have got this good a start of you
you can hear the sound of them eating in the whole field and it sounds
like a brushfire. They are a bad menace but they are not as hard to
control as the weevil. You mix arsenic poison with a sorry grade of
flour and dust the plants late of an evening (afternoon) or soon of a
morning (pre-morning); and the dew makes a paste of it that won't
blow off.

It is only in a very unusual year that you do well with both of the
most important crops, the two life mainly depends on, because they
need rain and sun in such different amounts. Cotton needs a great deal
less rain than corn; it is really a sun flower. If it is going to get a superflux of rain, that will best come before it is blooming; and if it has got
to rain during that part of the summer when a fairsized field is blooming a bale a day, it had best rain late in the evening when the blooms
are shutting or at night, not in the morning or the mid day: for then the
bloom is blared out flat; rain gets in it easy and hangs on it; it shuts
wet, sours, and sticks to the boll; next morning it turns red and falls.
Often the boll comes off with it. But the boll that stays on is sour and

---

* If I remember rightly, people never learned any successful method against him, and it is some
insect, whose name and kind I forget, who holds him in check.

rotted and good for nothing. Or to put it the other way around, it can take just one rain at the wrong time of day at the wrong time of summer to wreck you out of a whole bale.

It is therefore not surprising that they are constant readers of the sky; that it holds not an ounce of 'beauty' to them (though I know of no more magnificent skies than those of Alabama); that it is the lodestone of their deepest pieties; and that they have, also, the deep storm-fear which is apparently common to all primitive peoples. Wind is as terrifying to them as cloud and lightening and thunder: and I remember how, sitting with the Woods, in an afternoon when George was away at work, and a storm was building, Mrs. Gudger and her children came hurrying three quarters of a mile beneath the blackening air to shelter among company. Gudger says: 'You never can tell what's in a cloud.'

Picking season

Late in August the fields begin to whiten more rarely with late bloom and more frequently with cotton and then still thicker with cotton, a sparkling ground starlight of it, steadily bursting into more and more millions of points, all the leaves seeming shrunken smaller; quite as at night the whole frontage of the universe is more and more thoroughly printed in the increasing darkness; and the wide cloudless and tremendous light holds the earth clamped and trained as beneath a vacuum bell and burningglass; in such a brilliance that half and two thirds of the sky is painful to look into; and in this white maturing oven the enlarged bolls are streaked a rusty green, then bronze, and are split and splayed open each in a loose vomit of cotton. These split bolls are now *burrs*, hard and edged as chiseled wood, pointed nearly as thorns, spread open in three and four and five gores or cells. It is slow at first, just a few dozen scattered here and there and then a few tens of dozens, and then there is a space of two or three days in which a whole field seems to be crackling open at once, and at this time it seems natural that it must be gone into and picked, but all the more temperate and experienced tenants wait a few days longer until it will be fully worth the effort: and during this bursting of bolls and this waiting, there is a kind of quickening, as if deep under the ground, of all existence, toward a climax which cannot be delayed much longer, but which is held in the tensions of this reluctance, tightening, and delay: and this can be seen equally in long, sweeping drivings of a car between these spangling fields, and in any one of the small towns or the county seats, and in the changed eyes of any one family, a kind of tightening as of an undertow, the whole world and year lifted nearly upon its crest, and soon beginning the long chute down to winter: children, and once in a while a very young or a very old woman or man, whose work is scarcely entered upon or whose last task and climax this may be, are deeply taken with an excitement and a restlessness to begin picking, and in the towns, where it is going to mean money, the towns whose existence is for it and depends on it, and which in most times of year are sunken in sleep as at the bottom of a sea: these towns are sharpening awake; even the white hot streets of a large city are subtly changed in this season: but Gudger and his wife and Ricketts and Woods, and most of the heads of the million and a quarter families who have made this and are to do the working of taking it for their own harm and another's use, they are only a little more quiet than usual, as they might be if they were waiting for a train to come in, and keep looking at the fields, and judging them; and at length one morning (the Ricketts women are already three days advanced in ragged work), Gudger says, Well:

Well; I reckin tomorrow we'd better start to picking:

And the next morning very early, with their broad hats and great sacks and the hickory baskets, they are out, silent, their bodies all slanted, on the hill: and in every field in hundreds of miles, black and white, it is the same: and such as it is, it is a joy which scarcely touches any tenant; and is worn thin and through in half a morning, and is gone for a year.

It is simple and terrible work. Skill will help you; all the endurance you can draw up against it from the roots of your existence will be thoroughly used as fuel to it: but neither skill nor endurance can make it any easier.

Over the right shoulder you have slung a long white sack whose half length trails the ground behind. You work with both hands as fast and steadily as you can. The trick is to get the cotton between your fingertips at its very roots in the burr in all three or four or five gores at once so that it is brought out clean in one pluck. It is easy enough with one burr in perhaps ten, where the cotton is ready to fall; with the rest, the fibers are more tight and tricky. So another trick is, to learn these several different shapes of burr and resistance as nearly as possible by instinct, so there will be no second trying and delay, and none left wasted in the burr; and, too, as quickly to judge what may be too rotted and dirtied to use, and what is not yet quite ready to take: there are a lot suspended between these small uncertainties, and there should be no delay, no need to use the mind's judgement, and few mistakes. Still another trick is, between these strong pulls of efficiency, proper judgement, and maximum speed, not to hurt your fingers on the burrs any worse than you can help. You would have to try hard, to break your flesh on any one burr, whether on its sharp points or its edges; and a single raindrop is only scarcely instrumental in ironing a mountain flat; but in each plucking of the hand the fingers are searched deep in along these several sharp, hard edges. In two hours' picking the hands are just well limbered up. At the end of a week you are favoring your fingers, still in the obligation of speed. The later of the three to five times over the field, the last long weeks of the season, you might be happy if it were possible to exchange them for boils. With each of these hundreds of thousands of insertions of the hands, moreover, the fingers are brought to a small point, in an action upon every joint and tendon in the hand. I suggest that if you will try, three hundred times in succession, the following exercise: touch all five fingertips as closely as possible into one point, trying meanwhile to hold loose cotton in the palm of the hand: you will see that this can very quickly tire, cramp and deteriorate the whole instrument, and will understand how easily rheumatism can take up its strictures in just this place.

Meanwhile, too, you are working in a land of sunlight and heat which are special to just such country at just that time of year: sunlight that stands and stacks itself upon you with the serene weight of deep sea water, and heat that makes the jointed and muscled and fine-structured body glow like one indiscriminate oil; and this brilliant weight of heat is piled upon you more and more heavily in hour after hour so that it can seem you are a diving bell whose strained seams must at any moment burst, and the eyes are marked in stinging sweat, and the head, if your health is a little unstable, is gently roaring, like a private blowtorch, and less gently beating with aching blood: also the bag, which can hold a hundred pounds, is filling as it is dragged from plant to plant, four to nine burrs to a plant to be rifled swiftly, and the load shrugged along another foot or two and the white row stretched ahead to a blur and innumerably manifolded in other white rows which have not yet been touched, and younger bolls in the cleaned row behind already breaking like slow popcorn in the heat, and the sack still heavier and heavier, so that it pulls you back as a beast might rather than a mere dead weight: but it is not only this: cotton plants are low, so that in this heat and burden of the immanent sun and of the heavying sack you are dragging, you are continuously somewhat stooped over even if you are a child, and are bent very deep if you are a man or a woman. A strong back is a godsend, but not even the strongest back was built for that treatment, and there combine at the kidneys, and rill down the thighs and up the spine and athwart the shoulders the ticklish weakness of gruel or water, and an aching that is increased in geometric progressions, and at length, in the small of the spine, a literal and persistent sensation of yielding, buckling, splintering, and breakage: and all of this, even though the mercy of nature has hardened your flesh and has anesthetized your nerves and your powers of reflection and of imagination, yet reaches in time the brain and the more mirror-like nerves, and thereby is redoubled upon itself much more powerfully than before: and this is all compounded upon you during each successive hour of the day and during each successive day in a force which rest and food and sleep only partly and superficially refresh: and though, later in the season, you are relieved of the worst of the heat, it is in exchange at the last for a coolness which many pickers like even less well, since it so slows and chills the lubricant garment of sweat they work in, and seriously slows and stiffens the fingers which by then at best afford an excruciation in every touch.

The tenants' idiom has been used ad nauseam by the more unspeakable of the northern journalists but it happens to be accurate: that picking goes on each day from can to can't: sometimes, if there is a feeling of rush, the Ricketts continue it by moonlight. In the blasting heat of the first of the season, unless there is a rush to beat a rain or to make up an almost completed wagonload, it is customary to quit work an hour and a half or even two hours in the worst part of the day and to sit or lie in the shade and possible draft of the hallway or porch asleep or dozing after dinner. This time narrows off as the weeks go by and a sense of rush and of the wish to be done with it grows on the pickers and is tightened through from the landlord. I have heard of tenants and pickers who have no rest period and no midday meal, * but those I am acquainted with have it. It is of course no parallel in heartiness and variety to the proud and enormous meals which farm wives of the wheat country prepare for harvest hands, and which are so very zestfully regarded by some belated virgilians as common to what they like to call the American Scene. It is in fact the ordinary every day food,

---

* On the big plantations, where a good deal of the picking is done by day labor and is watched over by riding bosses, all the equations of speed and unresting steadiness are of course intensified; the whole nature of the work, in the men and women and their children, is somewhat altered. Yet not so much as might at first seem. A man and his family working alone are drawn narrowly together in these weeds even within themselves, and know they are being watched: from the very first, in town, their landlords are observant of which tenants bring their cotton first to gin and of who is slow and late; also, there is nearly always, in the tenant's family, the exceedingly sharp need of cottonseed money.

with perhaps a little less variety than in the earlier summer, hastily thrown together and heated by a woman who has hurried in exhausted from the field as few jumps as possible ahead of her family, and served in the dishes she hurriedly rinsed before she hurried out on the early morning as few jumps as possible behind them. When they are all done, she hurries through the dish washing and puts on her straw hat or her sunbonnet and goes on back into the field, and they are all at it in a strung-out little bunch, the sun a bitter white on their deeply bent backs, and the sacks trailing, a slow breeze idling in the tops of the pines and hickories along the far side but the leaves of the low cotton scarcely touched in it, and the whole land, under hours of heat still to go, yet listed subtly forward toward the late end of the day. They seem very small in the field and very lonely, and the motions of their industry are so small, in range, their bodies so slowly moving, that it seems less that they are so hard at work than that they are bowed over so deeply into some fascination or grief, or are as those pilgrims of Quebec who take the great flights of stairs upon their knees, slowly, a prayer spoken in each step. Ellen lies in the white load of the cotton-basket in the shade asleep; Squinchy picks the front of his dress full and takes it to his mother; Clair Bell fills a hat time after time in great speed and with an expression of delight rushes up behind her mother and dumps the cotton on all of her she can reach and goes crazy with laughter, and her mother and the girls stop a minute and she is hugged, but they talk more among themselves than the other families, they are much more quiet than is usual to them, and Mrs. Ricketts only pauses a minute, cleaning the cotton from her skirts and her hair and putting it in her sack, and then she is bowed over deeply at work again. Woods is badly slowed by weakness and by the pain in his shoulder; he welcomes any possible excuse to stop and sometimes has to pause whether there is any excuse or not, but his wife and her mother are both strong and good pickers, so he is able to get by without a hired hand. Thomas is not old enough yet to be any use. Burt too is very young for it and works only by fits and starts; little is expected of children so small, but it is no harm what little they do; you can't learn them too young. Junior is not very quick with it at best. He will work for a while furiously hard, in jealousy of Louise, and then slacken up with sore hands and begin to bully Burt. Katy is very quick. Last summer, when she was only eight, she picked a hundred and ten pounds in a day in a race with Flora Merry Lee. This summer she has had runarounds and is losing two fingernails but she is picking steadily. Pearl Woods is big for her age and is very steadily useful. Louise is an extraordinarily steady and quick worker for her age; she can pick a hundred and fifty pounds in a day. The two Ricketts boys are all right when their papa is on hand to keep them at their work; as it is, with Ricketts at the sawmills they clown a good deal, and tease their sisters. Mrs. Gudger picks about the average for a woman, a hundred and fifty to two hundred pounds a day. She is fast with her fingers until the work exhausts her; 'last half of the day I just don't see how I can keep on with it.' George Gudger is a very poor picker. When he was a child he fell in the fireplace and burnt the flesh off the flat of both hands to the bone, so that his fingers are stiff and slow and the best he has ever done in a day is a hundred and fifty pounds. The average for a man is nearer two hundred and fifty. His back hurts him badly too, so he usually picks on his knees, the way the others pick only when they are resting. Mrs. Ricketts used to pick three hundred and three hundred and fifty pounds in a day but sickness has slowed her to less than two hundred now. Mrs. Ricketts is more often than not a fantast, quite without realizing, and in all these figures they gave me there may be inaccuracy — according to general talk surrounding the Rust machine a hundred pounds a day is good picking — but these are their own estimates of their own abilities, on a matter in which tenants have some pride, and that seems to me more to the point than their accuracy. There are sometimes shifts into gayety in the picking, or a brief excitement, a race between two of the children, or a snake killed; or two who sit a few moments in their sweat in the shaded clay when they have taken some water, but they say very little to each other, for there is little to say, and are soon back to it, and mainly, in hour upon hour, it is speechless, silent, serious, ceaseless and lonely work along the great silence of the unshaded land, ending each day in a vast blaze of dust on the west, every leaf sharpened in long knives of shadow, the clay drawn down through red to purple, and the leaves losing color, and the wild blind eyes of the cotton staring in twilight, in those odors of work done and of nature lost once more to night whose sweetness is a torture, and in the slow, loaded walking home, whose stiff and gentle motions are those of creatures just awakened.

The cotton is ordinarily stored in a small structure out in the land, the cotton house; but none of these three families has one. The Gudgers store it in one of the chambers of their barn, the Woods on their front porch, raising planks around it, the Ricketts in their spare room. The Ricketts children love to play in it, tumbling and diving and burying each other; sometimes, it is a sort of treat, they are allowed to sleep in it. Rats like it too, to make nest-es * in, and that draws ratsnakes. It is not around, though, for very long at a time. Each family has a set of archaic iron beam scales, and when these scales have weighed out fourteen hundred pounds of cotton it is loaded, if possible during the first of the morning, onto the narrow and high-boarded wagon, and is taken into Cookstown to gin.

It is a long tall deep narrow load shored in with weathered wagonsides and bulged up in a high puff above these sides, and the mule, held far over to the right of the highway to let the cars go by, steps more steadily and even more slowly than ordinary, with a look almost of pomp, dragging the hearse-shaped wagon: its iron wheels on the left grince in the slags of the highway, those on the right in clay: and high

---

* Mrs. Gudger's word. Her saying of it was, 'rats likes it to make nest-es in.' It is a common pluralization in the south. There is no Cuteness in it, of speaking by diminutives, and I wonder whether this is not Scottish dialect, and whether they, too, are not innocent of the 'itsybitsying' which the middle-class literacy assumes of them. *Later.* On the proof-sheets is the following note, which I use with thanks: 'Isn't it the Middle-English plural? Chaucer used it for this same word and as a usual plural ending.'

upon the load, the father at the reins, the whole of the family is sitting, if it is a small family, or if it is a large, those children whose turn it is, and perhaps the mother too. The husband is dressed in the better of his work clothes; the wife, and the children, in such as they might wear to town on saturday, or even, some of them, to church, and the children are happy and excited, high on the soft load, and even a woman is taken with it a little, much more soberly, and even the man who is driving, has in the tightness of his jaws, and in his eyes, which meet those of any stranger with the curious challenging and protective, fearful and fierce pride a poor mother shows when her child, dressed in its best, is being curiously looked at; even he who knows best of any of them, is taken with something of the same: and there is in fact about the whole of it some raw, festal quality, some air also of solemn grandeur, this member in the inconceivably huge and slow parade of mule-drawn, crawling wagons, creaking under the weight of the year's bloodsweated and prayed-over work, on all the roads drawn in, from the utmost runners and ramifications of the slender red roads of all the south and into the southern highways, a wagon every few hundred yards, crested this with a white and this with a black family, all drawn toward those little trembling lodes which are the gins, and all and in each private and silent heart toward that climax of one more year's work which yields so little at best, and nothing so often, and worse to so many hundreds of thousands:

The gin itself, too, the wagons drawn up in line, the people waiting on each wagon, the suspendered white-shirted men on the platform, the emblematic sweep of the grand-shouldered iron beam scales cradling gently on the dark doorway their design of justice, the landlords in their shirt-sleeves at the gin or relaxed in swivels beside the decorated safes in their little offices, the heavy-muscled and bloodfaced young men in baseball caps who tumble the bales with short sharp hooks, the loafers drawn into this place to have their batteries recharged in the violence that is in process here in the bare and weedy outskirts of this bare and brutal town; all this also in its hard, slack,

nearly speechless, sullen-eyed way, is dancelike and triumphal: the big
blank surfaces of corrugated metal, bright and sick as gas in the sunlight, square their darkness round a shuddering racket that subsumes
all easy speaking: the tenant gets his ticket and his bale number, and
waits his turn in the long quiet line; the wagon ahead is emptied and
moves forward lightly as the mule is cut; he cuts his own load heavily
under as the gin head is hoisted; he reaches up for the suction pipe
and they let it down to him; he swings and cradles its voracity down
through the crest of and round and round his stack of cotton, until the
last lint has leapt up from the wagon bed; and all the while the gin is
working in the deafening appetites of its metals, only it is his work the
gin is digesting now, and standing so close in next its flank, he is intimate with this noise of great energy, cost and mystery; and out at the
rear, the tin and ghostly interior of the seed shed, against whose roof
and rafters a pipe extends a steady sleet of seed and upon all whose
interior surfaces and all the air a dry nightmare fleece like the false
snows of Christmas movies hangs shuddering as it might in horror of
its just accomplished parturition: and out in front, the last of the cotton snowlike relaxing in pulses down a slide of dark iron into the com-
press its pure whiteness; and a few moments merely of pressure under
the floor level, the air of an off-stage strangling; and the bale is lifted
like a theater organ, the presses unlatched, the numbered brass tag
attached, the metal ties made fast: it hangs in the light breathing of the
scales, his bale, the one he has made, and a little is slivered from it, and
its weight and staple length are recorded on his ginning slip, and it is
caught with the hooks and tumbled out of the way, his bale of cotton,
depersonalized forever now, identical with all others, which shall be
melted indistinguishably into an oblivion of fabrics, wounds, bleedings,
and wars; he takes his ginning slip to his landlord, and gets his cottonseed money, and does a little buying; and gathers his family together;
and leaves town. The exodus from town is even more formal than the
parade in was. It has taken almost exactly eighteen minutes to gin each
bale, once the waiting was over, and each tenant has done almost ex-

actly the same amount of business afterward, and the empty, light grinding wagons are distributed along the roads in a likewise exact collaboration of time and space apart, that is, the time consumed by ginning plus business, and the space apart which, in that time, a mule traverses at his classic noctambular pace. It is as if those who were drawn in full by the sun and their own effort and sucked dry at a metal heart were restored, were sown once more at large upon the slow breadths of their country, in the precisions of some mechanic and superhuman hand.

That is repeated as many times as you have picked a bale. Your field is combed over three, four or five times. The height of the ginning season in that part of the country is early October, and in that time the loaded wagons are on the road before the least crack of daylight, the waiting is endless hours, and the gin is still pulsing and beating after dark. After that comes hog-killing, and the gristing of the corn and milling of the sorghum that were planted late to come ready late; and more urgent and specific meditation of whether or not to move to another man, and of whether you are to be kept; and settlement time; and the sky descends, the air becomes like dark glass, the ground stiffens, the clay honeycombs with frost, the corn and the cotton stand stripped to the naked bone and the trees are black, the odors of pork and woodsmoke sharpen all over the country, the long dark silent sleeping rains stream down in such grieving as nothing shall ever stop, and the houses are cold, fragile drums, and the animals tremble, and the clay is one shapeless sea, and winter has shut.

Intermission

Conversation in the Lobby

In May 1939, the Partisan Review sent to a number of writers the questionnaire on the opposite page. It happened succinctly to represent a good deal that made me angry, and I promptly and angrily replied to it. My anger and speed made my answers intemperate, inarticulate, and at times definitely foolish: but my later attempts to do the same job more reasonably seemed, in the very fact of the reasonableness, to do such questions more honor than they deserved. I decided to let the answers stand and, in so far as they were an image of my foolishness, to let them accuse me.

It was not pleasant to do this, for I knew and liked (and like) some of the editors, and felt, also, some respect for some of what they were doing; and I thought it likely that my reply would be regarded as a personal attack. It was; and the reply was not printed, on the grounds that no magazine is under obligation to print an attack on itself, and that I had not answered the questions. That I differ with both opinions is a point worth mentioning but not worth arguing.

Readers who think that in printing this here I am (*a*) digressing from the subject of this volume, or (*b*) indulging in a literary quarrel, are welcome to their thoughts.

I wish to thank Mr. Dwight Macdonald for his decency in returning the manuscript to me, knowing how I would use it; and to express my regret over every misunderstanding, unpleasantness, and difference of opinion that is implicit in the incident, or that has arisen from it.

Some Questions Which
Face American Writers Today

1. Are you conscious, in your own writing, of the existence of a 'usable past'? Is this mostly American? What figures would you designate as elements in it? Would you say, for example, that Henry James's work is more relevant to the present and future of American writing than Walt Whitman's?

2. Do you think of yourself as writing for a definite audience? If so, how would you describe this audience? Would you say that the audience for serious American writing has grown or contracted in the last ten years?

3. Do you place much value on the criticism your work has received? Would you agree that the corruption of the literary supplements by advertising – in the case of the newspapers – and political pressures – in the case of the liberal weeklies – has made serious literary criticism an isolated cult?

4. Have you found it possible to make a living by writing the sort of thing you want to, and without the aid of such crutches as teaching and editorial work? Do you think there is any place in our present economic system for literature as a profession?

5. Do you find, in retrospect, that your writing reveals any allegiance to any group, class, organization, region, religion, or system of thought, or do you conceive of it as mainly the expression of yourself as an individual?

6. How would you describe the political tendency of American writing as a whole since 1930? How do you feel about it yourself? Are you sympathetic to the current tendency toward what may be called 'literary nationalism' – a renewed emphasis, largely uncritical, on the specifically 'American' elements in our culture?

7. Have you considered the question of your attitude toward the possible entry of the United States into the next world war? What do you think the responsibilities of writers in general are when and if war comes?

In reply to your questions:

In your letter you say: 'These questions, we think, are central to any discussion of American literature today.'

Then God help 'American' or any other 'literature.' Or else let both suspect words become your property and that of your inferiors. The good work will meanwhile be done by those who can use neither word.

You are supposed to be and I guess are the best 'American' 'literary' and 'critical' magazine. In other words, these questions, the best you can ask, prove a lot about American literature and criticism and about you, the self-assumed 'vanguard.' They prove you as bad for, or irrelevant to, good work, as The New Masses or The Saturday Review or Clifton Fadiman or all the parlor talkers or the publishers or most of the writers themselves.

It sounds like a meeting of the Junior League of Nations at Wellesley; or the Blairstown Conference; or a debate between an episcopal and a unitarian minister on the meaning of god in human experience.

The questions are so bad and so betraying they are virtually unanswerable; and are indeed more interesting as betrayals, that you only think you know what good work is, and have no right to your proprietary attitude about it.

1. A 'usable past'? (The polite substitute for 'tradition.' Academic; philosophic; critics' language.) Beethoven 'used' the 'past': but do you think he ever sat down to wonder, What am I using: What is useful?

All of the past one finds useful is 'usable' because it is of the present and because both present and past are essentially irrelevant to the whole manner of 'use.' Moreover, things are 'usable' only by second-rate people and worse. To those who really perceive them they are too hot to handle in any utilitarian way. These same things 'use' the good people because they have become a part of their identity.

You want to 'use' these people of the past in the same way you want to 'use' the writers and others of the present. A lot of the imitation good ones love to be used. Some of the better ones use you, but you don't know it: you think you are using them.

Each of these 'usable' people are of their time and place, certainly: but essentially they are timeless (or near it), and international neither in the League-of-Nations nor the Esperanto nor the 'Marxian' sense, but because they recognize themselves as members and liberators of the human race.

'Usable': Every good artist; every record of the past; and more particularly, all of the present and past which exists in the 'actual,' 'unrecreated' world of personal or speculative experience.

Christ: Blake: Dostoyevsky: Brady's photographs: everybody's letters: family albums: postcards: Whitman: Crane: Melville: Cummings: Kafka: Joyce: Malraux: Gide: Mann: Beethoven: Eisenstein: Dovschenko: Chaplin: Griffith: von Stroheim: Miller: Evans: Cartier: Levitt: Van Gogh: race records: Swift: Céline:

Some you 'study'; some you learn from; some corroborate you; some 'stimulate' you; some are gods; some are brothers, much closer than colleagues or gods; some choke the heart out of you and make you dubious of ever reading or looking at work again: but in general, you know yourself to be at least by knowledge and feeling, of and among these, a member in a race which is much superior to any organization or Group or Movement or Affiliation, and the bloody enemy of all such, no matter what their 'sincerity,' 'honesty,' or 'good intentions.'

And all the bad and the confused and self-deceiving stuff: Life; The Reader's Digest; any daily paper; any best-seller; the Partisan Review; the Museum of Modern Art: you learn as much out of corruption and confusion and more, than out of the best work that has ever been done. Only after a while you begin to know certain sectors by heart and in advance, and then they are no further use to you.

And why does it have to do with 'American' writing, present or future, when Whitman, Beethoven, Blake, Christ, Céline, and Tolstoy have so much in common?

2. What do you mean, 'audience'? It draws in to the point of a pin and it spreads out flat like a quoit. Some of the time you are writing for all men who are your equals and your superiors, and some of the time for all the deceived and captured, and some of the time for nobody. Some of the time you are trying to communicate (not necessarily to please); some of the time you are trying to state, communication or none. In the terms you are setting it, no decent writer can possibly be interested in the question. And what sort of conception of 'audience' and of 'serious' writing can you have, that you can wonder, journalistically, whether this past or any other ten years can make any but an illusory and dangerous difference to it?

3. Do I place much value on criticism. I sometimes place value on the criticism of a few whom I respect, in one way or another. Few of these happen to be writing critics. I would agree that the literary supplements and the liberal weeklies are corrupted: but more by the corruption of the minds which hold forth in them than by any amount of advertising or politics. I will have to add that in this respect of unsound mind I think nearly everything I have read in the Partisan Review is quite as seriously corrupting, and able further to corrupt the corruptible.

4. No; no living. Nor do I think there is any place in our etcetera for 'literature' as a 'profession,' unless you mean for professional litterateurs, who are a sort of high-class spiritual journalist and the antichrist of all good work. Nor do I think your implied desire that under a 'good system' there would be such a place for real 'writers' is to be respected or other than deplored. A good artist is a deadly enemy of society; and the most dangerous thing that can happen to an enemy, no matter how cynical, is to become a beneficiary. No society, no matter how good,

could be mature enough to support a real artist without mortal danger to that artist. Only no one need worry: for this same good artist is about the one sort of human being alive who can be trusted to take care of himself.

5. 'I find, in retrospect,' that I have felt forms of allegiance or part-allegiance to catholicism and to the communist party. I felt less and less at ease with them and I am done with them. I feel sufficiently intense allegiance toward certain shapes of fact and toward certain ideas that I prefer not to speak of them here, beyond saying that no organization of thought or of persons has ever held them, that they are antipathetic to any such, and that I feel a rarity but by no means a lack of company, and that this company is made up entirely of men who do not breathe one another's breath nor require anything of one another: but are of the only free human beings (and being such, are the only conceivable liberators of others): and that this freedom appears to me impossible under a 'democracy' or in any self-compromising, 'co-operative' effort. I am most certainly 'for' an 'intelligent' 'communism'; no other form or theory of government seems to me conceivable; but even this is only a part of much more, and a means to an end: and in every concession to a means, the end is put in danger of all but certain death. I feel violent enmity and contempt toward all factions and all joiners. I 'conceive of' my work as an effort to be faithful to my perceptions. I am not interested in 'expressing' 'myself' as an 'individual' except when it is suggested that I 'express' someone else.

6. 'The political tendency of American writing as a whole since 1930' smells no more nor less to heaven than all the other tendencies of all the tendential sheep who make up the bulk of what they please to call literature and who are perhaps the worst of all poisoners of the air against good writing and the most effective secondary stimulants toward the development of ferocity in personal integrity. No, I don't like 'literary nationalism' either. Nor 'peace,' nor 'democracy,' nor 'war,' nor 'fascism,' nor 'science,' nor 'art,' nor your evident self-assurance that by the act of talking in favor of the 'necessary independence of the rev-

olutionary artist' you know any more about it than Granville Hicks does.

7. I have often considered this question (though I might better respect a writer who hadn't done so in the least); first glibly ('on no condition will I enter a war'); later with more and more perplexity, distress, and immediate interest, fascination, and fear. I think I know that I would do one of the following: 1) Enlist in that part of the war which seemed most dangerous, least glamorous, least relevant to any choice I might have through 'education,' 'class,' 'connections,' or personal craftiness. This either for personal-'religious' reasons or out of an 'artist's' curiosity, or more likely both. 2) Join the stalinist party and do as I was told or Bore from Within it. 3) Stay wherever I happened to be, mind my own business, refuse every order, and take the consequences. 4) Stay wherever I happened to be, and write what I thought of the War, the Pacifists, etc., wherever I could get it printed. 5) Escape from it by whatever means possible and by the same means continue to do my own work. Of these I believe my likeliest efforts would be between 1, 3, and 5. On my 'responsibility *as a writer,*' I suspect 1 or 5 would be my choice, and that the steepest responsibility would favor 5. 2 is least attractive to me. I am worst confused between 'responsibilities' as a 'writer' and as a 'human being'; which I would presume are identical, yet which involve constant 'inhumanity' even in times of no official war. Or, in other words, I consider myself to have been continuously at war for some years, and can imagine no form of armistice. In that war I feel 'responsible.' I doubt any other form of war could make me feel more so. *

---

* I would now (fall of 1940) have to add to this a belief in non-resistance to evil as the only possible means of conquering evil. I am in serious uncertainty about this belief; still more so, of my ability to stand by it. I also uncertainly question whether a draft — or even registration — should not be resisted on still other grounds: i.e., whether the State can properly require the service, or even the registration, of the individual. Or, put more immediately, whether an individual can in good conscience serve, or register, by any requirement other than his own.

April 1941: To leave this whole question so tamely and inadequately dealt with is shameful, but I hope less so than to do in haste what I see no immediate prospect of having time to attempt properly.

Part Three

Inductions

I will go unto the altar of God:
Even unto the God of my joy and gladness.

Give sentence with me, O God, that I may hear thee, and defend my cause against the ungodly people: O deliver me from the deceitful and wicked man:

For thou art the God of my strength: why hast thou put me from thee: and why go I so heavily while the enemy oppress me?

O send out thy light and thy truth that they may lead me, and bring me unto thy holy hill and to thy dwelling:

For I will go unto the altar of God, even unto the God of my joy and gladness, and upon the harp will I give thanks unto thee, O God, my God:

Why art thou so heavy, O my soul, and why art thou so disquieted within me?

O put thy trust in God, for I will yet give him thanks, which is the help of my countenance, and my God.

Inductions

I remember so well, the first night I spent under one of these roofs:

We knew you already, a little, some of you, most of you:

First

First meetings

Down in front of the courthouse Walker had picked up talk with you, Fred, Fred Ricketts (it was easy enough to do, you talk so much; you are so insecure, before the eyes of any human being); and there you were, when I came out of the courthouse, the two of you sitting at the base of that pedestal wherefrom a brave stone soldier, frowning, blows the silence of a stone bugle searching into the North; and we sat and talked; or rather, you did the talking, and the loudest laughing at your own hyperboles, stripping to the roots of the lips your shattered teeth, and your vermilion gums; and watching me with fear from behind the glittering of laughter in your eyes, a fear that was saying, 'o lord god please for once, just for once, don't let this man laugh at me up his sleeve, or do me any meanness or harm' (I think you never got over this; I suppose you never will); while Walker under the smoke screen of our talking made a dozen pictures of you using the angle finder (you never caught on; I notice how much slower white people are to catch on than negroes, who understand the meaning of a camera, a weapon, a stealer of images and souls, a gun, an evil eye): and then two men came up and stood shyly, a little away; they were you, George, and you, Mr. Woods, Bud; you both stood there a little off side, shy, and taciturn, George, watching us out of your yellow eyes, and you, Woods, quietly modeling the quid between your molars and your cheek; and this was the first we saw of you:

You had come down to see if you could get relief or relief work, but there is none of that for your kind, you are technically employed; and now we all stood there, having introduced ourselves, talking a little, and the eyes of people on us, and you gained a little confidence in us when I met these eyes with a comic-contemptuous stare and a sneering smile; and we drove you out home: out to your home, Ricketts, the furthest along that branch road: and there you showed us your droughted corn, for you could not get it out of your head that we were Government men, who could help you: and there on the side porch of the house Walker made pictures, with the big camera; and we sat around and talked, eating the small sweet peaches that had been heating on a piece of tin in the sun, and drinking the warm and fever-tasting water from the cistern sunk beneath the porch; and we kept you from your dinners an hour at least; and I was very sorry and ashamed of that then, and am the same at all times since to think of it:

And it was here that we first saw most of you, scarcely knowing you by families apart: I can remember it so clearly, as if it were five minutes ago, and we were just drawn away from your company, and were riding the light ridges of the winding road, in the silence before we were able to speak a word of you, when the whole time was like one chord and shock of music: how you, Paralee, came up a path barefooted carrying two heavy buckets, a cornshuck hat on the back of your head; you were wearing a dress that had been torn apart a dozen times and sewn together again with whatever thread was handy; so far gone, so all-the-way broken down into a work dress, there had been no sense to wash it in a year; it had a big ruffle of wrecked curtain lace down the breast; and as you came toward us you looked at us shyly yet very directly and smiling through your friendly and beautiful, orange-freckled black eyes; and I shall not forget you soon, your courtesy, your dreadful and unanswerable need; your manure-stained feet and legs as you stood in the path and smiled at us; nor God knows, you, Margaret, a year and a whole world more hopeless; nor you children: you started out from behind bushes and hid behind one another and flirted at us and ridiculed us like young wild animals, and even then we knew you were wonderful, and yet it is amazing to me now how relatively lightly we realized you then: I think it was that there was so much going on, so richly, and so disturbing: such a strangeness of meaning and precariousness of balance, which I was wishing so much as never before to make secure; chiefly in one: in you, Mrs. Ricketts:

You realized what the poor foolishness of your husband had let you all in for, shouting to you all to come out, children sent skinning barefooted and slaver-mouthed down the road and the path to corral the others, the Woods and the Gudgers, all to stand there on the porch as you were in the average sorrow of your working dirt and get your pictures made; and to you it was as if you and your children and your husband and these others were stood there naked in front of the cold absorption of the camera in all your shame and pitiableness to be pried into and laughed at; and your eyes were wild with fury and shame and fear, and the tendons of your little neck were tight, the whole time, and one hand continually twitched and tore in the rotted folds of your skirt like the hand of a little girl who must recite before adults, and there was not a thing you could do, nothing, not a word of remonstrance you could make, my dear, my love, my little crazy, terrified child; for your husband was running this show, and a wife does as she is told and keeps quiet about it: and so there you stood, in a one-piece dress made of sheeting, that spread straight from the hole where the head stood through to the knee without belting, so that you knew through these alien, town-dressed eyes that you stood as if out of a tent too short to cover your nakedness: and the others coming up: Ivy, blandly, whom nothing could ever embarrass, carrying her baby, her four-year child in a dress made of pillowsack that came an inch below his navel; he was carrying a doll; Pearl, with her elegant skin, her red-brown sexy eyes; Miss-Molly: and Walker setting up the terrible structure of the tripod crested by the black square heavy head, dangerous as that of a hunchback, of the camera; stooping beneath cloak and cloud of wicked cloth, and twisting buttons; a witchcraft preparing, colder than keenest ice, and incalculably cruel: and at least you could do, and you did it, you washed the faces of your children swiftly and violently with rainwater, so that their faces were suddenly luminous stuck out of the holes of their clothes, the slightly dampened hair swept clean of the clear and blessed foreheads of these flowers; and your two daughters, standing there in the crowding porch, yielding and leaning their heads profound against the pulling and entanglements, each let down their long black hair in haste and combed and rearrayed it (but Walker made a picture of this; you didn't know; you thought he was still testing around; there you all are, the mother as before a firing squad, the children standing like columns of an exquisite temple, their eyes straying, and behind, both girls, bent deep in the dark shadow somehow as if listening and as in a dance, attending like harps the black flags of their hair): and we, the men meanwhile, Woods and George and I (Fred was in the lineup, talking over and over about being in the funny papers and about breaking the camera with his face, and laughing and laughing and laughing), we were sitting at the roots of a tree talking slowly and eating one small peach after another and watching, while I was spreading so much quiet and casualness as I could; but all this while it was you I was particularly watching, Mrs. Ricketts; you can have no idea with what care for you, what need to let you know, oh, not to fear us, not to fear, not to hate us, that we are your friends, that however it must seem it is all right, it is truly and all the way all right: so, continually, I was watching for your eyes, and whenever they turned upon me, trying through my own and through a friendly and tender smiling (which sickens me to disgust to think of) to store into your eyes some knowledge of this, some warmth, some reassurance, that might at least a little relax you, that might conceivably bring you to warmth, to any ease or hope of smiling; but your eyes upon me, time after time, held nothing but the same terror, the same feeling at very most, of 'if you are our friend, lift this weight and piercing from us, from my children' (for it was of them and of your husband that you had this care, at all times; I don't believe one could ever persuade you such a thing can exist as a thought for yourself); and at length, and just once, a change, a softening of expression; your eyes softened, lost all their immediate dread, but without smiling; but in a heart-broken and infinite yet timid reproachfulness, as when, say, you might have petted a little animal in a trap, beyond its thorntoothed fierceness, beyond its fear, to quiet, in which it knows, of your blandishments: you could spring free the jaws of this iron from my wrist; what is this hand, what are these kind eyes; what is this gentling hand on the fur of my forehead: so that I let my face loose of any control and it showed you just what and all I felt for you and of myself: it must have been an ugly and puzzling grimace, God knows no use or comfort to you; and you looked a moment and withdrew your eyes, and gazed patiently into the ground, in nothing but sorrow, your little hand now loosened in your dress.

If I were going to use these lives of yours for 'Art,' if I were going to dab at them here, cut them short here, make some trifling improvement over here, in order to make you worthy of The Saturday Review of Literature; I would just now for instance be very careful of Anticlimax which, you must understand, is just not quite nice. It happens in life of course, over and over again, in fact there is no such thing as a lack of it, but Art, as all of you would understand if you had had my advantages, has nothing to do with Life, or no more to do with it than is thoroughly convenient at a given time, a sort of fair-weather

friendship, or gentleman's agreement, or practical idealism, well understood by both parties and by all readers. However, this is just one of
several reasons why I don't care for art, and I shan't much bother, I'm
afraid. There was an anticlimax. The picture-making was still going on
when your children, George, came along, you, Louise, and you, Junior,
and Burt. You had been sent for; there were going to be pictures taken;
and you came so late, not only because your house was so far and
because Burt was so slow, whimpering and crying trying to keep up
with you; but also because your mother had taken time to wash you all
and to put a clean dress on you, Louise, and a ribbon in your hair. It
was the best dress you had, a prettier one than I was to see you wear
again; it looked almost though not quite like the 'party-dress' of a little
girl your age in town, of people whose mothers are so nice they would
never speak to yours unless about putting less starch in the cuffs,
please: white, and standing-out, and so soft, and translucent in the sunshine like your own soul, and one could only tell it from a really good
party-dress by the intense sleaziness and fragility of the cloth, through
which your body was visible, and the safety-pinned floursack you wore
for a clout; and by the ribbling hard narrow cheapness of the ribbon,
and meagerness of the sash which was trying to look like a great blown
sunlit bow at the small of your back and yet to save five or ten cents:
and by the stitching, which was done partly by a sewingmachine with
the gallops and partly by hand: and by a sort of uncertain embar-
rassedness in which this whole sweet artifact set itself around the animal litheness of your country body. And then, too, you yourself gave it
away, Louise, for your skin was a special quiet glowing gold color,
which can never come upon the skin of nicely made little girls in towns
and cities, but only to those who came straight out of the earth and are
continually upon it in the shining of the sun, active and sweating, and
toughening into work that has already made your clear ten-year-old
mouth resolute and unquestioning of personal desire: your skin shines
like a sober lamp in outdoor noon in all this whiteness; your feet and
legs are bare, they were washed, but already they carry the fine orange
pollen of the clay; it is entirely obvious that you are not what this dress

is pretending you are, Louise, and that the whole thing is a put-up job. But as a matter of fact I am noticing all this less than your eyes. Again, as with the Ricketts children, I am slow, but even so, it would be hard to see them at all and not have lost at least half your soul to them, even before you knew it: and already, though as yet I scarcely realize it, we have begun this looking-at-each-other of which I am later to become so conscious I am liable to trembling when I am in the same room with you. It is scary: scary as hell, and even more mysterious than frightening; and so tentative as I, who am a painfully tentative person, have never been before: yet somehow there is nothing shy about it, in either of us: it is frequent and, through all its guards, wide open: but what it is open upon, Lord only knows: there is no other blankness like you, like these temperatureless, keen, serene and wise and pure gray eyes of yours, set so wide, between your square young temples: and this as I said I am beginning only very faintly to realize now; so that I have become quiet in your presence and watchful, yet hardly know this beyond some feeling: here is a good child, here is a damned thoroughly good child. And so you three stand there, out at the side, near me, and near your father; Junior flickering glances at me which I fear in another way, shooing the flies from the scabs of one foot with the other foot, which is also scabby; Burt sniffling and beginning to talk to himself a little; and you, Louise, between them solid and stolid, looking straight ahead of you (I can rarely tell where your eyes are focused, save when they look at mine), and; well, and there you all are, in good order, under the shade of the tree. Your father will not let you get into the pictures on the porch: your picture will be later, to yourselves. (He is not unfriendly or 'pointed' about this, just open, and quiet.) And Mrs. Ricketts has seen you prepared as you are, and separate from those on the porch, and she is all tightened up again, and I know I have lost whatever shameful little I had gained for her, and it is now hard for me to meet her eyes at all, the whole thing has become so complicated and so shameful. (It occurs to me now as I write that I was as helpless as she; but I must confess I don't want to make anything of it.)

So in the course of time the work is done; they drift apart along

the porch and break loose along the dirt of the yard, in a sort of relaxation and loudness after tension: the children, that is; Mrs. Ricketts
goes directly into the house; and now George has begun to set things
in motion for his picture. He doesn't want it around here at the side of
the house where everything is trashed and ugly, but with a good background; and in this and in the posing of the picture he gets his way. It
is perfectly in one of the classical traditions: that of family snapshots
made on summer sunday afternoons thirty to forty years ago, when the
simple eyes of family-amateurs still echoed the daguerreotype studios.
The background is a tall bush in disheveling bloom, out in front of the
house in the hard sun: George stands behind them all, one hand on
Junior's shoulder; Louise (she has first straightened her dress, her hair,
her ribbon) stands directly in front of her father, her head about to his
breastbone, her hands crossed quietly at the joining of her thighs, looking very straight ahead, her eyes wide open in spite of the sun; Burt sits
at her feet with his legs uncrossing and his mind wandering (Louise
had helped him cross his legs, but no one can keep either them or his
attention in place); and there again they are; the three older of them
thoroughly and quietly serious, waiting for the shutter to release them:
and it is while I am watching you here, Louise, that suddenly yet very
quietly I realize a little more clearly that I am probably going to be in
love with you: while I am watching you in this precious imposture of a
dress, standing up the strength of your father and looking so soberly
and so straight into the plexus of the lens through those paralyzing
eyes of yours, and being so careful to hold perfectly still, and under sufficient tension of behavior that twice, and then again, I see you swal-
low, and your mouth twitch a little, trying very hard first not to do this,
then to manage it without appearing to move: and it is this sobriety,
and stolidity and resolute dutifulness in the sunshine, and the way your
mouth and throat worked, which has done the job on me:

And this was the last we had any particular reason to think we
would see either of you or any of these others: yet at the very last, just
as we left, the unforgiving face, the eyes, of Mrs. Ricketts at her door:

which has since stayed as a torn wound and sickness at the center of my chest, and perhaps more than any other thing has insured what I do not yet know: that we shall have to return, even in the face of causing further pain, until that mutual wounding shall have been won and healed, until she shall fear us no further, yet not in forgetfulness but through ultimate trust, through love.

Second

Gradual

And so it was that during the next days, the next weeks, we found ourselves coming back and back while we worked: it was so that we could not drive along the highway past those wandlike posts between which your road leads off along the hill without during the next mile feeling in our chests a pulling eastward alongside and behind us where you were, and a silence or some comment or questioning upon you: this is not a time to tell of this fully as it happened, and I shall here say only, how several times we visited you, Woods, learning you to be the shrewdest and the wisest, to talk to you, to explain ourselves, to seek your help through others to whom you might direct us in this country, and at length to lay ourselves fully before you and to ask you whether among you all, wherever it might be best convenient, we might live, paying our room and board, but with nothing at all changed because we were there: this is not the place to tell of these negotiations, nor of their subtlety and slowness: of how, long before you ceased to mistrust us, you were liking us, and were looking forward to our visits; nor of how very much we came to like and to look forward to you, so that you became in what our whole lives were then involved in a sort of father to us, with this half-recognized yet never made open among the three of us; nor of how a strange sort of community and understanding developed among us which we had with none of the others, in that we were all three of a reflective and skeptical cast of mind, and more particularly in our recognition of one another as criminals: neither these, nor the long and guarded, ironic yet friendly slowdrawling talks we held along the afternoons where you sat half naked on your unmade bed and scratched your body and spoke seditious truths in naïve elaborations of irony and glittered your eyes at us: none of these things are to be developed here; I can only say here how at length it was you who helped us arrange it, that we were to stay, not with you but at your son-in-law's, where there was room, and also because, well, you fellers know, got me this woman, here, not that I don't *trust* yuns (glittering merrily) but some way don't look right, couple young fellers, old man like me; don't know's I could stick up fer my rights, as you might say, if they turned out any funny-business, you might say. You understand, taint I don't *trust* yuns, but I know, young feller git too nigh a womurn, may not know hisself what he's lible to do next. Don't want to take no chanstes. — Sure; sure: we understand that: lot rather have it that way ourselves. And meantime Ivy is sitting on the scrapheap ice cream chair with her hands in her lap and her thick bare ankles crossed, one foot bent under along the floor, and she is smiling to herself, wearing also the face of one who would say, I am not hearing a word: and indeed we are all smiling back and forth, cautiously and respectfully, and yet openly. There has really been no need in his putting it so delicately: Ivy is a strong, young, goodlooking woman, he is a weakening and nearly old man, and she knows and he does, and we do, and we all know of the knowledge of each other, that she is also a serenely hot and simple nymph, whose eyes go to bed with every man she sees; and of how he has guarded her (but of that more in its place). So now, this is all quickly and simply spoken-of and agreed-upon: we and her husband understand each other in a thoroughly amused and almost affectionate way: and it is as if to seal the agreement, and the needlessness of talking further of it, that he purses his mouth, cocks his body, and baptizes with tobacco-amber the pink half-naked spine-feathered little abominable subpullet who eight feet away is scratching the stone fireplace full of trash and the sourness of dead fire: who, startled, shakes herself squeaking, lets out a wet weak nervous turd, calms, and goes on eating quids and meat rinds.

Reversion

But before this there has occurred an incident which helped determine it: that which I spoke of saying, 'I remember so well, the first night I spent under one of these roofs,' when 'We knew you already, a little, some of you, most of you': it was in a time about at the most intense, the most nearly insane, of our frustrations; a time by which already, according to our employers' standards of speed, I should have been back at my typewriter and Walker at his tanks, and when we were still involved to suffocation in the inanities of the 'contacts' and obligations they had wished on us, and were under the nearly incommunicable weight of paralysis which constant dissimulation, and slowing to alien pace, beneath the white grates of that summer sky, can bring upon one: and had not as yet found anything which could satisfy our hope, our need, our determination to do truly: so that for the moment we had broken all but entirely and had prescribed ourselves a medicine, a day or two in Birmingham, where, we said to ourselves and to each other, there would be a hotel bathroom black enough for Walker to develop some test interiors; and where we might get help from a New Deal architect whose goodness and understanding Walker felt some certainty of in advance; and where we might get help through some communists I had seen in Tarrant City; but we knew well enough that it was less for these things we went than that we might have the infinite relief of talking more nearly in our own language to others, to those who at least were also spies, and enemies of our enemies; and that we might at the same time use rooms and beds and bathrooms and eat foods and walk through lobbies whose provincial slickness we could simultaneously rest upon and ridicule and in both ways delight in; and that we might walk in the dynamic and heartening streets of a populous city, a relatively condensed and sophisticated civilization, whose ways we might stroll by the hour without the pressure upon us, the following, the swerving, of the slow blue dangerous and secret small-town eyes. We went, we sought out and talked with these people, a regular hemorrhage of talking which must have alarmed them but which also stimulated their own terrific loneliness as well as ours, and which was otherwise useless, we ate bloody foods in chilled rooms and drank liquors, we ate up the streets, their façades, their show-windows, the distributions of traffic and people along these troughs, their lights at night, their odors of soft coal and auto exhausts, the faces and forms of their women, as men starved or dried to husks in a desert might eat and drink, and this cruel great spread-out country town was so grateful a metropolis to me as I had never known since New York was virgin before me at fifteen, and I first walked in the late brilliant June dusk into the blinding marvel of Times Square, watching the Covered Wagon cross the river Platte in electric lights, over and over and over, my heart nearly breaking for joy here where all the shows of every kind on the otherwise rural round planet were spread at once before me, a giant tray of choiring diamonds.

But it is now sunday morning; late; we sit high in the Hotel Tutwiler; behind the gray of an opposite screen two floors beneath us a woman is shifting from nightgown through nakedness to day clothing but the sun is spread strongly enough on that tall windowed wall that we can see scarcely anything; little pennons and serpents of black smoke and white steam wave like handkerchiefs above the complex roofs of the lowspread city; it is transferred to us how hot the tar-paper roofs of these buildings are beneath the sun by a special sort of pallor on their blackness; our fan is drilling a steady hole and column of relative coolness straight from the center of the ceiling to the center of the floor:

We found out what train Walker would follow me down on and drank some more sloe gin tepid while we finished reading the Spanish news and the funny papers. I decided to shave and put on a clean shirt. We tried the radio and all we could get was church services. Down beneath us on the nearly smokeless hot sunlight, some tower of bells was still belting out a hymn tune. I had intended to get away by the middle of the morning but it was hot and we talked a good deal, and by the time we got downstairs I saw that I might as well eat first and get one more good meal inside me before resuming the bad ones that were all I could get where I was going back to.

In the bright sunday noon the airconditioned coffee shop of this business-men's big hotel had the deaf horror of a vacuum. Two sunday-clothed middle-class southerners and their adolescent daughter ate at a hard black table in the dead middle of the room, talking very little. When they spoke it was as if they were embarrassed at the loudness of their quieted voices; and their silver was sharp and loud in the brittle cold of ugly air. Waitresses stood at the walls in pastel-shaded brittle dresses and hard, fresh makeup, useless and restless but restrained, their restraint making them still more angry at spending a sunday this way. We ate a large, cold, expensive lunch slowly and with sick gentle-ness, the way you might unbandage treat and dress some complicated wound on your body, and it was one-forty before I finally got going.

Twenty-four hours of every day for weeks now I had been in the company of another person, and now I was alone, driving in this bright day. I knew now how much greater the strain had been than I had been able, while under it, to realize; for I have never known more complete pleasure and relief at being alone. Thinking over the good day and night Walker would be spending alone in Birmingham, I was almost equally glad on his account. The heat and the pleasure together soft-ened me all over and made me drowsy and I lay down into the driving as if into a hot bath, paying very little attention to anything except the road in front and in my mirror, and pleasurably holding the car, along these first sixty miles of narrow and twisted concrete, up against the thin margin of danger. Except for tobacco and the pleasure of speed, almost none of my appetites were awake; I was just watching the road disinvolve itself from the concealing country and run under me with its noise and the tires and the motor. From time to time I would go over

some part of some piece of music I knew, and I enjoyed it, but without
any real edge. I knew I very badly wanted, not to say needed, a piece
of tail, and remembered the place ahead of me where we had talked
with the whore; but neither the want nor the need nor her proximity
much impressed me: I felt only that it is too bad so seldom to feel the
want of a thing at its keenest when it is available. As I got nearer the
filling-station-lunch-house where we had seen her, my mind ran on
ahead and slowed around her. It lounged around and talked dialect
with her and made out what it could about her and where she had
come from; then it took her out to an iron bed in one of the pine log
cabins out back. The sun stenciled an astronomical chart on the drawn,
cracked windowshade and slivered through chinks in the logs, and in
the odor and shade of heated pine a wasp aligned his nervous noise. I
found her body heavy, sour, and wet with the heat on the squealing
bed, spongy and so discouraging I was good for nothing, while she
grunted lines like got it in good, honey, and, sock it to me, shugah. So,
as the place came in sight, sooner than I had expected it, I slowed the
car only a little, watching out for her with the tagends of sharp but
sleepy appetite on the chance that my eyes would tell me different from
my imagination. She was loafed up heavily against the flank of a
Plymouth, one thick thigh lifted, lowheeled slipper on the running-
board, loosening out like hair her thick whore's dialect upon the white-
hatted driver as he drank his dope, and I was glad for good and all that
I was not going to move in on that piece of head-cheese in such a guy's
tracks, and stepped up the car again. It was the same with Estelle, thinking of her now: not worth the sacrifice of this solitude however well it
probably wouldn't work out, and in spite of the vapor-lamp quality of
her lavender and inappeasable eyes. I didn't even slow and go through
the street her store was on but went straight on through the middle of
town and cut south; and as I drew out fast along the road south of
Cherokee City, began to realize where it was I was going in such a
hurry and what day it was, and slowed down a little, and then I really
did begin to realize it. Of all the christbitten places to spend a few free

hours alone, and of all the days to do it on. I thought of driving on back
to Cherokee City and putting up at some hotel there, for any town is a
pleasure until you know it well enough to hate it or like it, and I knew
neither of these towns that well; but I knew I was going to Centerboro
and no further, and kept right on going there, on road and through
country now that I knew by heart, raising a long ruche of orange dust
behind me, and wondering what I might read or write in the hotel
room, or whether to get hold of some liquor, or whether I might not go
deep enough down into the Prairie to make it safe and manage to get
into some negro church meeting; and by now here I was, much sooner than I expected, god knows much sooner than I wanted, already
piercing the shallow outskirts of Centerboro, and a little ahead of me
would be the main street and all the narrow, mean white faces that
turned slowly after me watching me and wishing to God I would do
something that would give them the excuse, * and the sun blistering
down on the business block: I brought the car down to a slow float and
swung into it.

It was different from what I had foreseen, for I had thought of it
in terms of weekdays, and this was sunday. There was no one at all in
sight in the block, and no cars moving, only two parked cars so cooked
in the sun they looked as if they might take fire of it any minute. There
are no trees in that block, and not even the shadow of the low buildings even partially shut the wound; the sun was hitting every surface in
sight, and all of them were bare and hard, and the street and walks
were white. The light shrank my eyes half shut, and in the street
between the two lines of buildings it was like lime working in a trough.
A small hound took the street, trying to go slow because he felt slow
and was born slow, but using his feet staccato because the pavement
hurt them. It was as hot as all the days of the week piled one on top of
another, or as if they were a series of burning-glasses through which
this sunday struck. As soon as I slowed and swung into this street, the

---

* The excuse to make me trouble, as a northern investigator.

sweat sprang out and ran on me, and I suddenly knew what a terrible event a summer sunday is in a southern small town, and how strongly influential on its victims and their civilization, and that for miles and hundreds on hundreds of miles all around me in any direction I cared to think, not one human being or animal in five hundred was stirring, nor even the leaves of the trees and the crops except in the slow twisting of some white and silent nightmare. There was nothing in the air that could be called a wind or even a breeze: the air lay all over this land like flesh, and when it moved at all the movement was senseless, without direction and frightening, like the flexions of an amoeba. The sun had lost its edge and size and occupied half the sky with a platinum light that shriveled the eye, and at any horizon along the road I had traveled I now remembered the dry, thin steam that had been drawn in toward the sun.

The wind of the plain speed of movement had walled me away as though with the glass of a bathysphere from the reality of this heat; but now the glass was broken and the deep sea stood in upon me; I was a part once more of the pace and nature of this country.

Slowed a long way down into this nearly noiseless floating at five miles an hour I went both ways the whole length of the main street in the shade of the trees that overhung nearly all but the business block and there was not a stir of life anywhere: every last soul in all these shaded, jigsawed, wooden houses must be dead asleep under the weight of the hot greasy sunday dinner in shaded rooms, not even a sheet over them, whose added weight would break them open; and the houses themselves, withdrawn in their dark green, half-bald, twiggy lawns, were numb with sleep as ruins in the dappling and scarce twisting of their tree shade. All the porches were empty, beyond any idea of emptiness. Their empty rockers stood in them; their empty hammocks hung in them. Through windows could be seen details of rooms furnished twenty to forty years ago, and at the same time the window surfaces gave back pieces of street and patterns of leaves on light. Not even a negress cook stole out delicately by the back way in her white slippers on the lawn and her hat and her white sunday dress; she was gone long ago, or asleep by the simmering of the kitchen range. It was silent as the crossing of an old-fashioned ferryboat, where no motor was used and the flat barge, attached to a rope, is swung on the bias of the flat stream's relaxation. On the cool, gray-painted, shaded boards of one of these middle-class porches my body stretched its length and became the loose and milky flesh of its childhood who listened, hours long in the terrible space and enlargement of silence, while the air lay in the metal magnolia leaves asleep, once in a while moving its dreaming mouth on the shapeless word of a dream or lifting and twisting one heavy thigh and creating in the leaves a chaffering and dry chime, and I, this eleven-year-old, male, half-shaped child, pressing between the sharp hip bone and the floor my erection, and, thinking and imagining what I was able of the world and its people and my grief and hunger and boredom, lay shaded from the bird-stifling brilliance of the afternoon and was sullen and sick, nearly crying, striking over and over again the heel of my bruised hand against the sooty floor and sweating and shaking my head in a sexual and murderous anger and despair: and the thought of my grandfather, whose house this now was, and of his house itself, and of each member of his family, and of all I knew so keenly and could never say and of those I too did damage to, and of the brainless strength and mystery behind all that blaze of brightness, all at once had me so powerfully by the root of the throat that I wished I might never have been born: and then this passed, all this, as quickly as it had come, and I was again in Centerboro driving on the slow flotation of silence, door by door and yard by yard in all its detail home by home in a town I hated that was drained, drenched, drowned in the desperateness of sunday. It held even those who were awake under its power, the few, the few, stragglers in the shaded quarters of the street, whose feet dragged in the rich boredom as if in flypaper, making a loud shuffle or swinging scrape on the silence and whose voices here in the open, white-hot air, were subdued and sick to hear. There was no more reason to be walking than to be on beds in the square shadow of screened and blinded rooms. There was not only nothing to do but nothing to talk about and nothing to think about or to have the vitality to desire; there was not even any reason to exist, nor was there enough energy to care that there was no reason. I knew that miles out the red road at the swimming pool there would be girls whose bright legs, arms and breasts in the thick clay water warmth would be comforting to look at as they lolled or lifted, but I knew too that they would be inaccessible, and that I would hate them, and myself, if they were accessible, and that even in their laughter and flirtation there would be the subdual of this sunday deathliness in whose power was held the whole of the south, everything between Birmingham and the smallest farmhouse, and the whole of a continent, and much of the earth. It was like returning several thousand years after the end of the world, when nothing but the sun was left, faithfully blasting away upon the dead earth as it twisted up, like a drowned body swollen light and lifted to the surface, the surfaces of its body and the exactitudes of those scars and lesions it had sustained in the course of its active life. But it was worse. For this was not the end of the world, it was contemporary, the summer of nineteen-thirty-six, and this dread was imposed by sunday, only for a space, and this was what life was like, the only world we have. Tomorrow of these millions each single, destroyed individual would resume the shape of his living just where he had left off; and there was nothing pleasing in the memory of that sure fact.

I went into Gaffney's Lunch. It was nearly cool and its fan drowsed. At the far end of the counter three hard-built, crazy-eyed boys of eighteen lounged in a slow collapse like dough, talking low in sexual voices and sniggering without enthusiasm; sick and desperate with nothing to do and with the rotting which the rightborn energy of their souls could by no chance have escaped. They looked at me with immediate and inevitable enmity. I looked back impersonally, almost wishing there might for their sake and mine be a fight, though I was unable to hate them and am not yet fully over my physical cowardice. They resumed their talk, glancing at me once in a while. I could not hear what they said but by its tone I knew it had nothing to do with me. I decided to assume no disguise in mannerism, but to be just as I was, which was what they would hate, and to let them make what they wanted of it and to take whatever might come. I ate a tomato sandwich as slowly as I possibly could and then another and drank three coca-colas fast and one slow and smoked three cigarettes, while I looked at all the no-credit wisecrack signs, extinct dance announcements, ads, tobacco cans, and packages of tobacco and candy and fig newtons and cigarettes that I could see in front of me and in the mirror. The tone of the talk was not changing and did not change. I was just as glad as not and then I knew I was a little gladder than not. I had nothing against them, I would have got hell beat out of me by even one of them, to say nothing of three, and after such a fight I could have got nowhere with work from this town. I bought two packs of cigarettes and went out into the silent sun again. There was in the bright light a sensation of shadow and I looked at the sky and it was unchanged, stark naked, and I looked lower. Huge thunderheads were barely lifted on the horizon, their convolutions a scarcely discernible brain-shape of silver in the strength of the light. They were no use; they were a trick a drought sun likes to play; and gets away with over and over again. They ride up looking rich as doom, and darken; the look of the earth is already dark purple, olivegreen and wealthy under their shadow and the air goes cold and waits. They let loose drops as big as teacups, about a dozen to the square rod, of which you hear the palpable splash and break; and list off to one side. The sun, which has meanwhile lowered a very little, shines again and the dirt is hard and blue where the drops have hit it; it steams and stinks as if you had spit on a stove. I got on into the car. It had collected such heat while it stood that my eyes were almost immediately blind with sweat and I could feel the tickling of the sweat like rapid insects as it ran on my belly, but I didn't start the car; I was unable to move. I sat looking out through the windshield at the white concrete in the sun, and did not light the cigarette that grew wet and weak between my fingers. There was nothing in the world I wanted so much as a girl, but she must not be a whore or a bitch, nor any girl I knew well either, but a girl nearly new to me. Between us we had only newly established physical understanding and confidence and much was still exploratory, and she would know enough to be quiet and to talk lazily. We would not try anything drastic but would lie in the shade where the grass was short and cold, and perhaps drink weak drinks slowly, fully clothed but without many clothes on in all this heat, and very lazily meddle around with each other's bodies, and talk some. It would be pleasant if we were in the course of becoming in love with each other, so long as that wasn't too strenuous, and this fact would from time to time overtake our cool and lazy, semierotic talk with its serious and honorable joy. This girl would have a good body in a thin, white cotton dress, and her flesh would have the talent for being cool no matter how closely you touched it, in this hot afternoon, and she would feel as much as I did the seaweight of broad leaves the summer had brought out above us and how they hung on the air, and the sense of the damned south spread under and around us, miles and hundreds of miles, millions and millions of people, in this awful paralysis of sunday, and the sense of death. And if, putting my forehead against her cold throat and feeling against my face through her dress the balance and goodness of her breasts, knowing suddenly my weakness and the effort and ugliness and sorrow of the beautiful world, I should almost in silence cry the living blood out of myself, this girl would not only know what it was about but would know that in the only way I would stand for anyone to know it, and we would still be companions in the fall of the afternoon, though we might never find such good of each other again.

I took the car out the Madrid road, and soon the excessive heat was breezed out of it that had assembled in it while it stood frying, and I was lifting a line of dust again while the sun leaned to my left with all its heat still in it and stood like a poultice on my left face and shoulder.

All these houses I hurried past were familiar, uhuh; uhuh; on a few of the front porches there were people. They looked after me and the car, turning their heads very slowly, too far gone even subconsciously to be grateful even for so small and meaningless a variant. God damn such a life. I began thinking of the girl again. She was all right but what the hell, fantast. Where was I going to get her and would I want her if I had her. If I was ever in my life going to do one page of decent writing or one good minute of movies that was all in hell I wanted and I knew I wouldn't; not by any chance; and that didn't make much difference either. Who the hell am I. I don't even want a drink, and I don't even much want to die. I wish there was no one in all my life I had ever come close enough to to harm, or change the life of, the least little bit, and what is there to do about that. There is nothing that exists, or in imagination, that is not much more than beautiful, and a lot I care about that, and existence goes on under pressures more terrible than can ever be done a thing for, and a lot I care again. I could put my foot to the floor right now and when it had built up every possible bit of speed I could twist the car off the road, if possible into a good-sized oak, and the chances are fair that I would kill myself, and I don't care much about doing that either. That would do Via some bad damage, just as continuing to live with her is bound to, and just as leaving her is bound to. My father, my grandfather, my poor damned tragic, not unusually tragic, bitched family and all these millions of each individual people that only want to live in kindness and decency, you never live an inch without involvement and hurting people and — ing yourself everlastingly and only the hard bastards come through, I'm not born and can't be that hard apparently and God — Genius and Works of Art anyway and who the hell am I, who in Jesus' name am I. This is a beautiful country. You can take that and good art and love together and stick them up your —. And if you think da dialectic is going to ring any conceivably worthwhile changes, you can stick that and yourself up after. Just an individualizing intellectual. Bad case of infantilism. And — you, too.

As soon as I got on the slag above Madrid, I started watching for the church. It turned up a couple of miles later. I slowed down and turned to the right between the two peeled posts and took the sharp little hill in high. The man on the porch of the relatively prosperous little farmhouse on my right turned his head after the car. I had wished for better luck, but all right.

The one I wanted to see was Gudger, to himself, or anyhow just with his family. His yellow eyes and very slow way of talking had stayed with me most and some of the things he had said made it possible that he had at least heard of the union. He was the most direct talker and seemed the sorest and most intelligent and I wanted to learn more about him; but I didn't know where he lived. I wanted to avoid involvement today with the Ricketts and with Woods, and if possible I would be glad if they never knew I was there, for any one of the three families was pretty sure to be sensitive and jealous. If I had to see Gudger at the price of involvement with them or of setting them against me I was not at all sure I wanted to, today.

I went on past the row of gray houses and up the second hill and was on the nearly flat top. Out at a distance I could see Ricketts' house. I went on quietly, not very fast, looking at the cotton and the side of the road and the road, and checking on the thunderheads that now stood up all over the sky on my right.

Some woods ran by on my left and I saw Woods' house, back from the road about a hundred yards; nobody in sight except one of the babies on the porch.

I didn't know about this at all. I didn't feel like meeting people, talking, bothering anyone or myself a bit. I wanted to look around and keep quiet.

Woods' low, dry cotton went by and then his corn. His house fell away behind as I took the curve and reappeared a moment in my mirror, and here was the Ricketts' house right by the road only a hundred yards off, and now, its side porch and all the filthy lard cans and the hard dirt scattered with hen turds; nobody there. I would drive on out the road farther than I had been and see what I could find. I slowed the car a little and lifted my foot and tried to coast by quietly.

Out of the bum, low potatoes on my left one of the Ricketts boys stood up fast and grinning and shouted Hello, grinning with joy all over his face, and sure I had come to see them. The other boy and one of the little girls stood up waving and grinning. I waved and smiled and put on the brakes. They floundered out fast through the plants and ran up to the car close to me at the window, feet on the running-board and quick bodies clamped close against the hot flank of the car, panting with the grinning look of dogs, their eyes looking straight, hard, and happy into mine. (Jesus, what could I ever do for you that would be enough.) For a second I was unable to say anything, and just looked back at them. Then I said, taking care to say it to all three, Is your Daddy around? They said nawsuh he was still to meetnen so was Mama but ParlLee was yer they would git her fer me. I told them, No, thanks, I didn't want to make any bother because I couldn't stay any time today; I just wanted to ask their Daddy would he tell me where Mr. George Gudger lived. They said he didn' live fur, he lived jist a piece down over the heel I could walk it easy. Not wanting to leave the car here to have to come back for, I asked if I could be sure of the path. They told me, You go awn daown the heel twhur Tip Foster's haouse is ncut in thew his barn nfoller the foot paff awn aout thew the corn tell ye come to a woods, take the one awn the right nanexunawn a liyuf nye come aout at the high een un a cotton patch, cut awn thew the cotton patch, you'll see the foot paff, ngo awn daown na heeln he's rat thur, the only haouse. I pretended to be confused more than I was and said, Is they any way of getting an auto in? The other little girl had come up on the other side of the car; she was leaning in the window on her folded, slender arms and looking at me smiling gladly but furtively. They said, Shore, ye tuck it a way awn back most t-tha high way twhur they was a ole gravel pit awn my left that wasn't used no more (I remembered it), turn to the left in round the gravel pit and a-past the nigger haouses and keep on a-goin' tell I couldn' go no furdern I would be thur. I thanked them a lot and told them to tell their Mama and Daddy hello for me and that I hoped I would git up and see them all soon; the little girl on my right was giggling and the other one started to giggle, neither of them in at all an unfriendly way. The towhead of the two boys shook his head and laughed snortily like a horse with pleasure; the other kept his eyes on mine and smiled steadily, and suddenly they all yelled, Yer's Daddy, *Dad Dy!* (O Christ!) and ran to meet him.

He was swinging up the road behind us limping on both his equally sore feet and saw who it was and came faster, and I opened the door and lounged one leg out, waiting to get his eye to nod and grin and say hello. He came on up already talking and we shook hands, and I told and asked him what I had told and asked his children (suddenly and vividly remembering how when I was a child that had been repeated over me, taken out of my hands, and how I had known my childhood was mistrusted; and now knowing the children must feel I mistrusted their efforts to be accurate). Ricketts was giving me back five words for every one, grinning and gleaming his eyes and wrinkling his forehead like a house afire and, from behind his eyes, watching for his effect and for my true intention, which he feared. He said he would go along in the car and show me, in such a way, and so many times, that I knew I risked the complete loss of any possible confidence or liking, and of any access to his family, if I should refuse, so I exaggerated the size of the favor he was doing me and thanked him in proportion, and opened the door on his side and turned the car around, waved at the children, and started on back down the road. No distance down the road his wife came toward us barefooted in a black cotton sunday dress. I put my hand up as if to the hat I did not have on and smiled, slowing the car. She saw who I was and made a small smile over a face that had doubt, a little hostility, and two degrees of fear, the tremulous and the dreadful. I told Ricketts how sorry we had been the way it had turned out awhile back, getting her and the children all lined up and taking pictures without giving her any explanation, and keeping them all from their dinners, and he said she didn't keer nothn about none of that, in a tone which without unkindness meant that she didn't have a right to, so if she did it made no difference. I told him I couldn't be a bit sure yet just where our work was going to be taking us, but I hoped we would be seeing them all some more. He said, any time, they were always right there. Then he said, any time, they were always right there. Then he laughed very loudly and said, yes sir, any time at all, they was sure God always right there. Then he laughed very loud and long and said, yes sir, they was always right there all right, any time at all, and kept on laughing while, out of the back of his eyes, he watched me. That is the pattern of almost anything Ricketts says.

Yet all this city-business, you can see; you can see how it was not really satisfactory: it was as alien, indeed as betraying, of the true and only possible satisfaction of our need and purpose as when, unable to sustain any instant longer of the effort, the pain, the loneliness, to do the piece of work you would give all your blood to do, and aside from which no hope of peace can reside, a would-be 'artist' breaks down, plays it out by the hour on a piano, sees a movie, takes sex or alcohol as if an enemy by the throat to devour it, seeks out friends and talks them half dead before they crawl to bed, and the bore, trembling and half crazy with need, self-recrimination, sorrow of what he has betrayed and of the persons he has used, begins that awful stoneheeled peripatation of the enchanted streets, watching lights in unknown windows tall in walls, grieving for an open bar, beating his thigh or the sides of buildings with his fist as he walks, doping himself with memories of music, which ends only in an exhaustion final beyond the lifting of one foot before the other, sometimes still in darkness, sometimes in breaking of the dawn, sometimes in clean full-swollen morning stare with the lamps long shut, or a subway ride, in barrenness of gold straw seats, among those tin-pailed, each lonesome soldiers, gentle and as if sorrowful still with sleep, who have lifted once more the burden whence they drooped it in the water, with night still streaming from it to the floor: and so, cold, cold, to coffee and the daylit bed:

All it had brought me, was this terrible frustration, which had in its turn drawn me along these roads and to this place scarce knowing why I came, to the heart and heart's blood of my business and my need:

and so was I satisfied, as how can I dream to tell you, first in one incident, so fully it seemed there could be no more, then in a second so
rich, so plain and fair, so incalculably peaceful, that the first in retrospect seemed of the ordinary body of events: it was quite as if again as
of Birmingham it was thirst: as if in some inconceivable thirst and blaze
of aridity, you had been satisfied twice over, twice differently, with the
first not in the least detracting from the second; two 'dreams,' 'come
true,' true like those that tortured my adolescence, and as if then some
one of them for whose shadow I gnawed at my wrist, had quietly, within the next few moments, materialized before me, smiling gently yet
gaily, abolishing all fear save that which is in wonder and in joy, that I
might behold and touch and smell and taste her, speak to her, worship
her, and hear her words, show her places I had found in walking, music
I knew and loved, find that she, too, in a distant city had seen that
movie whom few others had noticed and no one cared for; and that by
some cause inexplicable to her as well as to me, she too as well as I
could never hear in our heads the words and the music of 'tramp,
tramp, tramp, the boys are marching, cheer up comrades they will
come,' without breaking apart inside, I suppose where the heart is, into
a shuddering of sweet tears, though our images were disparate; hers,
she being enough younger, of the World War, and of the poor soldiers
who, imprisoned far from home, among those who did not even speak
their same language, heard their brothers marching in a band, and
could not go out and march with them, play with them, die with them;
mine of that last war in which there was much nobility, the Civil War,
the War Between the States, when dark-bearded, coal-eyed, narrow-fea-
tured men of it seems a different race, yet who were our grandparents,
whose broken old gentleness still trembles along the flagged streets of
late spring, were meeting in glades in a level sleet of lead to take each
other's souls out: of a camp, a prison camp, Andersonville whose pictures I had seen, a great stiff clay in winter, closed in a stockade, tents
smoking, the ground striped with shallow snow, the feet, the joints,
bandaged in pitiful rags, the eyes like skulls; the guards pacing, meet-

ing, pacing, the odors of southern winter, and all centered upon these
captives that slow, keen, special, almost weeping yearning of terror
toward brutality, in the eyes, the speech, which is peculiar to the men
of the south and is in their speech; and beyond this, north, a continent:
a continent of southern clay, stiffgrassed, thin-housed, deep-frozen,
down which from sheeted snows advanced a blackness and brave
string, earnest and gallant, bugles blithing, the bravery of whose feet is
known advancing, a hundred, a thousand miles, oh, kind, brave, resolute, oh, some day, some time, dangers braved, all armies cut through,
past, to the rescue: cheer up; comrades: they will come: and beneath
the starry flag we shall see our homes again, *and* the loved ones we left
so far away: so far away: whom also I know, my soldiers, and their
homes, those delicate frames, white in the white light snow, the bead-
ed women, whose jaws like eggs are rounded next the hair, their serious eyes, creatures of a nation which has never learned loving and
happy living, seated there waiting in the deepskirted secret whiteness
of their sex; and the softmouthed children, dark-clothed and ruffed,
whose dark jelly eyes regard the camera so mildly, so severely; and
thou, deepcrafted, rude-boned, mistaken Christ, who sank in an incongruous pietà before a Good Friday farce, those reins left loose whose
raving runs six decades nor shall ever cure: we shall treat them as if
they had never been away: 'we have lost our best friend': 'I laugh
because I must not cry; that's all; that's all.'

 I must excuse myself this apparent digression because you of
whom I write are added to the meaning of this song, and its meaning
to yours: for here, here, in this time; on this vast continental sorrowful
clay it is I see you, encamped, imprisoned, each in your pitiably decorated little unowned ship of home, ten million, patient, ignorant, grievous, ruined, so inextricably trapped, captured, guarded; in the patience
of your lives; and though you cannot know it you like these prisoners
are constantly waiting; and though you cannot hear it yet like them you
do hear; how on the stone of this planet there is a marching and reso-
nance of rescuing feet which shall at length all dangers braved, all

armies cut through, past, deliver you freedom, joy, health, knowledge like an enduring sunlight: and not to you alone, whose helpless hearts have been waiting and listening since the human world began, but to us all, those lovable and those hateful all alike. And whether this shall descend upon us over the steep north crown I shall not know, but doubt: and after how many false deliverances there can be no hopeful imagining: but that it shall come at length there can be no question: for this I know in my own soul through that regard of love we bear one another: for there it was proved me in the meeting of the extremes of the race.

But this refreshment was as if, to this thirsting man, without warning or teasing of gradualness the sky became somber and opened its heart upon him, and stood itself forth upon the earth, and more rain fell than heaven might carry, and he stood beneath the roaring of its streaming, head back, eyes on the falling wheaten sky, mouth wide to take its falling, and all the earth yielding up that sound of applause which is beyond politeness, beyond reward, beyond acclaim, beyond all such vulgarity, and is the simple roaring of all souls for joy before God, as I have seen occur a few times when Beethoven through Toscanini has imparted his full mind (he who truly hears my music can never know sorrow again).

And secondly, quite different, quite so silent, and so secret, as the other was wild, it is in this same thirst the sudden transport, the finding of one's self in the depth of woods, beside a spring: a spring so cold, so clean, so living, it breaks on the mouth like glass: whereto I prostrate myself as upon a woman, to take her mouth: and here I see, submerged, stones, the baroque roots of a tree, fine dust of leaves, gray leaves, so delicate, laid and laid among this dust a quilt, the feathering of a bird, whose plumage I cherish nor shall in my drinking disturb: and standing from the heart, a twindling, slender, upward spine (it is a column of gnats at evening, the column of the stars of all universes), that little stream of sand upon whose stalk this clean wide flower has spread herself: or better, since this joy is human, it is not in a woodland I stand, but in a springhouse, of plain boards, straddling a capacious spring, a place such as that which was at my grandfather's farm, with the odor of shut darkness, cold, wet wood, the delighting smell of butter; and standing in this spring, the crocks, brimmed with unsalted butter and with cream and milk; the place is shut behind me, but slit through with daylight, but the lighting comes as from a submerged lamp, that is, from the floor of the spring of which half is beyond shelter of the house: and here on this floor, too, I see these leaves, drifted and deep like snow, and driven, even beneath the house: and between two sweating stones, sitting there, watching me, shining with wet in the dark, with broad affronted eyes, the face and shoulders and great dim belly of a black and jade and golden bullfrog, big as a catcher's mitt, his silver larynx twitching constantly with scarcely controllable outrage.

Introit

All the way down from Ricketts' the wind had been lifting, taking up little spirals of dust among the shaken cotton along our left, twisting and treating them roughly, blowing them to pieces, and by the time we had drawn round the tip of the gravel pit to the left and were taking the car for my first time among the difficulties of that broken little road of which I was to learn each trick, forward and backward, like a piece of music; it was tightened full of clay dust, gravel, splinters, twigs, the meager firstlings of the grand impounded rain which slivered horizontals along the blinded windshield, so that all the left flank of the metal car was steadily bombarded with little sharpnesses so rapidly, so intensely, as by electrons. We sank a rooty slope and crossed a branch (whose thin sheet shimmering was shirred all over the road) and opened on the left in a grim olive light a field of corn all slashed one way, the leaves out level in great loudness, the olive light suffused with a dim red gold, which was the substance of the earth; melons like hogs, their dust backs sliced with water; peanut plants twittering as under the scathe of machine-gun fire, or alternate frames cut from a stretch of film; and among woods again, the sanded road resumed in rooted clay, uphill, ravine-like, wrenching a last hump free (the car listing steep as the Vestris), and delivered in suddenness upon wide space of light on torsive clays where stands, first seen to me, your holy house, George, cloven, expectant of storm, the dust sunken about it like sucked-back smoke of magic, the plants released erect and trembling as flesh at end of shock of surgery, the house quiet save one blind creaking, a bull waiting the hammer: for in this last quarter-mile the wind has suddenly sunken as if cut, the dry storm being over, the orchestra arrested of its bullying *tutti*, and among the quivering flocculence of vegetation, which knows well to expect another blow, no sound as such at all, yet a quality of withdrawal, of tension, which is part smell, part temperature, part sound, a motion of withdrawal as of wide hands armed with cymbals: the exhausting odor that breeds of dynamos, a searching change to coldness, a sound from all the air as of a sizzling fuse, a blind blattering of thunder and brightness, silence again, so steep, and down it, water like trays that bursts four inches wide in a slapping of hands, broad-separate drops; and as we draw up across your yard in rapid second, a new cold rushing in the air, a gray roar that runs out of the woods behind your house and takes the field in a stride to meet us where we stop in such a welter that, in the fifteen feet between the lean-to where we leave the car and the porch we sprint for, the clothing is stuck along shoulders and thighs like tissue paper and we stand on the porch against the wall in a quiet of blockaded wind which feels illegal, and the reeking of rain is so outrageous all round that I can scarcely hear half what Ricketts is saying, though the scare and pleasure of storm has brought his voice into a high shout: and we stand, watching, beneath the field, the embattled trees, which are scarcely visible, all thrashing, yet some struck, each as if singled out for it, a great blow across the shoulders and base of the skull that beats it down with an *oooooh* rather than groan, beaten low among the shoulders of his brethren where, arms stretched, he bruises his forehead among them to weep, and a foam running and skipping as foam on surf along their crests, and a regiment of crests suddenly sprung loose, each leaf a catapult in the bumpy wind, smacking their sheen of water up at a wild angle of which wind shears off the top, and the rigid trunks themselves swaying even from their strong footholds in a strong and vertical oscillation as of wharved masts, and George comes out, to see who is here, not at all exhilarated as we are, yet tense; and is much surprised to see me, and we shake hands; and my natural inclination is to stay and watch the rain, but he is as much ready to draw back into his shell as if we were all standing in it, or as if this were an impropriety he could be courteous but not too patient with; and we go back through the open hall (which frames at its far end a barnyard one emblazoned blizzard), and stepping quickly into the kitchen he takes a lamp from the table, and at the opposite door he knocks; and the door is unbuttoned from inside which had been secured in a thoughtless reflex of fear, and we all hurry in, and he buttons the door to again as promptly as to shut out a following beast, and here in this room we are in a near dead darkness, in which at first I know, only, that it is full of people, whom I do not yet see. Through two walls of this shuttered room and parts of the ceiling daylight is let in short lead slivers; there is the sound of a loud falling trickle and of many assorted paces of dripping water; and even here in this dry and windless place the air is bristly with sieved rain: I begin to see around me a little; George draws out a chair at the fireplace and I sit down; I see there are on the bed and floor a woman and children, none of whom makes a sound or says a word, nor can I yet make out their faces or their eyes; George is scratching a match; it glints and dies; another; dead wet pulp; another, flares; he guards it in his palm, he touches the wick; the dark flame climbs shapeless in braiding of oleaginous smoke; he sets the chimney round it, brings it trim, the flame pales, takes shape, brightens and swells to level, and stands there in glass; I look around me: the sobriety of its fragrant light is spread not quite to the two far walls but on all surfaces of wood more near, details of furniture, bed iron, bodies, faces:

The wood frame of the fireplace is whitewashed. The white wash is scarred with matches. The hearth is full of sweepings and char. Water drops in a steady spatter on the middle of this heap, and the broken black stones of the chimney-back are crawled with its shimmering in the lamp. A small outer hearth of foot smoothed sandstone is let into the floor; one leg of my hickory-bottom chair stands in it. The floor is so beautiful in the light of the lamp. The planks are pine; they must be each a foot wide. It is all wood around me, and except for the white-washing it is all bare and untouched; it is all pine; wide boards of it; held together against a structure of two-by-fours, some of them splintery, some smoothed with planes. The door we entered is of broad pine vertical boards nailed together by a transverse and two horizontals, hung from hinges: a thick wood button latch, its edges softened with a knife, a twenty-penny nail stuck through its center has made upon the wood of the solid wall and swinging door a circular shadow of its usage. (Later I am to see on much of the wood of this house the arched breath of the saws.) The foot of the bed is iron; dark; the paint is gone from it; and like moist whetstone to the touch: its several rods stand upward to a curving of iron, a little like a lyre, and the head, in darkness, is the same thing taller. The lamp stands on a little table next the fireplace, and this little table is spread with a piece of floursack whose printing is still faint in it and through which the cheapest available kinds of pink and blue shining threads have been drawn in a designing of embroidery which was not completed. The bed is sheeted white, and beyond, more dimly, is another plain of white, and the iron of a somewhat more ornate bed. Between my feet and George's, at the juncture of outer hearth and floor there is a rapid little splittering of water which I can see falling between our eyesight, a little less swift than a continuous stream. Somewhere behind him a bigger dropping is going on, with the loudness and force exactly of a finger nail struck as hard and rapidly as possible against wood. Back in the darkness there is a folding and glad noise as of a forest brook. By lamplight and by day I see, beneath the door, water slide and spread along the wood floor. A large and slow-collected drop breaks now and then on my right knee. I do not move to avoid it but I shade with my hand so that this foolishness shall not be noticed. I see George's feet in their bluchered workshoes, planted in the boards of the floor. I watch his eyes while he watches mainly at nothing, and at the fear of waiting in them as he tries to create a saving rhythm against the unpredictable thunder. I watch these others who in the dark are drawn into a rondure: Junior, sitting on the floor, at the foot of the bed, his teeth working at the root of his thumb nail, watching me constantly with his hidden look: Louise, sitting straight upright at the edge of a hickory chair by the bed and near me, holding a baby close yet lightly against her prescient body; watching me: Burt, on the bed, on his side, his knees drawn tight, his body drawn in a tight curve round the seated hips of his mother, his face jammed against her thin buttock, crying very quietly, twisting his forehead tighter and tighter against her, chewing the cloth of her skirt: you, Annie Mae, whose name I do not yet know, and whom I have never yet seen, and who I gather, are George's wife (though there has been no foolishness of 'introductions,' nor any word spoken, of any such kind): it is you I was first aware of from when first I came into this room, before you were yet a shadow out of the darkness, and you I have had on my mind while we have sat here, and so much cared toward, how from the first you not only never spoke but have not once lifted your face, your head, where you hold it there bowed deep, your sharp elbows on your sharp knees, the heels of the hands clamped to your ears, your eyes I feel sure through the tension of your body so tightly shut they must ache with it. All that I see now is this posture, the sharpness of your bent spine through your dress, the black top of your head locked in your hands and the white broken part down the center of the skull, and a little of your forehead: the wincing, and the narrow moan you yield in each bellowing of thunder: at which time George winces too, not at all ashamed of his fear, studious to hold it in bounds only for the sake of his family, that they may have something to count on, to look toward for their own courage. No one has anything to say in all this absorption in terror and patience of waiting except now and again Ricketts who, since he must always talk most when he fears most, finds this silence an unbearably frightening trial: so that now and again, out of a silence in which he has been breathing quicker and quicker, he darts a loud-voiced and trembling, joking comment, to which George makes little or no answer, almost as if it were obscene in this context, and which I try to ease into silence with a 'yeah: sure is,' or a smile or short laugh. He remarks how Annie Mae is all squinched up on the bed like the devil was after her, a-har-har-har-har, devil hisself, and George says yes that she sure is afeared of the thunder and the lightning; Louise tightens her arms round the baby, looking at me: after a little Ricketts says again, look at Annie Mae; skeered like devil hisself was after her, yes sir, devil hisself. No one answers him. Yes sir, all squinched up like devil hisself was on her tracks; never seed a woman so skeered a thunder; and he quiets again. There is a scratching at the door, without whimpering; nothing is done about it. It keeps up; pauses; resumes in much more urgency; quits; and is done with. After a minute George says: arn draws lightnin. Arn, and dawgs. I offer them another round of cigarettes. Ricketts as before refuses: he keeps on spitting in the fireplace, stooping forward far in his chair to indicate that he is taking due care in a home not his own and for the same reason spitting quietly and rather delicately. George, as before, takes one with thanks. I realize later that he likes machine-made cigarettes less well than those he rolls for himself, but he is fond of the meaning and distinction which is in their price, and would probably always use them if he could afford them. All this while something very important to me is happening, and this is between me and Louise. She sits squarely and upright in her chair, as I have told, silent, and careful of the child, and apparently no more frightened than I, and scarcely even excited by the storm, watching me, without smiling, whether in her mouth or her eyes: and I come soon to realize that she has not once taken her eyes off me since we entered the room: so that my own are drawn back more and more uncontrollably toward them and into them. From the first they have run chills through me, a sort of beating and ticklish vacuum at the solar plexus, and though already I have frequently met them I cannot look into them long at a time without panic and quick withdrawal, fear, whether for her or for myself I don't know. Inevitably I smile a little, quietly, whenever I meet her eyes, but that is all. I meditate, but cannot dare a full and open smile, in any degree which presupposes or hopes for an answer, not only because I realize how likely she would be not to 'return' it, which, needing her liking so much, I could not bear, but because too I feel she is a long way above any such disrespect, and I want her respect also for myself. There are kinds of friendliness: and of love, and of things a long way beyond them, which are communicable not only without 'smiling,' but without anything denominable as 'warmth' in the eyes, and after thinking a little about it, endeavoring to bring myself to dare to, and to lose my conscience, I let all these elements, in other words all that I felt about her, all I might be able to tell her in hours if words could tell it at all, collect in my eyes, and turned my head, and stood them into hers, and we sat there, with such a vibration increasing between us as drove me half unconscious, so that I persisted rather than ran as one might in war or round a pylon, blindly and deafly, and gained a second strength wherein I felt as of a new level, a new world, and kept looking at her, and she at me, each 'coldly,' 'expressionlessly,' I with a qualifying protectiveness toward her from myself, she without fear nor wonder, but with extraordinary serene reception and shining and studiousness, and yielding of no remotest clue, whether of warmth, hatred or mere curiosity; and at length it was she who let her eyes relax away, slowly, with dignity, and gazed down along the flat chest of her dress, and upon her wrist, and I continue to watch her; and after a little, not long at all, she raises her eyes again, and an almost imperceptibly softened face, shy, as if knowledgeable, but the eyes the same as before; and this time it is I who change, to warmth, so that it is as if I were telling her, good god, if I have caused you any harm in this, if I have started within you any harmful change, if I have so much as reached out to touch you in any way you should not be touched, forgive me if you can, despise me if you must, but in god's name feel no need to feel fear of me; it is as if the look and I had never been, so far as any harm I would touch you with, so far as any way I would not stand shelter to you: and these eyes, receiving this, held neither forgiveness nor unforgiveness, nor heat nor coldness, nor any sign whether she understood me or no, but only this same blank, watchful, effortless excitation; and it was I who looked away.

Every few minutes George would get up and open the door a foot or so, and it showed always the same picture: that end of the hallway mud and under water, where the planks lay flush to the ground: the opposite wall; the open kitchen; blown leaves beyond the kitchen window; a segment of the clay rear yard where rain beat on rain beat on rain beat on rain as would beat out the brains of the earth and stood in a bristling smoky grass of water a foot high; a corner of the henhouse; the palings of the garden; the growth of the garden buffeted; a tree by the palings with shearing of rain through it; open land beyond and beyond that trees in a line; the rain moving along the open land in tall swift columns of smoke, the trees lashing and laboring like rooted waves; and in all this time I have talked of, such steady rave of rain and such breakage of thunder as I shall not try to tell: the thunder, at length, has diminished first, and now after a long time further, the rain too, and now we sit with the door a little ajar and watch it follow itself in a frieze of tall forward-leaning figures on the field, and this smokiness faints slowly out of the air, and the yard dirt is needled, not battered; the thunder is growling well off to the west and the air, though completely clouded, is softly shiny; and there is everywhere such a running and rustling, gargling sound of water as might be heard if the recession of the late parts of a wave were magnified; and in all this I now see Louise's face in the strange blend of lamp with daylight; and Burt relaxes, and looks for a little while as if asleep; and Ricketts begins talking again more steadily; and now for the first time in all this hour we have sat here, Annie Mae takes her stiff hands from her ears and slowly lifts her beautiful face with a long stripe of tears drawn, vertical, beneath each eye, and looks at us gravely, saying nothing. After a minute she leans across toward her daughter (every line of her body sharp and straight as if drawn by a ruler), and asks, how's Squinchy?

She is really asking for him. Louise knows this, and gives him over to her, and she takes him against her body and gazes carefully into his face, smoothing on his bulged forehead her russet hand. He is asleep, and has been asleep in all this time, but now beneath her hand he comes awake, and cries a little, and begins to smile, and much more to comfort herself than her child, she turns away from us, and draws her dress away from her breast, and nurses him.

The shutters are opened. The lamp is drawn down, blown out. The room is clear with light and breathes coolness like a lung: it is filled with the odors of the rain on the earth and of wood, pork, bedding, and kerosene, and is cleaned of the exhaustion of our breathing. Our faces are no longer subsumed but are casual and they and I look at each other more casually yet shyly, much more sharply aware than before of the strangeness of my presence here. Our voices and our bodies take shape and loosen, and we get up off our chairs and the bed and the floor, and come out of the room to see what the rain has done. There still are no 'introductions'; there is no kind of social talk at all, but as if a definite avoidance of any of these issues as too complicated to try to cope with; but quietness, casualness, courtesy, friendliness, of a sort that make me feel at ease, only careful: and I see how they are very careful toward me, puzzled by me, yet glad rather than not to see me, and not troubled by me.

But from where I say, 'The shutters are opened,' I must give this up, and must speak in some other way, for I am no longer able to speak as I was doing, or rather no longer able to bear to. Things which were then at least immediate in my senses, I now know only as at some great and untouchable distance; distinctly, yet coldly as through reversed field-glasses, and with no warmth or traction or faith in words: so that at best I can hope only to 'describe' what I would like to 'describe,' as at a second remove, and even that poorly:

The room was all shut-in, full of shut odors. The door let in light, but only across one end of this room; so that as I have told the faces

were held in two lights at once, in two temperatures also, and in two
kinds of air. With even this amount of the light and odor of day there
was change; we were all widened apart, and more aware of each other,
in the diminished storm: our ordinary egoism and watchfulness of a
curious human situation was somewhat restored in each of us, and with
this, something happy that came of the air itself, not very different from
the venturing and resumed loudness of small birds on the barnyard air,
whose pleated flight and song were brash as with dawn: The letting-
open of the blinds in two of the four blind walls then let the room full
of this cooled and happy light, wherein each piece of furniture stood
completed in its casual personality within these blockaded boards, and
where we found ourselves and saw each other hovered, no longer with
any reason here to be huddled, and sat a few moments as if blinking,
and as if embarrassed to be sitting; so that it was in part this embarrassment which, after those moments of shy glancing at one another,
broke us and brought us standing and strolling, chairs drawn back, and
broken apart along the porch: and I would wish most deeply to say,
how strange the natural day in a room can be, and how curiously, how
secretly, it can disturb those who find it broken upon them, and who
find themselves resumed each into his ordinary being, before he is
quite ready to reassume it, in a room whose walls have widened, have
opened once more their square eyes, upon sectors of country, in steadily thinning satin rain:

But the music of what is happening is more richly scored than this;
and much beyond what I can set down: I can only talk about it: the personality of a room, and of a group of creatures, has undergone change,
as if of two different techniques or mediums; what began as 'rem-
brandt,' deeplighted in gold, in each integer colossally heavily planted,
has become a photograph, a record in clean, staring, colorless light,
almost without shadow, of two iron sheeted beds which stand a little
away from the walls; of dislocated chairs; within cube of nailed house-
wood; a family of tenant farmers, late in a sunday afternoon, in a certain fold of country, in a certain part of the south, and of the lives of
each of them, confronted by a person strange to them, whose presence

and its motives are so outlandish there is no reason why any of it should be ever understood; almost as if there were no use trying to explain; just say, I am from Mars, and let it go at that: and this, as well as the lifted storm, the resumption of work in lack of fear, is happening in these minutes; each mind disaligned, and busy, in a common human timidity or fear; the fear in which a new acquaintance begins to be made. I wish I might remember the talk, or even the method and direction, the shape of the talk, but I can remember this scarcely at all. I explained myself a little, this single visit, that is, as simply as I might: such as it was it was not difficult to believe, and was well enough accepted; neither I nor either of the other men said much directly to Mrs. Gudger, nor she much to us; though, so far as I felt it would be allowed as proper, I turned what I said or replied to include her, and a few times directly her way. She became able to say a little how frightened she was of storms, but without apology and in next to no humor, just statement, a sort of implied courtesy of explanation to me, if I had thought it strange at all: I gave her indirect reason to know I did not in the least think it strange: I spoke a little to the two older children, as if it were natural to speak to children; they were puzzled by this but appeared rather to like it. Mrs. Gudger was very quietly courteous toward me in a deeply withdrawn way: as a wife, as a woman, it was not her place to show or even to feel any question who I was, why I might be there; that was the business of the man and her greatest courtesy lay in this observance: the children, though, I felt their eyes on me all the while. Nothing that was said made any difference of itself, but in each thing that was said there was all the difference in the world in the way I should meet or say it: I relied on quietness and occasional volunteering, and improvised on whatever seemed best to hand, and began to have the pleasure of realizing that though I remained inevitably somewhat mysterious, I was in each few minutes a little more comfortably accepted as friendly, as respectful toward them, as candid of my ignorance, my motives, and my regard, and as a person who need not at all be feared nor dealt toward in any lack of ease.

The yard dirt had no shape left to it at all; or had the shape the rain had given it; it looked like a relief map. The hens were out to their threshold or staggered out from under the house, talking worriedly, trembling, dry and sopping wet in patches. The hog was grunting and water swashed in his wallow; the cow let out a comment like a giant wooden flute: I looked, and saw her stretched head. Out in the edge of the cotton one of the three peach trees had been torn in half: we got pieces of wire and lifted its drenching weight and wired it together: the grass under these trees was littered full of the whole crop of peaches; hardly a dozen hung surviving; they were broken apart and bruised beyond any use. We collected them in buckets and a tub and with Mrs. Gudger and the children sorted apart those ripe and sufficiently whole to be used for eating and for drying, and those fit only for the hogs. Gudger was concerned that I should not muddy my sunday shoes, and (in re-erecting the tree) that I should not drench my clothes.

While we sorted peaches, the whole storm sank and the sun spread above its horizon and sank toward it: you know well enough how cleansed, and glad, and in what appearance of health and peace, every twig and leaf and all the shape of a country shine in such a light, and can fill you with love which has no traceable basis: well, this beyond such had come at the end of a long and cruel drought, and there was a movement and noise all round me of creatures and meanings where at length I found myself; and that I was not crying for joy was only that there was so much still to watch, to hear, and to wonder before, while we stood on the front porch and talked, George saying, over and over, while we looked out upon the resplendent country, how good a season it had been, a real good season, and how it seemed sure enough to have been an answer to prayer, for they had been praying for rain all these weeks now, more and more: and over to the left where the hill sank, there stood up among the tops of the thick woods a long thin wall of white and curving mist above loud water:

And he invited me, several times, to stay the night; of course the cooking was pretty plain, but stay the night; and each time in some paralyzing access of shyness before strong desire I thanked him and said

I had better not, knowing even while I said it how strongly I risked his misunderstanding, and his hurt, yet unable to say otherwise: and at length, and sure, and sick to hell, that I had hurt him, that I had seemed in my refusal to set myself above him, no matter how 'politely'; I told them good-bye and that I wanted to see them soon again, and Ricketts and I got into the car; and, dangerous in every moment of bogging in the clay, we took our way across the changed surface of his front yard and out of sight.

(I take Ricketts home. On the way back toward the highway, short still of the branch road that leads to the Gudgers':)

Third

Second Introit

Ricketts had shown me tricks of driving I shouldn't have dared or imagined along the clay, and now retracing it, alone, with the dark coming on, I followed my own ruts most of the time, often with my hands off the steering-wheel, holding the car in a light and somewhat swift second gear so that it seemed more to float and sail than to go on the ground, catching it lightly as possible in the instant of slewing and putting on speed rather than slowing and guiding beforehand, as I should have been more likely to do of myself. Half a dozen places we had come very near bogging, and here the clay was so wrought-up it was necessary each time to guess again. You can't afford to use brakes in this sort of material, and whatever steering you do, it must be as light-handed as possible; about the only thing to say of speed in such situations is to go a full shade faster most of the time than you can imagine is at all safe to go. It is different from snow and from any other mud I ‸now of, and it holds a dozen sudden differences within itself, all requiring quick modifications of technique and all more or less indescribably hidden among one another: driving, you feel less like an 'operator' than like a sort of passive-active brain suspended at the center of a machine, careful to let it take its own way, and to hold it at all in restraint only by little ticklings of an end of a whip: your senses are translated, they pervade the car, so that you are all four wheels as sensitively as if each were a fingertip; and these feel out a safe way through rather by force of will or wish than by any action. The joke of this was that my forces of will or of wish were crossed on themselves between the curiosity to manage this two miles of road, out of amateurish pride, and the regret that I was not at the Gudgers' and the desire to be there and to have a good excuse for being there: so that each time I got through a particularly tough stretch, it was in about as much amused regret as pleasure: so that at length, feeling the right rear wheel slew deeply toward the ditch; well, I didn't know then, and don't now, whether the things I was doing to save it were 'correct' or not, and whether or not it was by my will that I wrung the wheel and drove so deep that there was no longer any hope at all of getting it out: but I do know that as I felt it settle it was a thorough pleasure to me, an added pleased feeling of, well, I did all *I* could: I sat in the steep-tilted car maybe a full minute with the motor idling, feeling a smile all over the bones of my face as strange to me as greasepaint: set it in low, shifted the steering, gave it all modulations of power and of steering I could think of; they only foundered it deeper as I had begun to hope they might: and abruptly shut off the engine and the lights and lighted a cigarette and sat looking out at the country and at the sky, while the vanquished engine cooled with a tin noise of ticking.

There was the very darkest kind of daylight which can be called daylight at all, still on everything, and all through the air, a cold, blue-brown light of agate; and I was stationary in the middle of a world of which all members were stationary, and in this stasis, a sour odor of the earth and of night strengthened into me steadfastly until, at length, I felt an exact traction with this country in each twig and clod of it as it stood, not as it stood past me from a car, but to be stood in the middle of, or drawn through, passed, on foot, in the plain rhythm of a human being in his basic relation to his country. Each plant that fluted up in long rows out of the soil was native to its particular few square inches of rootage, and held relationship among these others to the work and living of some particular man and family, in a particular house, perhaps whose lamp I saw beneath this field; and each tree had now its own particular existence and personality, stood up branching out of its special space in the spreading of its blood, and stayed there waiting, a marked man, a tree: as different as the difference between a conducted tour of a prison and the first hours there as a prisoner: and all the while, it grew darker.

I took off my shoes and changed to sneakers (there was no sense in this, and I don't understand why), rolled the legs of my pants to the knee, took out an extra pack of cigarettes, two pencils, a small notebook, rolled up the windows, and locked the car: looked how deeply to the hub the wheel was sunk, and started off down the road, looking back at the car frequently from changed distances as if at a picture of myself, tilted up there helpless with its headlights and bumper taking what light was left. I began to feel laughter toward it as if it were a new dealer, a county dietitian, an editor of Fortune, or an article in the New Republic; and so, too, at myself, marveling with some scorn by what mixture of things in nature good and beneath nausea I was now where I was and in what purposes: but all the while I kept on walking, and all the while the bone center of my chest was beating with haste and hope, and I was watching for landmarks, less by need (for all I needed was to follow this road to a branching and the branch to its end) than for gratification in feeling them approach me once more in a changed pace and purpose and depth of feeling and meaning: for I now felt shy of them yet somehow as if I newly possessed or was soon to possess them, as if they silently opened and stood quiet before me to watch and evaluate and guard against me, yet at the same time, in a kind of grave aloofness of the defenseless, to welcome me: and yet again in all this I felt humble, and respectful, careful that I should not so much as set my foot in this clay in a cheapness of attitude, and full of knowledge, I have no right, here, I have no real right, much as I want it, and could never earn it, and should I write of it, must defend it against my kind: but I kept on walking: the crumpled edge of the gravel pit, the two negro houses I twisted between, among their trees; they were dark; and down the darkness under trees, whose roots and rocks were under me in the mud, and shin-deep through swollen water; and watched the steep-slanted corn, all struck toward me from my left, and nearly motionless now, while along my right and all upon me there was the rustling second rain of a trillion leaves relaxing the aftermath of storm, and a lithe, loud, rambling noise of replenished branches; thinking, how through this night what seepage in the porous earth would soon express this storm in glanded springs, deep wells refreshed; odors all round so black, so rich, so fresh, they surpassed in fecundity the odors of a woman; the cold and quiet sweating of hard walking; and so at last to the darkness of that upward ravine of road beyond which the land opens in a wave, and floats the house:

Up this ravine, realizing myself now near, I came stealthily, know-ing now I had at least half-contrived this, and after a misunderstood refusal, and for the first time realizing that by now, a half-hour fully dark, you must likely be in bed, through supper, done with a day, so that I must surely cause disturbance: slower, and slower, and two thirds ready to turn back, to spend the night in the car; and out into the cleared yard, silently, standing vertical to the front center of the house; it is dead black; not a light; just stands there, darker than its sur-roundings, perfectly quiet: and standing here, silently, in the demeanor of the house itself I grow full of shame and of reverence from the soles of my feet up my body to the crest of my skull and the leaves of my hands like a vessel quietly spread full of water which has sprung from in the middle of my chest: and shame the more, because I do not yet turn away, but still stand here motionless and as if in balance, and am aware of a vigilant and shameless hope that — not that I shall move for-ward and request you, disorder you — but that 'something shall hap-pen,' as it 'happened' that the car lost to the mud: and so waiting, in doubt, desire and shame, in a drawing-back of these around a vacuum of passive waiting, as the six walls of an empty room might wait for a sound: and this, or my breathing, or the beating of my heart, must have been communicated, for there is a sudden forward rush to the ledge of the porch of bellowing barking, and a dog, shouting his soul out against me: nothing else: and I think how they are roused by it and feel I have done wrong enough already, and withdraw a little, hoping that will quiet him, and in the same hope hold forward my hand and speak very quietly. He subdues to a growled snarling of bragging hate and fear and I am ready to turn and leave when a shadow heavily shuffles behind him, and in a stooped gesture of peering me out, Gudger's voice asks, who is it: ready for trouble. I speak before I move, telling him who I am, then what has happened, why I am here, and walk toward him, and how sorry I am to bother them. It is all right with him; come on in; he had thought I was a nigger.

I come up onto the porch shamefacedly, telling him again how sorry I am to have rousted them out like this. It's all right. They were just got to bed, none of them asleep yet. He has pulled on his overalls over nothing else and is barefooted. In the dark I can see him stooping his square head a little forward to study me. There is still antagonism and fear in his voice and in his eyes, but I realize this is not toward me, but toward the negro he thought I was: his emotions and his mind are slow to catch up with any quick change in the actuality of a situation. In a little more this antagonism has drained away and he is simply a tired and not unkind man taking care of a half-stranger at night who is also an anomaly; and thus he does as he has done before without any affectation of social grace: people plain enough take a much more profoundly courteous care of one another and of themselves without much if any surprise and no flurry of fussiness and a kind of respect which does not much ask questions. So it was there was neither any fake warmth and heartiness nor any coldness in his saying, Sure, come on in, to my asking could he put me up for the night after all, and he added, Better eat some supper. I was in fact very hungry, but I did all I was able to stop this, finally trying to compromise it to a piece of bread and some milk, that needn't be prepared; I'm making you enough bother already; but no; Can't go to bed without no supper; you just hold on a second or two; and he leans his head through the bedroom door and speaks to his wife, explaining, and lights the lamp for her. After a few moments, during which I hear her breathing and a weary shuffling of her heels, she comes out barefooted carrying the lamp, frankly and profoundly sleepy as a child; feeling disgusted to wake her further with so many words I say, Hello, Mrs. Gudger: say I want to tell you I'm *awful* sorry to give you all this bother: you just, honest I don't need much of anything, if you'd just tell me where a piece of bread is, it'll be *plenty*, I'd hate for you to bother to cook anything up for me: but she answers me while passing, looking at me, trying to get me into focus from between her sticky eyelashes, that 'tain't no bother at all, and for me not to worry over that, and goes on into the kitchen; and how quickly I don't understand, for I am too much occupied to see, with Gudger, and with holding myself from the cardinal error of hovering around her, or of offering to help her, she has built a pine fire and set in front of me, on the table in the hall, warmed-over biscuit and butter and blackberry jam and a jelly-glass full of buttermilk, and warmed field peas, fried pork, and four fried eggs, and she sits a little away from the table out of courtesy trying to hold her head up and her eyes open, until I shall have finished eating, saying at one time how it's an awful poor sort of supper and at another how it's awful plain, mean food; I tell her different, and eat as rapidly as possible and a good deal more than I can hold, in fact, all the eggs, a second large plateful of peas, most of the biscuit, feeling it is better to keep them awake and to eat too much than in the least to let them continue to believe I am what they assume I must be: 'superior' to them or to their food, eating only so much as I need to be 'polite'; and I see that they are, in fact, quietly surprised and gratified in my appetite.

But somehow I have lost hold of the reality of all this, I scarcely can understand how; a loss of the reality of simple actions upon the specific surface of the earth. This country, these roads, these odors and noises, the action of walking the dark in mud, the approach, just what a slow succession of certain trees past your walking can implant in you, can mean to you, the house as it stands there dark in darkness, the indecisiveness and the bellowing dog, the conversations of questioning, defense, assurance, acceptance, the subtle yet strong distinctions of attitude, the walking between the walls of wood and the sitting and eating, the tastes of the several foods, the weights of our bodies in our chairs, the look of us in the lamplight in the presence of the walls of the house and of the country night, the beauty and stress of our tiredness, how we held quietness, gentleness, and care toward one another like three mild lanterns held each at the met heads of strangers in darkness: such things, and these are just a few, I have not managed to give their truth in words, which are a soft, plain-featured, and noble music, each part in the experience of it and in the memory so cleanly and so simply defined in its own terms, striking so many chords and relationships at once, which I can but have blurred in the telling at all.

To say, then, how, as I sat between the close walls of this hallway, which opened upon wide night at either end, between these two somberly sleepy people in the soft smile of the light, eating from unsorted plates with tin-tasting implements the heavy, plain, traditional food which was spread before me, the feeling increased itself upon me that at the end of a wandering and seeking, so long it had begun before I was born, I had apprehended and now sat at rest in my own home, between two who were my brother and my sister, yet less that than something else; these, the wife my age exactly, the husband four years older, seemed not other than my own parents, in whose patience I was so different, so diverged, so strange as I was; and all that surrounded me, that silently strove in through my senses and stretched me full, was familiar and dear to me as nothing else on earth, and as if well known in a deep past and long years lost; so that I could wish that all my chance life was in truth the betrayal, the curable delusion, that it seemed, and that this was my right home, right earth, right blood, to which I would never have true right. For half my blood is just this; and half my right of speech; and by bland chance alone is my life so softened and sophisticated in the years of my defenselessness, and I am robbed of a royalty I can not only never claim, but never properly much desire or regret. And so in this quiet introit, and in all the time we have stayed in this house, and in all we have sought, and in each detail of it, there is so keen, sad, and precious a nostalgia as I can scarcely otherwise know; a knowledge of brief truancy into the sources of my life, whereto I have no rightful access, having paid no price beyond love and sorrow.

The biscuits are large and shapeless, not cut round, and are pale, not tanned, and are dusty with flour. They taste of flour and soda and damp salt and fill the mouth stickily. They are better with butter, and still better with butter and jam. The butter is pallid, soft, and unsalted, about the texture of cold-cream; it seems to taste delicately of wood and wet cloth; and it tastes 'weak.' The jam is loose, of little berries, full of light raspings of the tongue; it tastes a deep sweet purple tepidly watered, with a very faint sheen of a sourness as of iron. Field peas are olive-brown, the shape of lentils, about twice the size. Their taste is a cross between lentils and boiled beans; their broth is bright with seasoning of pork, and of this also they taste. The broth is soaked up in bread. The meat is a bacon, granular with salt, soaked in the grease of its frying: there is very little lean meat in it. What there is is nearly as tough as rind; the rest is pure salted stringy fat. The eggs taste of pork too. They are fried in it on both sides until none of the broken yolk runs, are heavily salted and peppered while they fry, so that they come to table nearly black, very heavy, rinded with crispness, nearly as dense as steaks. Of milk I hardly know how to say; it is skimmed, blue-lighted; to a city palate its warmth and odor are somehow dirty and at the same time vital, a little as if one were drinking blood. There is even in so clean a household as this an odor of pork, of sweat, so subtle it seems to get into the very metal of the cooking-pans beyond any removal of scrubbing, and to sweat itself out of newly washed cups; it is all over the house and all through your skin and clothing at all times, yet as you bring each piece of food to your mouth it is so much more noticeable, if you are not used to it, that a quiet little fight takes place on your palate and in the pit of your stomach; and it seems to be this odor, and a sort of wateriness and discouraged tepidity, which combine to make the food seem unclean, sticky, and sallow with some invisible sort of disease, yet this is the odor and consistency and temper and these are true tastes of home; I know this even of myself; and much as my reflexes are twitching in refusal of each mouthful a true homesick and simple fondness for it has so strong hold of me that in fact there is no fight to speak of and no faking of enjoyment at all. And even later, knowing well enough of such food what an insult it is to those who must spend their lives eating it, and who like it well enough, and when I am sick with it, I have also fondness for it, and when this fails, a funny kind of self-scorning determination that I shall eat for a few weeks what a million people spend their lives eating, and feel that whatever discomfort it brings me is little enough and willingly taken on, in the scale of all it could take to even us up.

All this while we are talking some: short of exact recording, which is beyond my memory, I can hardly say how: the forms of these plainest and most casual actions are the hardest I can conceive of to set down straight as they happen; and each is somewhat more beautiful and more valuable, I feel, than, say, the sonnet form. This form was one in which two plain people and one complex one who scarcely know each other discourse while one eats and the others wait for him to finish so they may get back to bed: it has the rhythms and inflections of this triple shyness, of sleepiness, of fast eating, of minds in the influence of lamplight between pine walls, of talk which means little or nothing of itself and much in its inflections: What is the use? What is there I can do about it? Let me try just a few of the surfaces instead. Just in the fact that they were drawn up out of bed to do me this natural kindness, one in overalls and one in a house dress slid on over nakedness, and were sitting here, a man and his wife, in an hour whose lateness is uncommon to them, there is a particular sort of intimacy between the three of us which is not of our creating and which has nothing to do with our talk, yet which is increased in our tones of voice, in small quiet turns of humor, in glances of the eyes, in ways even that I eat my food, in their knowledge how truly friendly I feel toward them, and how seriously I am concerned to have caused them bother, and to let them be done with this bother as quickly as possible. And the best in this — it will be hard to explain unless you know something of women in this civilization — is the experiencing of warmth and of intimacy toward a man and his wife at the same time (for this would seldom happen, it being the business of a wife to serve and to withdraw). I felt such an honor in her not just staying at more distance, waiting to clear up after me, but sitting near, almost equal in balance with her husband, and actually talking; and I began even through her deep exhaustion to see such pleasant and seldom warmth growing in her, in this shifted status and acceptance in it, and such a kindly and surprised current of warmth increasing through this between her husband and her, a new light and gentle novelty spreading a prettiness in her face that, beyond a first expostulation that she get back to her rest and leave me to clean off the table, I not only scarcely worried for her tiredness, or her husband's, but even somewhat prolonged the while we sat there, shamed though I was to do so, and they wakened, and warmed to talking, even while fatigue so much more heavily weighed them under, till it became in the scale of their sleeping an almost scandalously late-night conversation, in which we were all leaned toward each other in the lamplight secretly examining the growth of friendliness in one another's faces, they opening further speaking as often as I and more often: while nevertheless there stole up my quiet delight from the pit of my stomach a cold and sickening shame to be keeping them up, a feeling I had mistaken their interest and their friendliness, that it was only a desperate and nearly broken patience in a trap I had imposed in abuse of their goodness; and I broke through a little wait in what we were speaking, to say how sorry and ashamed I was, and that we must get to sleep; and this they received so genuinely, so kindly, that even in their exhaustion I was immediately healed, and held no fear of their feelings about it: and we drew back our chairs and got up and she cleared the table (no, beyond quickly stacking my dishes toward her I could not offer even to help her with this) and there followed a simple set of transitions which are beautiful in my remembrance and which I can scarcely set down: a telling me where I would sleep, in the front room; a spreading of pallets on the floor of the back bedroom; a waking and bringing-in of the children from their sleeping on the bed I was to have: they came sleepwalking, along bare floor toward lamplight, framed in the lighted upright planks of the door: the yielding-over to me of the lamp, which I accepted (there are courtesies you accept, though you are ashamed to), provided they should have used it first to get themselves to bed: they give me, meanwhile, their little tin night-light, which looks like the minutest kind of Roman lamp: I say good night to Mrs. Gudger and she to me, smiling sleepily and sadly in a way I cannot deduce, and goes on in; I button my door, that leads into their bedroom, and wait in this front room, new to me, with my night-light, sitting on the edge of the child-warmed bed, looking at the little sketches of carpentry I can see in my faint light, and at the light under their door and through seams in the wall, while in a confusion of shufflings and of muted voices which overspreads the sleeping of children like quiet wings; and rustlings of cloth, and sounding of bedsprings, they restore themselves for sleeping: then a shuffling, a sliding of light, a soft knock at the door; I come to it; Gudger and I exchange our lamps, speaking few words in nearly inaudible voices, while beyond his shoulder I feel the deep dark breathing a soft and quiet prostration of bodies: All right in year hain't you? – Ah, sure, fine. Sure am. – Annie Mae told me to say, she's sorry she ain't got no clean sheet, but just have to (*oh, no!*) make out best way you can. – Oh, no. No. You tell her I certainly do thank her, but, no, I'll be fine like this, *fine* like this – She just don't got none tell she does a warshin. – Sure; sure; I wouldn't want to dirty up a clean sheet for you, one night. Thanks a lot. Door, right head a yer bed, if you want to git out. I look, and nod:

Yeah; thanks.

Night:

Night:

The door draws shut.

*

I stand alone, and I find that, without my knowledge or will, my left arm has slowly extended, the lamp in the hand at the end of it, as far as I can stretch, and I turn upon the center of the room.

In the room: the Testament

Six sides of me, all pine: Floor supported; walls walled, stood vertical, joined at their four edges, at floor, at one another, and at roof: roof, above rafters, tilted tall, from eaves to crest. Between slats, the undersides of shingles. One wall is lapboard, that one which joins the other bedroom: the others, the skeleton and the inward surface of the outward skin of the house. A door to the bedroom: a door by my bed to the hallway: in the wall at the foot of my bed, a square window, shuttered; another in the wall next at right angles. On the floor beneath this window, a small trunk. To its left, stood across the corner, a bureau and mirror. To its right, stood across the corner, a sewing machine:

I have told of these: But here, and now, I was first acquainting myself of this room in a silence of wonder to match the silence of sleeping in the next room. Its fragrance was everywhere; its plainness and coloring were beautiful to me. The furniture stood, where I have begun to see, sober and naked to me in the solemn light, and seemed as might the furnishing of a box-car, a barn. This barn and box-car resemblance I use, it occurred to me then and since, as an indication of the bone-like plainness and as if fragility of the place; but I would not mislead or miscolor: this was a room of a human house, of a sort stood up by the hundreds of thousands in the whole of a country; the sheltering and home of the love, hope, ruin, of the living of all of a family, and all the shelter it shall ever know, and since of itself it is so ordinary, so universal, there is no need to name it as a barn, or as a box-car.

But here, I would only suggest how thin-walled, skeletal, and beautiful it seemed in a particular time, as if it were a little boat in the darkness, floated upon the night, far out on the steadiness of a vacant sea, whose crew slept while I held needless watch, and felt the presence of the country round me and upon me. I looked along the walls, how things which were pretty were stuck and pinned to the wood; and at the wood: I should find it hard to tire of watching plain wood which is in some human usage; of running my fingers upon it as it were skin; little tricks of glass and china, and of sewn cloths, which were created to be pretty, to be happy: the restings of furniture on the surface of the naked floor; various reflections of the room in the eaten mirror: the square, useless lamp which stood in the dark corner under the sewing-machine: the iron bed, whose sheets and coverlets Mrs. Gudger had drawn smooth for me, the mark of my butt on its edge, my shoes beside it, crazy with mud, worn out and sleeping as a pair of wrecked horses: how the shutters filled their squares of window and were held shut with strings and nails: crevices in the walls, stuffed with hemp, rags, newsprint, and raw cotton: large damp spots and rivulets on the floor, and on the walls, streams and crooked wetness; and a shivering, how chilly and wet the air is in this room: a shutting-off of these matters and mere 'touch' and listening, how the home was squared on us, and beyond on all sides the billion sleeping of the natural earth: sitting, where the table blocks the fireplace, watching the lamp, how the light stands up and the wick sleeps in the glass, and meditating those who sleep just beyond this wall: it was in this first night that I found, on the bureau, a bible; very cheap; bound in a limp brown fake-leather which was almost slimily damp; a family bible: I opened it up quietly in the lamplight, here and there through it: I quote from notes I made at that time:

The Title Page:

The New Testament

With the words spoken by Christ printed in red

(printed in red)

Malachi 4, v. 6.
And he shall turn the heart of the fathers to the children, and the heart of the children to their fathers, lest I come and smite the earth with a curse.

And elsewhere, printed in brown ink; the handwriting in pencil:

Presented to . . .

George Gudger

by *Annie Mae Gudger*

Family Record:

Parents' Names

Husband. *George Gudger*

Born. *September 11 – 1904*

Wife. *Annie Mae Gudger*

Born. *October 19, 197*

Married. *George G. and Annie Mae G. was married April 19th 1924*

Children's Names

Maggie Louise G. was born February 2nd 1926

George Junior Gudger was born Sepenber 4, 1927

Martha Ann G. was born

March 28 1931

Burt Westly Gudger

July 14 1932

Valley Few G

Dec, 26, 1936 ＊

Marriages:

George

Deaths: *Lulla Woods died*

June 7, 19x 29

Martha Ann G—

Died September 28, 1931

＊ It was written thus. He was born in 1934.

This bible was of some absorbent paper and lay slack, cold, and very heavy in the hand. It gave out a strong and cold stench of human excrement.

In the Room: In Bed

I put in my hand and it took the last warmth of the sleeping of the children. I sat on the edge of the bed, turned out the lamp, and lay back along the outside of the covers. After a couple of minutes I got up, stripped, and slid in between the sheets. The bedding was saturated and full of chill as the air was, its lightness upon me nervous like a belt too loosely buckled. The sheets were at the same time coarse and almost slimily or stickily soft: much the same material floursacks are made of. There was a ridgy seam down the middle. I could feel the thinness and lumpiness of the mattress and the weakness of the springs. The mattress was rustlingly noisy if I turned or contracted my body. The pillow was hard, thin, and noisy, and smelled as of acid and new blood; the pillowcase seemed to crawl at my cheek. I touched it with my lips: it felt a little as if it would thaw like spun candy. There was an odor something like that of old moist stacks of newspaper. I tried to imagine intercourse in this bed; I managed to imagine it fairly well. I began to feel sharp little piercings and crawlings all along the surface of my body. I was not surprised; I had heard that pine is full of them anyhow. Then, too, for a while longer I thought it could be my own nerve-ends; I itch a good deal at best: but it was bugs all right. I felt places growing on me and scratched at them, and they became unmistakable bedbug bites. I lay awhile rolling and tightening against each new point of irritation, amused and curious how I had changed about bedbugs. In France I used to wake up and examine a new crop each morning, with no revulsion: now I was squeamish in spite of myself. To lie there naked feeling whole regiments of them tooling at me, knowing I must be imagining two out of three, became more unpleasant than I could stand. I struck a match and a half-dozen broke along my pillow: I caught two, killed them, and smelled their queer rankness. They were full of my blood. I struck another match and spread back the cover; they rambled off by dozens. I got out of bed, lighted the lamp, and scraped the palms of my hands all over my body, then went for the bed. I killed maybe a dozen in all; I couldn't find the rest; but I did find fleas, and, along the seams of the pillow and mattress, small gray translucent brittle insects which I suppose were lice. (I did all this very quietly, of course, very much aware I might wake those in the next room.) This going-over of the bed was only a matter of principle: I knew from the first I couldn't beat them. I might more wisely not have done so, for I shouldn't have discovered the 'lice.' The thought of their presence bothered me much more than the bedbugs. I unbuttoned the door by my bed and went out into the hallway; the dog woke and sidled toward me on his toenails sniffing and I put my hand on his head and he wagged from the middle of his spine on back. I was closely aware of all the bare wood of the house and of the boards under my bare feet, of the damp and deep gray night and of my stark nakedness. I went out to the porch and pissed off the edge, against the wall of the house, to be silent, and stood looking out. It was dark, and mist was standing up in streaks, and the woods along my left and at the bottom of the field in front of me were darkest of any part of the night. Down under the strongest streak of mist along my left, in the deep woods, there was a steady thrusting and spreading noise of water. There were a few stars through thin mist, and a wet gray light of darkness everywhere. I went down the steps and out into the yard, feeling the clay slippery and very cold on my feet, and turned round slowly to look at the house. The instant I was out under the sky, I felt much stronger than before, lawless and lustful to be naked, and at the same time weak. I watched the house and felt like a special sort of burglar; but still more I felt as if I trod water in a sea whose floor was drooped unthinkably deep beneath me, and I was unsafely far from the wall of the ship. I looked straight up into the sky, found myself nodding at whatever it was I saw, and came back and scraped my feet on the steps, rubbed them dry with my hands, and, with one more slow look out along the sunken landscape went back into the bedroom. I put on my coat, buttoned my pants outside it, put my socks on, got into bed, turned out the lamp, turned up my coat collar, wrapped my head in my shirt, stuck my hands under my coat at the chest, and tried to go to sleep. It did not work out well. They got in at the neck and along my face and at my ankles, and along the wrists and knuckles. I wanted if I could to keep my hands and face clear. I wasn't used to these bugs. Their bites would show, and it might be embarrassing whether questions or comments were placed or not. After a little while I worked it out all over, bandaging more tightly and carefully at every strategic joint of cloth. This time I put the socks on my hands and wrapped my feet in my shorts, and once I was set, took great care to lie still. But they got in as before, and along my back and up my belly too: through my stiff, starved dozing I could feel them crawling captured under the clothes, safe against my getting at them, pricking and munching away: so in time, I revised my attitude. I stripped once more, scratched and cleaned all over, shook out all my clothes, dressed again, lay down outside all the covers, and let them take their course while I attended as well as I could to other things; that is, to my surroundings, to whatever was on my mind, and to relaxing for sleep. This worked better. I felt them nibbling, but they were seldom in focus, and I lay smoking, using one shoe for an ashtray and looking up at the holes in the roof. Now and then I reached out and touched the rough wood of the wall just behind me and of the wall along my right: or felt the iron rods of the bed with my hands, my feet, and the crown of my head; or ran the fingertips of my left hand along the grain of the floor: or tilting my chin, I looked back beyond my forehead through the iron at the standing-up of the wall: all the while I would be rubbing and desperately scratching, but this had become mechanical by now. I don't exactly know why anyone should be 'happy' under these circumstances, but there's no use laboring the point: I was: outside the vermin, my senses were taking in nothing but a deep-night, unmeditatable consciousness of a world which was newly touched and beautiful to me, and I must admit that even in the vermin there was a certain amount of pleasure: and that, exhausted though I now was, it was the eagerness of my senses quite as fully as the bugs and the itching which made it impossible for me to sleep and, sickly as I now strained toward sleep, it was pleasurable to stay awake. I dozed off and on, but had no realization of deeper sleep. I must have been pretty far gone, though, for when Gudger came in barefooted to take up the lamp, I feigned sleeping, and lacked interest to look at the furniture which was now visible by a sort of sub-daylight: and heard the sounds of dressing and movements in the house, and saw the wall of their room slit with yellow light, only with a deep and gentle sorrow, in some memory out of childhood which seemed now restored like the ghost of one beloved and dead: and was taken out of full sleep by the sound, a little later, of his shoes on the floor, as he came to the side of the bed and spoke to me.

The sun was not yet up, but the sky over the hill was like white china and it was full daylight now, everything hung with rain and letting it run off in large drops; the grain of wood in the wall of the house was yellow, red and fading blue-black (as of wet tortoise shell), which the sun would not bleach for several hours yet; the ground was drawn down close on itself with a somehow blue-sheened surface that looked hard as iron. The lamp was no longer giving any light beyond its own daylighted chimney, and Mrs. Gudger put it out. Even now, with the hot load of the breakfast inside me, I was stiff with cold and was not yet well awake.

We cut up across the hill field by the path their walking had laid in it; the path was all but rained out. In some parts it was packed hard enough to be slippery, the rest of the time it let our feet down as deep as plowed dirt itself and we lifted them out in each step with one to three inches of clay hung on them. The cotton plants brushed us at the knees so that in no time we were drenched there.

It was only a chance that the road and the ditch clay would have hardened enough during the night to make it possible to get the car out. With about ten minutes work, that brought up a shallow, stickily drying sweat in the cool of this morning, we managed to do it, and moving precariously in low and second as if walking a slackwire, with a couple of sideslips that nearly ditched us again, we got the car out to the slag and swung right and made speed on its slow rollercoaster lifts and falls while around us fields, with which I found I felt a strong new kind of familiarity, lilted and relaxed upon our motion.

After not more than three miles, just within first sight of Cookstown, low and diminutive, Gudger told me to turn right just this side of the grismill.

It was dirt road again, but wider, and thick enough with sand to be possible, though it was still good and wet. I managed about thirty-five on it, and the tires were very loud under us. This was new country to me, still totally poor, yet with something loosened and pastoral about it and as if self-sufficient and less hopelessly lonesome and abandoned; the early light and the cleanness and silence after the rain may have been responsible for this impression. There were more small, privately owned farms than on many roads I had driven over, none of them any richer-looking than tenant farms; yet living was a little different on them and a little less pointless. Even in the smoke that wrinkled up out of their chimneys and lavished lazily like the tail of a pleased cat and in the keen odors of fire and breakfast that lay occasionally across the road, there was a little more security than in these same on a tenant farm, and a little more of the sense of a family planted in one place and coming up like a tree, even if it was a starved tree.

Strung along at two out of three mail boxes, thinly along the road, men stood smoking and waited. I started to slow for the first and Gudger said the truck would be along. With all the equipment in the back we had room only for one more anyway. They looked at us coldly and shyly as we went past. To three or four Gudger lifted a hand, and these lifted a hand, not smiling.

We ran sharply up a hill with small black pines on it and at the top a small unpainted church and clay burial ground, and the hill ran down much more slowly. Gudger said turn right down there at the bottom. I swung right through a snowlike sludge of clay and righted the car along a rut between the deep ones and a light rut in the grass. It was harder going again. Wet blackberry brambles laid water on the windshield. In two hundred yards more the woods were up to one side of

us, a high field to the other, and the road was sand again, and Gudger
said to take the right fork, and it was as subduing as going into a tunnel. The pines and the soft-wooded and high trees and the oaks and
hickories were thick all around us and over us now, so that the air was
cold, dark and clear, and noisily hushed as I remember when, a child,
I used to crawl into a culvert, and sat down and listened. The sand road
was drenching wet and there was the mark of one car that had been
ahead of us, and ahead there was the rattling of a wagon, and we
rounded a heavy bush and saw it and slowed; the men looked round,
two black, one white, who lifted his hand as Gudger lifted his; the
negroes nodded. The whipped mules dragged the wagon on through a
flooded branch that submerged thirty yards of the road and stood up
around the bushes and tree-trunks on either side so that they had no
rootage, and I watched where and how deep the wheels went while I
idled the motor and lighted Gudger's and my own cigarette. It was
twenty-one past six. Gudger said, 'We got here in good time.' They got
the wagon on through and drew up along a patch of grass and roots at
the side of the road. I said thanks with hand and head, put the car into
low and then into second and, following their trail, which still creased
the water a little, went through pretty fast with a loud cold splitting and
crashing noise of the new water and was on solid land again. The white
man and I lifted hands as I went by and the negroes nodded again, but
more slightly. They were all three looking at us curiously and tenta-
tively. 'Left up yer ahead'; where there was wide light on the wet road.
We swung as if into the face of a powerful searchlight into a long grassy
clearing stacked down the middle with wet yellow lumber and full of
light which had, since we lost it to woods, greatly increased and which
came straight and low at us from the far end; we went past another
wagon and drew up at the side of the road in the heavy grass halfway
down the clearing. The wagon passed alongside and Gudger and the
men on the wagon lifted their hands and the men looked back non-
committally at me and Gudger and the sedan and the Tennessee
license. Gudger's watch made twenty-three past six.

We sat still in the car and finished the things we had been saying, very slowly and shyly on both sides, all through the drive; which were, very carefully keyed, chiefly about what the tenant farmer could do to help himself out of the hole he is in. Gudger made him another ciga- rette and we smoked, talking very little. We were not by any means at ease with each other, but he now felt he could trust me and we liked each other. While we talked, I was looking around slowly.

The sawmill was at the far end; it was still in the morning shadow of the woods. The sun had just cleared the tops of the pines beyond it so that they were still burnt away. Rising and twisting all through these close-growing pines, and on the high glittering grass and in long streams in the air, was the white smoke of the cold, now swiftly heat- ing, early morning, which the sun drew up, and the sun struck through this smoke and diffused it so that the air was clear, transparent and all but blinding bright, as if it had been polished. The wagon that had drawn aside from us in the woods road had come up and let off its men, and a truckload of negroes and white men arrived from Cooks- town, and the clearing was thickening but not by any means crowded with men and the sound of their talk and the noises of the beginning of a day's work: nearly every one of these men glanced at us more than once, carefully and with candor, yet they did not stare, and were only careful, not hostile. Over by the toolshed of fresh pine a negro, har- nessing his team, threw back his head and looked into the sun and sang, shouting, a phrase which sprang out of his throat like a wet green branch. Gudger said he was agoin to have to git on to work now. I told him I sure was obliged to him for taking me in last night and he said he was glad to have holp me.

END OF PART THREE

Shady Grove

Two Images

Shady Grove, Alabama, July 1936

Just beside it there is a large square white-painted church, which we got into. Bare benches of heavy pine, a lot of windows, partition-curtains of white sheeting run on wires, organ, chairs, and lectern.

The graveyard is about fifty by a hundred yards inside a wire fence. There are almost no trees in it: a lemon verbena and a small magnolia; it is all red clay and very few weeds.

Out at the front of it across the road there is a cornfield and then a field of cotton and then trees.

Most of the headboards are pine, and at the far end of the yard from the church the graves are thinned out and there are many slender and low pine stumps about the height of the headboards. The shadows are all struck sharp lengthwise of the graves, toward the cornfield, by the afternoon sun. There is no one anywhere in sight. It is heavily silent and fragrant and all the leaves are breathing slowly without touching each other.

Some of the graves have real headstones, a few of them so large they must be the graves of landowners. One is a thick limestone log erected by the Woodmen of the World. One or two of the others, besides a headpiece, have a flat of stone as large as the whole grave.

On one of these there is a china dish on whose cover delicate hands lie crossed, cuffs at their wrists, and the nails distinct.

On another a large fluted vase stands full of dead flowers, with an inch of rusty water at the bottom.

On others of these stones, as many as a dozen of them, there is something I have never seen before: by some kind of porcelain reproduction, a photograph of the person who is buried there; the last or the best likeness that had been made, in a small-town studio, or at home with a snapshot camera. I remember one well of a fifteen-year-old boy in sunday pants and a plaid pullover sweater, his hair combed, his cap in his hand, sitting against a piece of farm machinery and grinning. His eyes are squinted against the light and his nose makes a deep shadow down one side of his chin. Somebody's arm, with the sleeve rolled up, is against him; somebody who is almost certainly still alive: they could not cut him entirely out of the picture. Another is a studio portrait, close up, in artificial lighting, of a young woman. She is leaned a little forward, smiling vivaciously, one hand at her cheek. She is not very pretty, but she believed she was; her face is free from strain or fear. She is wearing an evidently new dress, with a mail-order look about it; patterns of beads are sewn over it and have caught the light. Her face is soft with powder and at the wings of her nose lines have been deleted. Her dark blonde hair is newly washed and professionally done up in puffs at the ears which in that time, shortly after the first great war of her century, were called cootie garages. This image of her face is split across and the split has begun to turn brown at its edges.

I think these would be graves of small farmers.

There are others about which there can be no mistake: they are the graves of the poorest of the farmers and of the tenants. Mainly they are the graves with the pine headboards; or without them.

When the grave is still young, it is very sharply distinct, and of a peculiar form. The clay is raised in a long and narrow oval with a sharp ridge, the shape exactly of an inverted boat. A fairly broad board is driven at the head; a narrower one, sometimes only a stob, at the feet. A good many of the headboards have been sawed into the flat simulacrum of an hourglass; in some of these, the top has been roughly rounded off, so that the resemblance is more nearly that of a head and shoulders sunken or risen to the waist in the dirt. On some of these boards names and dates have been written or printed in hesitant letterings, in pencil or in crayon, but most of them appear never to have been touched in this way. The boards at some of the graves have fallen slantwise or down; many graves seem never to have been marked except in their own carefully made shape. These graves are of all sizes between those of giants and of newborn children; and there are a great many, so many they seem shoals of minnows, two feet long and less, lying near one another; and of these smallest graves, very few are marked with any wood at all, and many are already so drawn into the earth that they are scarcely distinguishable. Some of the largest, on the other hand, are of heroic size, seven and eight feet long, and of these more are marked, a few, even, with the smallest and plainest blocks of limestone, and initials, once or twice a full name; but many more of them have never been marked, and many, too, are sunken half down and more and almost entirely into the earth. A great many of these graves, perhaps half to two thirds of those which are still distinct, have been decorated, not only with shrunken flowers in their cracked vases and with bent targets of blasted flowers, but otherwise as well. Some have a line of white clamshells planted along their ridge; of others, the rim as well is garlanded with these shells. On one large grave, which is otherwise completely plain, a blown-out electric bulb is screwed into the clay at the exact center. On another, on the slope of clay just in front of the headboard, its feet next the board, is a horseshoe; and at its center a blown bulb is stood upright. On two or three others there are insulators of blue-green glass. On several graves, which I presume to be those of women, there is at the center the prettiest or the oldest and most valued piece of china: on one, a blue glass butter dish whose cover is a setting hen; on another, an intricate milk-colored glass basket; on others, ten-cent-store candy dishes and iridescent vases; on one, a pattern of white and colored buttons. On other graves there are small and thick white butter dishes of the sort which are used in lunchrooms, and by the action of rain these stand free of the grave on slender turrets of clay. On still another grave, laid carefully next the headboard, is a corncob pipe. On the graves of children there are still these pretty pieces of glass and china, but they begin to diminish in size and they verge into the forms of animals and into homuncular symbols of growth; and there are toys: small autos, locomotives and fire engines of red and blue metal; tea sets for dolls, and tin kettles the size of thimbles: little effigies in rubber and glass and china, of cows, lions, bulldogs, squeaking mice, and the characters of comic strips; and of these I knew, when Louise told me how precious her china dogs were to her and her glass lace dish, where they would go if she were soon drawn down, and of many other things in that home, to whom they would likely be consigned; and of the tea set we gave Clair Bell, I knew in the buying in what daintiness it will a little while adorn her remembrance when the heaviness has sufficiently grown upon her and she has done the last of her dancing: for it will only be by a fortune which cannot be even hoped that she will live much longer; and only by great chance that they can do for her what two parents have done here for their little daughter: not only a tea set, and a cocacola bottle, and a milk bottle, ranged on her short grave, but a stone at the head and a stone at the foot, and in the headstone her six month image as she lies sleeping dead in her white dress, the head sunken delicately forward, deeply and delicately gone, the eyes seamed, as that of a dead bird, and on the rear face of this stone the words:

> We can't have all things to please us,
> Our little Daughter, Joe An, has gone to Jesus.

It is not likely for her; it is not likely for any of you, my beloved, whose poor lives I have already so betrayed, and should you see these things so astounded, so destroyed, I dread to dare that I shall ever look into your dear eyes again: and soon, quite soon now, in two years, in five, in forty, it will all be over, and one by one we shall all be drawn into the planet beside one another; let us then hope better of our children, and of our children's children; let us know, let us know there is cure, there is to be an end to it, whose beginnings are long begun, and in slow agonies and all deceptions clearing; and in the teeth of all hope of cure which shall pretend its denial and hope of good use to men, let us most quietly and in most reverent fierceness say, not by its captive but by its utmost meanings:

Our father, who art in heaven, hallowed be thy name: thy kingdom come: thy will be done on earth as it is in heaven: give us this day our daily bread: and forgive us our trespasses as we forgive those who trespass against us: and lead us not into temptation: but deliver us from evil: for thine is the kingdom: and the power: and the glory: for ever and ever: amen.

The last words of this book have been spoken and these that follow are not words; they are only descriptions of two images. One is of Squinchy Gudger and his mother as they are in the open hall; one is of Ellen Woods as she lies sleeping at the edge of the front porch: both in a silent, white hour of a summer day.

His mother sits in a hickory chair with her knees relaxed and her bare feet flat to the floor; her dress open and one broken breast exposed. Her head is turned a little slantwise and she gazes quietly downward past her son's head into the junctures of the earth, the floor, the wall, the sunlight, and the shade. One hand lies long and flat along her lap: it is elegantly made of bone and is two sizes too large for the keen wrist. With her other hand, and in the cradling of her arm and shoulder, she holds the child. His dress has fallen aside and he is naked. As he is held, the head huge in scale of his body, the small body ineffably relaxed, spilled in a deep curve from nape to buttocks, then the knees drawn up a little, the bottom small and sharp, and the legs and feet drifted as if under water, he suggests the shape of the word siphon. He is nursing. His hands are blundering at her breast blindly, as if themselves each were a new born creature, or as if they were sobbing, ecstatic with love; his mouth is intensely absorbed at her nipple as if in rapid kisses, with small and swift sounds of moisture; his eyes are squeezed shut; and now, for breath, he draws away, and lets out a sharp short whispered *ahh*, the hands and his eyelids relaxing, and immediately resumes; and in all this while, his face is beatific, the face of one at rest in paradise, and in all this while her gentle and sober, earnest face is not altered out of its deep slantwise gazing: his head is now sunken off and away, grand and soft as a cloud, his wet mouth flared, his body still more profoundly relinquished of itself, and I see how against her body he is so many things in one, the child in the melodies of the womb, the Madonna's son, human divinity sunken from the cross at rest against his mother, and more beside, for at the heart and leverage of that young body, gently, taken in all the pulse of his being, the penis is partly erected.

And Ellen where she rests, in the gigantic light: she, too, is completely at peace, this child, the arms squared back, the palms open loose against the floor, the floursack on her face; and her knees are flexed upward a little and fallen apart, the soles of the feet facing: her blown belly swimming its navel, white as flour; and blown full broad with slumbering blood into a circle: so white all the outward flesh, it glows of blue; so dark, the deep hole, a dark red shadow of life blood: this center and source, for which we have never contrived any worthy name, is as if it were breathing, flowering, soundlessly, a snoring silence of flame; it is as if flame were breathed forth from it and subtly played about it: and here in this breathing and play of flame, a thing so strong, so valiant, so unvanquishable, it is without effort, without emotion, I know it shall at length outshine the sun.

Let us now praise famous men.

Let us now praise famous men, and our fathers that begat us.

The Lord hath wrought great glory by them through his great power from the beginning.

Such as did bear rule in their kingdoms, men renowned for their power, giving counsel by their understanding, and declaring prophecies:

Leaders of the people by their counsels, and by their knowledge of learning meet for the people, wise and eloquent in their instructions:

Such as found out musical tunes, and recited verses in writing:

Rich men furnished with ability, living peaceably in their habitations:

All these were honoured in their generations, and were the glory of their times.

There be of them, that have left a name behind them, that their praises might be reported.

And some there be which have no memorial; who perished, as though they had never been; and are become as though they had never been born; and their children after them.

But these were merciful men, whose righteousness hath not been forgotten.

With their seed shall continually remain a good inheritance, and their children are within the covenant.

Their seed standeth fast, and their children for their sakes. Their seed shall remain for ever, and their glory shall not be blotted out.

Their bodies are buried in peace; but their name liveth for evermore.

Notes and Appendices

1.

Suggested:

Detail of gesture, landscape, costume, air, action, mystery, and incident throughout the writings of William Faulkner.

Many passages in Mark Twain, Thomas Wolfe, and Erskine Caldwell.

Sketches made in Georgia by David Friedenthal.

Stark Love, a motion picture, by Karl Brown.

Photographs in *Pellagra*, by Dr. A. Marie; The State Co., Publishers, Columbia, S.C.

Frontier, a motion picture, by Alexander Dovschenko.

Married Woman Blues, by Sleepy John Estes; Decca.

New Salty Dog and *Slow Mama Slow*, by Salty Dog Sam; Oriole.

Who Was John and *My Poor Mother Died Ashouting*, by Mitchell's Christian Singers; Decca.

American Photographs, by Walker Evans; Museum of Modern Art.

All southern city and small town newspapers and postcards.

Road maps and contour maps of the middle south.

2.

BEETHOVEN SONATA
HELD NO DISTURBANCE

San Francisco, Dec. 6 (A.P.).
— 'Beethoven,' said Judge Herbert Kaufman, 'cannot disturb the peace.'

So he freed Rudolph Ramat,
69 years old and blind, of a
charge of disturbing the peace by
playing his accordion on Market
Street.
　'Your honor,' Ramat pleaded
yesterday, 'I have worked
　　　— from the New York *Sun.* *

3.

A Note on the Photographs

Margaret Bourke-White Finds
Plenty of Time to Enjoy Life
Along With Her Camera Work

———

Famous Photographer Who Took Pictures for *You Have
Seen Their Faces* Discusses Experiences
Among Southern Share-Croppers

———

By May Cameron

(*Herschel Brickell's reviews of books appear in this space five days a week.*)
　It's difficult to know where to begin on Margaret Bourke-White,
because she is so many people rolled into one.
　"You can't possibly miss her," Miss Bourke-White's secretary told
me, "because she's wearing the reddest coat in the world."
　A superior red coat, Miss Bourke-White called it, and such fun. It
was designed for her by Howard Greer, and if you're as little up on
your movie magazines as I am, I'd better explain that the Greer label is
some pumpkins. You'd find it, if you could look, in the more glamorous
gowns of Dietrich and, among others, Hepburn.

---

* A conservative newspaper.

This famous photographer, just past thirty, can well afford Hollywood's best. In less than eight years she has climbed to the top of the heap in her profession and is now — movie actresses barred — one of the highest-paid women in America. Trying to imagine this made me a little dizzy, but here it is: for every minute — minute, mind you — of her working time today Margaret Bourke-White commands quite a few dollars.

And this is the young lady who spent months of her own time in the last two years traveling the back roads of the deep south bribing, cajoling, and sometimes browbeating her way in to photograph Negroes, share-croppers and tenant farmers in their own environments. Seventy-five of these photographs appear in *You Have Seen Their Faces*, a book for which Erskine Caldwell wrote the text.

. . . .

SNUFF, 'RELIGION' AND PATENT MEDICINE

Ingenuity such as she was never called upon to use in her years of industrial photography went into the making of many of the photographs included in the book. The striking photograph of a Negro preacher caught at the very height of his emotion and oratory Miss Bourke-White took on her knees right in front of the pulpit, the preacher's own emotion making him entirely oblivious to exploding flashlights. Her rare photographs of the "coming through" ritual, if it could be called a ritual, in a white Holiness church were possible only because the minister had never before had a photographer to deal with and he didn't know what to do about it.

The small-town orator-politician had already started talking when Margaret Bourke-White set up her tripod and went to work on him. She is certain that he wouldn't have posed for her, but, once he had started to orate, nothing, not even a strange photographer, could stop him. And to one of the last couples pictured in the book, Miss Bourke-White and Erskine Caldwell had to pay a bribe.

"So far as we could tell, they hadn't any food, but they begged for snuff, two kinds, Buttercup and Rooster snuff," Margaret Bourke-White explained. "They hoped we'd throw in a little coffee and maybe some chewing tobacco, but snuff came first. They tell you snuff's good when you are hungry or when you have a toothache or when you're just feeling generally low. They seem to live on snuff and religion — which has no real relation to religion — and patent medicine.

"Caldwell's new play, *Journeyman,* is concerned with one congregation of a white Holiness church. The Negro churches are not, somehow, so shocking, because you think of Negroes as being actors and emotional, but with the white people the whole business is so sordid and desperate and out of place. It isn't as though their church played any role, as we know religion. It's just a place where people go to shout and scream and roll on the floor. They are so beaten down and their lives are so drab and barren and lonely that they have nothing. This terrible thing every Sunday is their only emotional release."

. . . .

THE PICTURE OF TODAY'S SETUP

Miss Bourke-White, whose beautiful photographs of dynamos and cranes and turbines and girders and industrial fine points are known to every one, made several trips to Russia and, in observing an agricultural nation being turned into an industrial one, became tremendously interested in the man behind the machine.

"I loved the industrial photographs for their pictorial value and all the excitement of machinery, and I still do; but a couple of years ago I began to feel that if I was worth anything at all I wanted to do something really worth while, something lasting," she said. "In Russia I got the first glimpse of figuring out man's relationship to the machine and to his employer, and my eyes were opened tremendously. It's more complicated in America, of course, but now I am most interested in taking pictures of what's going on, not necessarily news, but just man's place in the whole setup of today.

"I'm tired of glorifying big business, tired of photographing beautiful, empty-headed models stepping into beautiful automobiles. I do only the industrial photographs that are interesting now, as, for example, my trip to Brazil last year to photograph coffee plantations, which had never been done, and to do airplane pictures, of which I do a great many.

"I believe, too, that photographs are a true interpretation. One photograph might lie, but a group of pictures can't. I could have taken one picture of share-croppers, for example, showing them toasting their toes and playing their banjos and being pretty happy. In a group of pictures, however, you would have seen the cracks on the wall and the expressions on their faces. In the last analysis, photographs really have to tell the truth; the sum total is a true interpretation. Whatever facts a person writes have to be colored by his prejudice and bias. With a camera, the shutter opens and it closes and the only rays that come in to be registered come directly from the object in front of you."

In the eight or nine years since she started selling photographs, while still in Columbia, Margaret Bourke-White has had the energy and made the time to find an awful lot of fun in just living. She's a tango expert; crazy about the theater; loves swimming, ice skating, skiing, and adores horseback riding. Sometimes, she explained, when she knows that the light will be right only a few hours of the day for whatever pictures she is taking, she has her horse brought around to "location" and rides until the light is right. Movies occupy whatever week-ends she spends in New York, often as many as five a day. Aside from a photographer's interest, she just likes the damn things. *

---

* Reprinted by courtesy of the New York *Post,* a liberal newspaper.

4.

A Definition

The generic word for tenant is tenant. In the vicinity of which we tell, however, and, it appears, generally throughout the south, the word is used to designate only one of the two chief classes of tenant, that is the man who, as distinguished from the man who owns nothing save, perhaps, some furniture, one or two eating or hunting animals, and the clothes on his back, owns a mule and some farm implements and who, not needing to be furnished these, can arrange to yield less of his two major crops in payment of rent to the landowner.

One name for the other chief sort of tenant, the man who, owning neither mule nor implements, must be furnished these as well as land and shelter, and must pay the landowner half his cotton and a third to half his corn, is sharecropper. He is also called a halvers-hand and is described as working on halves, or halvers. In the vicinity of which we tell and, it appears, generally throughout the south, the word sharecropper and its synonyms are used only of this class of tenant.

These usages do not differ from class to class, but are common to the language of landowner, tenant and sharecropper alike.

Of all the words which may be used to designate any sort of tenant, the word we heard used least frequently throughout our investigation, by landowners, storekeepers, townspeople, small farmers, tenants, sharecroppers, and all local human beings white or black, save only new dealers, communists, and various casts of liberal, was the word sharecropper.

In the north, however, and particularly in the seaboard north, where most of the writing and printing and reading of the United States is carried on, sharecropper has, through the agencies of print and the lectured word, become the generic term. Literally, of course, it describes both sorts of tenant, for each sort shares his crop: and it may be that through constant usage it will establish itself as generic. At present, however, it is in this generic spread unavailable to the mouth of anyone who would speak at all seriously of cotton tenants, and such a person will use it hesitantly if at all even in its specific and proper sense. For not only is the word inaccurately used save where it is indigenous, and not only is it a dialect word, to which a conscientious 'educated' person knows he has forfeited the right, even should he know its meaning accurately; and not only is it a dialect word inaccurately used by those who have no right to use it; but it has very swiftly, and within a very few years, absorbed every corruptive odor of inverted snobbery, marxian, journalistic, jewish, and liberal logomachia, emotional blackmail, negrophilia, belated transference, penis-envy, gynecological flurry and fairly good will which the several hundred thousand least habitable and scrupulous minds of this peculiarly psychotic quarter of the continent can supply to it: and is one of the words a careful man will be watchful of, and by whose use and inflection he may take clear measurement of the nature, and the stature, and the causes, and the timbre, of the enemy.

Note. Other anglosaxon monosyllables are god, love, loyalty, honor, beauty, duty, integrity, art, artist, religion, truth, science, poetry, culture, fascism, communism, dialectical-materialism, fellow-traveler, anarchist, philosophical-anarchist, marx, freud, semantic, loyalist, franco, hitler, duce, committee, friend, enemy, state, totalitarian state, mental state, statement, education, student, teacher, maestro, woman, man, Woman, Man, humanity, kidnap, vigilante, sex fiend, perversion, normal, genius, guarantee, peaceful-picketing, collective-bargaining, Negro, negro, Jew, jew, dinge, jig, boog, colored, jigaboo, nigger, darky, spade, eph, shine, smoke, hebe, kike, sheeny, eskimo, jewish, jow, joosh, anti-semitic, swing, cat, alligator, gator, icky, wacky, lick, hotlick, gutbucket, barrelhouse, bennygoodman, plumbing, stick, tea, lush, godbox, jitter-bug, tong, goddam, god damn, god damned, swell, oke, okay, lousy, superb, good, excellent, fine, nice, magnificent, bravo, bis, pooch, virgin, frigid, wife, husband, prick, pricque, box, bubs, jamsession, jive, silicosis, syphilis, wasserman, sex, sexual, sexuality, homosexual, heterosexual, bisexual, asexual, fairy, pansy, flit, headleigh, swish, les, lesbie, lesbian, labor, laborite, writer, author, musician, composer, workshop, studio, den, stuff, shot, pic, pix, angle, contact, leica, candid, Life, margaret bourke-white, maggie berkwitz, surrealism, photography, photographer, documentary, work, van gogh, dali, picasso, shakespeare, critic, reviewer, authority, book, publisher, gallery, show, theater, exhibition, stage, drama, tragedy, satire, sincerity, trotskyite, The Old Man, stalinist, liberal, minicam, henchman, the cape, the vineyard, flying, motoring, bathe, cue, revival, luntnfontanne, group theater, group, group consciousness, movement, john-ford, walt-disney, the dance, balletomane, leftist, editor, cub, hack, shop, inhibition, complex, regionalism, nationalism, jingoism, patriotism, americanism, altruism, schism, jizzum, hizzun, malnutrition, pare-lorentz, capital, thurman-arnold, veblen, mysticism, intellectual, emotional outlet, escapism, ideology, business, big business, big operator, layout, setup, pushover, scientist, scientific, medical, surgical, visceral, fiddle, prostie, frank, honest, incest, sponsor, cinematic, film, movie, talkie, moom pitcher, genitalia, parts, privates, idealist, psychotic, psychic, psyche, psychoanalysis, neothomist, physical, mental, emotional, spiritual, intuitive, esp, stooge, gross, clear, cleaned, communication, literature, understand, howdoyoufeelnow, sympathy, sympathizer, galleys, machine, laugh, sadisticanal, balls, nuts, nerts, bastid, taste, serve, deserve, fault, father, mother, dad, mummy, mumsy, mumpsypum, daddy, daddyboy, chickabiddy, comfy, cute, satisfactory, congratulations, congratters, sexual intercourse, fearful, dreadful, awful, godawful, nasty, nastiness, snotty, ghastly, great, greatness, greatest, best, worst, splendid, i mean, on the other hand, that is, for pete's sake, qxr, capehart, disk, disque, album, Jesus, Jesus Christ, Jesus Christ, Jesus H. Christ, Jeez, jeez fellas, jeez fellas, The Nazarene, The Nazarene Carpenter, The Galilean, Our Lord, Our Savior, Christ, christ, kee-rist, crissake, gawd, sacrosanct, sacrament, sacrilege, development, health, mental health, decadent, depravity, amoral, amorist, unethical, act of kind, coitus, relations, been with, live with, sleep with, mistress, lover, pubes, curse, fall off the roof, flagging, courses, unwell, period, friend, art treasure, American, democracy, munich betrayal, rape-of-czechoslovakia, battle-of-britain, determinism, guy, gal, person, class-consciousness, early-chaplin, late-beethoven, early-steinbeck, orson-welles, tom-wolfe, toscanini, fifth-column, reactionary, demagogue, blitzkrieg, defense.

5.

The tigers of wrath are wiser than the horses of instruction.

The road of excess leads to the palace of wisdom.

Prudence is a rich, ugly old maid courted by Incapacity.

Improvement makes straight roads, but the crooked roads without improvement are roads of Genius.

The eagle never lost so much time as when he submitted to learn of the crow.

The weak in courage are strong in cunning.

Listen to the fool's reproach; it is a kingly title.

The fox provides for himself, but God provides for the lion.

You never know what is enough until you know what is more than enough.

The Giants who formed this world into its sensual existence and now seem to live in it in chains are in truth the causes of its life and the sources of all activity, but the chains are the cunning of weak and tame minds which have power to resist energy, according to the proverb, the weak in courage are strong in cunning.

Thus one portion of being is the Prolific, the other the Devouring. To the devourer it seems as if the producer was in his

chains; but it is not so, he only takes portions of existence and fancies that the whole.

But the Prolific would cease to be Prolific unless the Devourer as a sea received the excess of his delights.

Some will say, Is not God alone the Prolific? I answer, God only Acts and Is, in existing beings or Men.

These two classes of men are always upon earth, and they should be enemies. Whoever tries to reconcile them seeks to destroy existence.

If the fool would persist in his folly he would become wise.

Everything possible to be believed is an image of truth.

One thought fills immensity.

Mutual forgiveness of each vice,
Such are the gates of Paradise.

Truth can never be told so as to be understood, and not be believed.

Everything that is is holy.

(On the Porch: 3

From these woods a good way out along the hill there now came a sound that was new to us.

All the darkness in near range of the earth as far as we were able to hear was strung with noises that were all one noise, and to this we had become so accustomed that this new sound came out of silence, and left an even more powerful silence behind it, so that with each return it, and the ensuing silence, gave each other more and more value, like the exchanges of two mirrors laid face to face.

Whereas we had been silent before, this sound immediately stiffened us into much more intense silence. Without exchange of word or glance we each received communication of a new opening of delight: but chiefly we now engaged in mutual listening and in analysis of what we heard, so strongly, that in all the body and in the whole range of mind and memory, each of us became all one hollowed and listening ear.

It was perhaps most nearly like the noise hydrogen makes when a match flame is passed across the mouth of a slanted test-tube. It was about the same height as this sound: soprano, with a strong alto illusion. It was colder than this sound, though: as cold and as chilling as the pupil of a goat's eye, or a low note on the clarinet. It ran eight identical notes to a call or stanza, a little faster than allegretto, in this rhythm and accent:

$$- - - - : - - : - - :$$

Every note was sharply, dryly, and cleanly accented, just short of staccato; and each was driven out with such strictness and restraint that there was in the short silence between each note an extreme tightness and mutual, organically shared tension. Each of the first seven notes was given exactly the same force; the seventh, hit harder, splayed open a fraction, and out of two things, the extra, hammer hardness it was hit with, and a barely discernible trailing-down at its end, gave the illusion of being a higher note.

This sound, then, started up, with great dramatic suddenness, at some indeterminable distance from us, a distance which in time became a little more determinable, though it was never at all possible accurately to locate it; for the ear always needs the help of the eye. It was from somewhere in the woods out to the left of the house at the bottom of our hill; and a little later it became clear that it was not in the low woods, but somewhere up the opposite slope; and after a little we got it in range within say twenty degrees of the ninety on the horizontal circle which at first it could have occupied any part of. It became clear that it would be between an eighth and a quarter mile away; and this became remarkable to us because at that considerable distance we could nevertheless hear, or rather by some equivalent to radioactivity strongly feel, the motions and tensions of the throat and body, the very tilt of the head, that discharged it.

Soon we were helped in locating it (as a second point in any geometry always is helpful, whereas one point alone can run you crazy) by the opening-up of a second call. This call was identical with the first but, coming from a good deal farther away, seemed higher, hollower, and thinner: scarcely more, yet very definitely more, than a loud clear echo.

Which of these calls seemed the more mysterious, it is not possible to say. Their quality was very different by virtue both of their difference in distance and of a distinct though indefinable difference in the personality of the callers. At one moment the more distant call was more exciting simply in its distance and because, by its secondary appearance and by its distance beyond the first caller in relation to us, we got the illusion that it was the thing sought by the other; the next, the nearer call took all the honors from it, by nearness; by having become the searcher with whom we had identified ourselves and taken sides and by having yet at the same time remained so entirely itself, without regard for us, no part of us, more alien to us, because it was alive and conscious and within our near perspective of kinship, than any stone or star. The fact is of course that these two series of calls, when they had been set going, enhanced each other quite as richly as each enhanced and received enhancement from its own, and the other's, interventions of silence, and a little later from its participation in, yet aristocratic distinction from, that plebeian, unanimous ringing of the air which had at no time ceased or diminished and which, now that we were listening so intently, became once more a part of the reality of hearing.

By use only of silences, without changing their stanzaic structure, these two calls went through any number of rhythmic-dramatic devices of delays in question and answer, of overlappings, of tricks of delay by which each pretended to show that it had signed off for the night or, actually, that it no longer even existed. There is an old, not specially funny vaudeville act in which the whole troupe builds up and burlesques a dramatic situation simply by different vocal and gesticulative colorations of the word 'you.' I thought of that now: but its present use was any amount better because the artists were subtler and what they had to say was more enigmatic and more exciting to the audience. Neither of them changed a note or a beat of his call; and if either allowed himself any change of tone or color whatever, it was so delicate that it is impossible to assign it to the callers save through the changefulness and human sentimentality of us who were listening and making what we could of it. But certainly, one way or the other, its meanings changed. One time it would be sexual; another, just a casual colloquy; another, a challenge; another, a signal or warning; another, a comment on us; another, some simple and desperate effort at mutual location; another, most intense and masterful irony; another, laughter; another, triumph; another, a masterpiece of parody of any one, any combination, or all of these assigned or implicit tones: but at all times it was beyond even the illusion of full apprehension, and was noble, frightening and distinguished: a work of great, private and unambitious art which was irrelevant to audience.

We were trying hardest of all to make out what animal or bird was making these sounds, but we had no clue, no anchorage in knowledge through whose help we might by comparative projections have taken it. I cannot even try to say how in the long run we concluded (perhaps in part through its sharpness, tightness out of the throat, and carnivorous timbre) that it was the voice of a fur-bearing animal and that the animal was on the small side and that he might most likely, then that he must, be a fox. It is this sort of mystery we should run against in all casual experience if we found ourselves without warning possessed of a new sense.

Now this is one of a universe of things which should be accepted and recorded for its own sake. The first entrance of this call was as perfect a piece of dramatic or musical structure as I know of: the context perfectly prepared, the entrance of the mysterious principal completely unforeseen yet completely casual, with none of the quality of studiousness in its surprise which hurts for instance some of the music of Brahms; and from its first entrance on, the whole world was frozen and fixed under its will as by the introduction of a precipitant; so that the identical entrance of the second voice carried with it an excitement almost beyond what is possible to bear.

When this second voice had spoken, the first did not answer, but froze just as we and our world had frozen. That which had called was listening intently too. And that which had called the caller was waiting and listening. And now after a long space of more and more tremendous silence (into which there arose, but very faintly, loosely, as natural and common as dew, the ramified ringing of frogs, insects, and night birds), after this long space of silence had extended itself beyond any degree of natural endurance, the second voice spoke a second time, identically, yet, because of the silence, the lack of answer, more imperious-sounding than at first. Then there was a wait, in whose first part the call repeated itself on the ear's memory silently yet keenly as print, and in whose latter expansion once again we were intense with waiting; and then, by some rhythmic genius a little, but only a very little, off-beat, off the beat of eccentrics our ear had of the sum of the calls computed, a very little before it was quite possible to expect it, there came the voice of the first creature; and it was with the breaking open of this voice that we too broke open, silently, our whole bodies broke open into a laughter that destroyed and restored us more even than the most absolute weeping ever can. This is a laughter I have experienced only rarely: listening to the genius of Mozart at its angriest and cleanest, most masculine fire; the sudden memory of some line of Shakespeare, 'Nymph, in thine orisons be all my sins remembered'; walking in streets or driving in country; watching negroes; or in that delicate stage of love when a girl, serious and scarcely tinged with smiling, her eyes muted and her head poised most immaculately, first begins, not in pleasure alone, but in a kind of fear and deep gentleness, to use her light, slow, frank hands upon your head and body: a phase so unassailably beyond any meaning of tenderness and of trust, so like the opening of first living upon the shining of the young earth in its first morning, that an overwhelming knowledge of God and of his non-existence fight in you and, all in this same quietness, you feel it impossible that you can look into her eyes one more moment and not be so distended by incredulous joy that you are of one size and ignorance and fleshlessness with space itself. *

And this phase of love, to anyone who holds love in the utmost esteem that is its due, must be beyond all comparison the cruelest and

---

* The essences of anguish and of joy are thus identical: they are the explosion or incandescence resulting from the incontrovertible perception of the incredible.

bitterest thing in human experience. Even within its own moments it draws you both irresistibly into those desperate battlings of the body which only in their first few seconds seem the greater joy they are not, and which so soon blunt and blind the delicate munificence of your exchange into their own beautiful but violent, charcoal-drawn terms. Out of this violence of flesh and of total mutual confidence it is not possible many times to withdraw into that quieter sphere of apposition in which the body, brain and spirit of each of you is all one perfectly focused lens and in which these two lenses devour, feed, enrich and honor each other; it is not possible because the violence blurs, feathers and distorts the essential constituency of the lens. And it is then, living in flushes of memory of a thing more excellent than you may much. hope to share between you again, that with scarcely conscious bravery and sorrow, and with measureless compassion, love must assume itself to be established and alive between you. There will be goodness and joy between you again, with wisdom and luck a great deal, more than enough, but not all the kind regard nor all the love within the scope of existence will ever restore you what for a while, and only that you might lose it in the blind service of nature, you had.

In the sound of these foxes, if they were foxes, there was nearly as much joy, and less grief. There was the frightening joy of hearing the world talk to itself, and the grief of incommunicability. In that grief I am now as then, with the small yet absolute comfort of knowing that communication of such a thing is not only beyond possibility but irrelevant to it; whereas in love, where we find ourselves so completely involved, so completely responsible and so apparently capable, and where all our soul so runs out to the loveliness, strength, and defenseless mortality, plain, common, salt and muscled toughness of human existence of a girl * that the desire to die for her seems the puniest and stingiest expression of your regard which you can, like a proud tomcat

---

* I would presume this to be quite as possible, and of no less dignity and valor, in homosexual as well as in heterosexual love.

with a slain fledgling, lay at her feet; in love the restraint in focus and the arrest and perpetuation of joy seems entirely possible and simple, and its failure inexcusable, even while we know it is beyond the power of all biology and even while, like the fading of flowerlike wonder out of a breast to which we are becoming habituated, that exquisite joy lies, fainting through change upon change, in the less and less prescient palm of the less and less godlike, more and more steadily stupefied, human, ordinary hand.

And so though this incident of the calling of two creatures should by rights be established at very least as a poem, or a piece of music, and though, even, I know that a more gifted human being, and even I myself, could come nearer giving it, I do not relinquish the ultimately hopeless effort with entire grief simply because that effort would be, above most efforts, so useless.

This calling continued, never repeating a pattern, and always with what seemed infallible art, for perhaps twenty minutes. It was thoroughly as if principals had been set up, enchanted, and left like dim sacks at one side of a stage as enormous as the steadfast tilted deck of the earth, and as if onto this stage, accompanied by the drizzling confabulation of nocturnal-pastoral music, two masked characters, unforetold and perfectly irrelevant to the action, had with catlike aplomb and noiselessness stept and had sung, with sinister casualness, what at length turned out to have been the most significant, but most unfathomable, number in the show; and had then in perfect irony and silence withdrawn.

It was after the ending of this that we began a little to talk. Ordinarily we enjoyed talking and of late, each absorbed throughout most of the day in subtle and painful work that made even the lightest betrayal of our full reactions unwise, we had found the fragments of time we were alone, and able to give voice to them and to compare and analyze them, valuable and necessary beyond comparison of cocaine. But now in this structure of special exaltation it was, though not unpleasant, thoroughly unnecessary, and obstructive of more pleasing usage. Our talk drained rather quickly off into silence and we lay thinking, analyzing, remembering, in the human and artist's sense praying, chiefly over matters of the present and of that immediate past which was a part of the present; and each of these matters had in that time the extreme clearness, and edge, and honor, which I shall now try to give you; until at length we too fell asleep.